SACRIFICE

AGE OF BRONZE

Volume 2

SACRIFICE

by Eric Shanower

image

Age of Bronze
Volume 2
Sacrifice
Copyright © 2004 by Eric Shanower. All rights reserved.

ISBN 1-58240-399-6
Published by Image Comics, Inc.
Office of Publication: 1942 University Ave., Suite 305
Berkeley, CA 94704
Image and its logos are ® and © by Image Comics, Inc. All rights reserved.

Erik Larsen *Publisher*
Todd McFarlane *President*
Marc Silvestri *CEO*
Jim Valentino *Vice-President*

Eric Stephenson *Executive Director*
Brett Evans *Production Manager*
Jim Demonakos *PR & Marketing Coordinator*
Allen Hui *Production Artist*
Joe Keatinge *Traffic Manager*
Mia MacHatton *Adminstrative Assistant*
Jonathan Chan *Production Assistant*

The story of *Sacrifice* was originally serialized in the comic book series
Age of Bronze, issues 10 though 19.

First printing July 2004
Second printing November 2005

Visit the *Age of Bronze* website at
www.age-of-bronze.com

Age of Bronze is a trademark of Eric Shanower.

Printed in Canada.

Friends of Troy is an organization for those interested in Troy and its legends.
It supports the ongoing activities of the International Troy Excavation Project.
All Friends of Troy receive the annual newsletter and updates on Troy-related news.
Friends are welcome at Troy and are given guided tours of the site and excavation.
If you would like to become a Friend of Troy, send your name and address to

Institute for Mediterranean Studies
7086 Aracoma Drive
Cincinnati, OH 45237
USA

Phone: 513/631-8049
Fax: 513/631-1715
E-mail: studies@usa.net
Website: www.studies.org
Or see: www.uni-tuebingen.de/troia/eng/freunde.html

For information on the TROIA — FOUNDATION which supports
the International Troy Excavation Project, see the website
www.uni-tuebingen.de/troia/eng/troiastiftung.html

For Dad,
whose ships don't go astray.

"I was cut off from hope in that sad place
   Which men call'd Aulis in those iron years:
My father held his hand upon his face;
   I, blinded with my tears,

"Still strove to speak: my voice was thick with sighs
   As in a dream. Dimly I could descry
The stern black-bearded kings with wolfish eyes,
   Waiting to see me die.

"The high masts flicker'd as they lay afloat;
   The crowds, the temples, waver'd, and the shore;
The bright death quiver'd at the victim's throat—
   Touch'd—and I knew no more."

                    —Alfred Lord Tennyson
                    "A Dream of Fair Women," 1833-53
                    lines 105-116

Contents

Maps
8

Our Story So Far
10

Sacrifice
13

Glossary of Names
216

Genealogical Charts
220

Bibliography
222

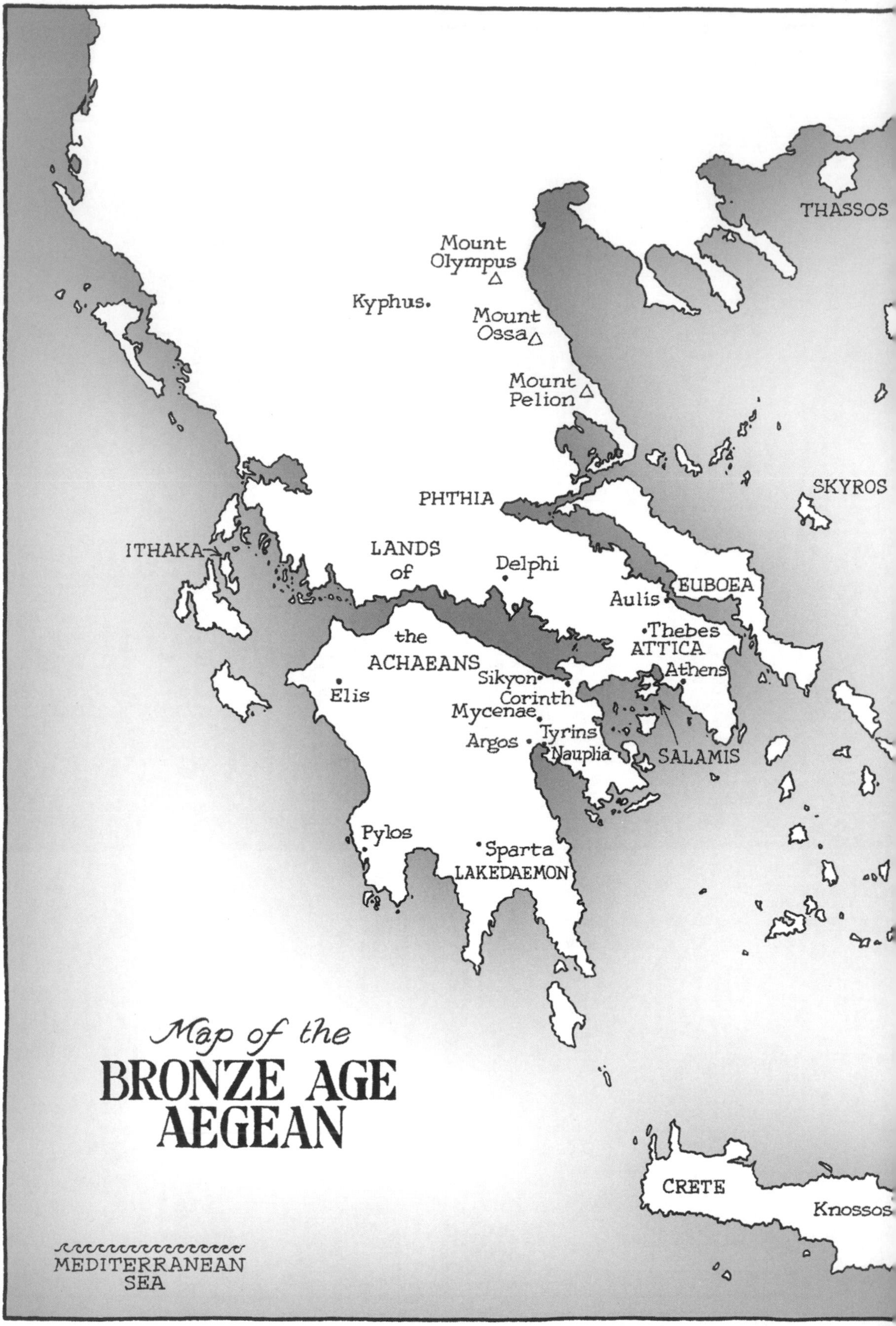
Map of the
BRONZE AGE
AEGEAN
THASSOS
Mount Olympus
Kyphus.
Mount Ossa
Mount Pelion
SKYROS
PHTHIA
ITHAKA
LANDS of the ACHAEANS
Delphi
EUBOEA
Aulis
Thebes
ATTICA
Athens
Sikyon
Elis
Corinth
Mycenae
Tyrins
Argos
Nauplia
SALAMIS
Pylos
Sparta
LAKEDAEMON
CRETE
Knossos
MEDITERRANEAN SEA

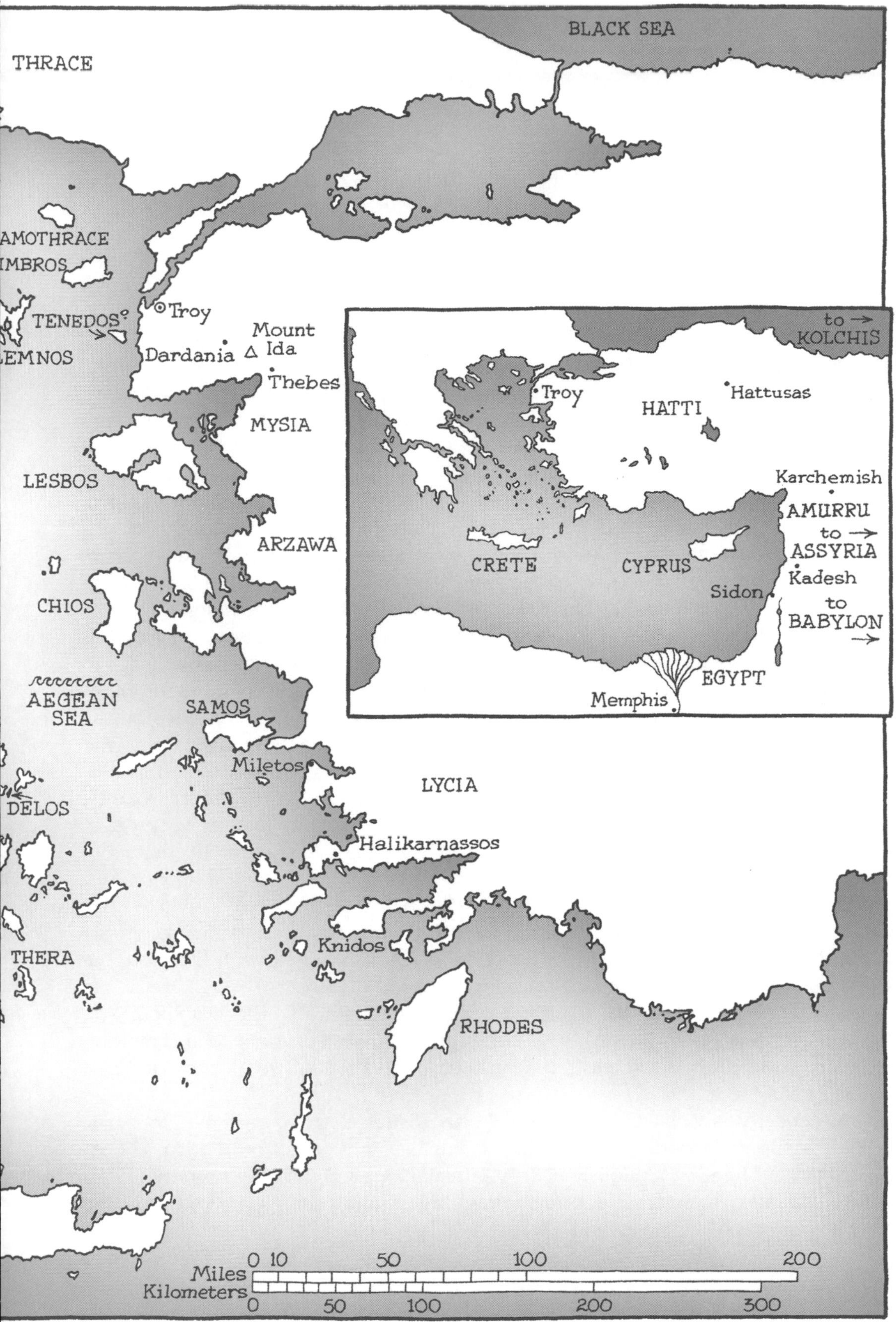

BLACK SEA
THRACE
SAMOTHRACE
IMBROS
TENEDOS
LEMNOS
Troy
Mount Ida
Dardania
Thebes
MYSIA
LESBOS
ARZAWA
CHIOS
AEGEAN SEA
SAMOS
Miletos
LYCIA
DELOS
Halikarnassos
THERA
Knidos
RHODES
to KOLCHIS
Troy
HATTI
Hattusas
Karchemish
AMURRU
to ASSYRIA
Kadesh
CRETE
CYPRUS
Sidon
to BABYLON
EGYPT
Memphis
Miles
Kilometers
0 10 50 100 200
0 50 100 200 300

Our Story So Far

During the Late Bronze Age—about the 13th century BCE—the powerful city of Troy flourishes under the Great King Priam's rule. Years before, Priam's sister Hesione was captured by Achaean raiders during an assault on Troy. Now Priam commands Paris, a prince of Troy recently reunited with his father and his mother Hekuba, to bring Hesione back. Priam's daughter Kassandra and her twin brother Helenus predict calamity, but no one takes their warnings seriously.

Accompanied by his cousin Aeneas, Paris sails to the Achaean city of Sparta where Menelaus is king. Paris forgets his pregnant lover, the mountain nymph Oenone, and ignoring his brother Hektor's warning to follow their father Priam's instructions, he seduces Menelaus's wife Helen away from Sparta with her serving women and infant son Pleisthenes. They sail to Cyprus, then to Sidon.

Helen's brothers Kastor and Polydeukes pursue, but are lost in a storm at sea.

Menelaus is eager to recover his wife, while his brother Agamemnon, king of Mycenae and High King of the Achaeans, is eager to gain Troy's control of rich trade routes through the Hellespont. So they summon the many Achaean kings who once swore an oath to help Helen's husband for her sake. At the bay at Aulis a massive army with hundreds of ships and thousands of men assembles. The army pledges to follow High King Agamemnon as commander in an attack on Troy.

The Achaean priestess Thetis foresees the death of her son Achilles at Troy. To circumvent this, she takes the boy from his teacher, the kentaur Cheiron, and hides him, disguised as a girl called Pyrrha, among the daughters of Lykomedes on the island of Skyros. There, Achilles rapes Lykomedes's eldest daughter Deidamia, who bears a son. Deidamia calls the child Pyrrhus; Achilles calls him Neoptolemus.

A prophecy foretells that if Odysseus, king of Ithaka, goes to Troy with the army, he'll return home to his wife Penelope and son Telemachus after twenty years, alone and unrecognized. To avoid this fate, Odysseus pretends to be mad. But Palamedes, prince of Nauplia, exposes Odysseus's ploy, thus earning his enmity.

Kalchas, Trojan priest of the sun god, has visions that show him Troy's fall. He joins the Achaeans, leaving his recently widowed daughter Cressida at Troy in the care of her uncle Pandarus. The Trojan prince Troilus falls in love with Cressida, but Pandarus discourages Troilus from pursuing her prematurely.

All signs point to eventual success for the Achaean army. The Delphic oracle predicts Achaean victory over Troy, contingent, however, upon conflict among Achaeans. And Kalchas foretells Achaean triumph in the tenth year, provided that Achilles joins the army.

Odysseus tricks Achilles into shedding his disguise and brings him to Aulis. Achilles assumes leadership of his father Peleus's Myrmidons from Phthia, choosing a short life fighting gloriously at Troy rather than a long life in obscurity.

After Palamedes remedies a food shortage by bringing supplies from Delos, the army at last sets sail for war with Troy.

SACRIFICE

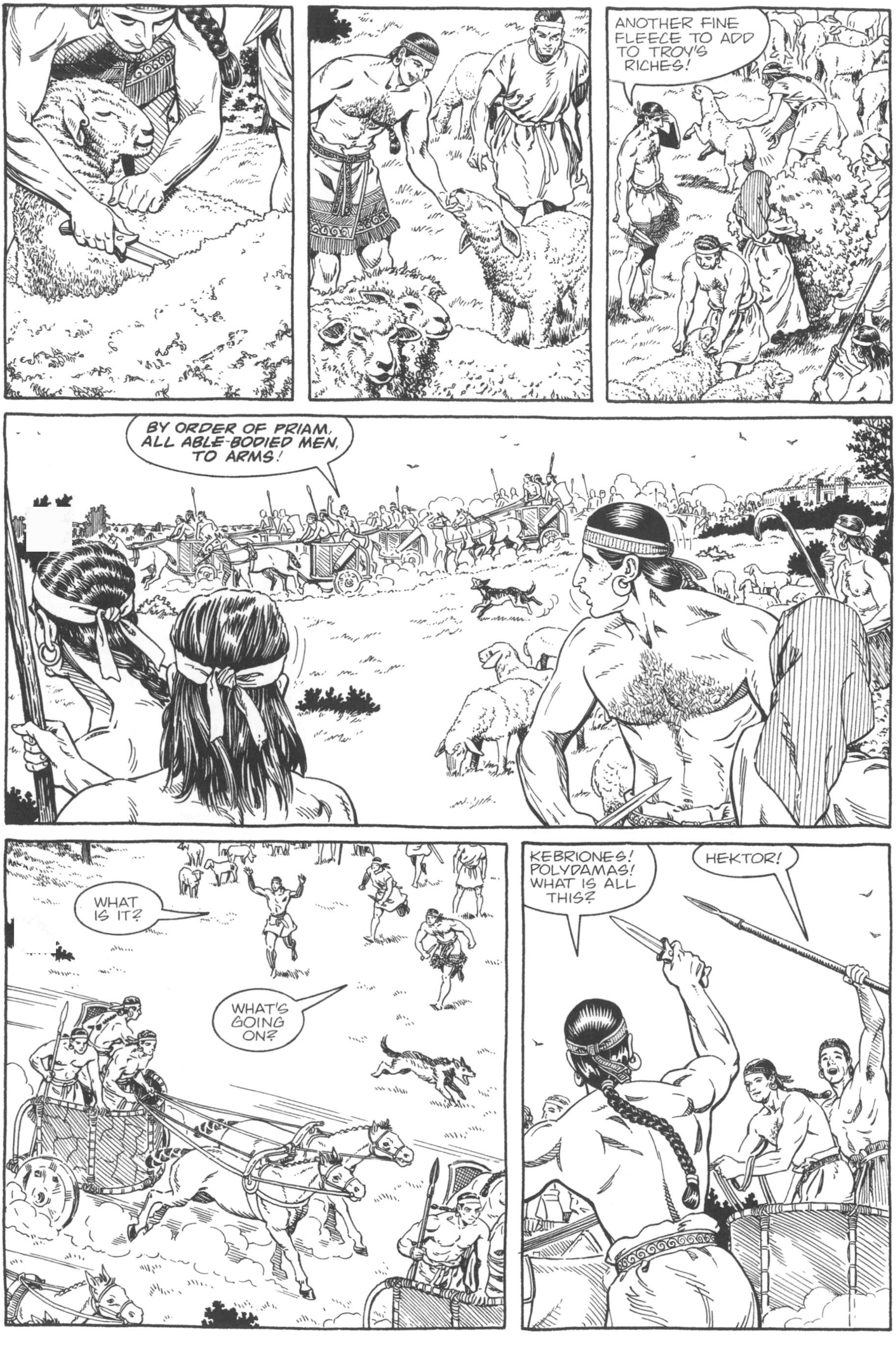
ANOTHER FINE FLEECE TO ADD TO TROY'S RICHES!
BY ORDER OF PRIAM, ALL ABLE-BODIED MEN, TO ARMS!
WHAT IS IT?
WHAT'S GOING ON?
KEBRIONES! POLYDAMAS! WHAT IS ALL THIS?
HEKTOR!

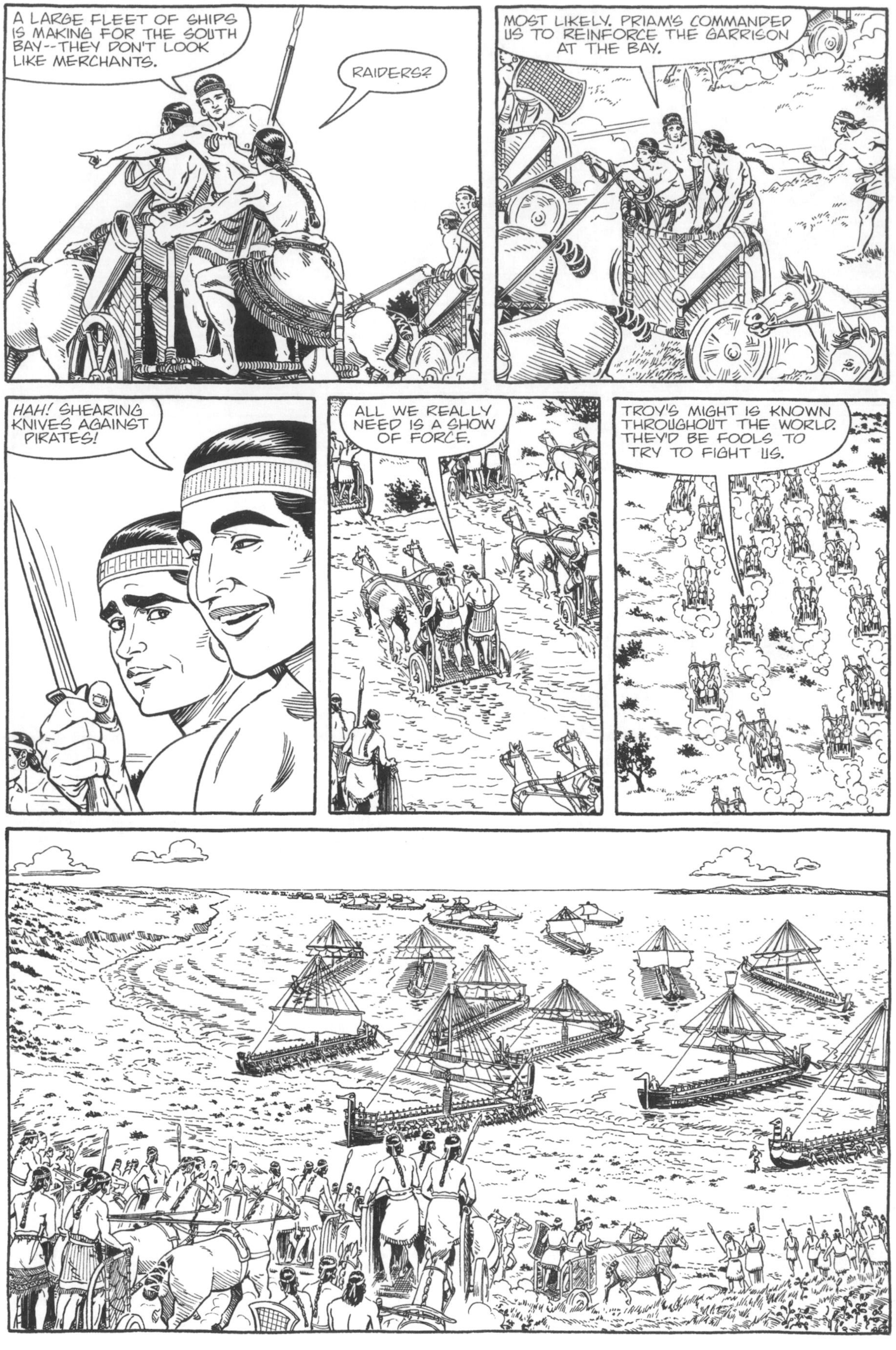

A LARGE FLEET OF SHIPS IS MAKING FOR THE SOUTH BAY--THEY DON'T LOOK LIKE MERCHANTS.
RAIDERS?
MOST LIKELY. PRIAM'S COMMANDED US TO REINFORCE THE GARRISON AT THE BAY.
HAH! SHEARING KNIVES AGAINST PIRATES!
ALL WE REALLY NEED IS A SHOW OF FORCE.
TROY'S MIGHT IS KNOWN THROUGHOUT THE WORLD. THEY'D BE FOOLS TO TRY TO FIGHT US.

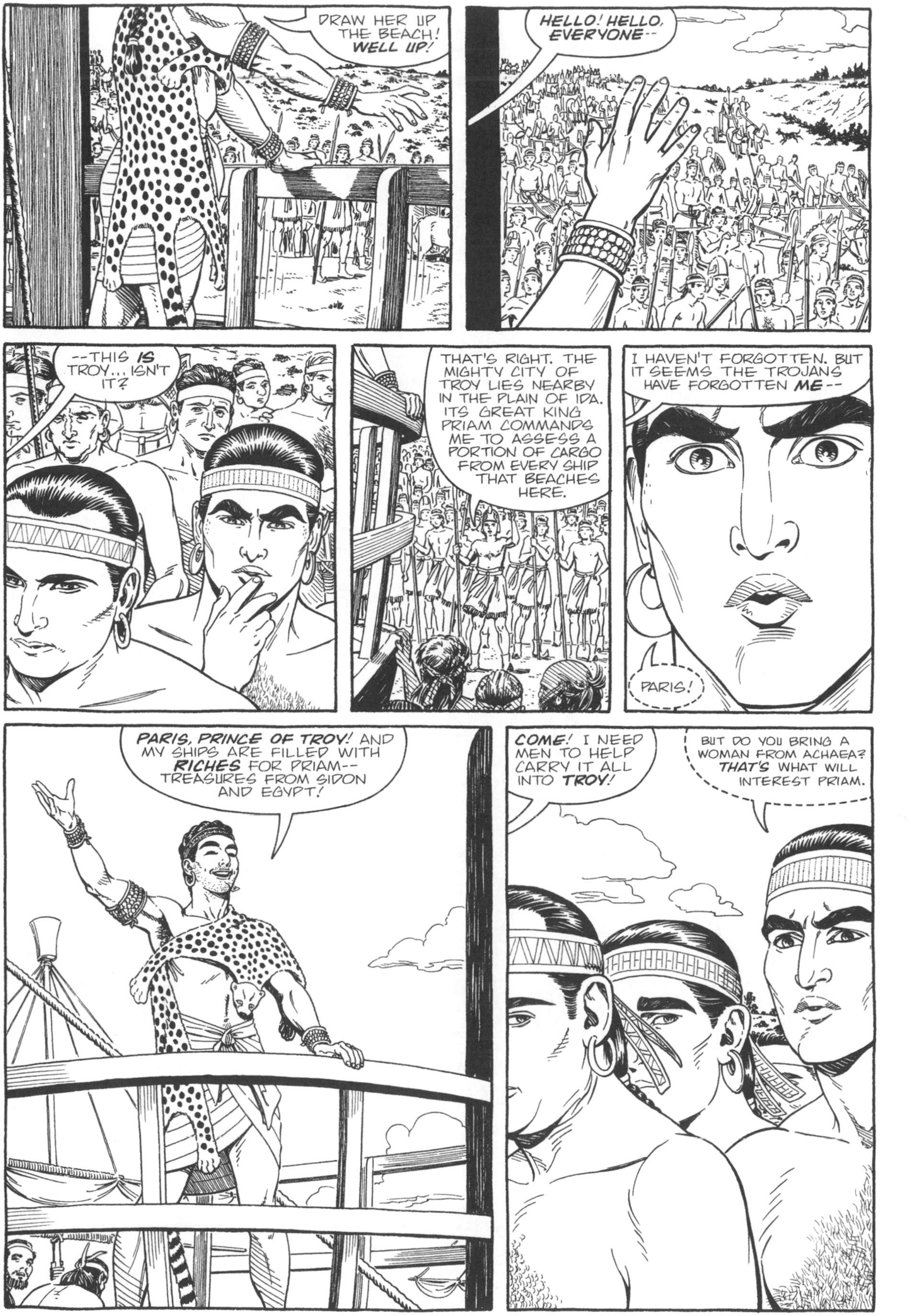
DRAW HER UP THE BEACH! WELL UP!
HELLO! HELLO, EVERYONE--
--THIS IS TROY... ISN'T IT?
THAT'S RIGHT. THE MIGHTY CITY OF TROY LIES NEARBY IN THE PLAIN OF IDA. ITS GREAT KING PRIAM COMMANDS ME TO ASSESS A PORTION OF CARGO FROM EVERY SHIP THAT BEACHES HERE.
I HAVEN'T FORGOTTEN. BUT IT SEEMS THE TROJANS HAVE FORGOTTEN ME--
PARIS!
PARIS, PRINCE OF TROY! AND MY SHIPS ARE FILLED WITH RICHES FOR PRIAM-- TREASURES FROM SIDON AND EGYPT!
COME! I NEED MEN TO HELP CARRY IT ALL INTO TROY!
BUT DO YOU BRING A WOMAN FROM ACHAEA? THAT'S WHAT WILL INTEREST PRIAM.

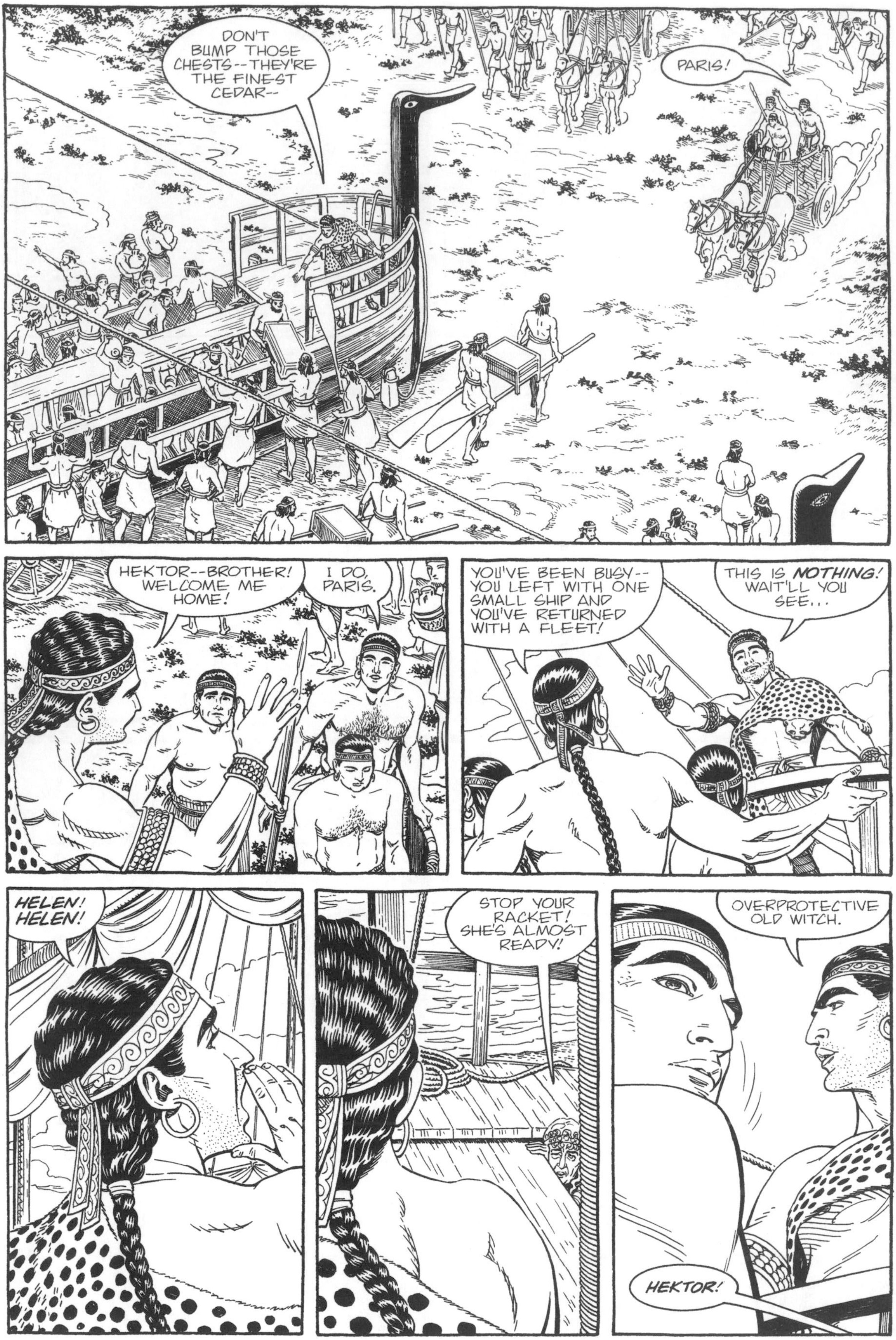
DON'T BUMP THOSE CHESTS--THEY'RE THE FINEST CEDAR--
PARIS!
HEKTOR--BROTHER! WELCOME ME HOME!
I DO, PARIS.
YOU'VE BEEN BUSY--YOU LEFT WITH ONE SMALL SHIP AND YOU'VE RETURNED WITH A FLEET!
THIS IS **NOTHING!** WAIT'LL YOU SEE...
HELEN! HELEN!
STOP YOUR RACKET! SHE'S ALMOST READY!
OVERPROTECTIVE OLD WITCH.
HEKTOR!

AENEAS--COUSIN!

IT'S BEEN TOO LONG, HEKTOR, *MUCH* TOO LONG. I WASN'T SURE I'D EVER SEE THE PLAIN OF IDA AGAIN.

HAVE YOU SENT ANYONE TO TELL PRIAM THAT WE'VE ARRIVED?

NO, NOT YET.

THEN LEND ME A CHARIOT AND *I'LL* GO!

RIGHT! KEBRIONES, DID YOU HEAR THAT?

WHAT'S HAPPENING NOW, AITHRA?

AENEAS IS RIDING OFF IN A CHARIOT--TO ANNOUNCE TO THE CITY OUR ARRIVAL, NO DOUBT.

CHECK MY BACK HAIR AGAIN, KLYMENE. AND IS MY MAKE-UP RIGHT? THIS LIGHT IS TOO DIM!

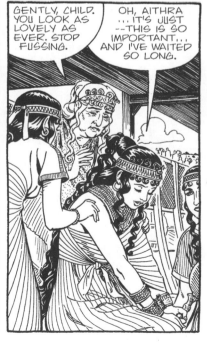

GENTLY, CHILD. YOU LOOK AS LOVELY AS EVER. STOP FUSSING.

OH, AITHRA ...IT'S JUST --THIS IS SO IMPORTANT... AND I'VE WAITED SO LONG.

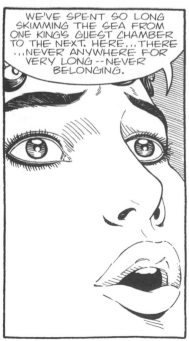

WE'VE SPENT SO LONG SKIMMING THE SEA FROM ONE KING'S GUEST CHAMBER TO THE NEXT. HERE...THERE ...NEVER ANYWHERE FOR VERY LONG--NEVER BELONGING.

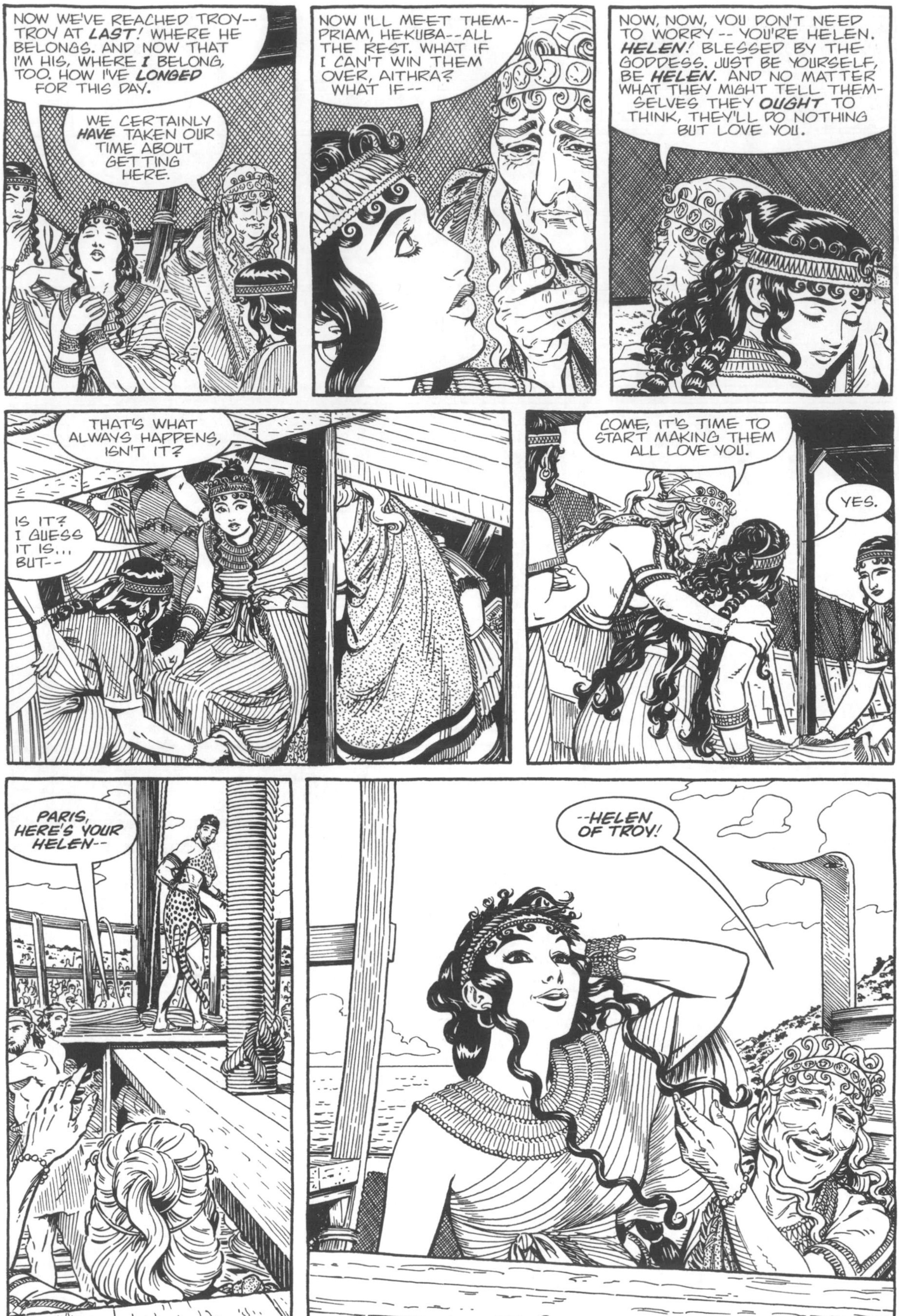
NOW WE'VE REACHED TROY-- TROY AT *LAST*! WHERE HE BELONGS. AND NOW THAT I'M HIS, WHERE *I* BELONG, TOO. HOW I'VE *LONGED* FOR THIS DAY.
WE CERTAINLY *HAVE* TAKEN OUR TIME ABOUT GETTING HERE.
NOW I'LL MEET THEM-- PRIAM, HEKUBA--ALL THE REST. WHAT IF I CAN'T WIN THEM OVER, AITHRA? WHAT IF--
NOW, NOW, YOU DON'T NEED TO WORRY -- YOU'RE HELEN. *HELEN*! BLESSED BY THE GODDESS. JUST BE YOURSELF, BE *HELEN*. AND NO MATTER WHAT THEY MIGHT TELL THEMSELVES THEY *OUGHT* TO THINK, THEY'LL DO NOTHING BUT LOVE YOU.
THAT'S WHAT ALWAYS HAPPENS, ISN'T IT?
IS IT? I GUESS IT IS... BUT--
COME, IT'S TIME TO START MAKING THEM ALL LOVE YOU.
YES.
PARIS, HERE'S YOUR HELEN--
--HELEN OF TROY!

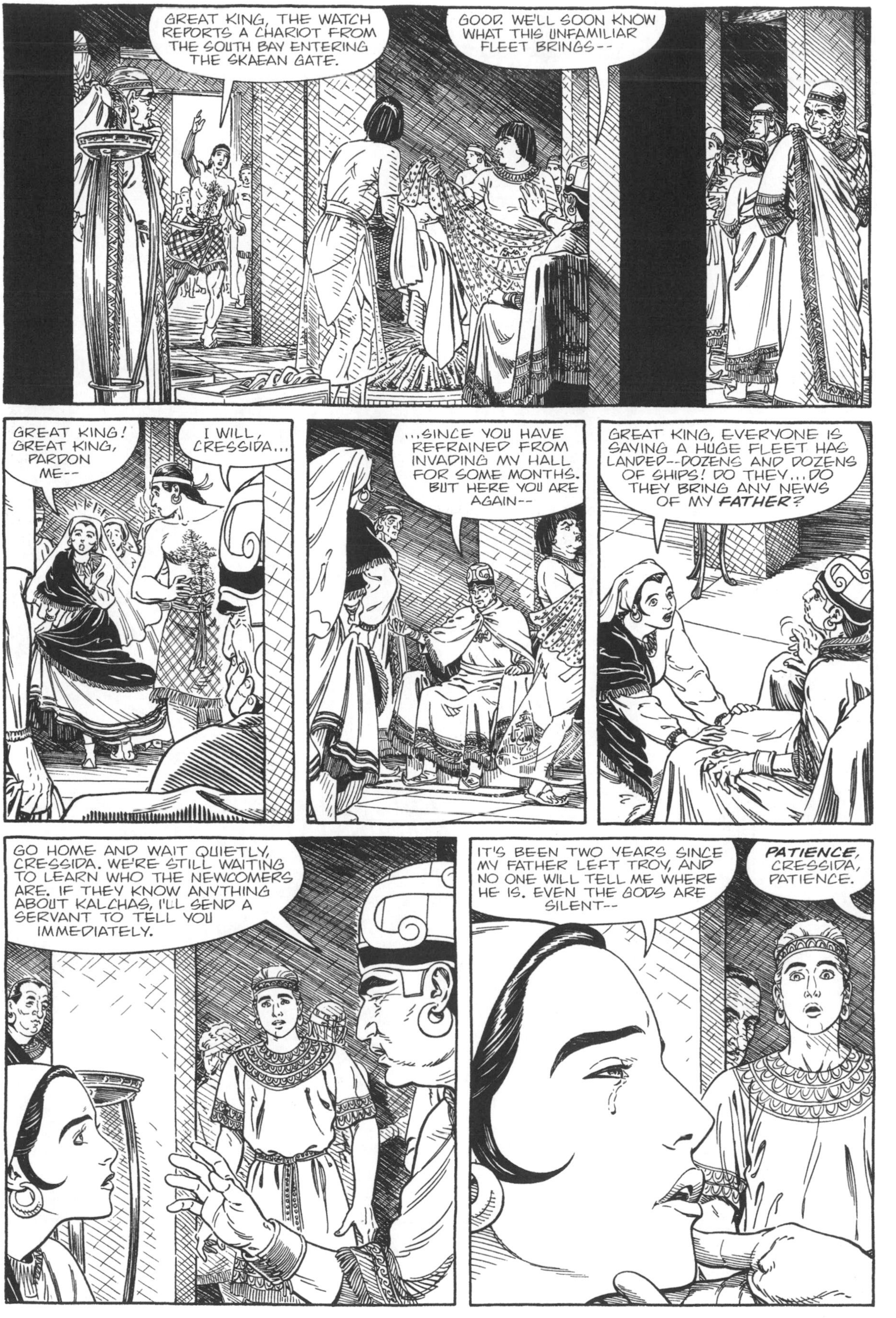
GREAT KING, THE WATCH REPORTS A CHARIOT FROM THE SOUTH BAY ENTERING THE SKAEAN GATE.
GOOD. WE'LL SOON KNOW WHAT THIS UNFAMILIAR FLEET BRINGS--
GREAT KING! GREAT KING, PARDON ME--
I WILL, CRESSIDA...
...SINCE YOU HAVE REFRAINED FROM INVADING MY HALL FOR SOME MONTHS. BUT HERE YOU ARE AGAIN--
GREAT KING, EVERYONE IS SAYING A HUGE FLEET HAS LANDED--DOZENS AND DOZENS OF SHIPS! DO THEY...DO THEY BRING ANY NEWS OF MY FATHER?
GO HOME AND WAIT QUIETLY, CRESSIDA. WE'RE STILL WAITING TO LEARN WHO THE NEWCOMERS ARE. IF THEY KNOW ANYTHING ABOUT KALCHAS, I'LL SEND A SERVANT TO TELL YOU IMMEDIATELY.
IT'S BEEN TWO YEARS SINCE MY FATHER LEFT TROY, AND NO ONE WILL TELL ME WHERE HE IS. EVEN THE GODS ARE SILENT--
PATIENCE, CRESSIDA, PATIENCE.

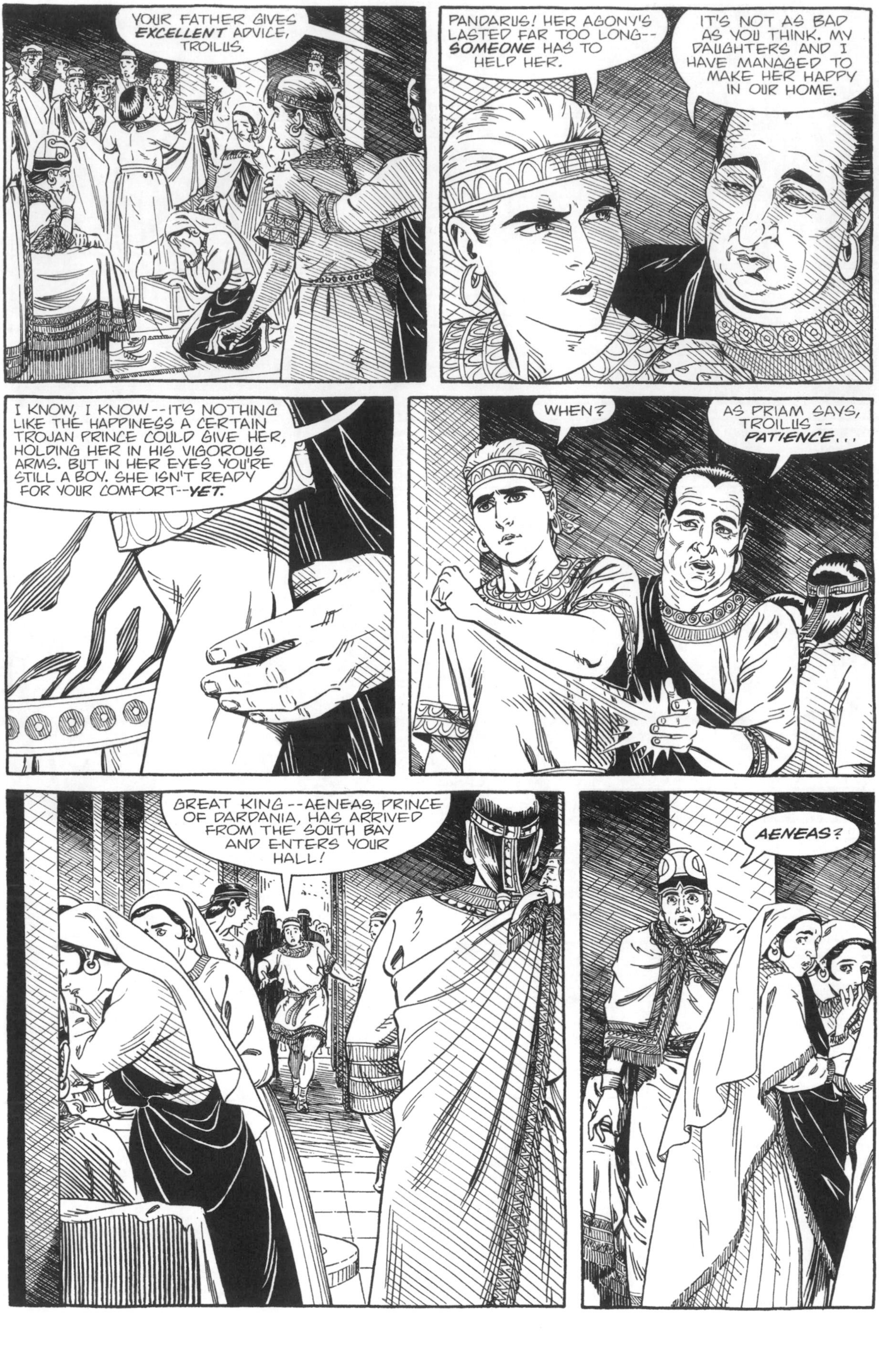
YOUR FATHER GIVES **EXCELLENT** ADVICE, TROILUS.
PANDARUS! HER AGONY'S LASTED FAR TOO LONG-- **SOMEONE** HAS TO HELP HER.
IT'S NOT AS BAD AS YOU THINK. MY DAUGHTERS AND I HAVE MANAGED TO MAKE HER HAPPY IN OUR HOME.
I KNOW, I KNOW--IT'S NOTHING LIKE THE HAPPINESS A CERTAIN TROJAN PRINCE COULD GIVE HER, HOLDING HER IN HIS VIGOROUS ARMS. BUT IN HER EYES YOU'RE STILL A BOY. SHE ISN'T READY FOR YOUR COMFORT--**YET.**
WHEN?
AS PRIAM SAYS, TROILUS -- **PATIENCE**...
GREAT KING--AENEAS, PRINCE OF DARDANIA, HAS ARRIVED FROM THE SOUTH BAY AND ENTERS YOUR HALL!
AENEAS?

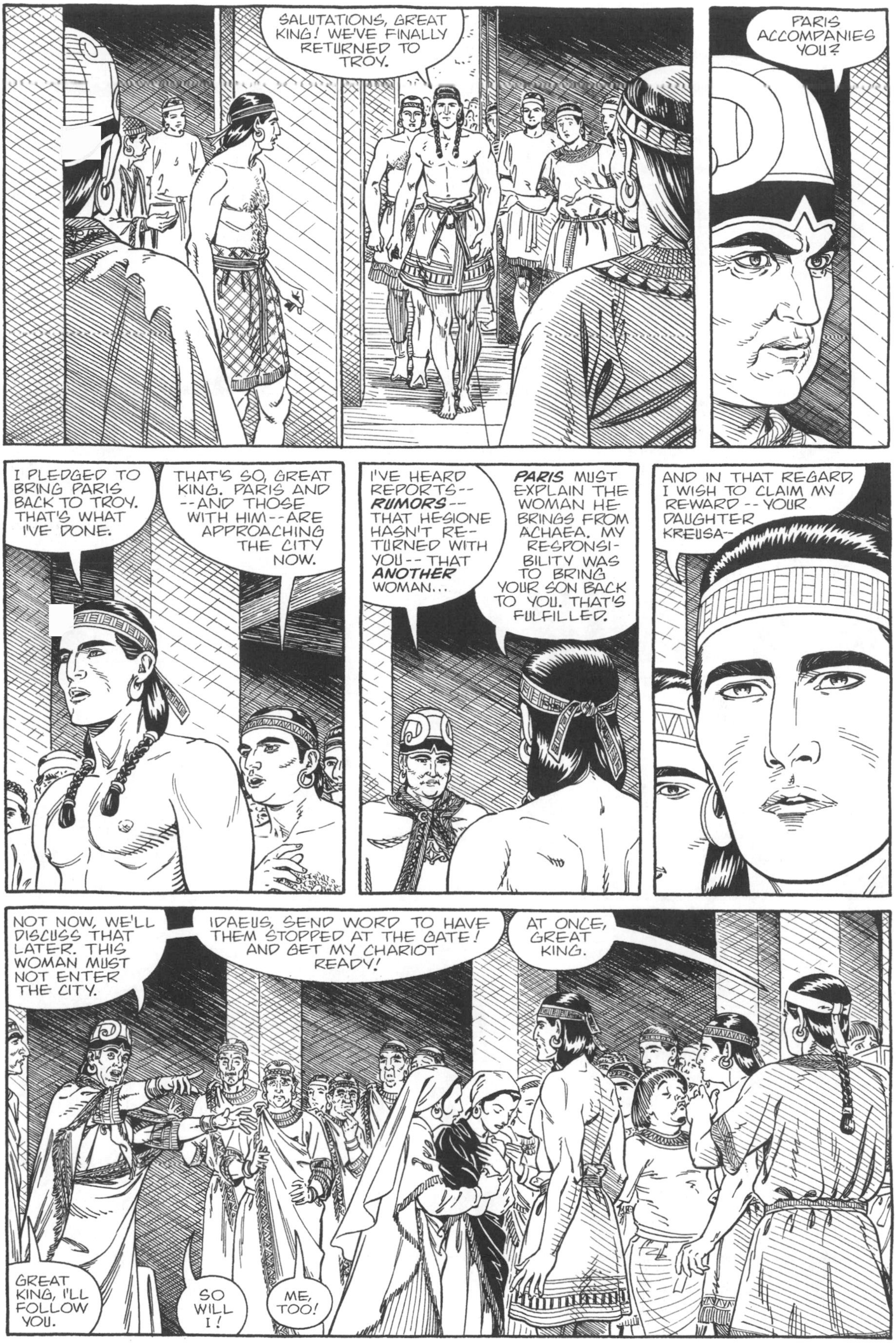
SALUTATIONS, GREAT KING! WE'VE FINALLY RETURNED TO TROY.
PARIS ACCOMPANIES YOU?
I PLEDGED TO BRING PARIS BACK TO TROY. THAT'S WHAT I'VE DONE.
THAT'S SO, GREAT KING. PARIS AND --AND THOSE WITH HIM--ARE APPROACHING THE CITY NOW.
I'VE HEARD REPORTS-- **RUMORS**-- THAT HESIONE HASN'T RETURNED WITH YOU-- THAT **ANOTHER** WOMAN...
PARIS MUST EXPLAIN THE WOMAN HE BRINGS FROM ACHAEA. MY RESPONSIBILITY WAS TO BRING YOUR SON BACK TO YOU. THAT'S FULFILLED.
AND IN THAT REGARD, I WISH TO CLAIM MY REWARD -- YOUR DAUGHTER KREUSA--
NOT NOW, WE'LL DISCUSS THAT LATER. THIS WOMAN MUST NOT ENTER THE CITY.
IDAEUS, SEND WORD TO HAVE THEM STOPPED AT THE GATE! AND GET MY CHARIOT READY!
AT ONCE, GREAT KING.
GREAT KING, I'LL FOLLOW YOU.
SO WILL I!
ME, TOO!

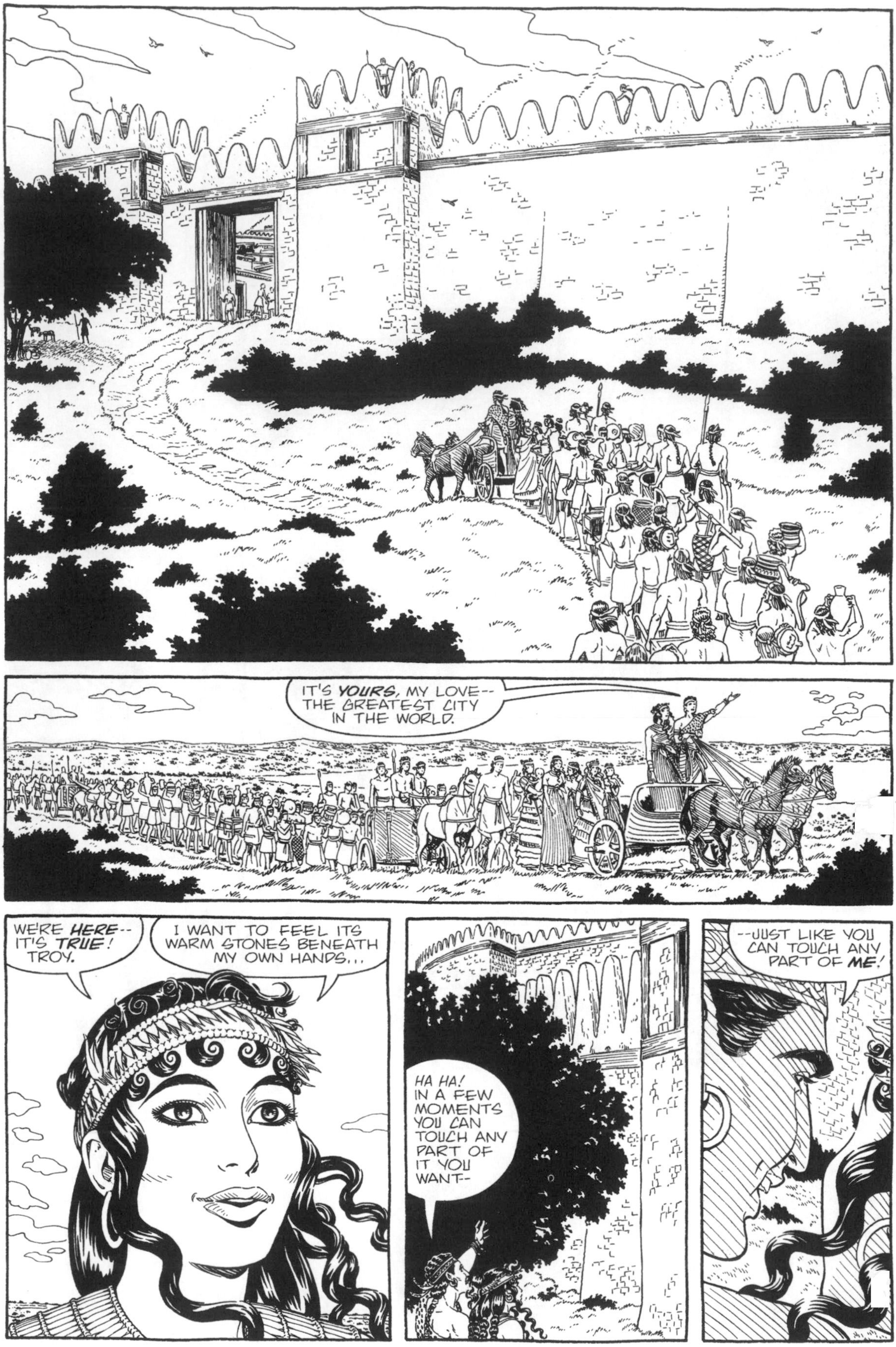
IT'S **YOURS**, MY LOVE-- THE GREATEST CITY IN THE WORLD.
WE'RE **HERE**-- IT'S **TRUE**! TROY.
I WANT TO FEEL ITS WARM STONES BENEATH MY OWN HANDS...
HA HA! IN A FEW MOMENTS YOU CAN TOUCH ANY PART OF IT YOU WANT-
--JUST LIKE YOU CAN TOUCH ANY PART OF **ME**!

PARIS!

GREAT KING! FATHER!

I CAME TO SEE WHETHER THE NEWS OF YOUR RETURN COULD REALLY BE TRUE--YOU'VE BEEN AWAY SO LONG.

IT LOOKS LIKE EVERYONE ELSE HAD THE SAME IDEA.

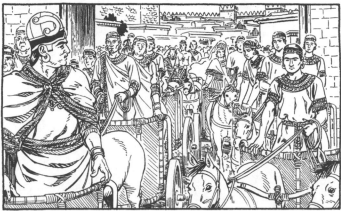

LOOK, HELEN! THE WHOLE CITY'S COME TO WELCOME US!

WHAT DO THEIR MURMURS MEAN? ARE THEY WEL- COMING ME? OR JUDGING ME?

SO *THAT'S* WHAT AN ACHAEAN WOMAN LOOKS LIKE!

IF THEY'RE ALL LIKE HER, LET'S BRING OVER SOME *MORE!*

NO WOMAN'S WORTH STARTING A *WAR* OVER.

SHE'D KEEP A MAN WARM AT NIGHT, THOUGH.

LOOK AT HER HAIR SHINE IN THE SUNLIGHT!

EASY TO LOOK AT ON THE OUTSIDE, BUT HARD AS BRONZE INSIDE. I KNOW THE TYPE.

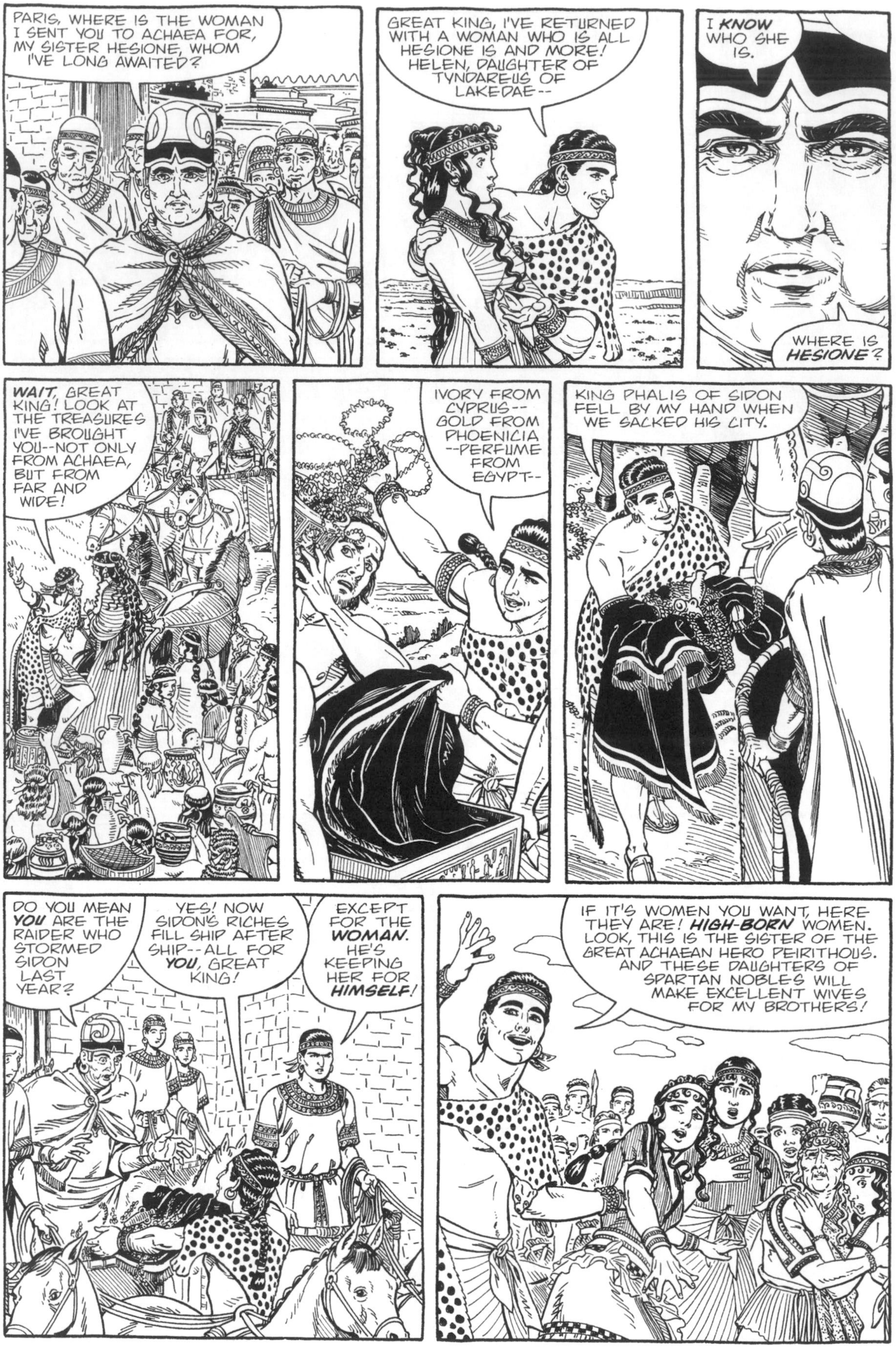
PARIS, WHERE IS THE WOMAN I SENT YOU TO ACHAEA FOR, MY SISTER HESIONE, WHOM I'VE LONG AWAITED?
GREAT KING, I'VE RETURNED WITH A WOMAN WHO IS ALL HESIONE IS AND MORE! HELEN, DAUGHTER OF TYNDAREUS OF LAKEDAE--
I **KNOW** WHO SHE IS.
WHERE IS **HESIONE**?
WAIT, GREAT KING! LOOK AT THE TREASURES I'VE BROUGHT YOU--NOT ONLY FROM ACHAEA, BUT FROM FAR AND WIDE!
IVORY FROM CYPRUS-- GOLD FROM PHOENICIA --PERFUME FROM EGYPT--
KING PHALIS OF SIDON FELL BY MY HAND WHEN WE SACKED HIS CITY.
DO YOU MEAN **YOU** ARE THE RAIDER WHO STORMED SIDON LAST YEAR?
YES! NOW SIDON'S RICHES FILL SHIP AFTER SHIP--ALL FOR **YOU**, GREAT KING!
EXCEPT FOR THE **WOMAN**. HE'S KEEPING HER FOR **HIMSELF**!
IF IT'S WOMEN YOU WANT, HERE THEY ARE! **HIGH-BORN** WOMEN. LOOK, THIS IS THE SISTER OF THE GREAT ACHAEAN HERO PEIRITHOUS. AND THESE DAUGHTERS OF SPARTAN NOBLES WILL MAKE EXCELLENT WIVES FOR MY BROTHERS!

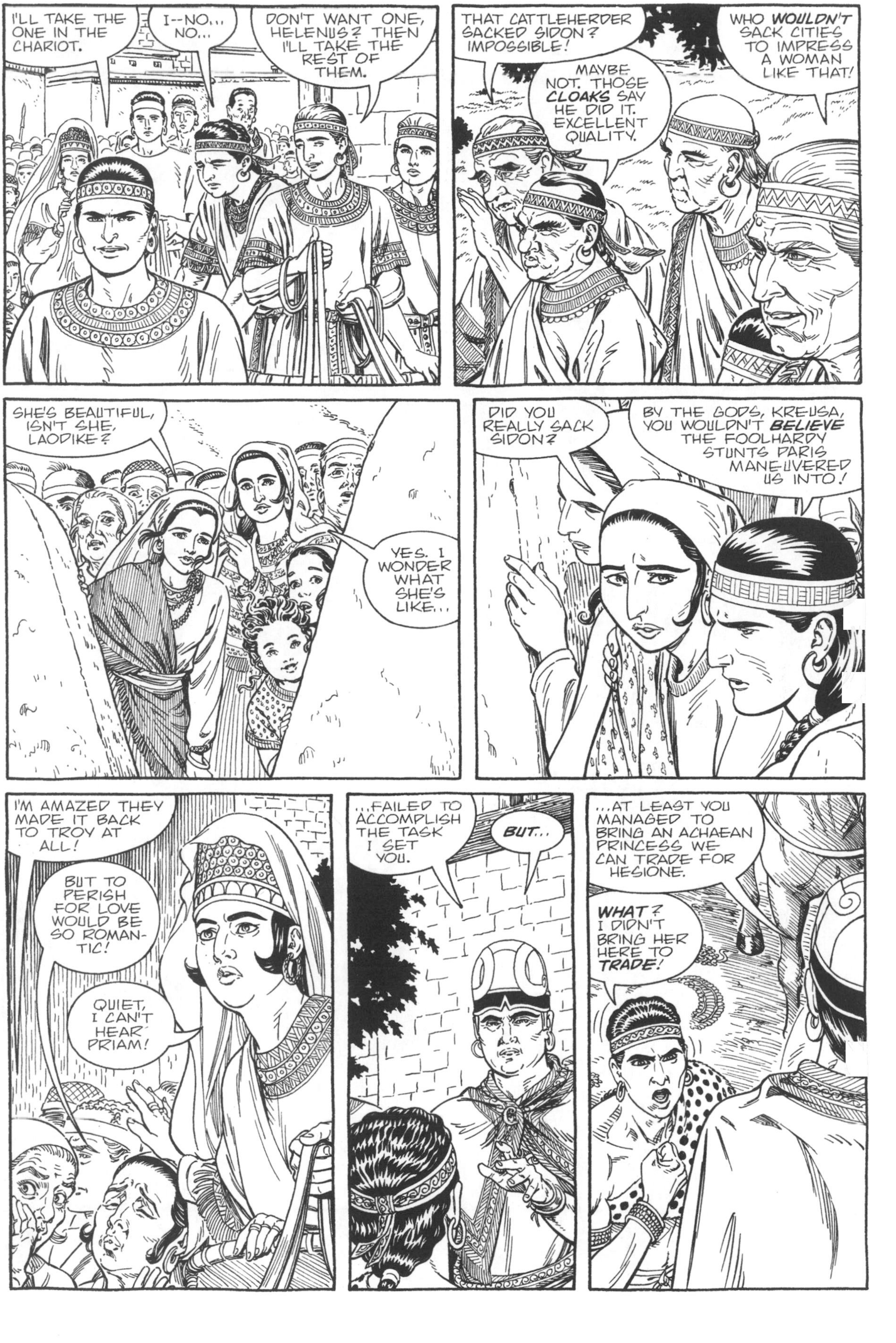
I'LL TAKE THE ONE IN THE CHARIOT.
I--NO... NO...
DON'T WANT ONE, HELENUS? THEN I'LL TAKE THE REST OF THEM.
THAT CATTLEHERDER SACKED SIDON? IMPOSSIBLE!
MAYBE NOT. THOSE CLOAKS SAY HE DID IT. EXCELLENT QUALITY.
WHO WOULDN'T SACK CITIES TO IMPRESS A WOMAN LIKE THAT!
SHE'S BEAUTIFUL, ISN'T SHE, LAODIKE?
YES. I WONDER WHAT SHE'S LIKE...
DID YOU REALLY SACK SIDON?
BY THE GODS, KREUSA, YOU WOULDN'T BELIEVE THE FOOLHARDY STUNTS PARIS MANEUVERED US INTO!
I'M AMAZED THEY MADE IT BACK TO TROY AT ALL!
BUT TO PERISH FOR LOVE WOULD BE SO ROMANTIC!
QUIET, I CAN'T HEAR PRIAM!
...FAILED TO ACCOMPLISH THE TASK I SET YOU.
BUT...
...AT LEAST YOU MANAGED TO BRING AN ACHAEAN PRINCESS WE CAN TRADE FOR HESIONE.
WHAT? I DIDN'T BRING HER HERE TO TRADE!

PARIS, A MAN WHO CARRIES OFF A KING'S WIFE IS CERTAINLY **BRAVE**, BUT NOT VERY SMART. PRIAM KNOWS BEST. DO AS HE SAYS.
NO! HELEN IS MY **WIFE**!
SHE IS NOT YOUR WIFE UNLESS **I** SAY SO!
WAIT.
PRIAM OF TROY, GREAT KING...

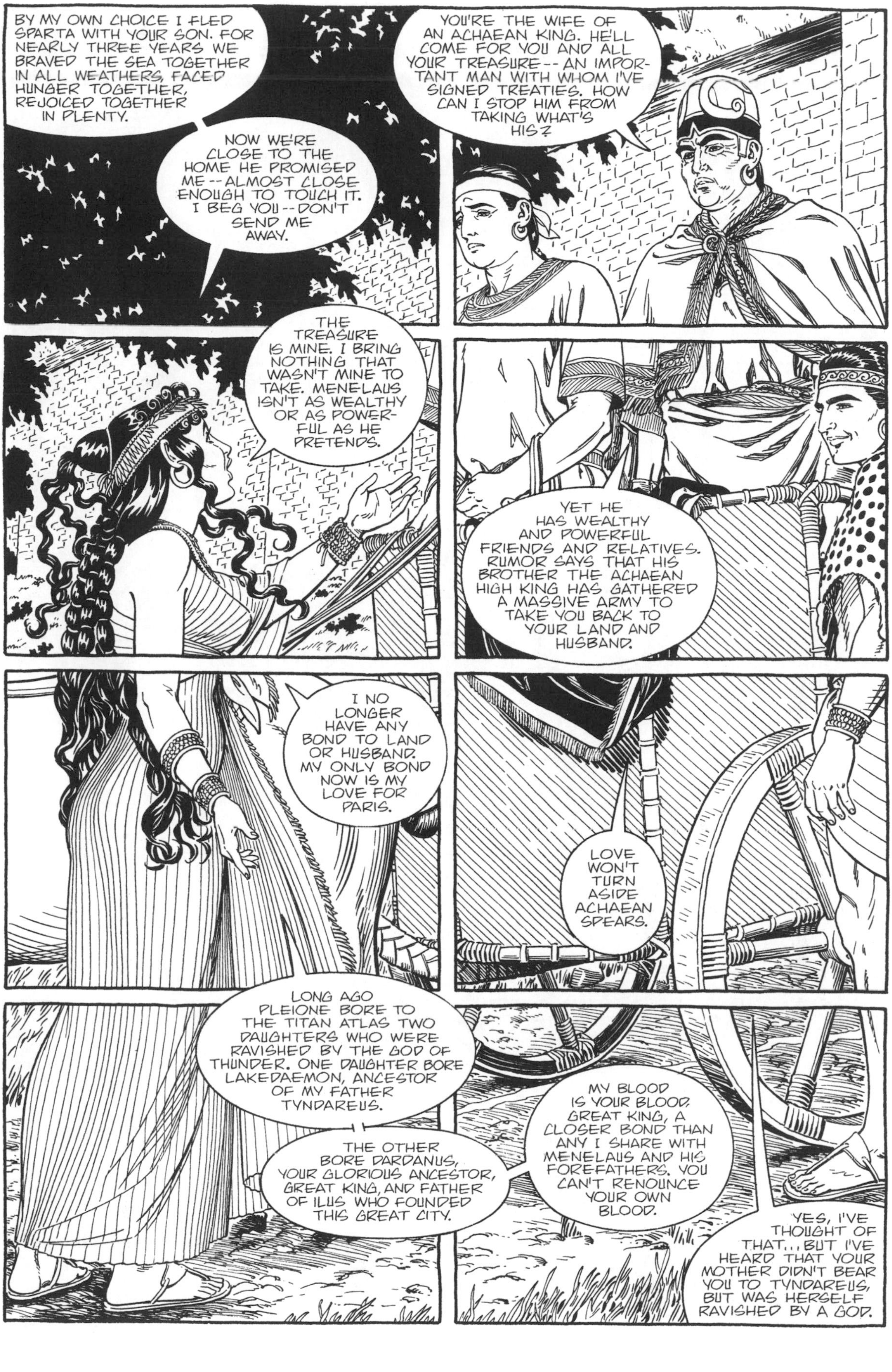
BY MY OWN CHOICE I FLED SPARTA WITH YOUR SON. FOR NEARLY THREE YEARS WE BRAVED THE SEA TOGETHER IN ALL WEATHERS, FACED HUNGER TOGETHER, REJOICED TOGETHER IN PLENTY.
NOW WE'RE CLOSE TO THE HOME HE PROMISED ME--ALMOST CLOSE ENOUGH TO TOUCH IT. I BEG YOU--DON'T SEND ME AWAY.
YOU'RE THE WIFE OF AN ACHAEAN KING. HE'LL COME FOR YOU AND ALL YOUR TREASURE--AN IMPORTANT MAN WITH WHOM I'VE SIGNED TREATIES. HOW CAN I STOP HIM FROM TAKING WHAT'S HIS?
THE TREASURE IS MINE. I BRING NOTHING THAT WASN'T MINE TO TAKE. MENELAUS ISN'T AS WEALTHY OR AS POWERFUL AS HE PRETENDS.
YET HE HAS WEALTHY AND POWERFUL FRIENDS AND RELATIVES. RUMOR SAYS THAT HIS BROTHER THE ACHAEAN HIGH KING HAS GATHERED A MASSIVE ARMY TO TAKE YOU BACK TO YOUR LAND AND HUSBAND.
I NO LONGER HAVE ANY BOND TO LAND OR HUSBAND. MY ONLY BOND NOW IS MY LOVE FOR PARIS.
LOVE WON'T TURN ASIDE ACHAEAN SPEARS.
LONG AGO PLEIONE BORE TO THE TITAN ATLAS TWO DAUGHTERS WHO WERE RAVISHED BY THE GOD OF THUNDER. ONE DAUGHTER BORE LAKEDAEMON, ANCESTOR OF MY FATHER TYNDAREUS.
THE OTHER BORE DARDANUS, YOUR GLORIOUS ANCESTOR, GREAT KING, AND FATHER OF ILUS WHO FOUNDED THIS GREAT CITY.
MY BLOOD IS YOUR BLOOD, GREAT KING, A CLOSER BOND THAN ANY I SHARE WITH MENELAUS AND HIS FOREFATHERS. YOU CAN'T RENOUNCE YOUR OWN BLOOD.
YES, I'VE THOUGHT OF THAT... BUT I'VE HEARD THAT YOUR MOTHER DIDN'T BEAR YOU TO TYNDAREUS, BUT WAS HERSELF RAVISHED BY A GOD.

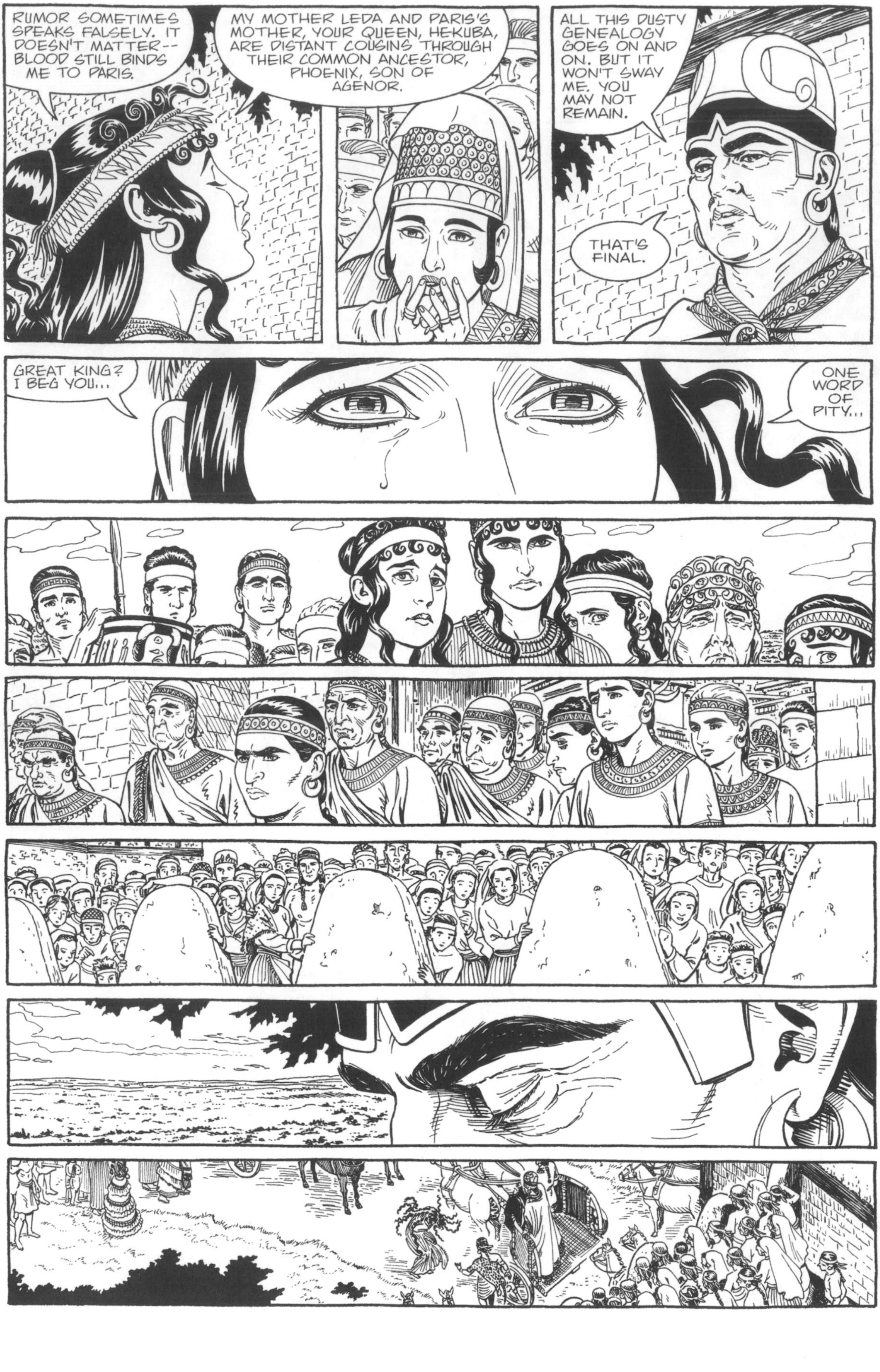
RUMOR SOMETIMES SPEAKS FALSELY. IT DOESN'T MATTER-- BLOOD STILL BINDS ME TO PARIS.
MY MOTHER LEDA AND PARIS'S MOTHER, YOUR QUEEN, HEKUBA, ARE DISTANT COUSINS THROUGH THEIR COMMON ANCESTOR, PHOENIX, SON OF AGENOR.
ALL THIS DUSTY GENEALOGY GOES ON AND ON. BUT IT WON'T SWAY ME. YOU MAY NOT REMAIN.
THAT'S FINAL.
GREAT KING? I BEG YOU...
ONE WORD OF PITY...

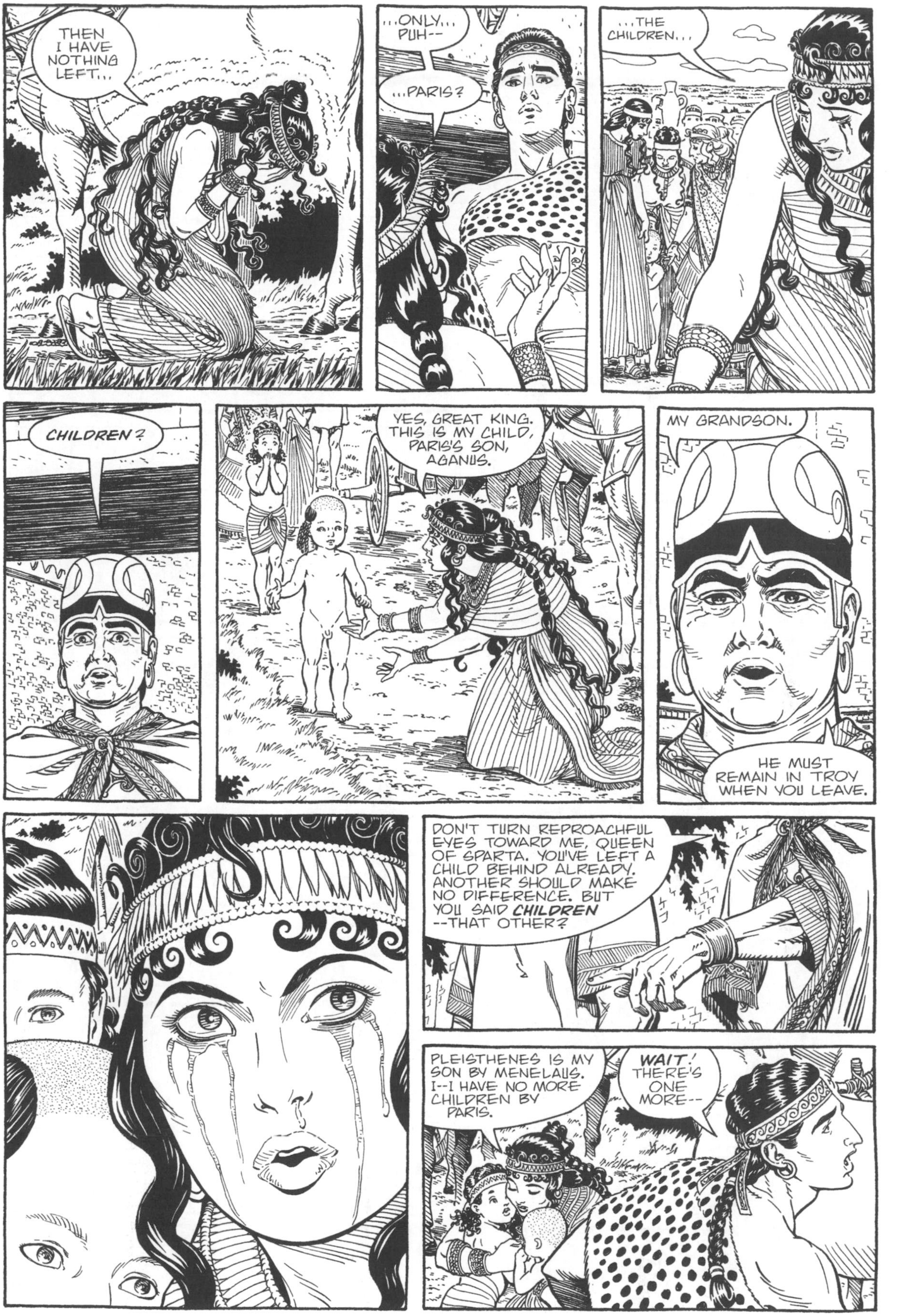

THEN I HAVE NOTHING LEFT...
...ONLY... PUH--
...PARIS?
...THE CHILDREN...
CHILDREN?
YES, GREAT KING. THIS IS MY CHILD, PARIS'S SON, AGANUS.
MY GRANDSON.
HE MUST REMAIN IN TROY WHEN YOU LEAVE.
DON'T TURN REPROACHFUL EYES TOWARD ME, QUEEN OF SPARTA. YOU'VE LEFT A CHILD BEHIND ALREADY. ANOTHER SHOULD MAKE NO DIFFERENCE. BUT YOU SAID CHILDREN --THAT OTHER?
PLEISTHENES IS MY SON BY MENELAUS. I--I HAVE NO MORE CHILDREN BY PARIS.
WAIT! THERE'S ONE MORE--

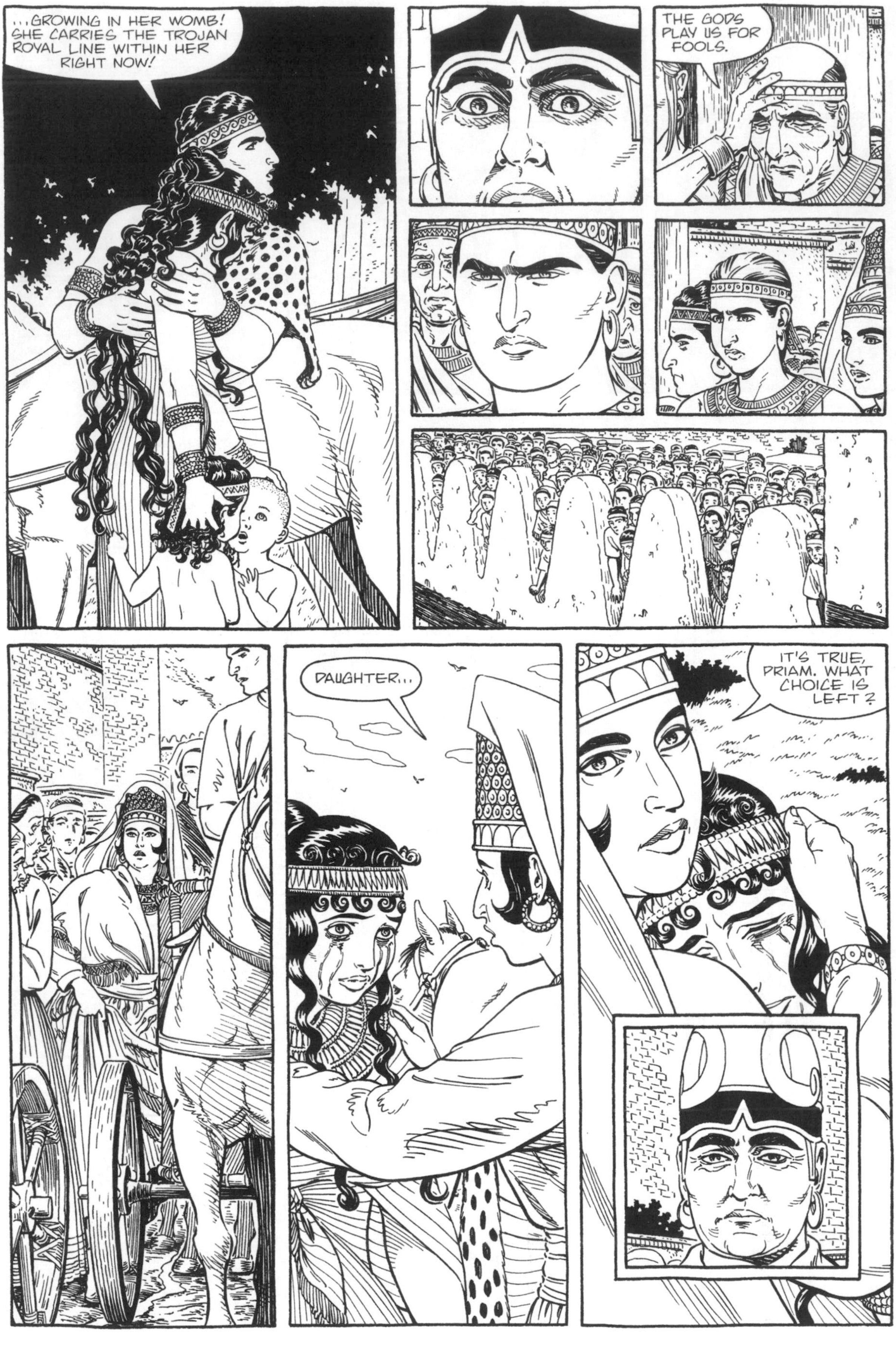
...GROWING IN HER WOMB! SHE CARRIES THE TROJAN ROYAL LINE WITHIN HER RIGHT NOW!
THE GODS PLAY US FOR FOOLS.
DAUGHTER...
IT'S TRUE, PRIAM. WHAT CHOICE IS LEFT?

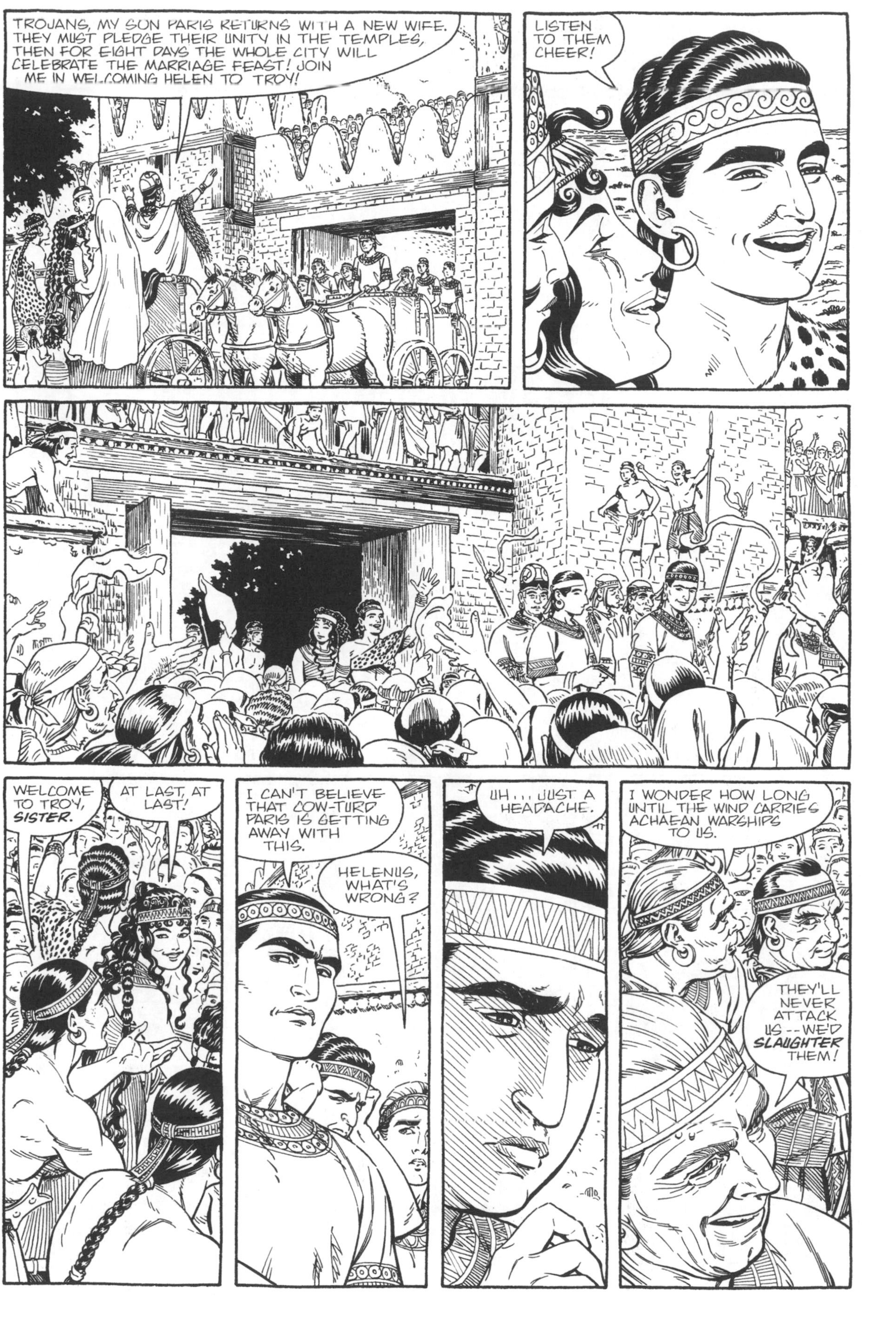
TROJANS, MY SON PARIS RETURNS WITH A NEW WIFE. THEY MUST PLEDGE THEIR UNITY IN THE TEMPLES, THEN FOR EIGHT DAYS THE WHOLE CITY WILL CELEBRATE THE MARRIAGE FEAST! JOIN ME IN WELCOMING HELEN TO TROY!
LISTEN TO THEM CHEER!
WELCOME TO TROY, SISTER.
AT LAST, AT LAST!
I CAN'T BELIEVE THAT COW-TURD PARIS IS GETTING AWAY WITH THIS.
HELENUS, WHAT'S WRONG?
UH... JUST A HEADACHE.
I WONDER HOW LONG UNTIL THE WIND CARRIES ACHAEAN WARSHIPS TO US.
THEY'LL NEVER ATTACK US--WE'D SLAUGHTER THEM!

GREAT KING, I PRAY THAT TROY WON'T COME TO REGRET THIS DAY.

THE GODS HAVE DECIDED, ANTENOR. TROY'S FATE RESTS IN THEIR HANDS.

BUT WHATEVER HAPPENS, I HAVE TO ADMIT I LIKE HER. YOU SAW THE WAY SHE STOOD UP TO ME...

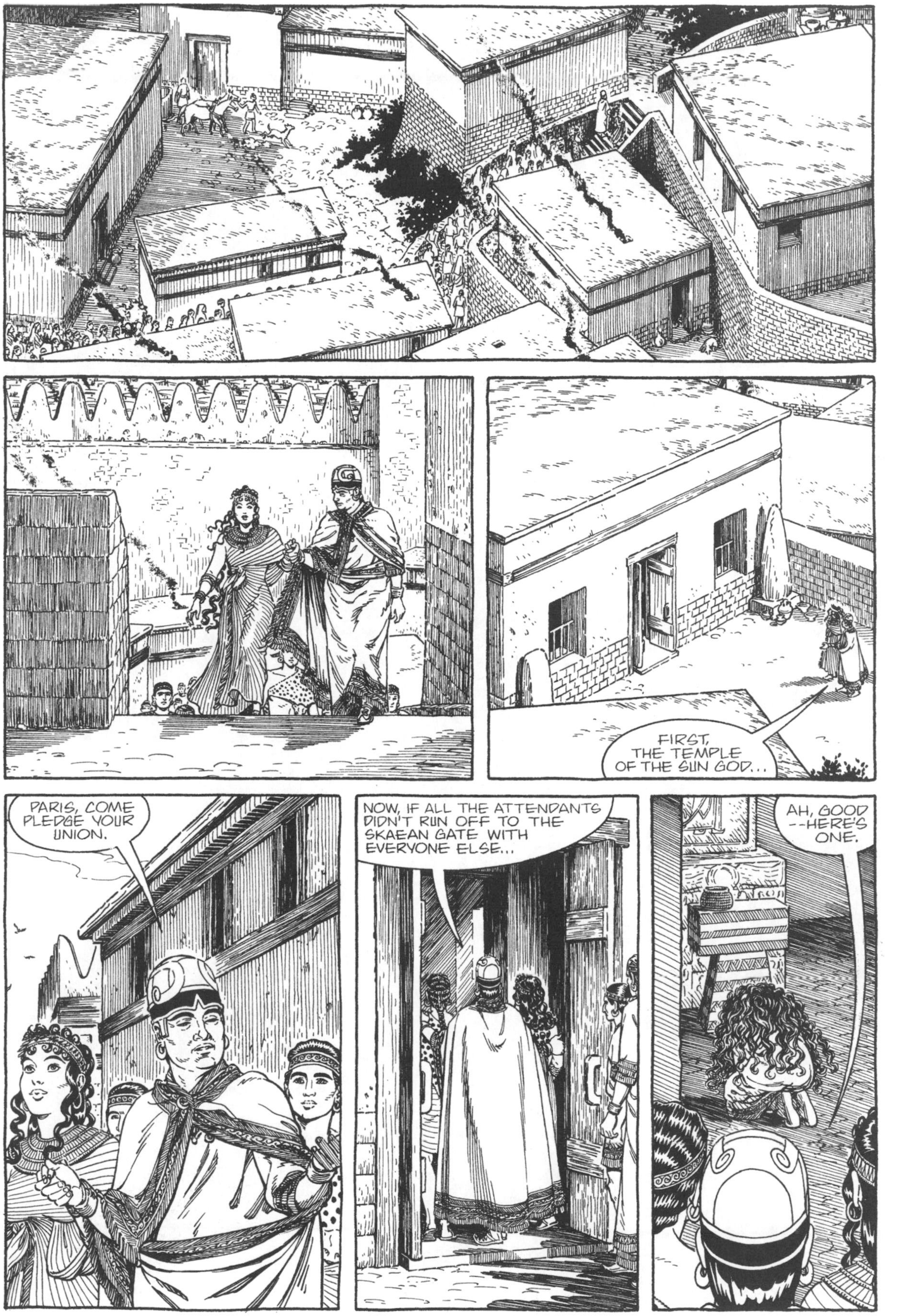
FIRST, THE TEMPLE OF THE SUN GOD...
PARIS, COME PLEDGE YOUR UNION.
NOW, IF ALL THE ATTENDANTS DIDN'T RUN OFF TO THE SKAEAN GATE WITH EVERYONE ELSE...
AH, GOOD --HERE'S ONE.

FIRE!

FIRE AND DESTRUCTION!

KASSANDRA!

YOU'LL KILL US ALL!

WHAT'S HAPPENING? WHAT'S WRONG WITH HER?

DON'T WORRY, HELEN. SHE HAS FITS SOMETIMES. SHE DID THE SAME THING WHEN I FIRST--

AND YOU! PLUCKED FROM YOUR ROUNDED HUSK TO LEAD THE SCALY SERPENT ACROSS THE FLOOD!

STOP THAT NOISE AT ONCE, KASSANDRA! I'LL HAVE YOU HAULED OUT--

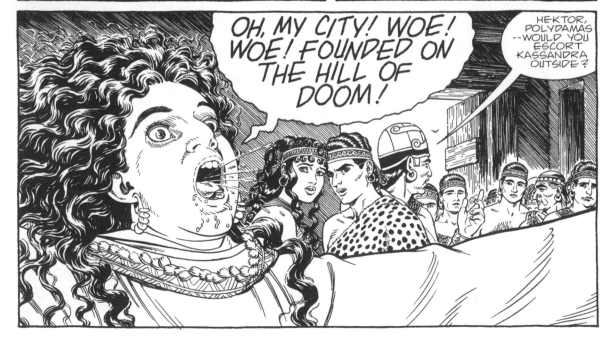

OH, MY CITY! WOE! WOE! FOUNDED ON THE HILL OF DOOM!

HEKTOR, POLYDAMAS --WOULD YOU ESCORT KASSANDRA OUTSIDE?

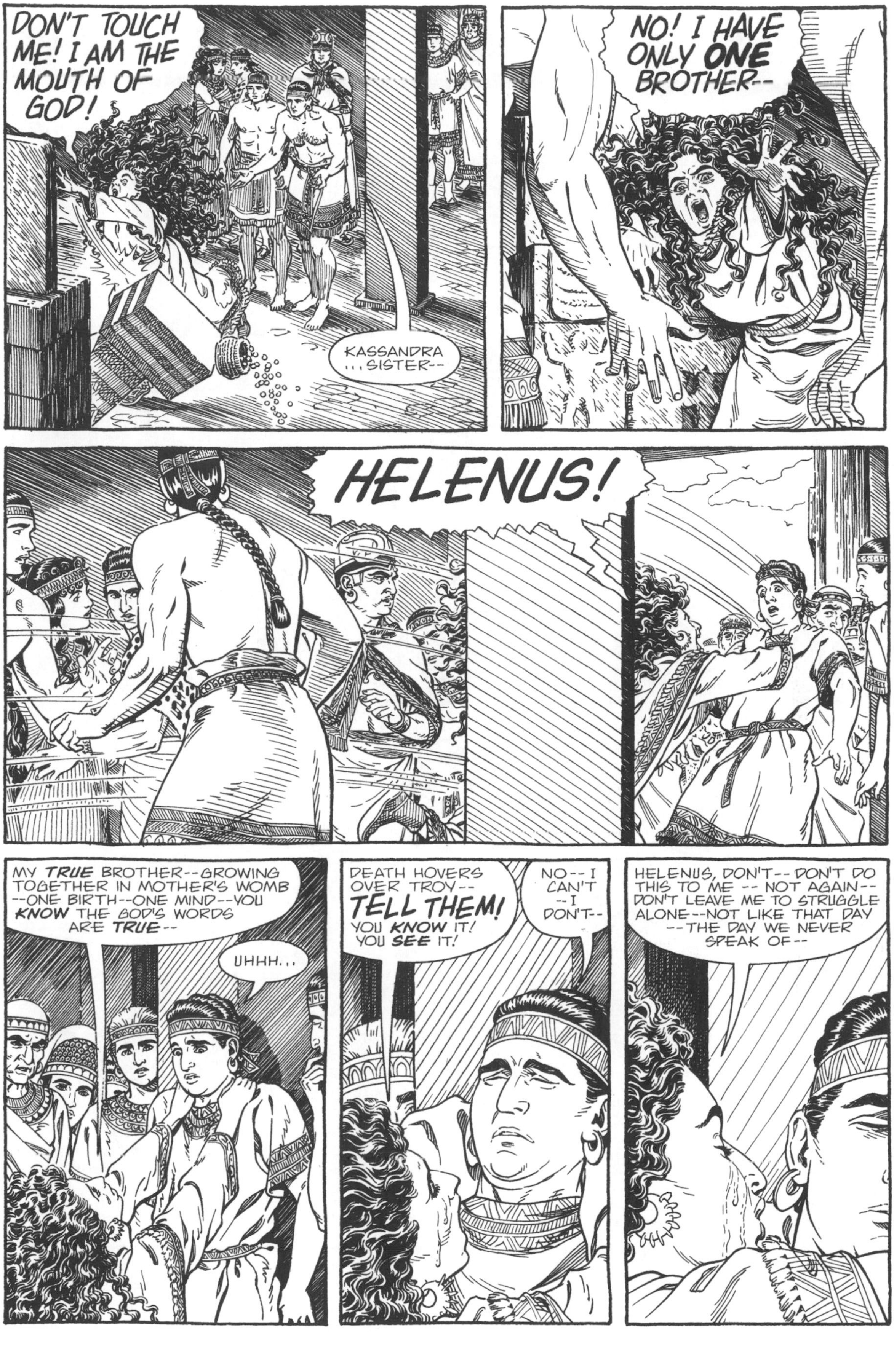
DON'T TOUCH ME! I AM THE MOUTH OF GOD!
KASSANDRA ...SISTER--
NO! I HAVE ONLY ONE BROTHER--
HELENUS!
MY TRUE BROTHER--GROWING TOGETHER IN MOTHER'S WOMB --ONE BIRTH--ONE MIND--YOU KNOW THE GOD'S WORDS ARE TRUE--
UHHH...
DEATH HOVERS OVER TROY-- TELL THEM! YOU KNOW IT! YOU SEE IT!
NO--I CAN'T --I DON'T--
HELENUS, DON'T--DON'T DO THIS TO ME --NOT AGAIN-- DON'T LEAVE ME TO STRUGGLE ALONE--NOT LIKE THAT DAY --THE DAY WE NEVER SPEAK OF--

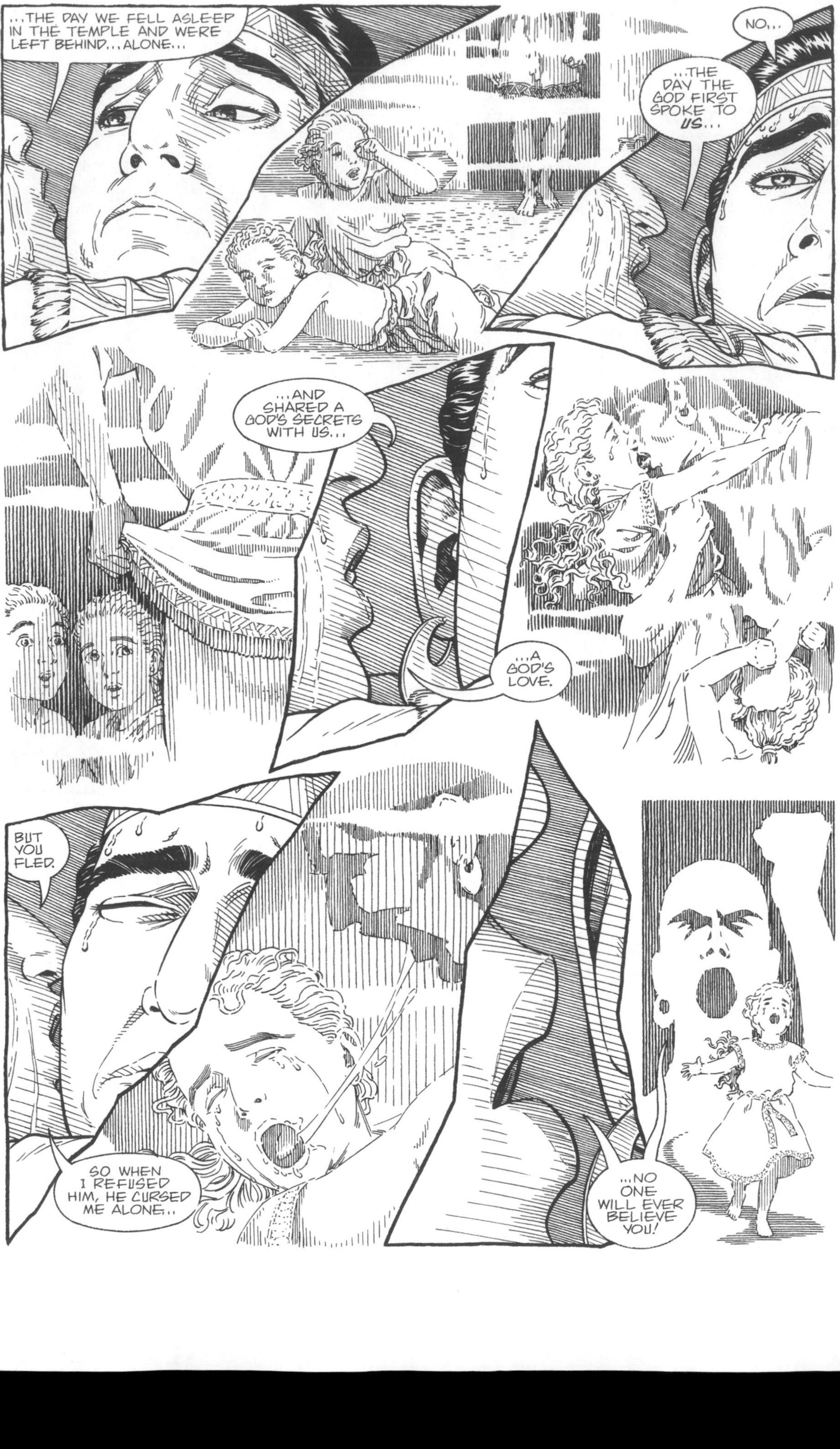
...THE DAY WE FELL ASLEEP IN THE TEMPLE AND WERE LEFT BEHIND... ALONE...
NO,..
...THE DAY THE GOD FIRST SPOKE TO US...
...AND SHARED A GOD'S SECRETS WITH US...
...A GOD'S LOVE.
BUT YOU FLED.
SO WHEN I REFUSED HIM, HE CURSED ME ALONE...
...NO ONE WILL EVER BELIEVE YOU!

THAT CURSE HAS LINGERED EVER SINCE --LIKE THE TASTE OF HIS SALIVA IN MY MOUTH. BUT YOU ESCAPED THE CURSE, MY BROTHER, MY TWIN, MY UNCURSED SELF.

TELL THEM! *TELL THEM!* THEY'LL *BELIEVE YOU!* TELL THEM!

UNH!

KASSANDRA...

HELENUS! DON'T DESERT ME!

KASSANDRA...

NOAAAAAAAAAAAAAAAAAAAAA

CONFINE HER TO HER ROOM. IDAEUS, I WANT SOMEONE WATCHING HER DAY AND NIGHT.

YES, GREAT KING.

≷AHUH≷
≷HAAH≷
≷KAH≷
≷AHUH≷

PEOPLE OF TROY, WE ARE HERE TO FULFILL A DECREE OF THE GODS--A SACRED UNION--

--WHICH MARKS THE START OF THE WEDDING FEAST!

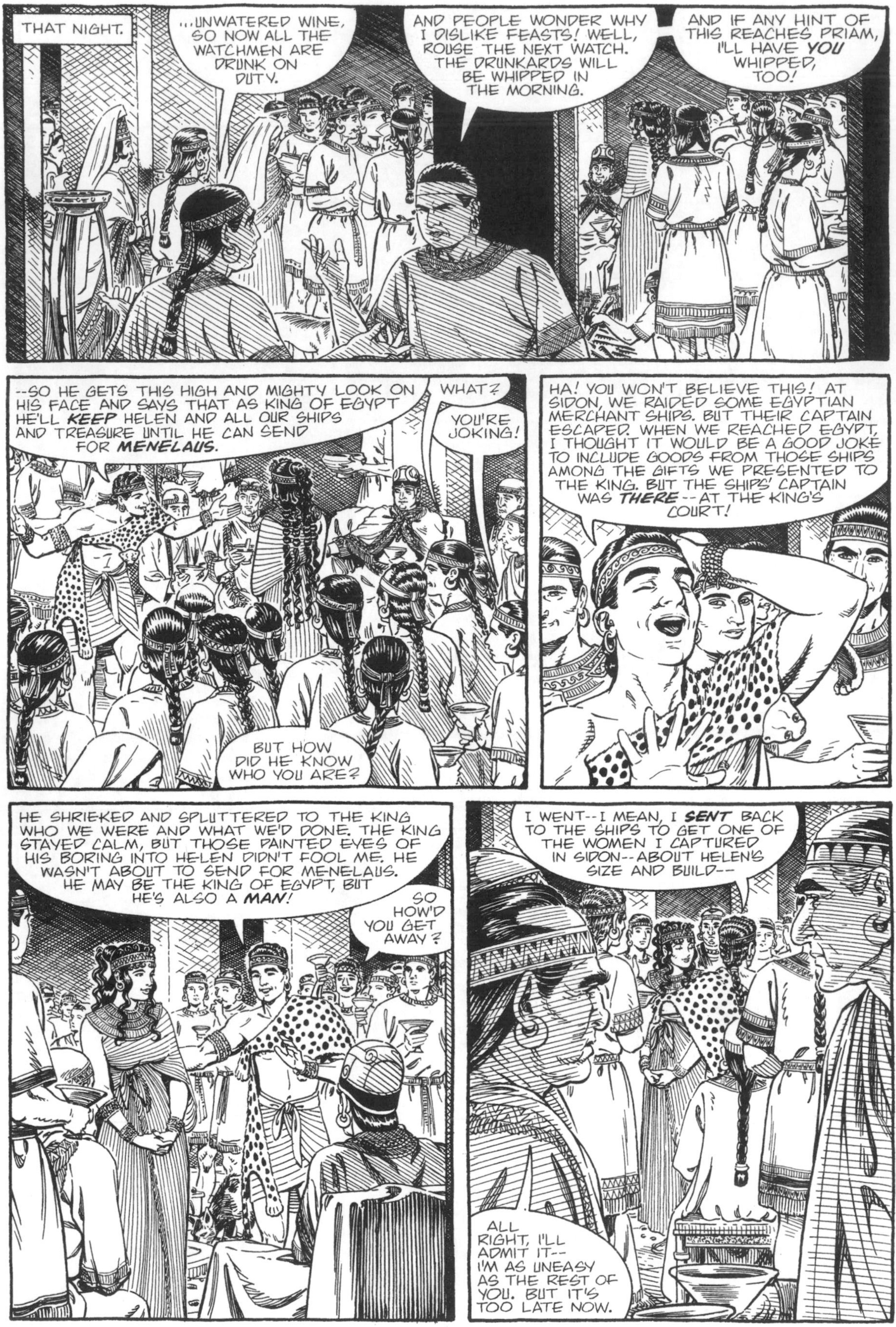
THAT NIGHT.
...UNWATERED WINE, SO NOW ALL THE WATCHMEN ARE DRUNK ON DUTY.
AND PEOPLE WONDER WHY I DISLIKE FEASTS! WELL, ROUSE THE NEXT WATCH. THE DRUNKARDS WILL BE WHIPPED IN THE MORNING.
AND IF ANY HINT OF THIS REACHES PRIAM, I'LL HAVE *YOU* WHIPPED, TOO!
--SO HE GETS THIS HIGH AND MIGHTY LOOK ON HIS FACE AND SAYS THAT AS KING OF EGYPT HE'LL **KEEP** HELEN AND ALL OUR SHIPS AND TREASURE UNTIL HE CAN SEND FOR **MENELAUS**.
WHAT?
YOU'RE JOKING!
BUT HOW DID HE KNOW WHO YOU ARE?
HA! YOU WON'T BELIEVE THIS! AT SIDON, WE RAIDED SOME EGYPTIAN MERCHANT SHIPS. BUT THEIR CAPTAIN ESCAPED. WHEN WE REACHED EGYPT, I THOUGHT IT WOULD BE A GOOD JOKE TO INCLUDE GOODS FROM THOSE SHIPS AMONG THE GIFTS WE PRESENTED TO THE KING. BUT THE SHIPS' CAPTAIN WAS **THERE**--AT THE KING'S COURT!
HE SHRIEKED AND SPLUTTERED TO THE KING WHO WE WERE AND WHAT WE'D DONE. THE KING STAYED CALM, BUT THOSE PAINTED EYES OF HIS BORING INTO HELEN DIDN'T FOOL ME. HE WASN'T ABOUT TO SEND FOR MENELAUS. HE MAY BE THE KING OF EGYPT, BUT HE'S ALSO A **MAN**!
SO HOW'D YOU GET AWAY?
I WENT--I MEAN, I **SENT** BACK TO THE SHIPS TO GET ONE OF THE WOMEN I CAPTURED IN SIDON--ABOUT HELEN'S SIZE AND BUILD--
ALL RIGHT, I'LL ADMIT IT--I'M AS UNEASY AS THE REST OF YOU. BUT IT'S TOO LATE NOW.

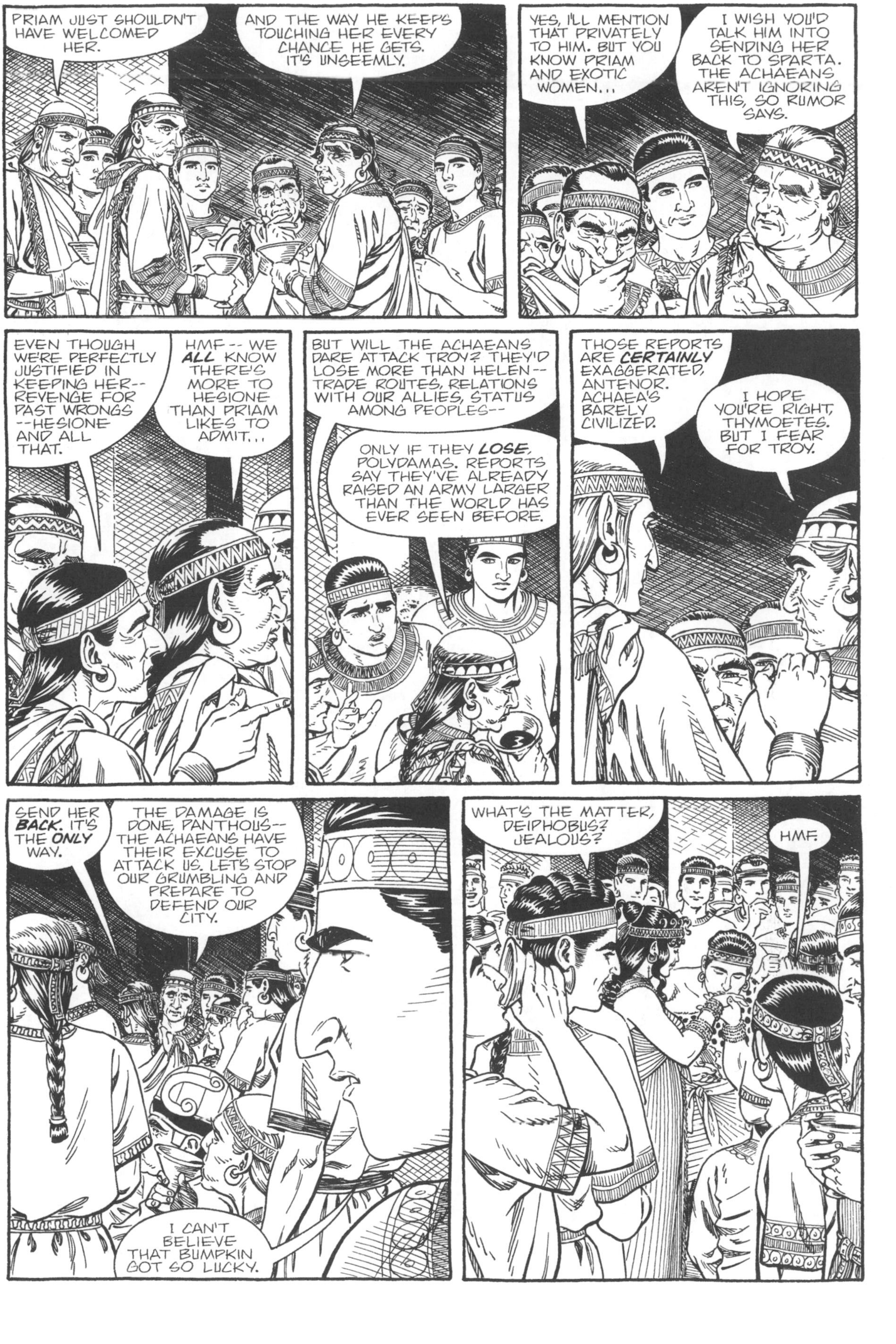
PRIAM JUST SHOULDN'T HAVE WELCOMED HER.
AND THE WAY HE KEEPS TOUCHING HER EVERY CHANCE HE GETS. IT'S UNSEEMLY.
YES, I'LL MENTION THAT PRIVATELY TO HIM. BUT YOU KNOW PRIAM AND EXOTIC WOMEN...
I WISH YOU'D TALK HIM INTO SENDING HER BACK TO SPARTA. THE ACHAEANS AREN'T IGNORING THIS, SO RUMOR SAYS.
EVEN THOUGH WE'RE PERFECTLY JUSTIFIED IN KEEPING HER-- REVENGE FOR PAST WRONGS --HESIONE AND ALL THAT.
HMF-- WE ALL KNOW THERE'S MORE TO HESIONE THAN PRIAM LIKES TO ADMIT...
BUT WILL THE ACHAEANS DARE ATTACK TROY? THEY'D LOSE MORE THAN HELEN-- TRADE ROUTES, RELATIONS WITH OUR ALLIES, STATUS AMONG PEOPLES--
ONLY IF THEY LOSE, POLYDAMAS. REPORTS SAY THEY'VE ALREADY RAISED AN ARMY LARGER THAN THE WORLD HAS EVER SEEN BEFORE.
THOSE REPORTS ARE CERTAINLY EXAGGERATED, ANTENOR. ACHAEA'S BARELY CIVILIZED.
I HOPE YOU'RE RIGHT, THYMOETES. BUT I FEAR FOR TROY.
SEND HER BACK. IT'S THE ONLY WAY.
THE DAMAGE IS DONE, PANTHOUS-- THE ACHAEANS HAVE THEIR EXCUSE TO ATTACK US. LET'S STOP OUR GRUMBLING AND PREPARE TO DEFEND OUR CITY.
I CAN'T BELIEVE THAT BUMPKIN GOT SO LUCKY.
WHAT'S THE MATTER, DEIPHOBUS? JEALOUS?
HMF.

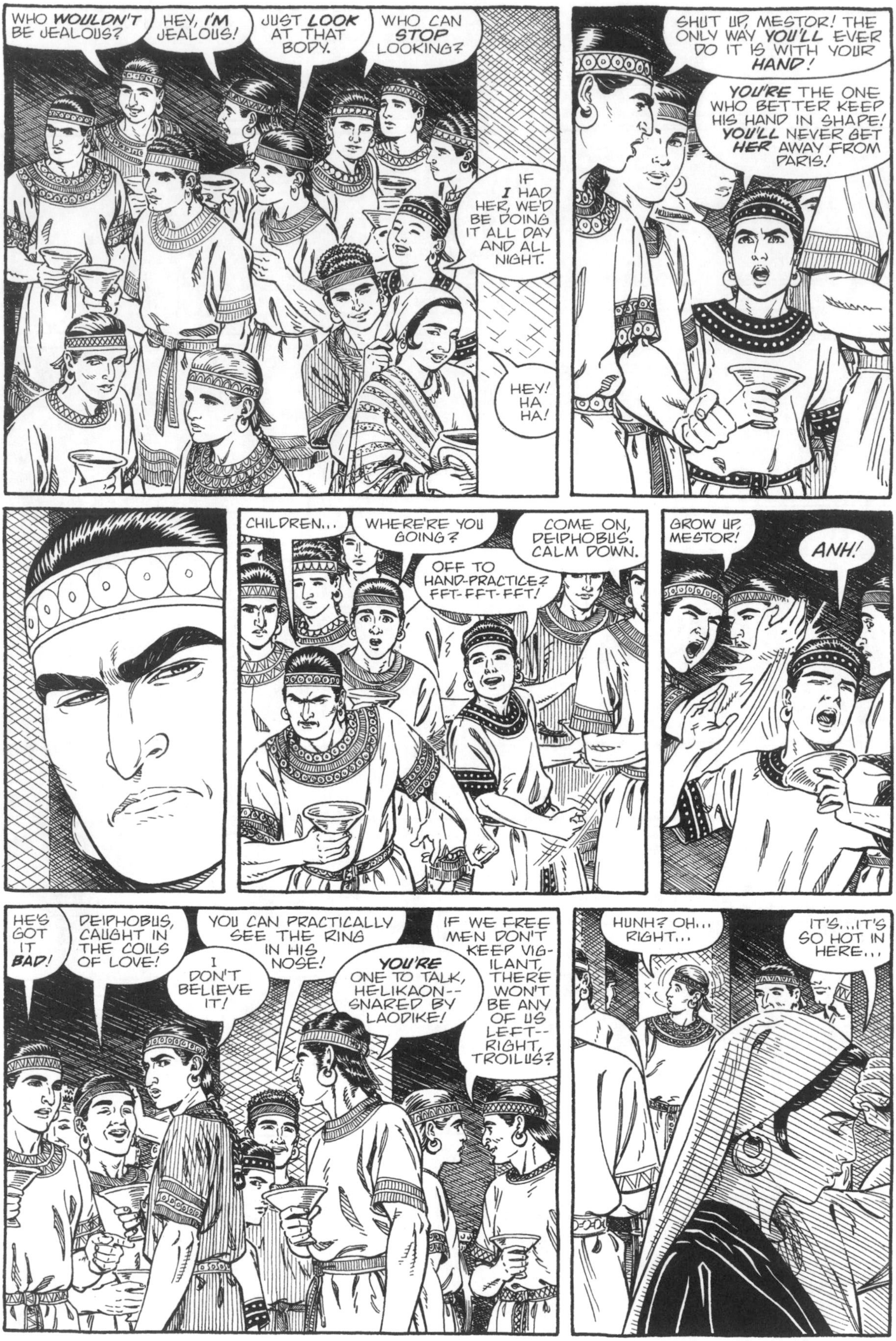

WHO WOULDN'T BE JEALOUS?
HEY, I'M JEALOUS!
JUST LOOK AT THAT BODY.
WHO CAN STOP LOOKING?
IF I HAD HER, WE'D BE DOING IT ALL DAY AND ALL NIGHT.
HEY! HA HA!
SHUT UP, MESTOR! THE ONLY WAY YOU'LL EVER DO IT IS WITH YOUR HAND!
YOU'RE THE ONE WHO BETTER KEEP HIS HAND IN SHAPE! YOU'LL NEVER GET HER AWAY FROM PARIS!
CHILDREN...
WHERE'RE YOU GOING?
COME ON, DEIPHOBUS. CALM DOWN.
OFF TO HAND-PRACTICE? FFT-FFT-FFT!
GROW UP, MESTOR!
ANH!
HE'S GOT IT BAD!
DEIPHOBUS, CAUGHT IN THE COILS OF LOVE!
YOU CAN PRACTICALLY SEE THE RING IN HIS NOSE!
I DON'T BELIEVE IT!
YOU'RE ONE TO TALK, HELIKAON-- SNARED BY LAODIKE!
IF WE FREE MEN DON'T KEEP VIGILANT, THERE WON'T BE ANY OF US LEFT-- RIGHT, TROILUS?
HUNH? OH... RIGHT...
IT'S...IT'S SO HOT IN HERE...

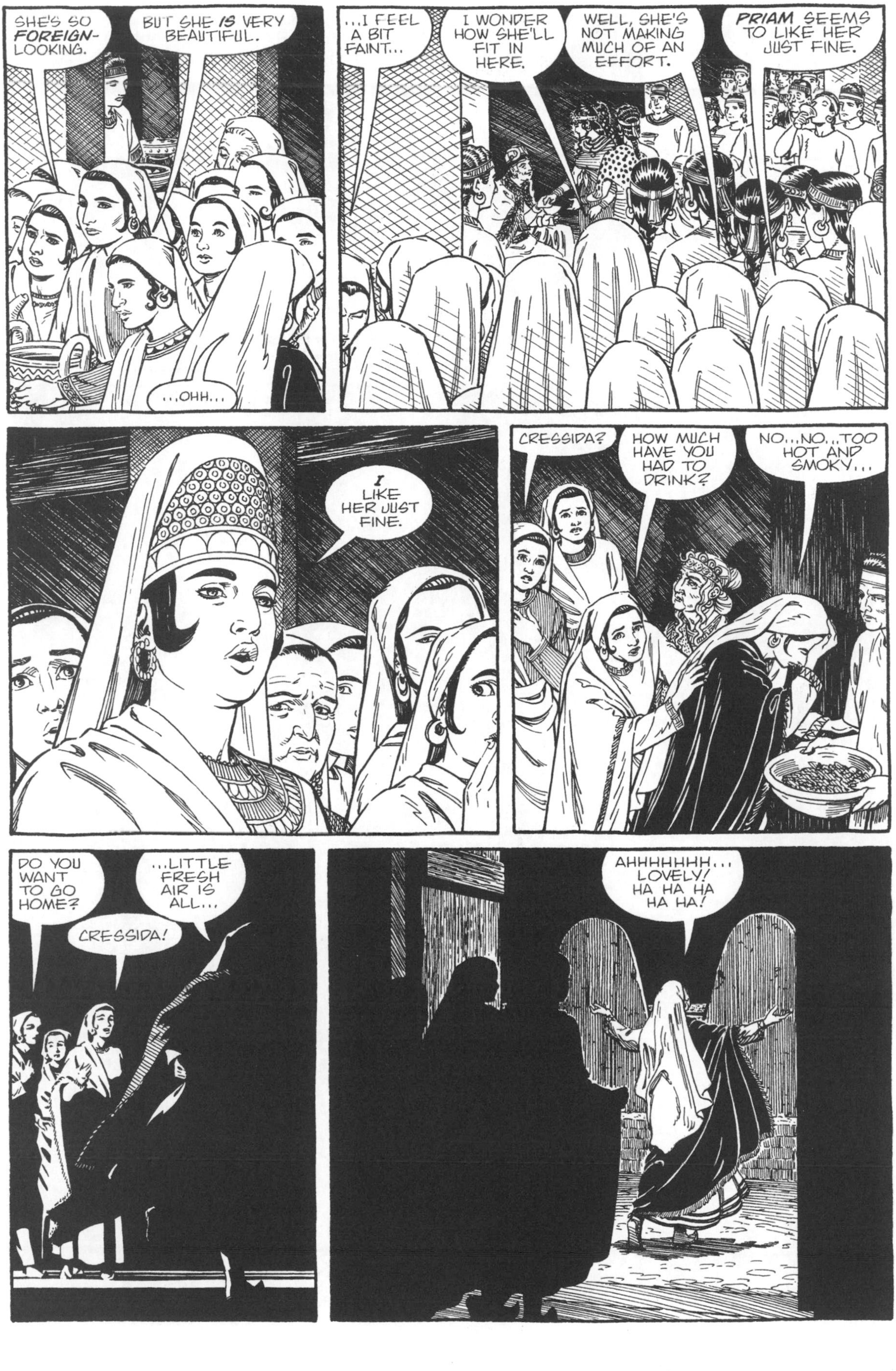
SHE'S SO *FOREIGN*-LOOKING.
BUT SHE *IS* VERY BEAUTIFUL.
...OHH...
...I FEEL A BIT FAINT...
I WONDER HOW SHE'LL FIT IN HERE.
WELL, SHE'S NOT MAKING MUCH OF AN EFFORT.
PRIAM SEEMS TO LIKE HER JUST FINE.
I LIKE HER JUST FINE.
CRESSIDA?
HOW MUCH HAVE YOU HAD TO DRINK?
NO...NO...TOO HOT AND SMOKY...
DO YOU WANT TO GO HOME?
CRESSIDA!
...LITTLE FRESH AIR IS ALL...
AHHHHHHH... LOVELY! HA HA HA HA HA!

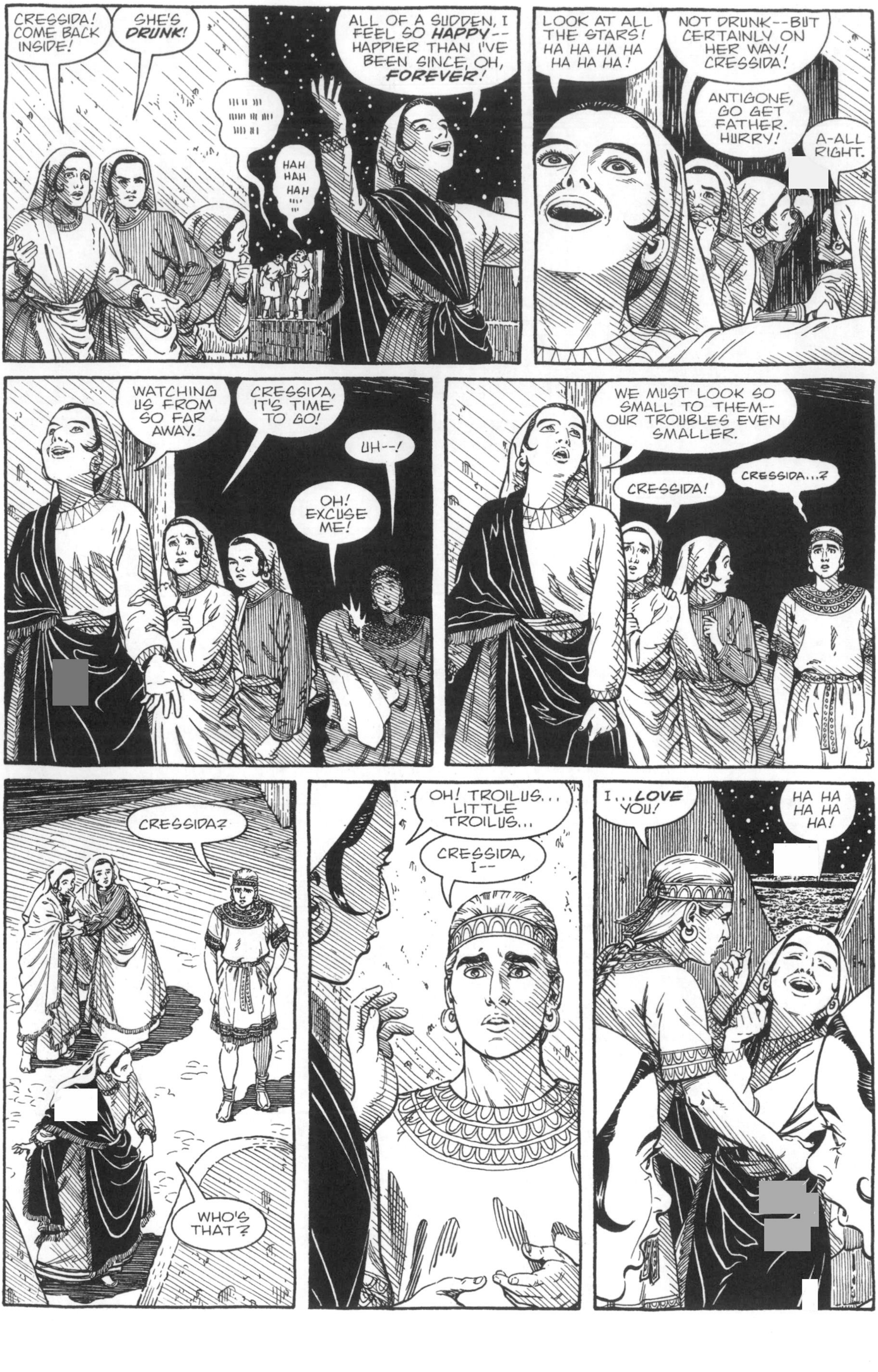
CRESSIDA! COME BACK INSIDE!
SHE'S **DRUNK**!
HAH HAH HAH
ALL OF A SUDDEN, I FEEL SO **HAPPY**-- HAPPIER THAN I'VE BEEN SINCE, OH, **FOREVER**!
LOOK AT ALL THE STARS! HA HA HA HA HA HA HA!
NOT DRUNK--BUT CERTAINLY ON HER WAY! CRESSIDA!
ANTIGONE, GO GET FATHER. HURRY!
A-ALL RIGHT.
WATCHING US FROM SO FAR AWAY.
CRESSIDA, IT'S TIME TO GO!
UH--!
OH! EXCUSE ME!
WE MUST LOOK SO SMALL TO THEM-- OUR TROUBLES EVEN SMALLER.
CRESSIDA!
CRESSIDA...?
CRESSIDA?
WHO'S THAT?
OH! TROILUS... LITTLE TROILUS...
CRESSIDA, I--
I...**LOVE** YOU!
HA HA HA HA HA!

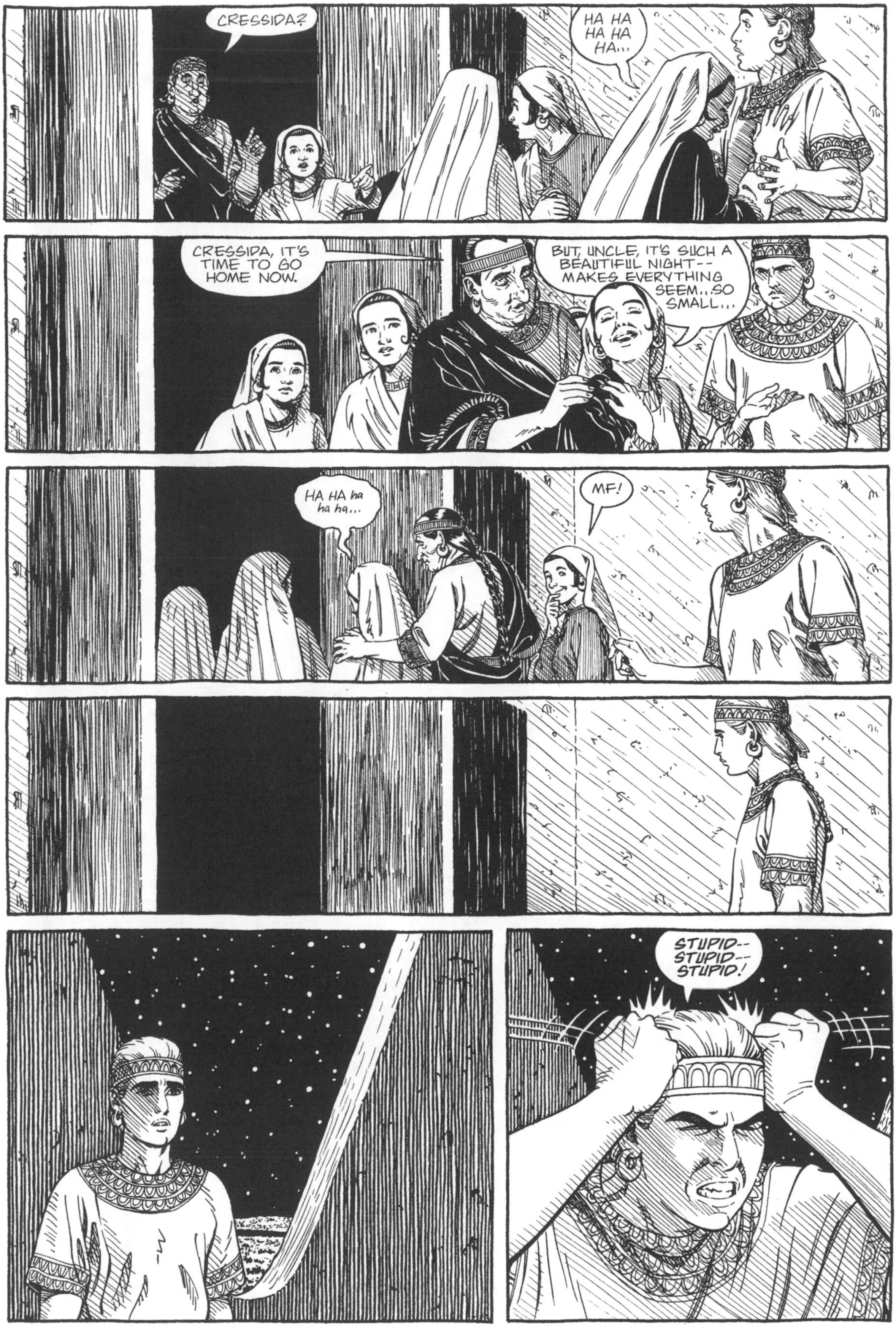
CRESSIDA?
HA HA HA HA HA...
CRESSIDA, IT'S TIME TO GO HOME NOW.
BUT, UNCLE, IT'S SUCH A BEAUTIFUL NIGHT-- MAKES EVERYTHING SEEM...SO SMALL...
HA HA ha ha ha...
MF!
STUPID-- STUPID-- STUPID!

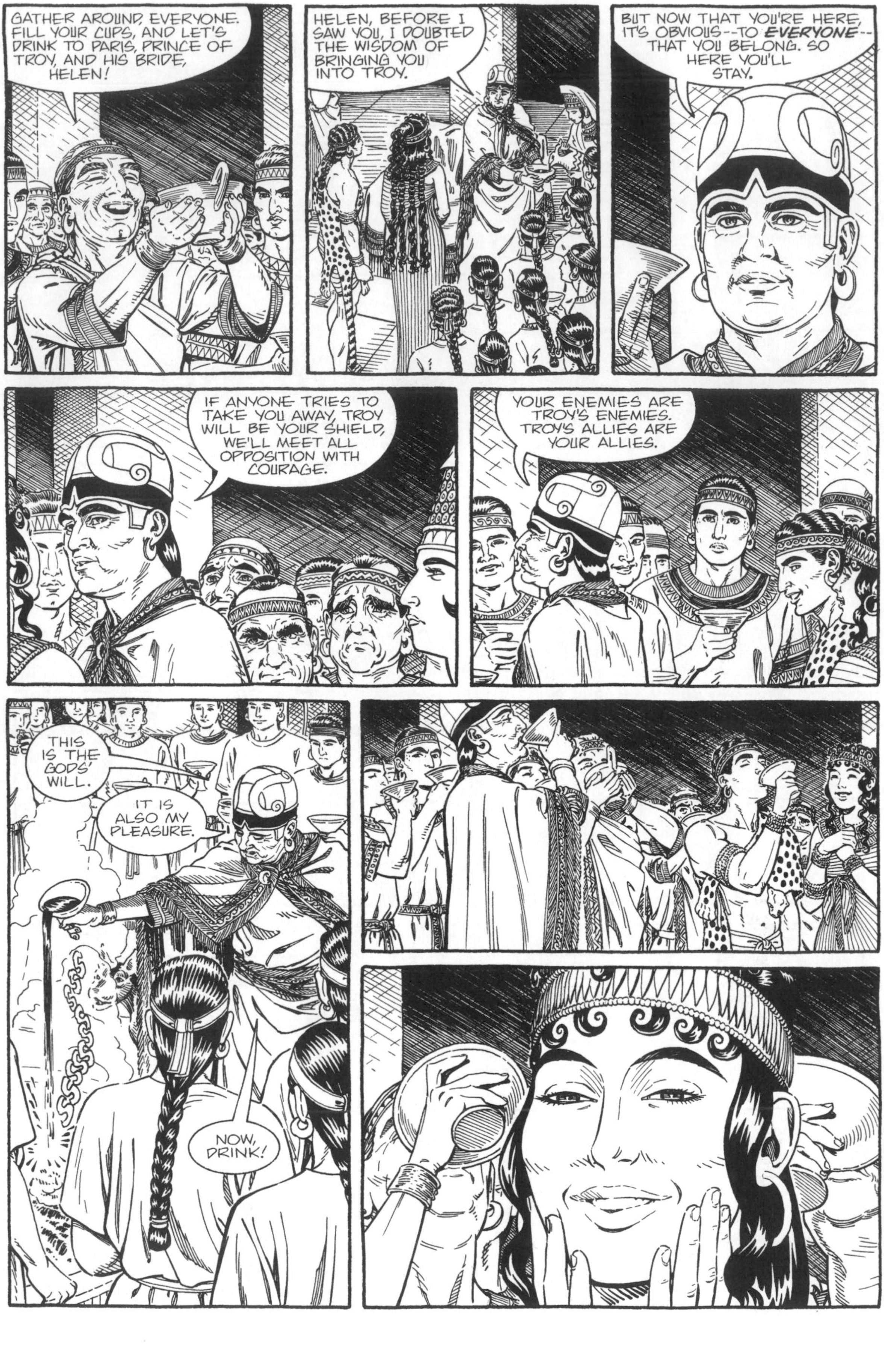
GATHER AROUND, EVERYONE. FILL YOUR CUPS, AND LET'S DRINK TO PARIS, PRINCE OF TROY, AND HIS BRIDE, HELEN!
HELEN, BEFORE I SAW YOU, I DOUBTED THE WISDOM OF BRINGING YOU INTO TROY.
BUT NOW THAT YOU'RE HERE, IT'S OBVIOUS--TO EVERYONE--THAT YOU BELONG. SO HERE YOU'LL STAY.
IF ANYONE TRIES TO TAKE YOU AWAY, TROY WILL BE YOUR SHIELD, WE'LL MEET ALL OPPOSITION WITH COURAGE.
YOUR ENEMIES ARE TROY'S ENEMIES. TROY'S ALLIES ARE YOUR ALLIES.
THIS IS THE GODS' WILL.
IT IS ALSO MY PLEASURE.
NOW, DRINK!

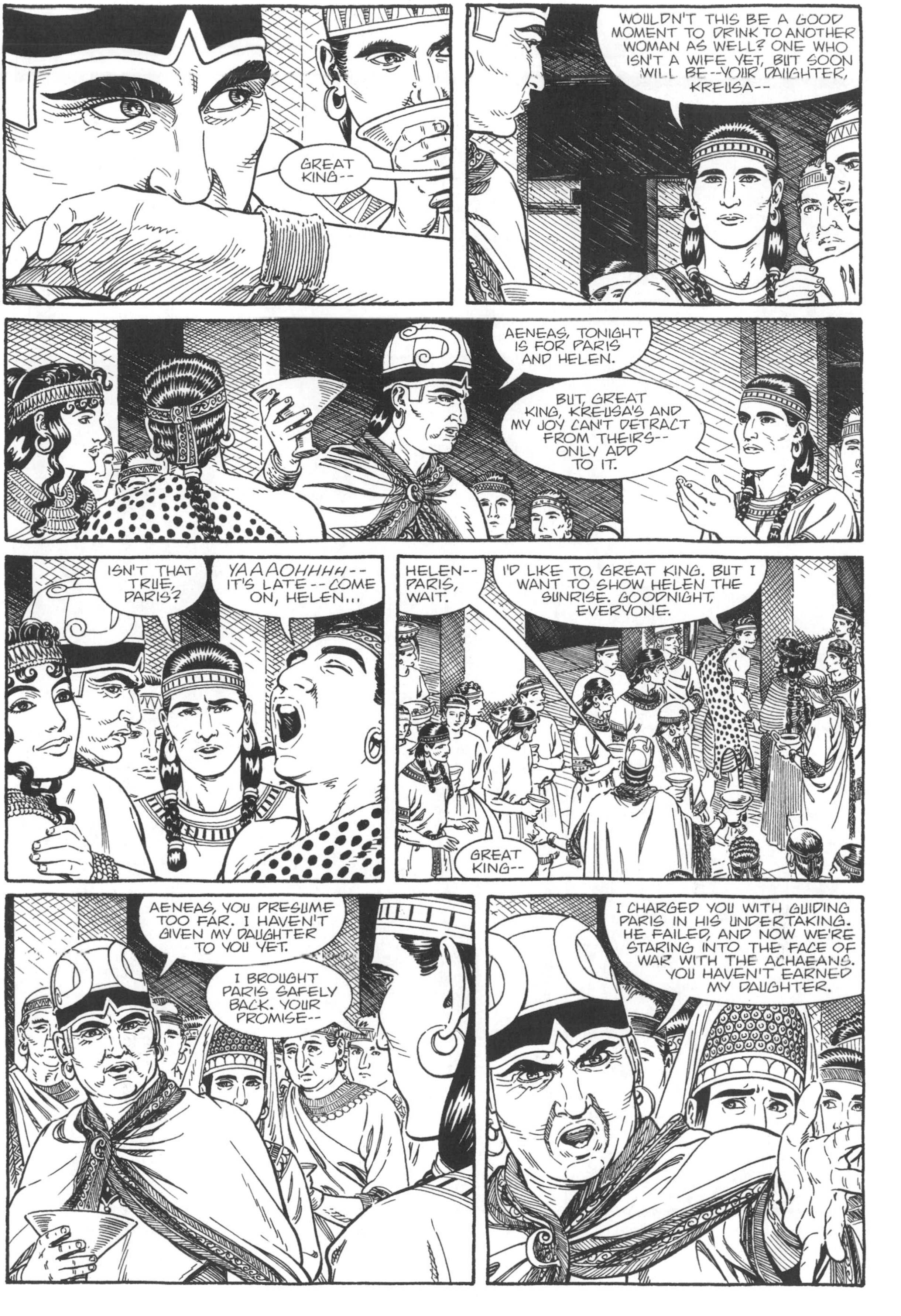
GREAT KING--
WOULDN'T THIS BE A GOOD MOMENT TO DRINK TO ANOTHER WOMAN AS WELL? ONE WHO ISN'T A WIFE YET, BUT SOON WILL BE--YOUR DAUGHTER, KREUSA--
AENEAS, TONIGHT IS FOR PARIS AND HELEN.
BUT, GREAT KING, KREUSA'S AND MY JOY CAN'T DETRACT FROM THEIRS-- ONLY ADD TO IT.
ISN'T THAT TRUE, PARIS?
YAAAOHHHH-- IT'S LATE--COME ON, HELEN...
HELEN-- PARIS, WAIT.
I'D LIKE TO, GREAT KING. BUT I WANT TO SHOW HELEN THE SUNRISE. GOODNIGHT, EVERYONE.
GREAT KING--
AENEAS, YOU PRESUME TOO FAR. I HAVEN'T GIVEN MY DAUGHTER TO YOU YET.
I BROUGHT PARIS SAFELY BACK. YOUR PROMISE--
I CHARGED YOU WITH GUIDING PARIS IN HIS UNDERTAKING. HE FAILED, AND NOW WE'RE STARING INTO THE FACE OF WAR WITH THE ACHAEANS. YOU HAVEN'T EARNED MY DAUGHTER.

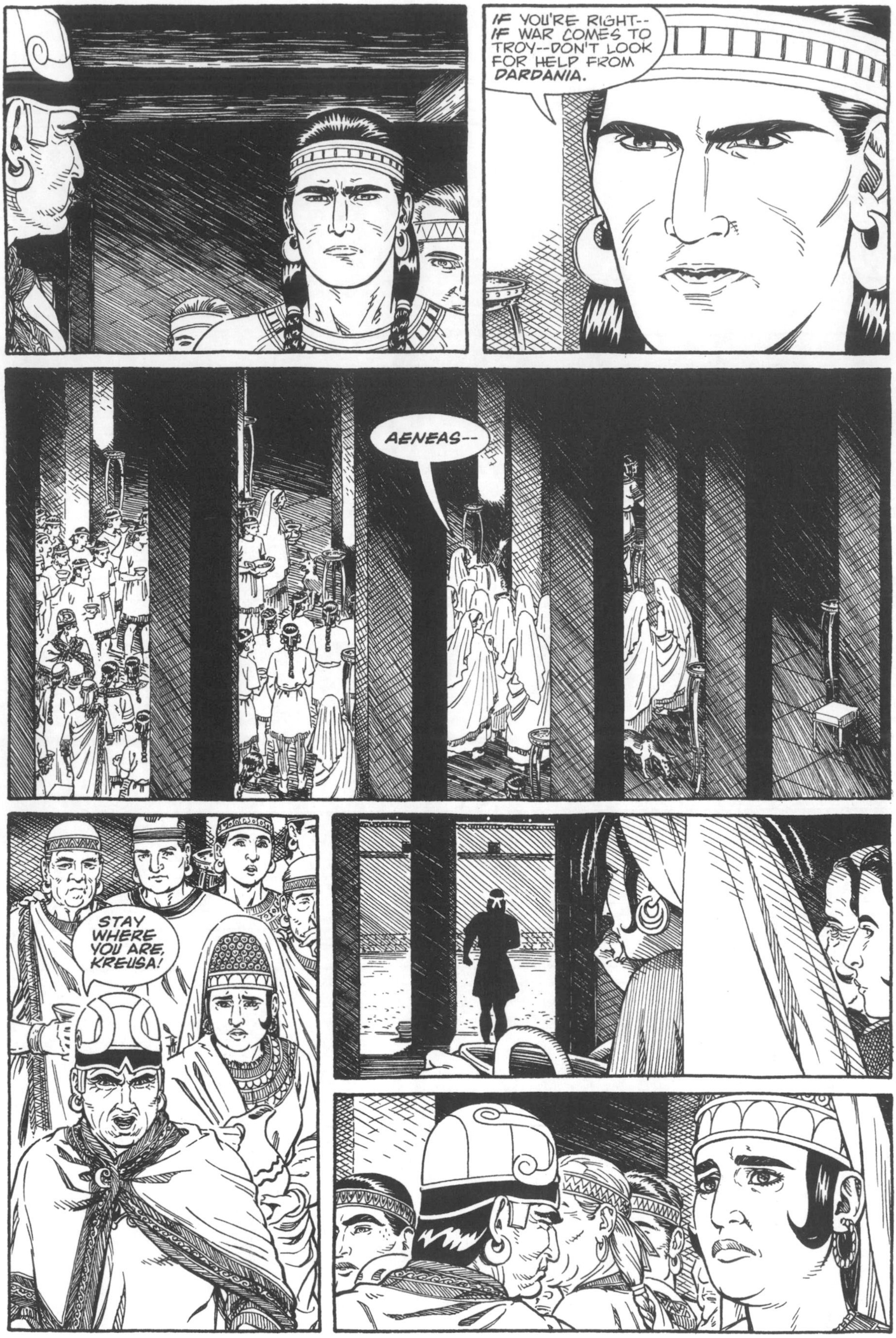
IF YOU'RE RIGHT-- IF WAR COMES TO TROY--DON'T LOOK FOR HELP FROM DARDANIA.
AENEAS--
STAY WHERE YOU ARE, KREUSA!

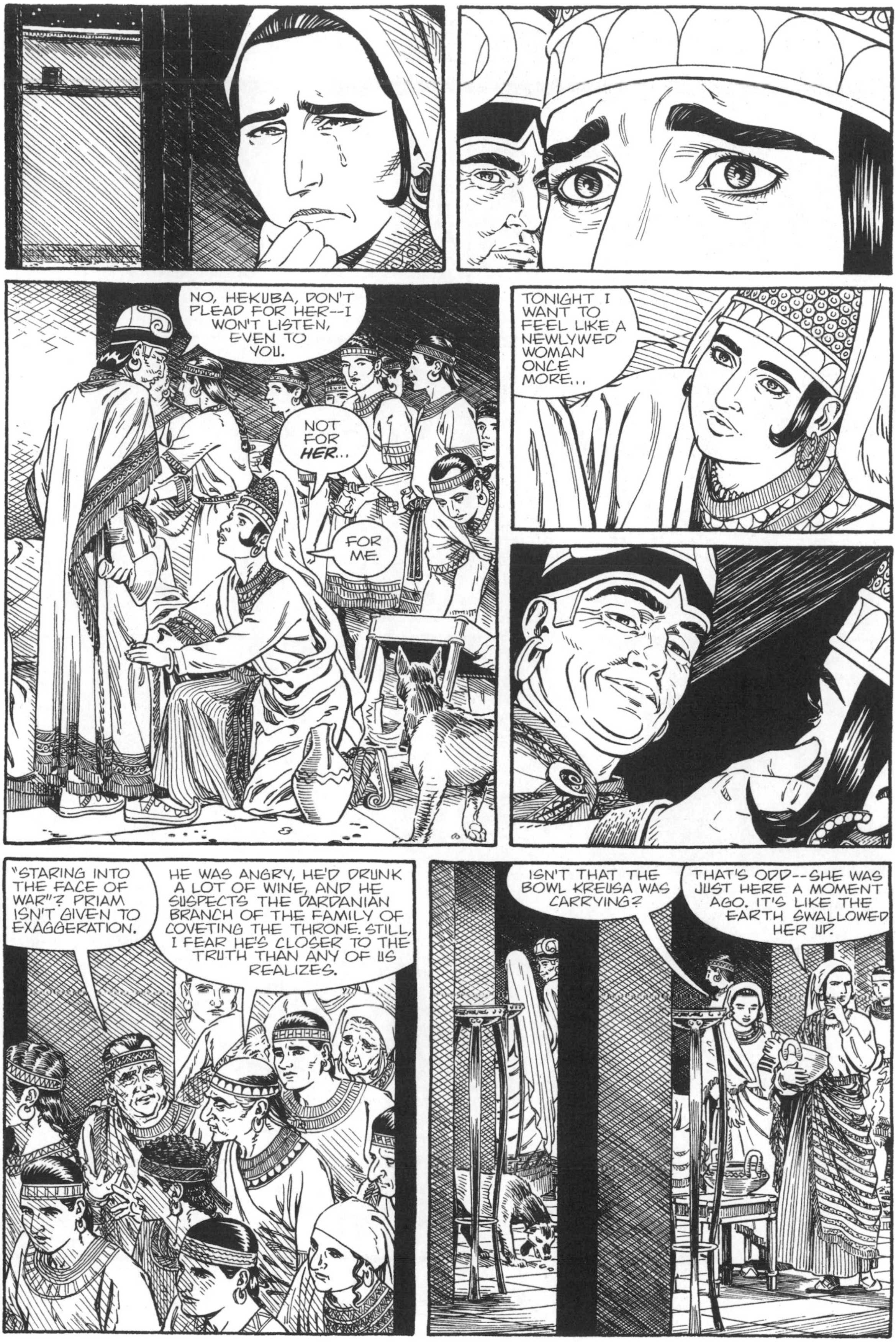
NO, HEKUBA, DON'T PLEAD FOR HER--I WON'T LISTEN, EVEN TO YOU.
NOT FOR HER...
FOR ME.
TONIGHT I WANT TO FEEL LIKE A NEWLYWED WOMAN ONCE MORE...
"STARING INTO THE FACE OF WAR"? PRIAM ISN'T GIVEN TO EXAGGERATION.
HE WAS ANGRY, HE'D DRUNK A LOT OF WINE, AND HE SUSPECTS THE DARDANIAN BRANCH OF THE FAMILY OF COVETING THE THRONE. STILL, I FEAR HE'S CLOSER TO THE TRUTH THAN ANY OF US REALIZES.
ISN'T THAT THE BOWL KREUSA WAS CARRYING?
THAT'S ODD--SHE WAS JUST HERE A MOMENT AGO. IT'S LIKE THE EARTH SWALLOWED HER UP.

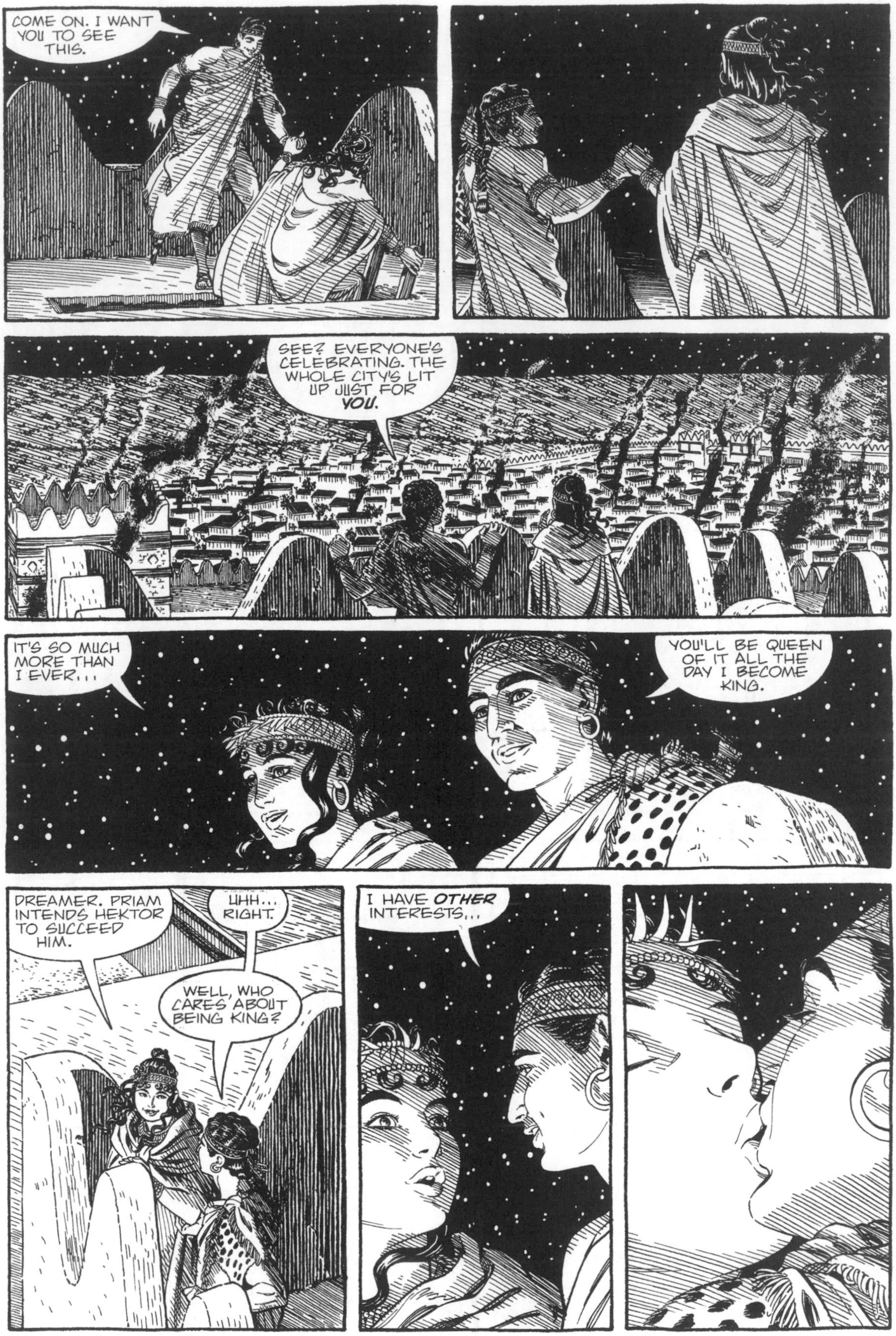
COME ON. I WANT YOU TO SEE THIS.
SEE? EVERYONE'S CELEBRATING. THE WHOLE CITY'S LIT UP JUST FOR YOU.
IT'S SO MUCH MORE THAN I EVER...
YOU'LL BE QUEEN OF IT ALL THE DAY I BECOME KING.
DREAMER. PRIAM INTENDS HEKTOR TO SUCCEED HIM.
UHH... RIGHT.
WELL, WHO CARES ABOUT BEING KING?
I HAVE OTHER INTERESTS...

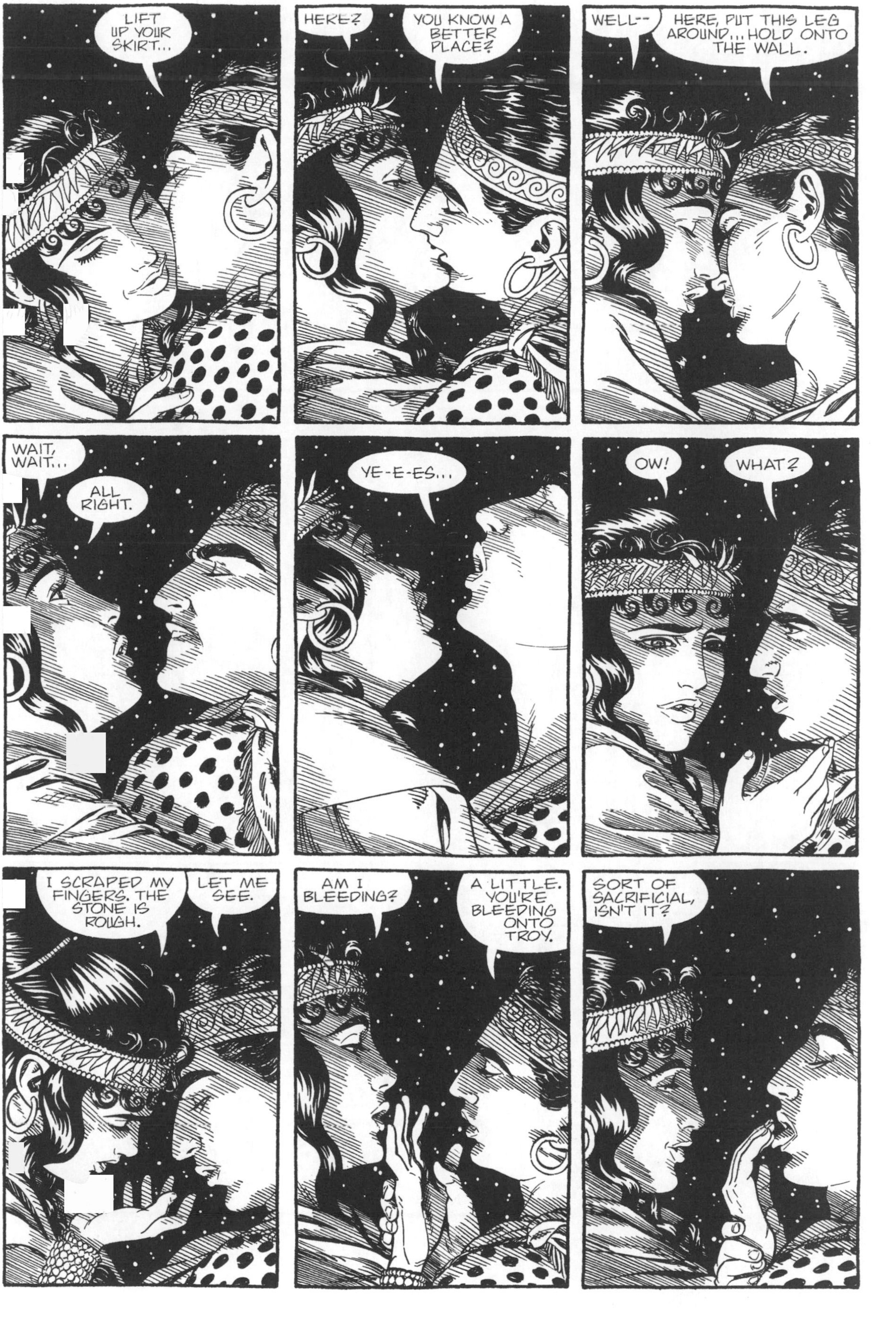
LIFT UP YOUR SKIRT...
HERE?
YOU KNOW A BETTER PLACE?
WELL--
HERE, PUT THIS LEG AROUND,.. HOLD ONTO THE WALL.
WAIT, WAIT...
ALL RIGHT.
YE-E-ES...
OW!
WHAT?
I SCRAPED MY FINGERS. THE STONE IS ROUGH.
LET ME SEE.
AM I BLEEDING?
A LITTLE. YOU'RE BLEEDING ONTO TROY.
SORT OF SACRIFICIAL, ISN'T IT?

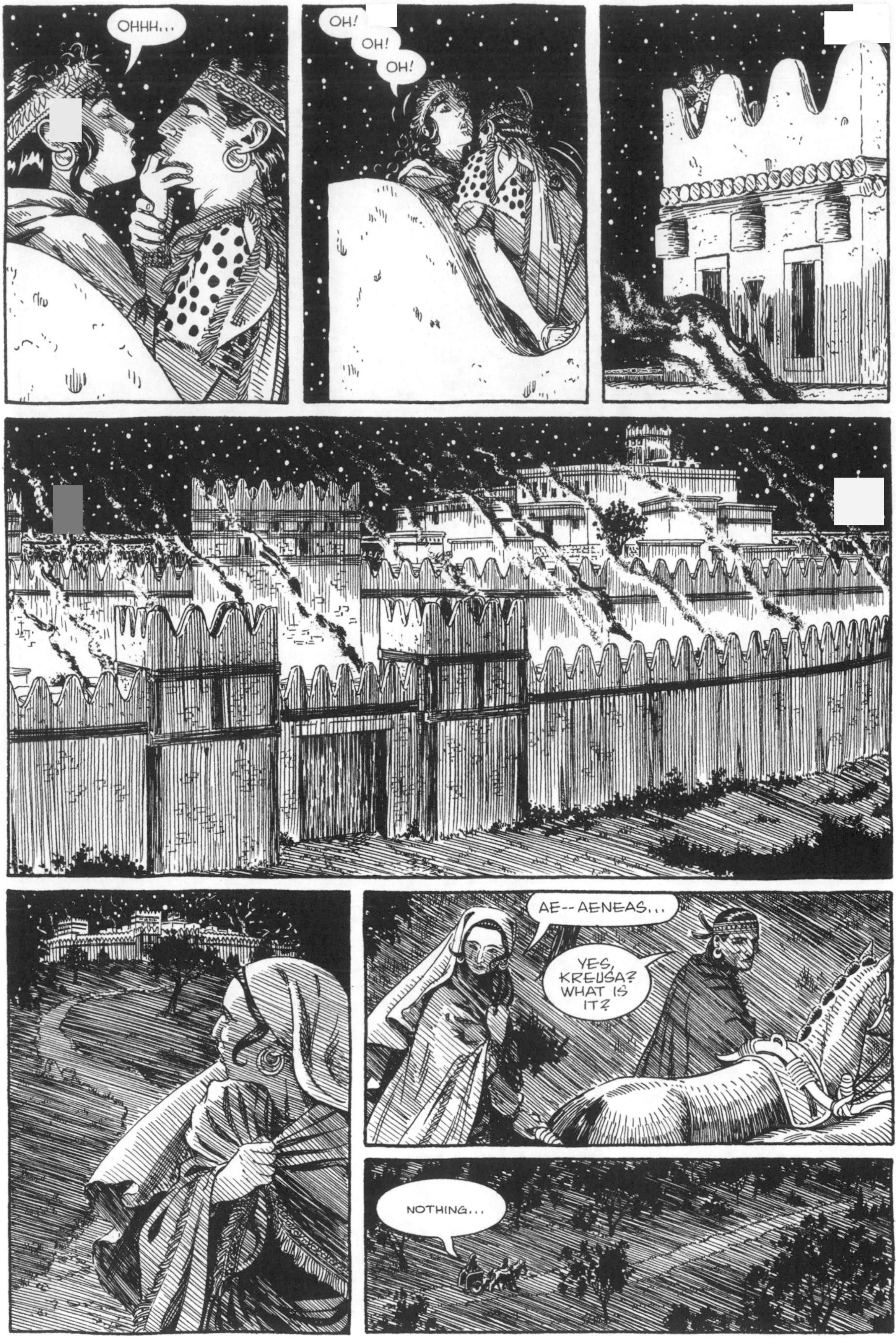
OHHH...
OH!
OH!
OH!
AE--AENEAS...
YES, KREUSA? WHAT IS IT?
NOTHING...

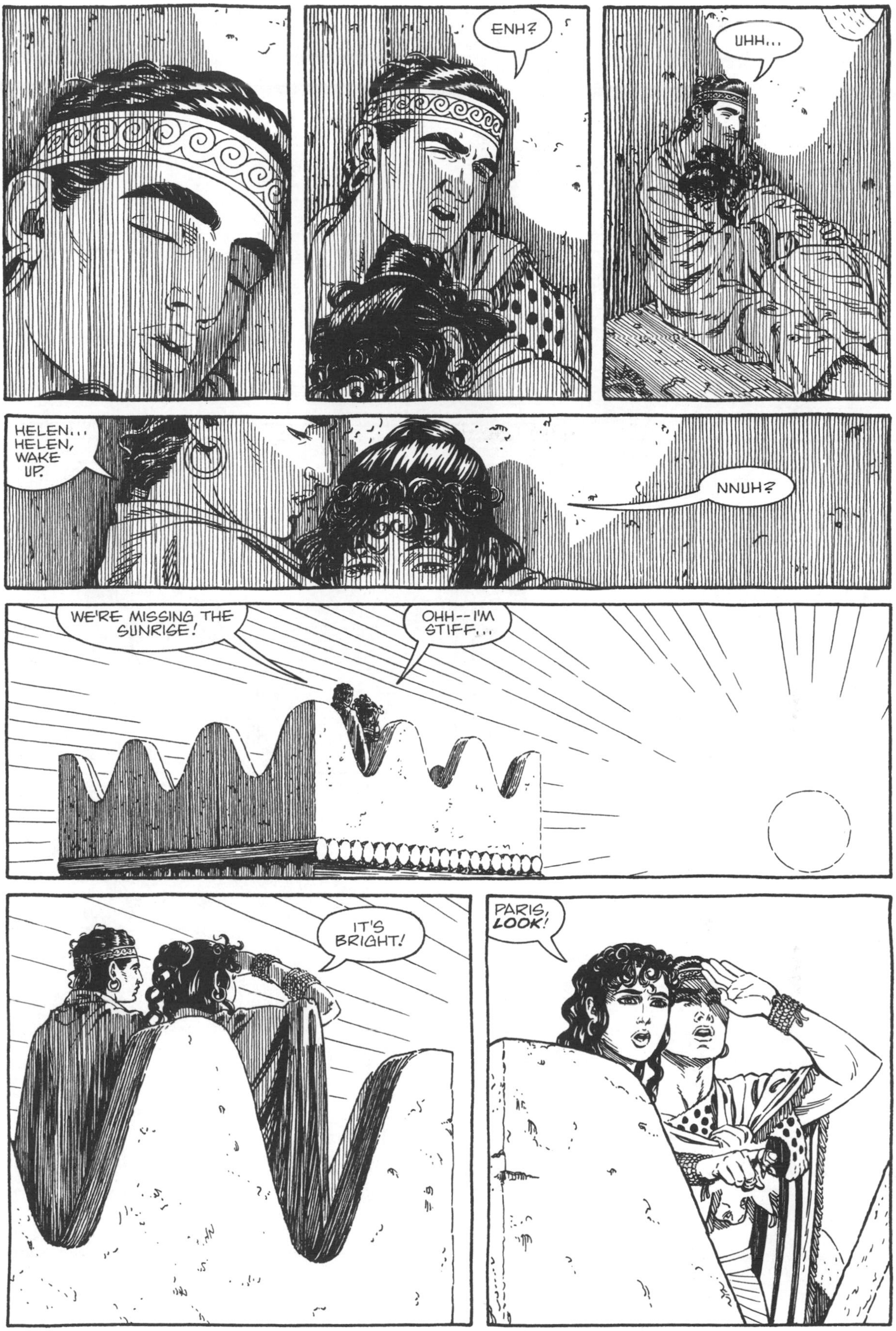
ENH?
UHH...
HELEN... HELEN, WAKE UP.
NNUH?
WE'RE MISSING THE SUNRISE!
OHH--I'M STIFF...
IT'S BRIGHT!
PARIS, **LOOK**!

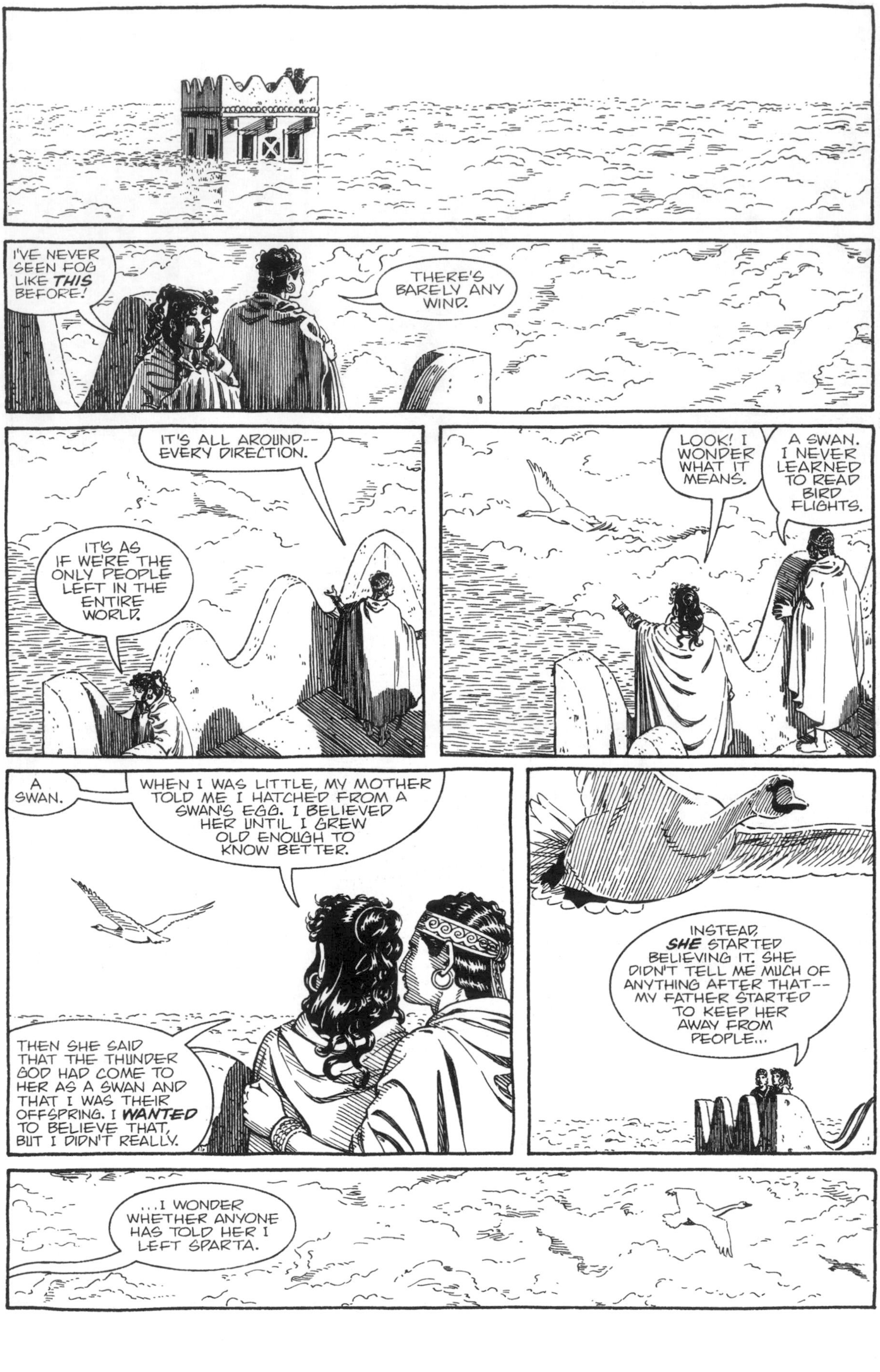
I'VE NEVER SEEN FOG LIKE THIS BEFORE!
THERE'S BARELY ANY WIND.
IT'S ALL AROUND-- EVERY DIRECTION.
IT'S AS IF WE'RE THE ONLY PEOPLE LEFT IN THE ENTIRE WORLD.
LOOK! I WONDER WHAT IT MEANS.
A SWAN. I NEVER LEARNED TO READ BIRD FLIGHTS.
A SWAN.
WHEN I WAS LITTLE, MY MOTHER TOLD ME I HATCHED FROM A SWAN'S EGG. I BELIEVED HER UNTIL I GREW OLD ENOUGH TO KNOW BETTER.
THEN SHE SAID THAT THE THUNDER GOD HAD COME TO HER AS A SWAN AND THAT I WAS THEIR OFFSPRING. I WANTED TO BELIEVE THAT, BUT I DIDN'T REALLY.
INSTEAD, SHE STARTED BELIEVING IT. SHE DIDN'T TELL ME MUCH OF ANYTHING AFTER THAT-- MY FATHER STARTED TO KEEP HER AWAY FROM PEOPLE...
...I WONDER WHETHER ANYONE HAS TOLD HER I LEFT SPARTA.

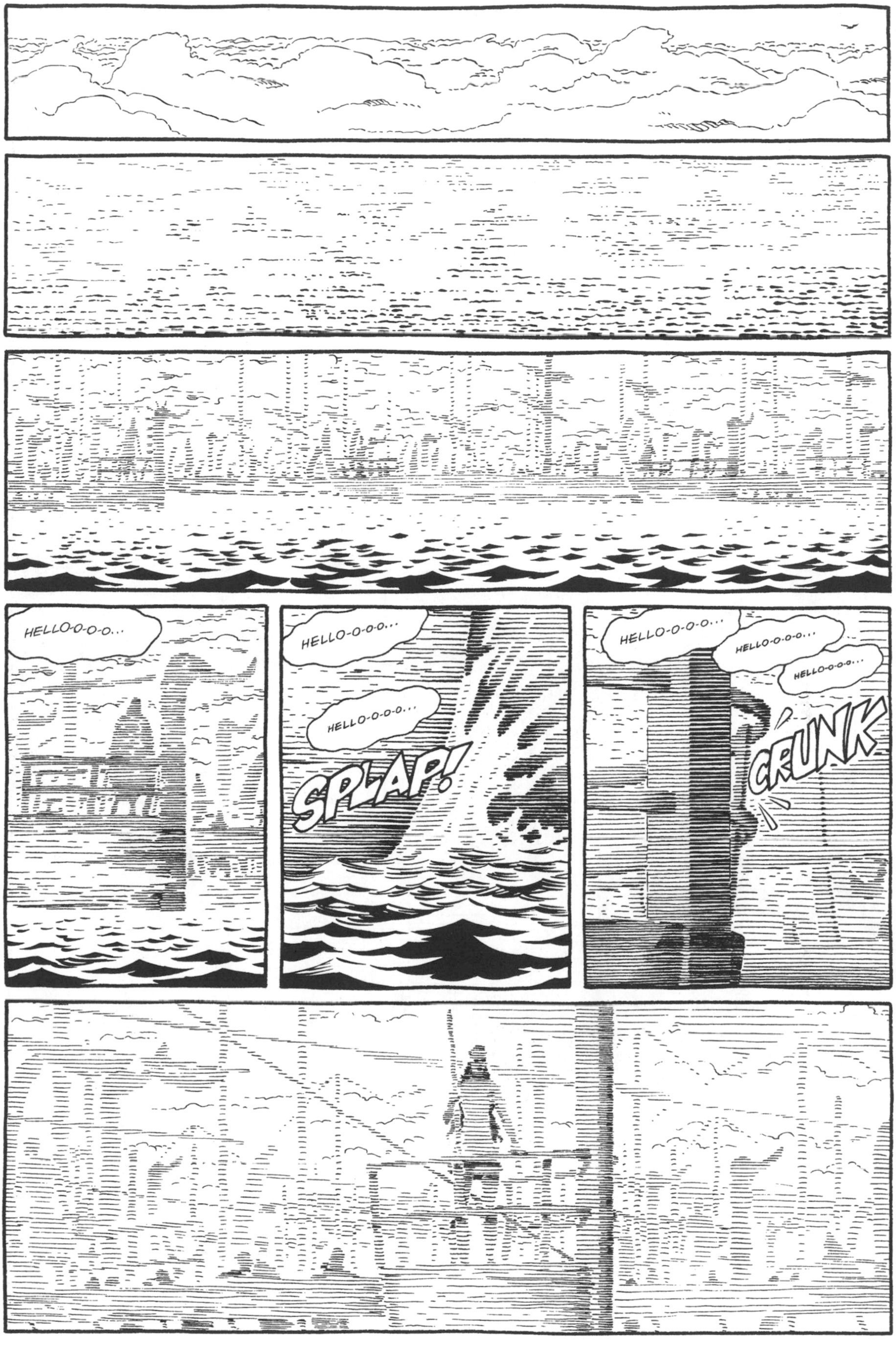
HELLO-O-O-O...
HELLO-O-O-O...
HELLO-O-O-O...
SPLAP!
HELLO-O-O-O...
HELLO-O-O-O...
HELLO-O-O-O...
CRUNK

HELLO-O-O-O-O...

ACHILLES, ARE YOU GOING TO STARE INTO THE FOG ALL DAY?

LAST NIGHT AT COUNCIL WHEN MENELAUS SAID OUR DAYS OF SAILING WOULD END TODAY AT TROY, I DECIDED MY SHIPS WOULD LAUNCH *FIRST* AT DAWN.

BUT THIS *FOG*... THIS *DRIFTING*...

HELLO-O-O-O...

HELLO-O-O-O...

HELLO-O-O-O...

FETCH MORE WINE, AUTOMEDON. I'LL OFFER YET *ANOTHER* LIBATION TO THE SUN GOD --NO! THIS TIME TO THE GOD OF FIRE --TO *BURN* THIS FOG AWAY!

WHY NOT TO YOUR GRANDFATHER, THE SEA--TO CARRY US TO LAND? *ANY* LAND.

THE ONLY LAND *I* WANT TO SEE IS TROY.

HELLO-O-O-O!

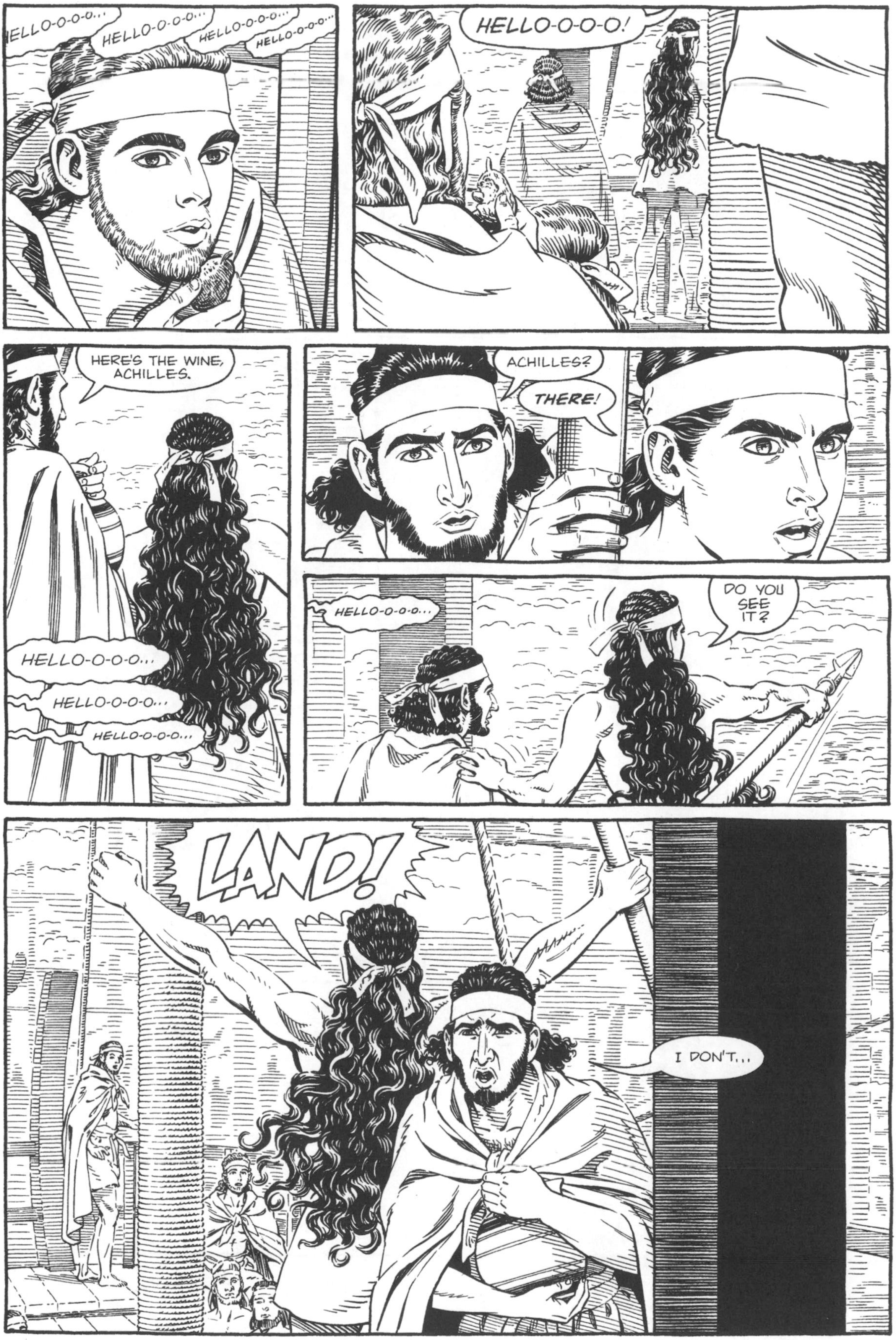

HELLO-O-O-O...
HELLO-O-O-O...
HELLO-O-O-O...
HELLO-O-O-O...
HELLO-O-O-O!
HERE'S THE WINE, ACHILLES.
HELLO-O-O-O...
HELLO-O-O-O...
HELLO-O-O-O...
ACHILLES?
THERE!
HELLO-O-O-O...
DO YOU SEE IT?
LAND!
I DON'T...

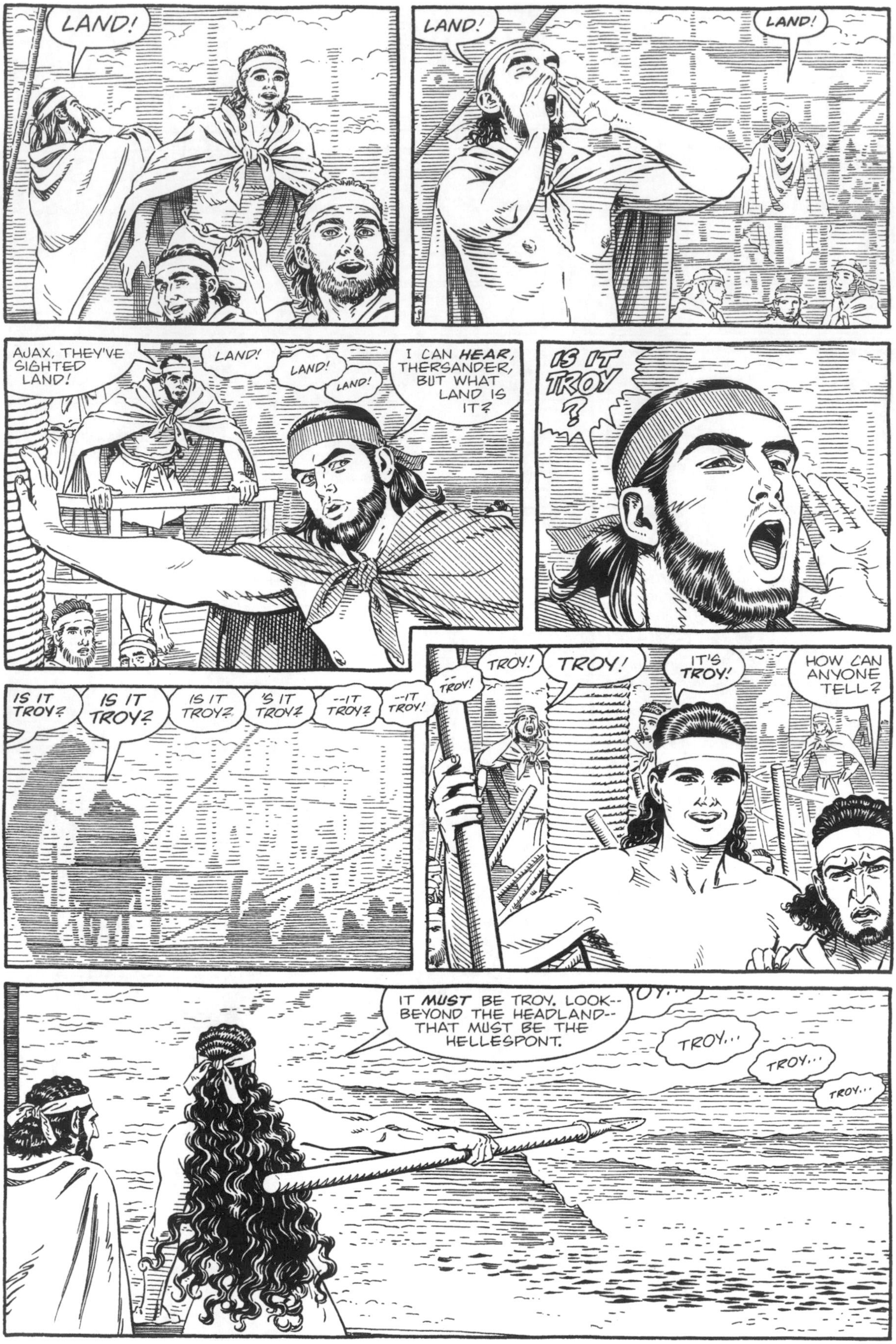
LAND!
LAND!
LAND!
AJAX, THEY'VE SIGHTED LAND!
LAND!
LAND!
LAND!
I CAN HEAR, THERSANDER, BUT WHAT LAND IS IT?
IS IT TROY?
IS IT TROY?
IS IT TROY?
IS IT TROY?
'S IT TROY?
--IT TROY?
--IT TROY!
--TROY!
TROY!
TROY!
IT'S TROY!
HOW CAN ANYONE TELL?
IT MUST BE TROY. LOOK--BEYOND THE HEADLAND--THAT MUST BE THE HELLESPONT.
TROY...
TROY...
TROY...

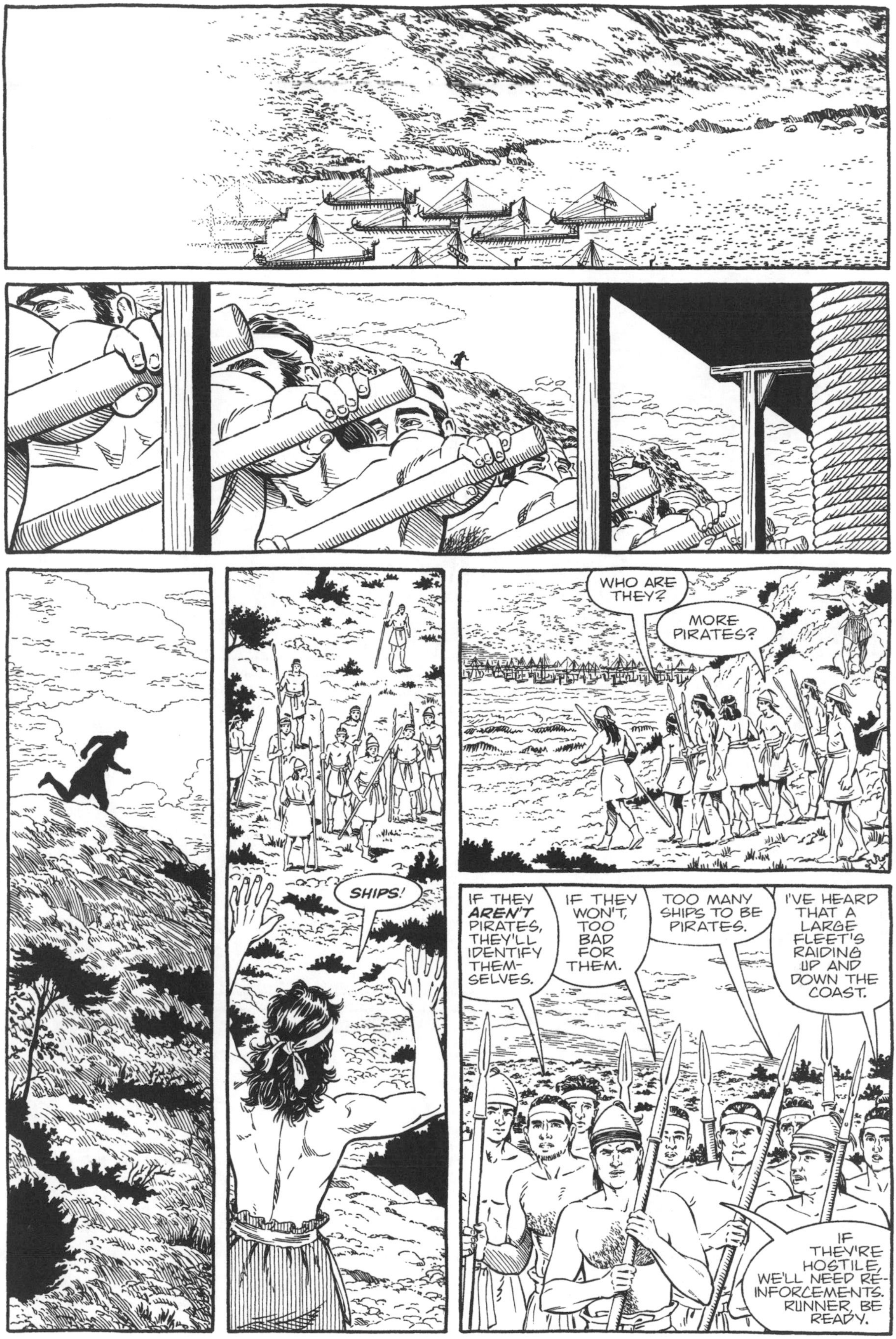
SHIPS!
WHO ARE THEY?
MORE PIRATES?
IF THEY *AREN'T* PIRATES, THEY'LL IDENTIFY THEM-SELVES.
IF THEY WON'T, TOO BAD FOR THEM.
TOO MANY SHIPS TO BE PIRATES.
I'VE HEARD THAT A LARGE FLEET'S RAIDING UP AND DOWN THE COAST.
IF THEY'RE HOSTILE, WE'LL NEED RE-INFORCEMENTS. RUNNER, BE READY.

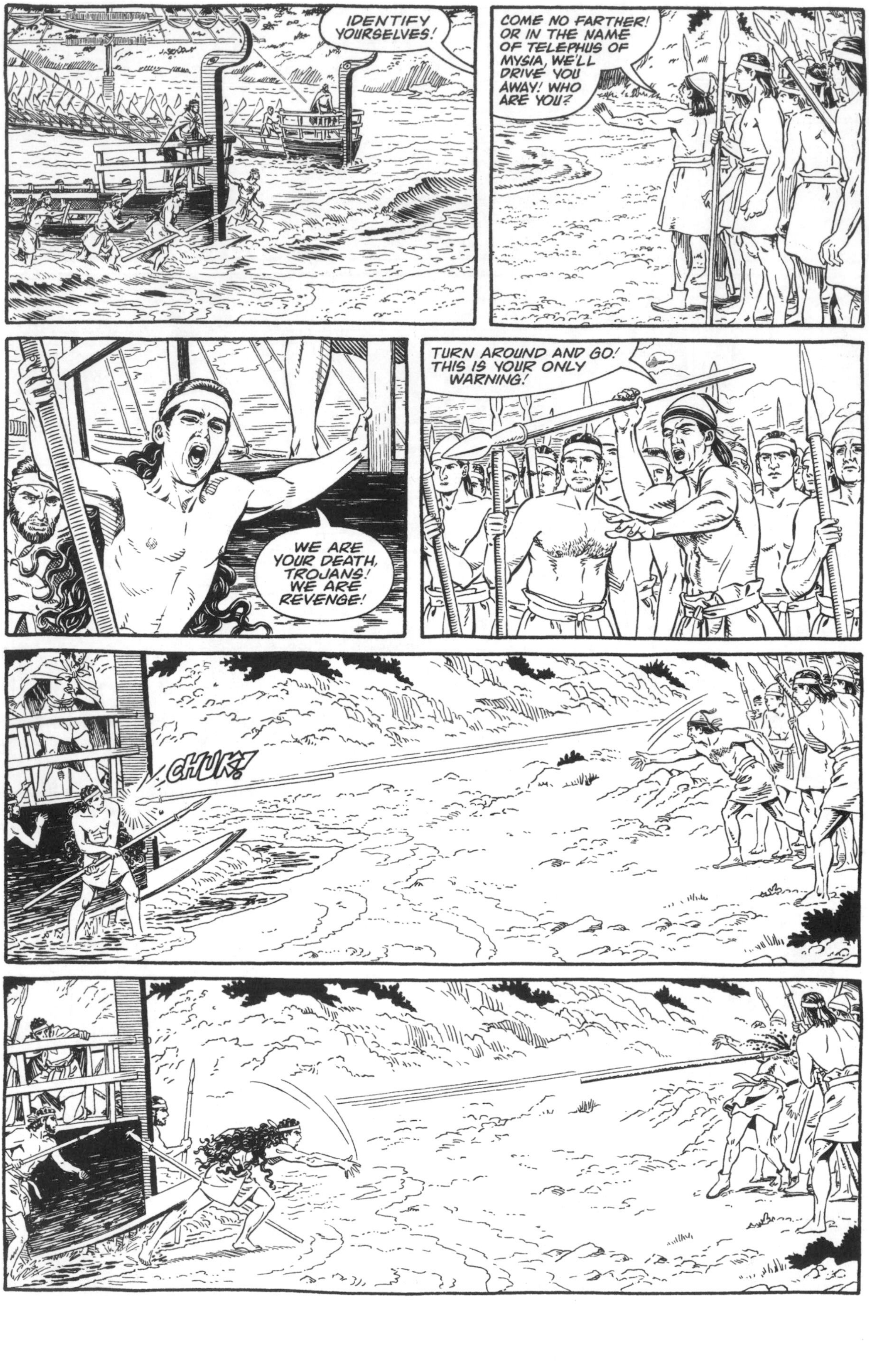
IDENTIFY YOURSELVES!
COME NO FARTHER! OR IN THE NAME OF TELEPHUS OF MYSIA, WE'LL DRIVE YOU AWAY! WHO ARE YOU?
WE ARE YOUR DEATH, TROJANS! WE ARE REVENGE!
TURN AROUND AND GO! THIS IS YOUR ONLY WARNING!
CHUK!

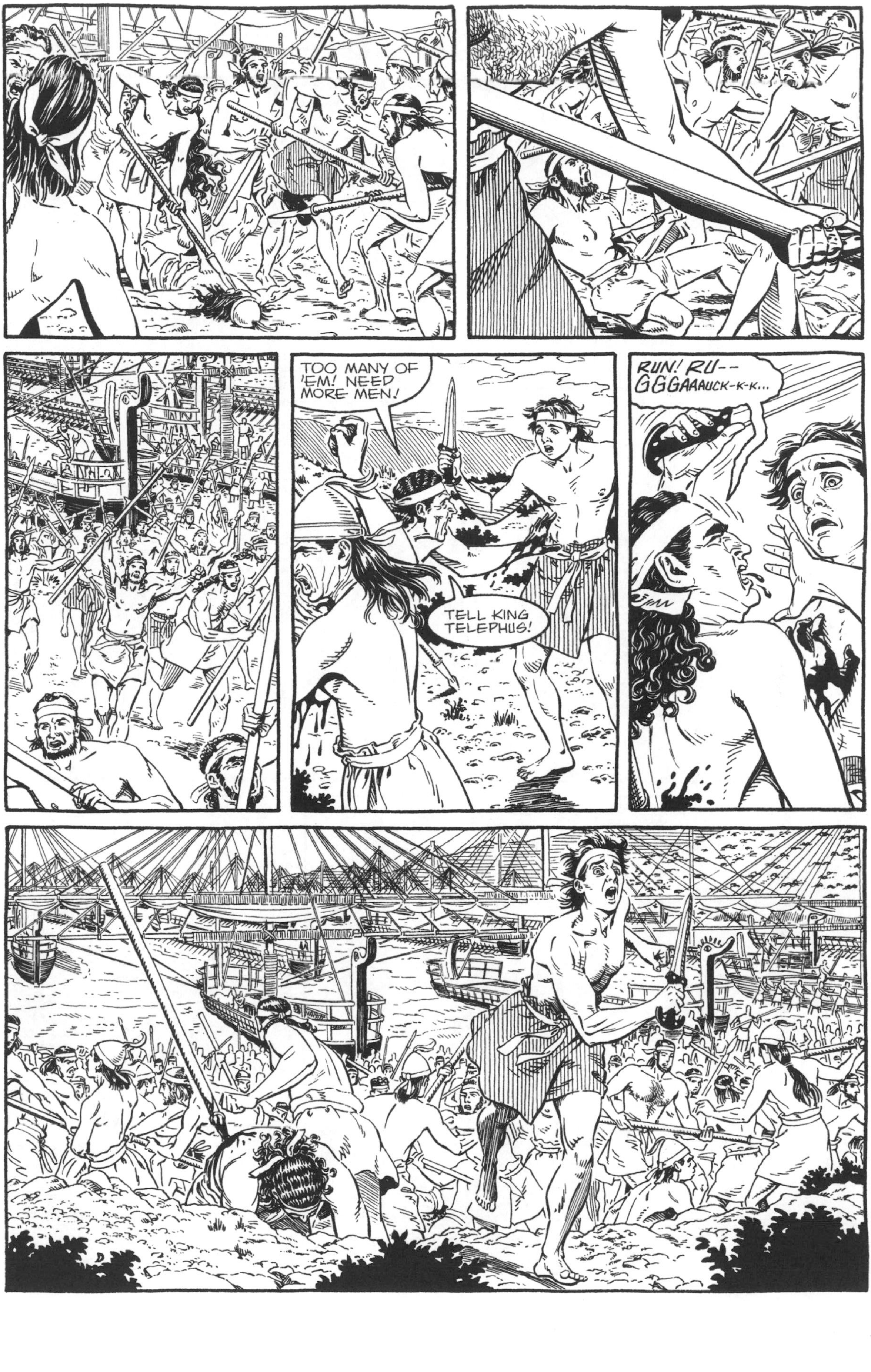
TOO MANY OF 'EM! NEED MORE MEN!
TELL KING TELEPHUS!
RUN! RU-- GGGAAAUCK-K-K...

TELEPHUS?

HIERA, NOT NOW. PIRATES ARE ATTACKING THE COAST. IF THEY'RE AS NUMEROUS AS REPORTED, YOU WILL NEED MANY WARRIORS TO DRIVE THEM AWAY.

YES, EVERY SHEPHERD, EVERY FARMER, EVERY FARMER'S *SON*-- ALL WHO CAN SWING CLUBS OR THROW STONES, BUT TRAINED *WARRIORS* ARE SCARCE IN MYSIA.

I'LL LEAD THE CHARIOTS, TEUTHRANIUS COMMANDS THE ARCHERS, AND-- AND I WILL LEAD MY--

YOU? YOU'LL STAY *HERE*-- DO YOU FORGET, TELEPHUS? BEFORE I CAME HERE TO BE YOUR WIFE, I WAS A WARRIOR-PRINCESS ALONG THE BLACK SEA COAST. THE MEN AND WOMEN WHO CAME HERE WITH ME WERE MY ARMY. TIME AND AGAIN WE TURNED BACK PIRATES FROM OUR SHORES. LET US SHOW YOU THAT WE ARE STILL WARRIORS.

HIERA..., YOU'RE NO LONGER A WARRIOR-PRINCESS. YOU'RE MY WIFE. GO AND WAIT WITH MY OTHER WIVES FOR MY RETURN FROM BATTLE.

AND IF YOU *DO NOT* RETURN? THEN BURN MY BODY WITH ALL THE HONOR AN EXCELLENT WIFE OWES HER KING AND HUSBAND.

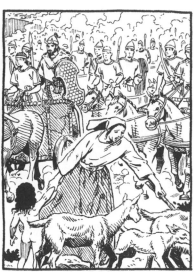

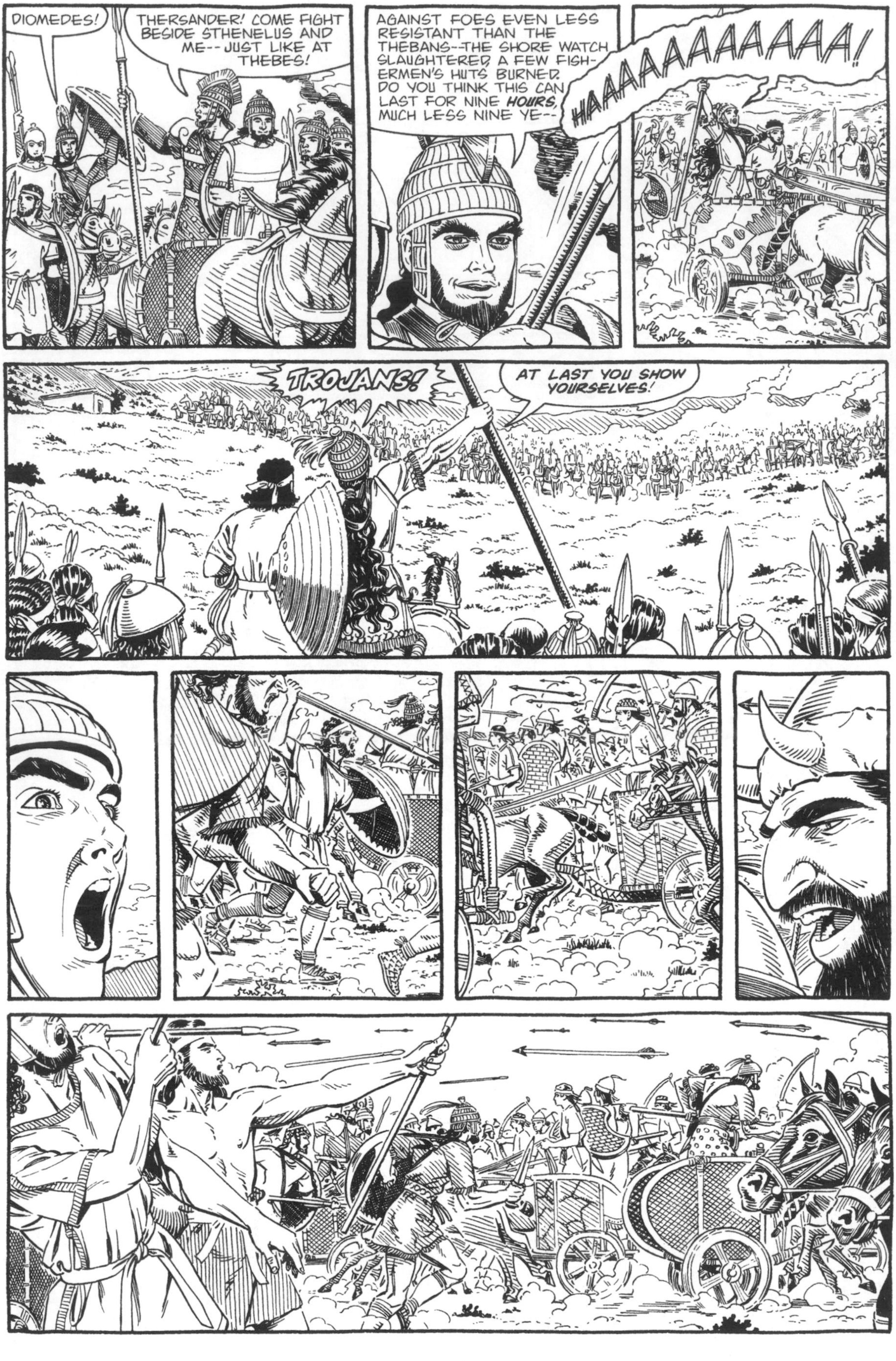

DIOMEDES!
THERSANDER! COME FIGHT BESIDE STHENELUS AND ME-- JUST LIKE AT THEBES!
AGAINST FOES EVEN LESS RESISTANT THAN THE THEBANS--THE SHORE WATCH SLAUGHTERED, A FEW FISHERMEN'S HUTS BURNED. DO YOU THINK THIS CAN LAST FOR NINE HOURS, MUCH LESS NINE YE--
HAAAAAAAAAAAAA!
TROJANS!
AT LAST YOU SHOW YOURSELVES!

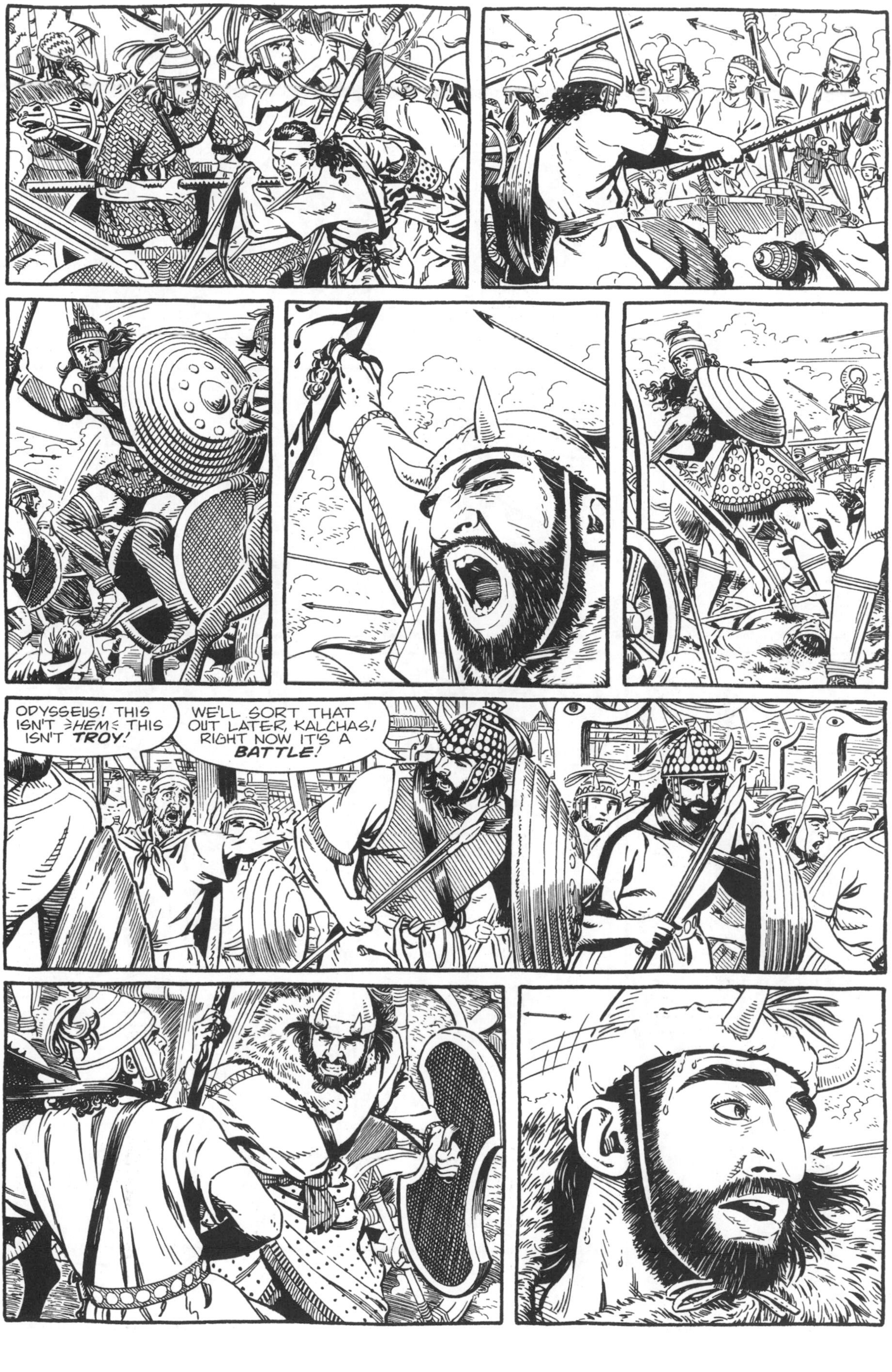
ODYSSEUS! THIS ISN'T ⋽HEM⋹ THIS ISN'T **TROY**!
WE'LL SORT THAT OUT LATER, KALCHAS! RIGHT NOW IT'S A **BATTLE**!

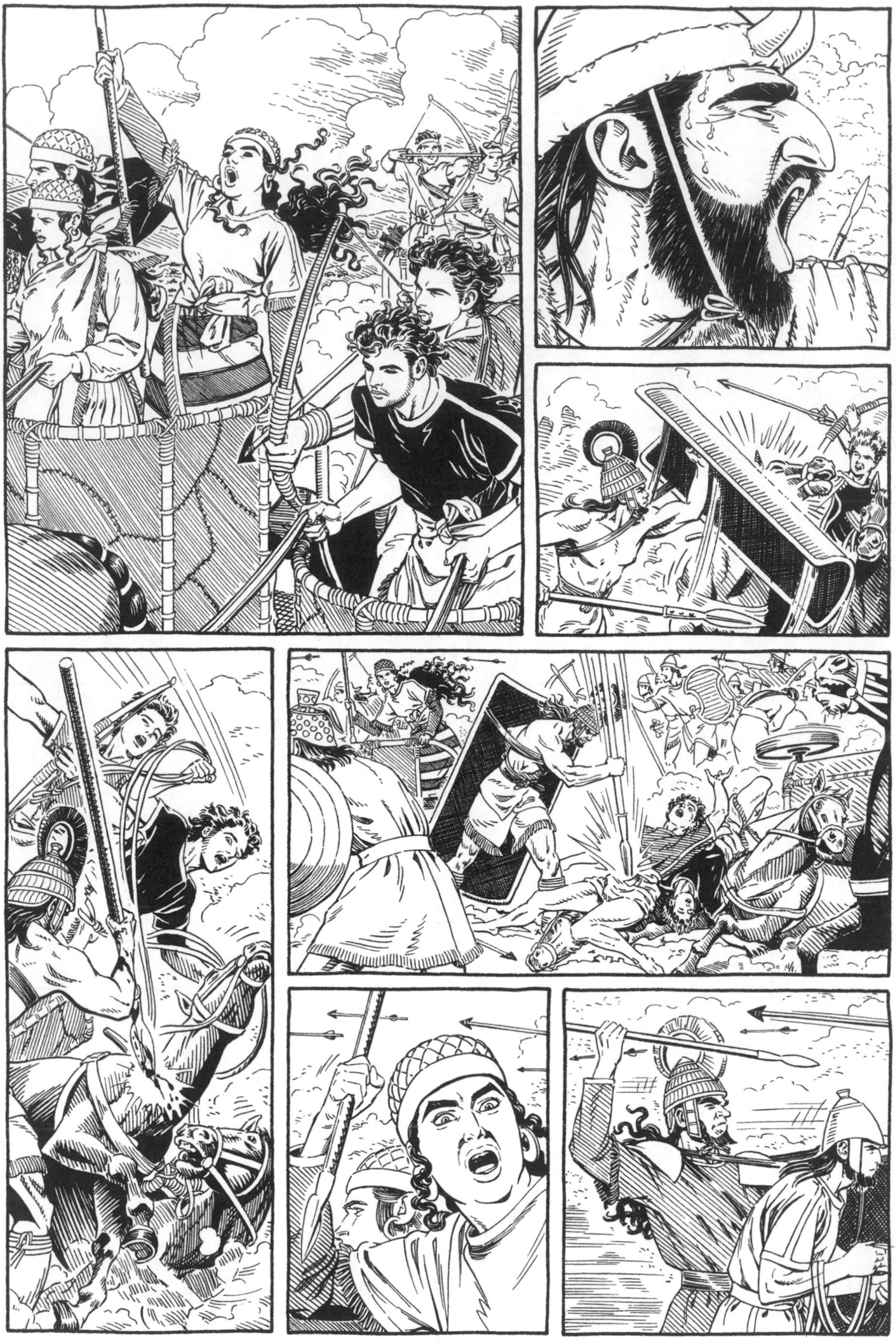

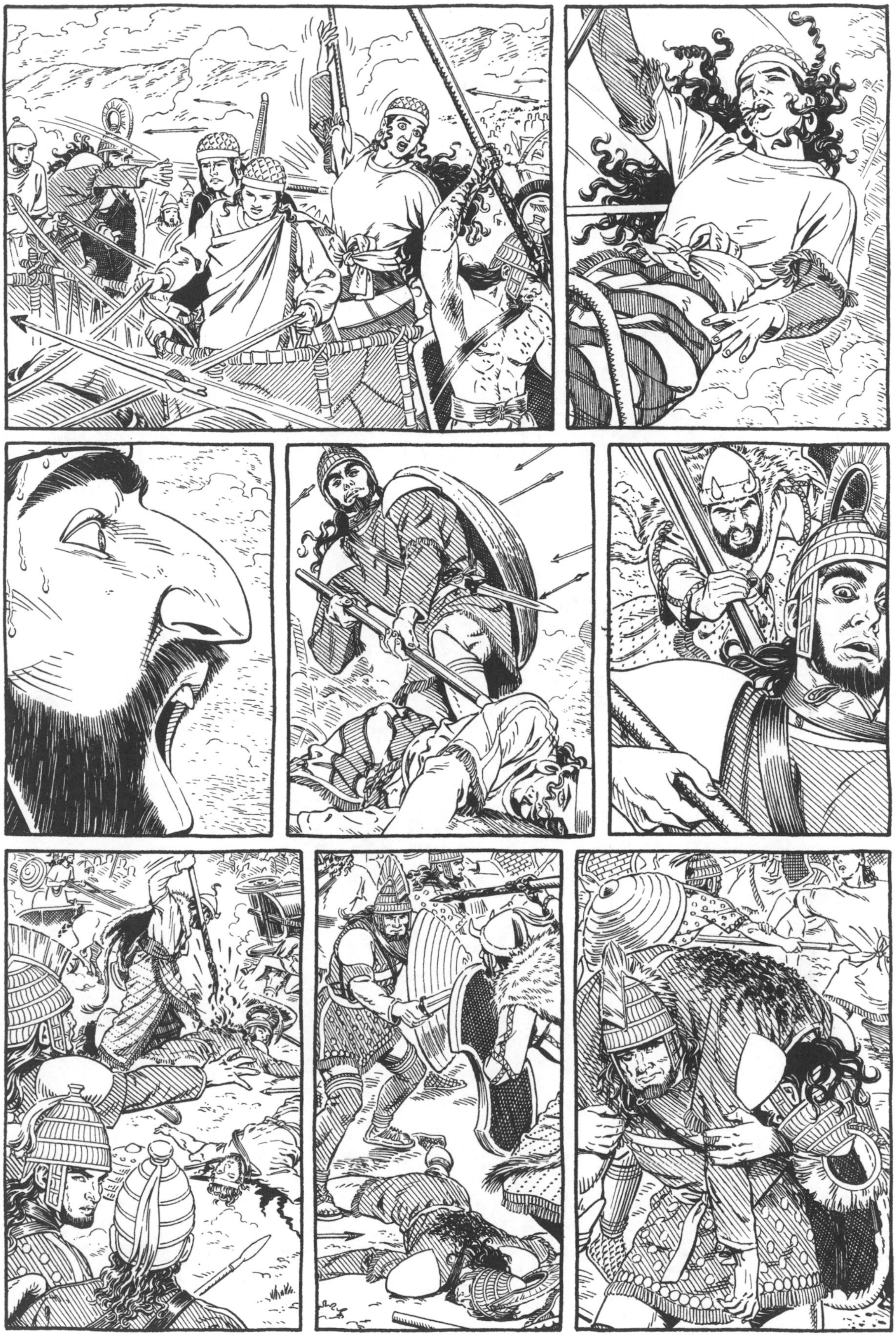

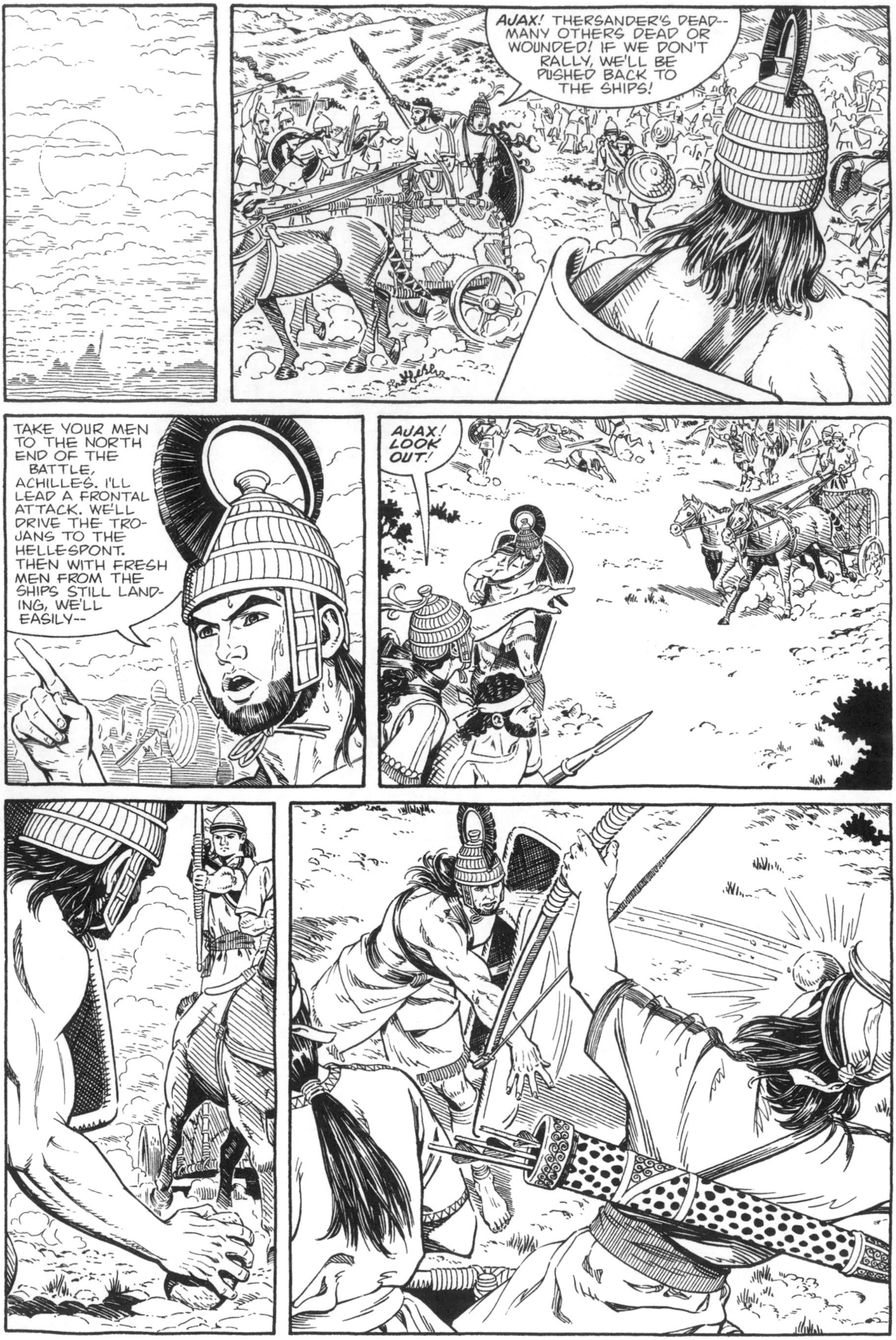
AJAX! THERSANDER'S DEAD-- MANY OTHERS DEAD OR WOUNDED! IF WE DON'T RALLY, WE'LL BE PUSHED BACK TO THE SHIPS!
TAKE YOUR MEN TO THE NORTH END OF THE BATTLE, ACHILLES. I'LL LEAD A FRONTAL ATTACK. WE'LL DRIVE THE TROJANS TO THE HELLESPONT. THEN WITH FRESH MEN FROM THE SHIPS STILL LANDING, WE'LL EASILY--
AJAX! LOOK OUT!

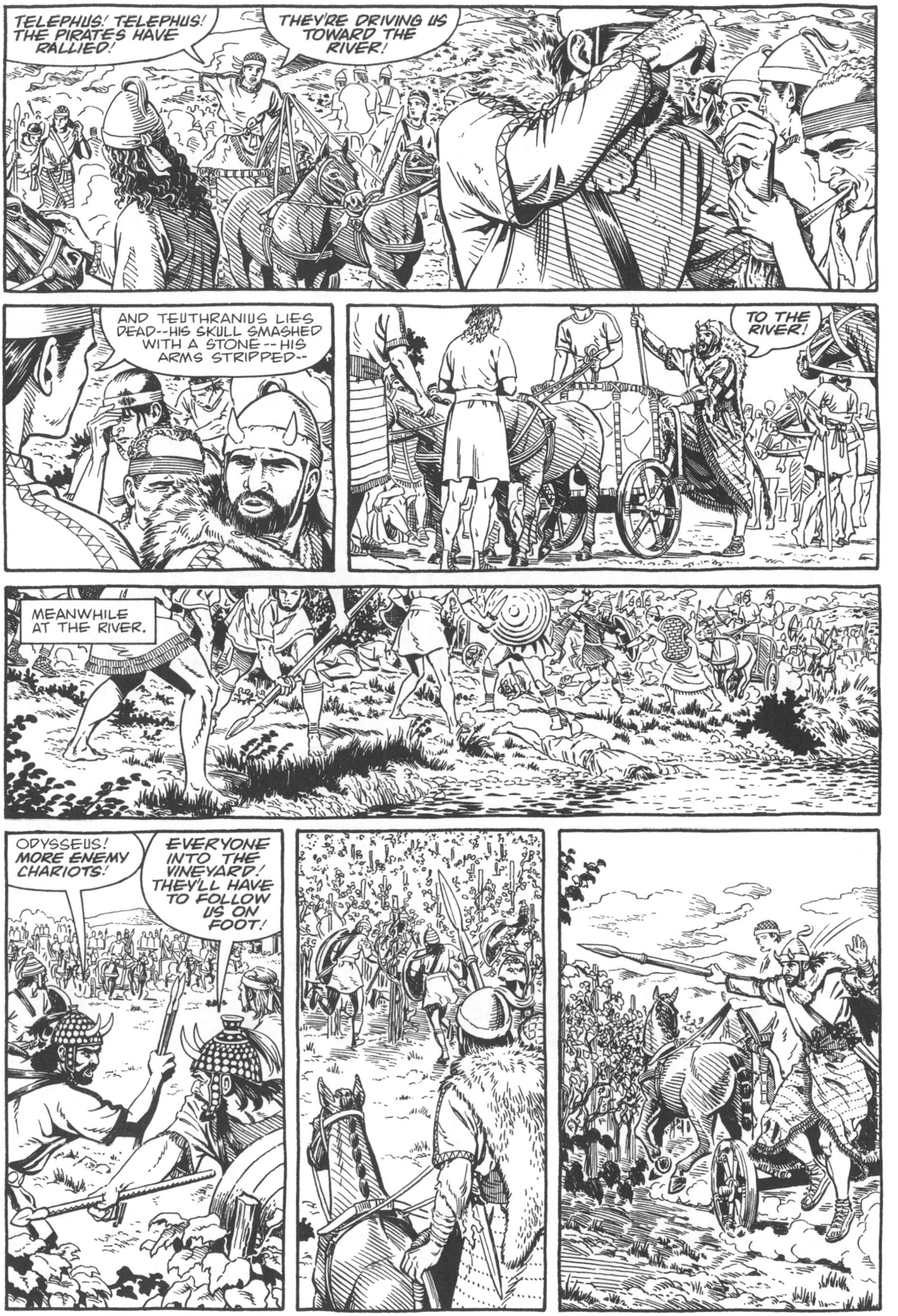

TELEPHUS! TELEPHUS! THE PIRATES HAVE RALLIED!
THEY'RE DRIVING US TOWARD THE RIVER!
AND TEUTHRANIUS LIES DEAD--HIS SKULL SMASHED WITH A STONE--HIS ARMS STRIPPED--
TO THE RIVER!
MEANWHILE AT THE RIVER.
ODYSSEUS! MORE ENEMY CHARIOTS!
EVERYONE INTO THE VINEYARD! THEY'LL HAVE TO FOLLOW US ON FOOT!

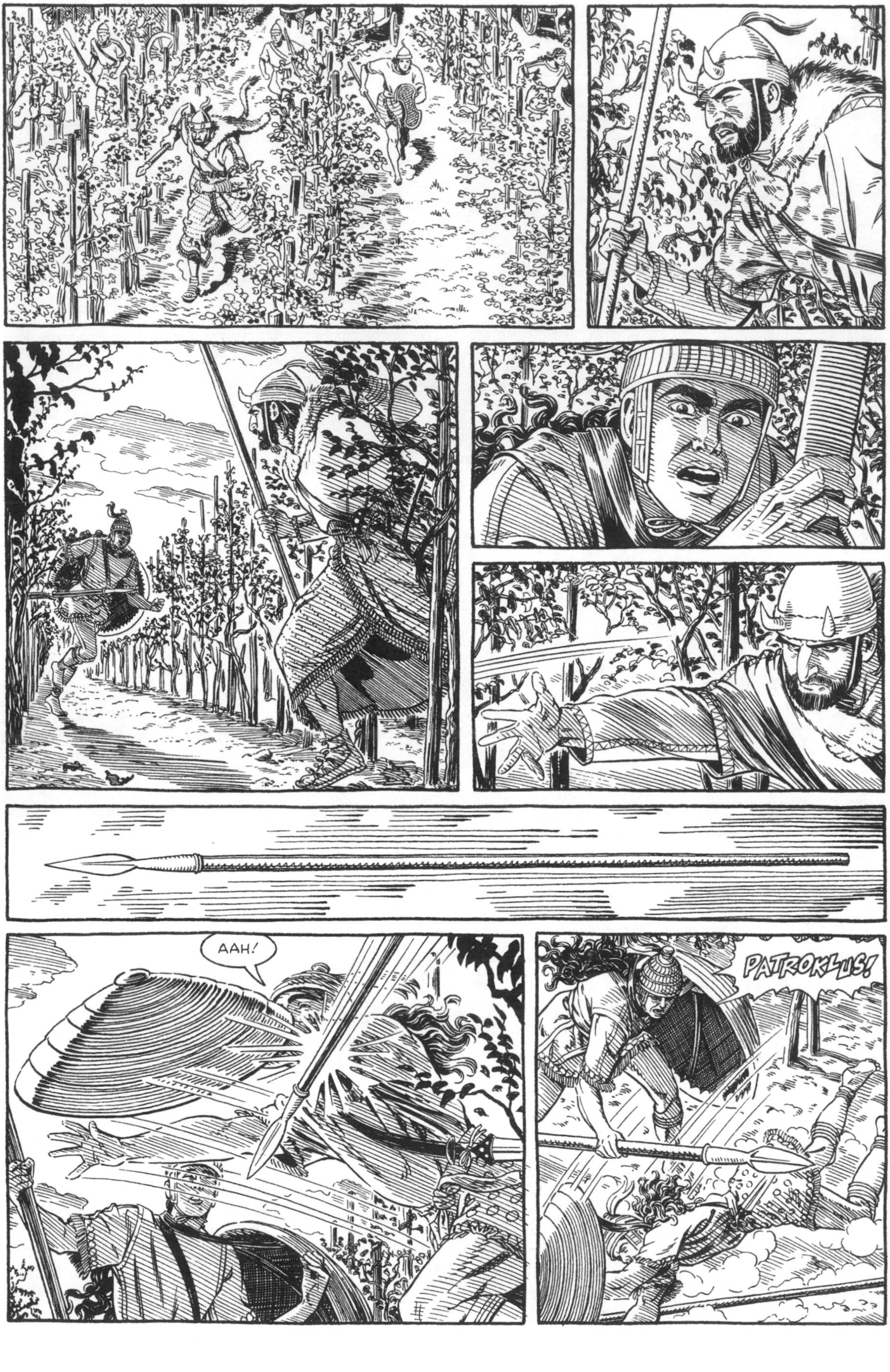
AAH!
PATROKLUS!

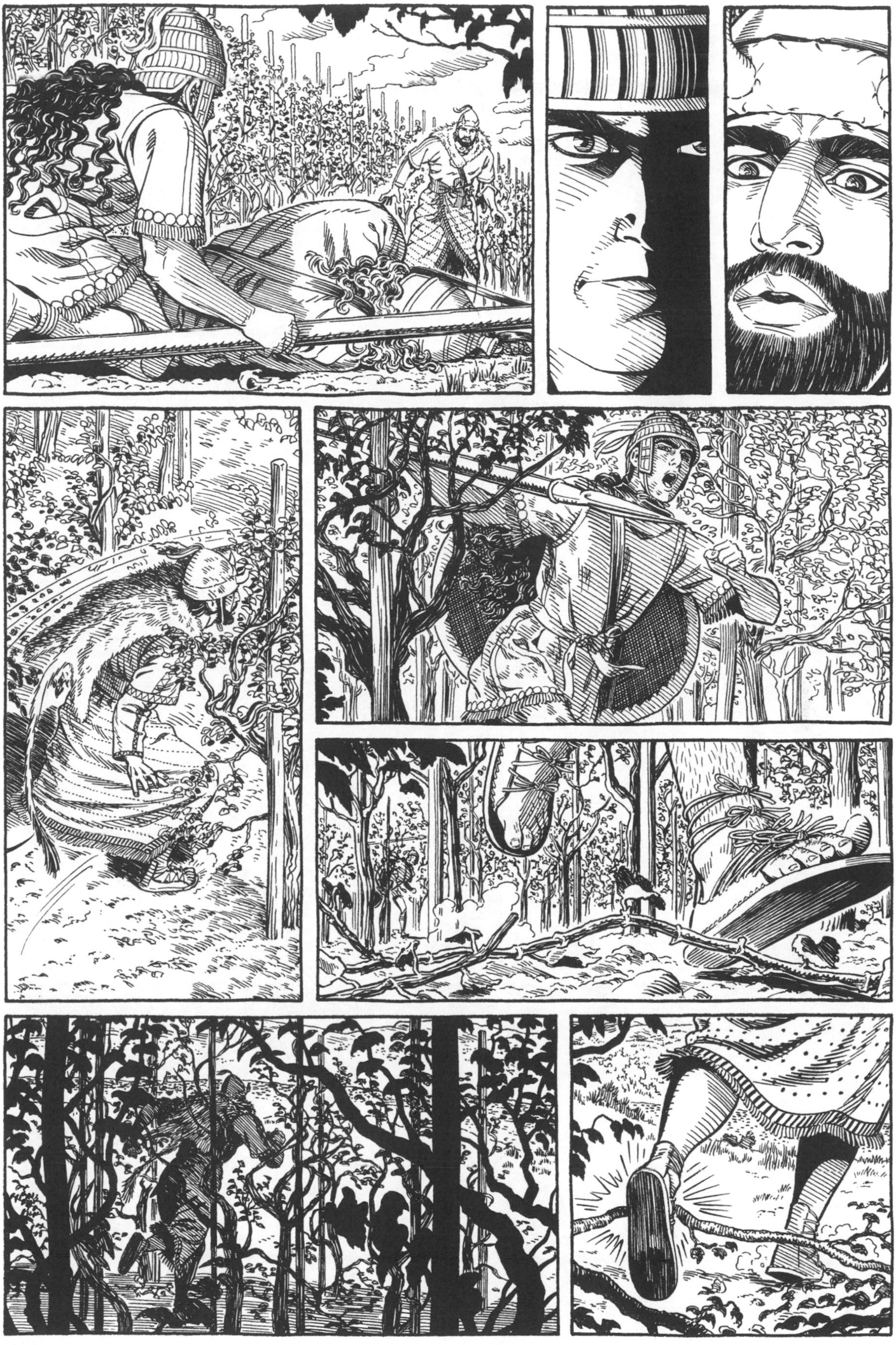

AAA
AA
GH!

ACHILLES! TROJAN CHARIOTS!

ACHILLES!

THEY AREN'T PURSUING.

NO...IT'S GETTING ...TOO DARK ...FOR ANY ...MORE... FIGHTING...

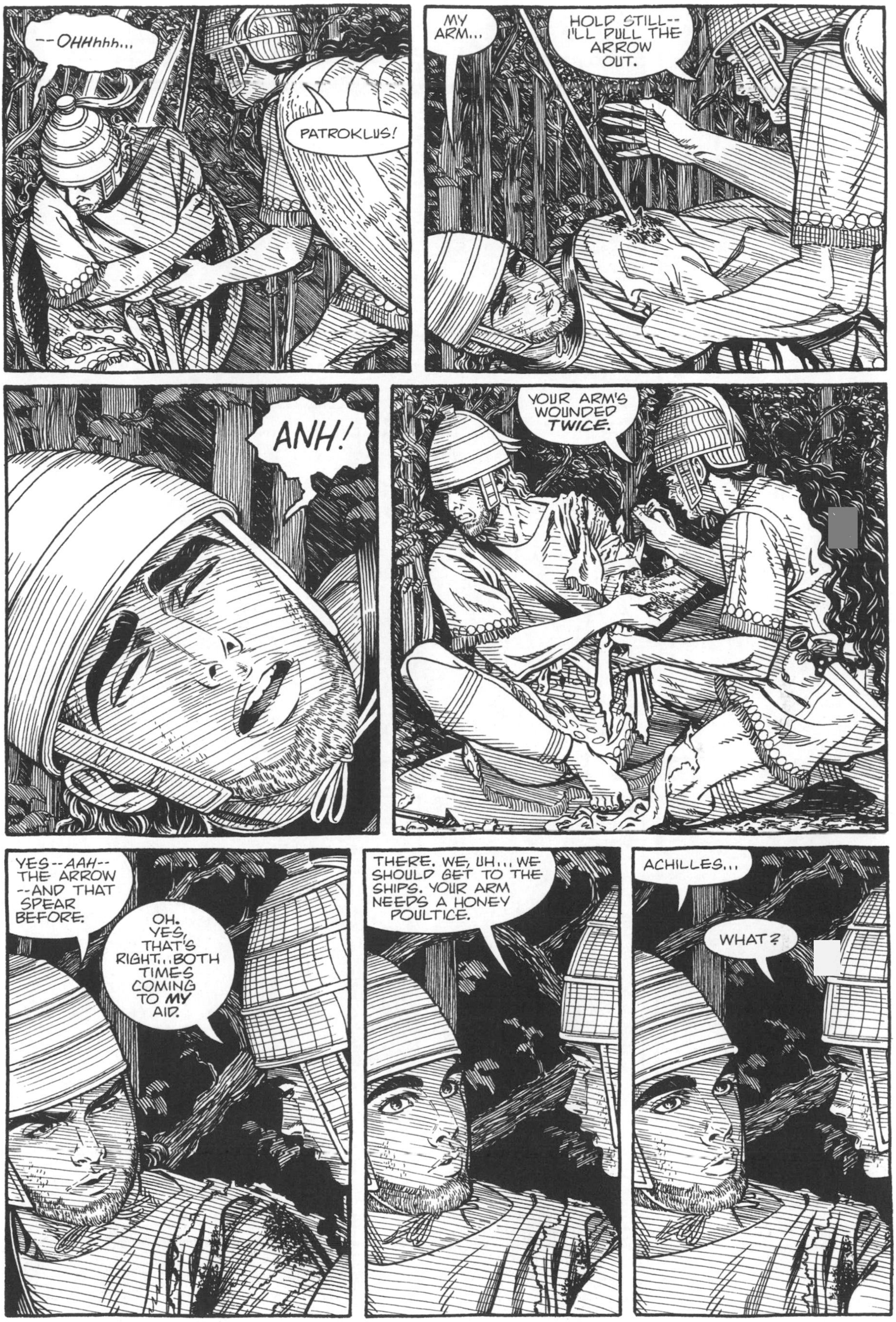
--OHHhhh...
PATROKLUS!
MY ARM...
HOLD STILL--
I'LL PULL THE ARROW OUT.
ANH!
YOUR ARM'S WOUNDED TWICE.
YES--AAH--THE ARROW--AND THAT SPEAR BEFORE.
OH. YES, THAT'S RIGHT...BOTH TIMES COMING TO MY AID.
THERE. WE, UH... WE SHOULD GET TO THE SHIPS. YOUR ARM NEEDS A HONEY POULTICE.
ACHILLES...
WHAT?

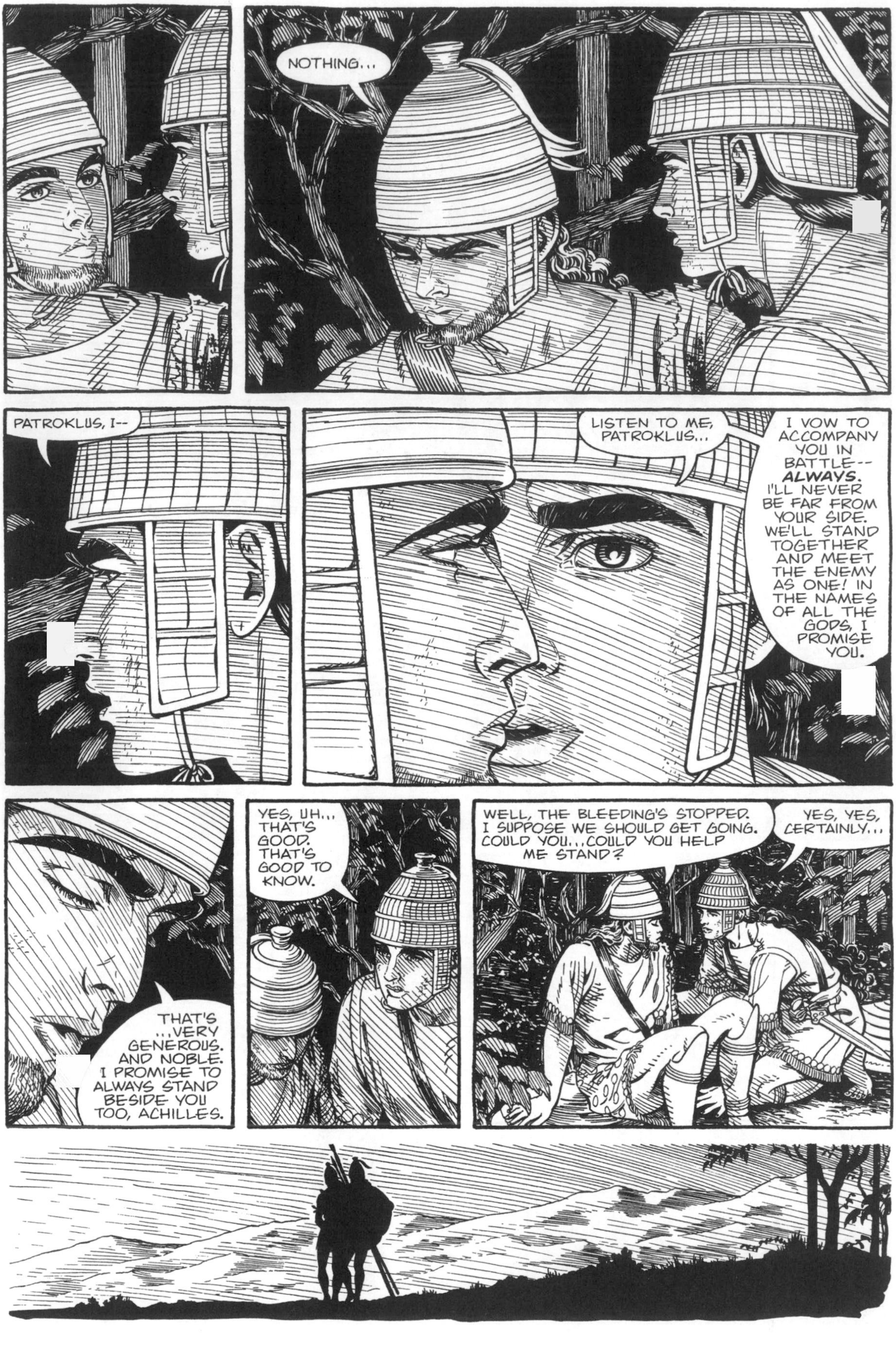
NOTHING...
PATROKLUS, I--
LISTEN TO ME, PATROKLUS...
I VOW TO ACCOMPANY YOU IN BATTLE-- ALWAYS. I'LL NEVER BE FAR FROM YOUR SIDE. WE'LL STAND TOGETHER AND MEET THE ENEMY AS ONE! IN THE NAMES OF ALL THE GODS, I PROMISE YOU.
THAT'S ...VERY GENEROUS. AND NOBLE. I PROMISE TO ALWAYS STAND BESIDE YOU TOO, ACHILLES.
YES, UH... THAT'S GOOD. THAT'S GOOD TO KNOW.
WELL, THE BLEEDING'S STOPPED. I SUPPOSE WE SHOULD GET GOING. COULD YOU...COULD YOU HELP ME STAND?
YES, YES, CERTAINLY...

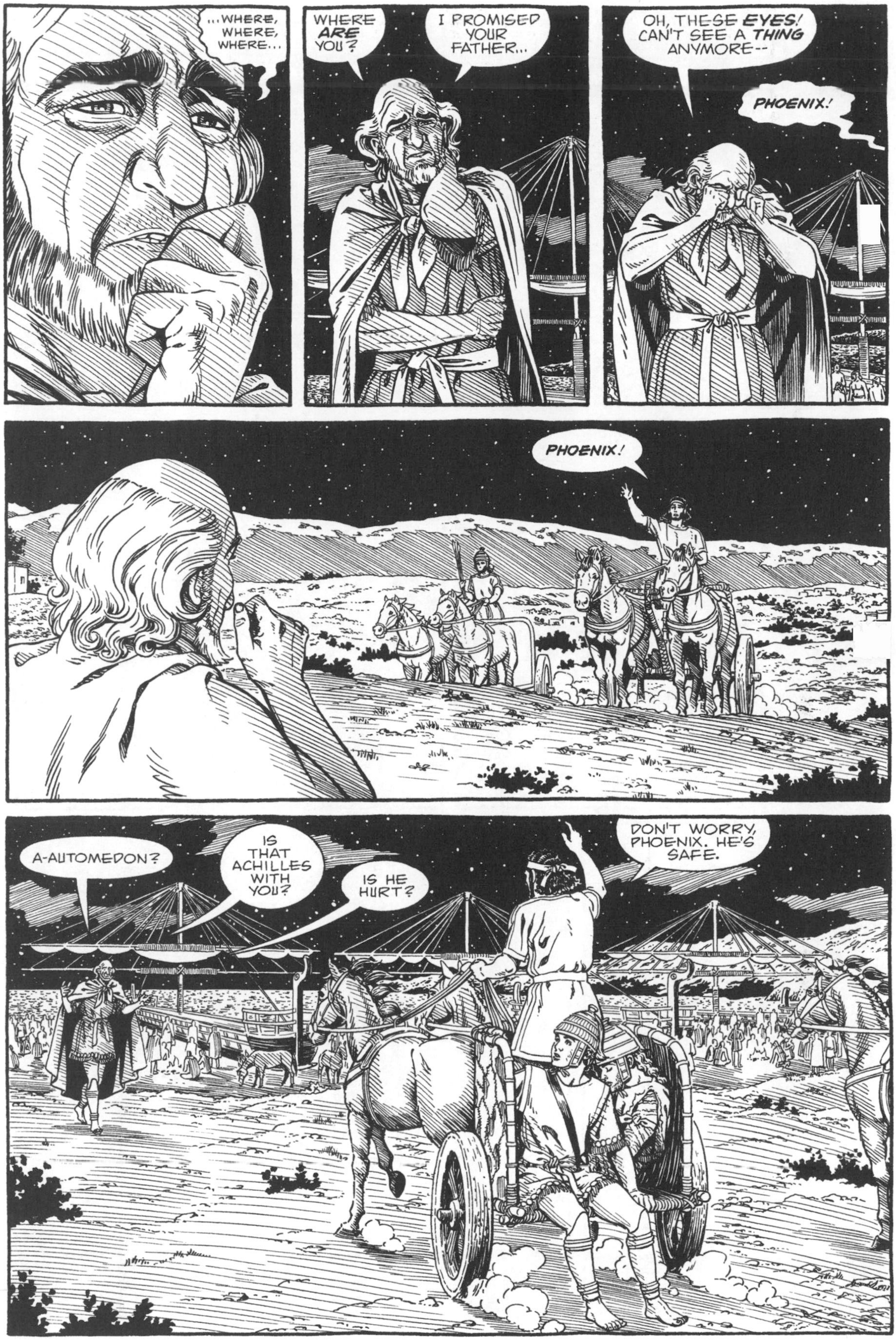

...WHERE, WHERE, WHERE...
WHERE ARE YOU?
I PROMISED YOUR FATHER...
OH, THESE EYES! CAN'T SEE A THING ANYMORE--
PHOENIX!
PHOENIX!
A-AUTOMEDON?
IS THAT ACHILLES WITH YOU?
IS HE HURT?
DON'T WORRY, PHOENIX. HE'S SAFE.

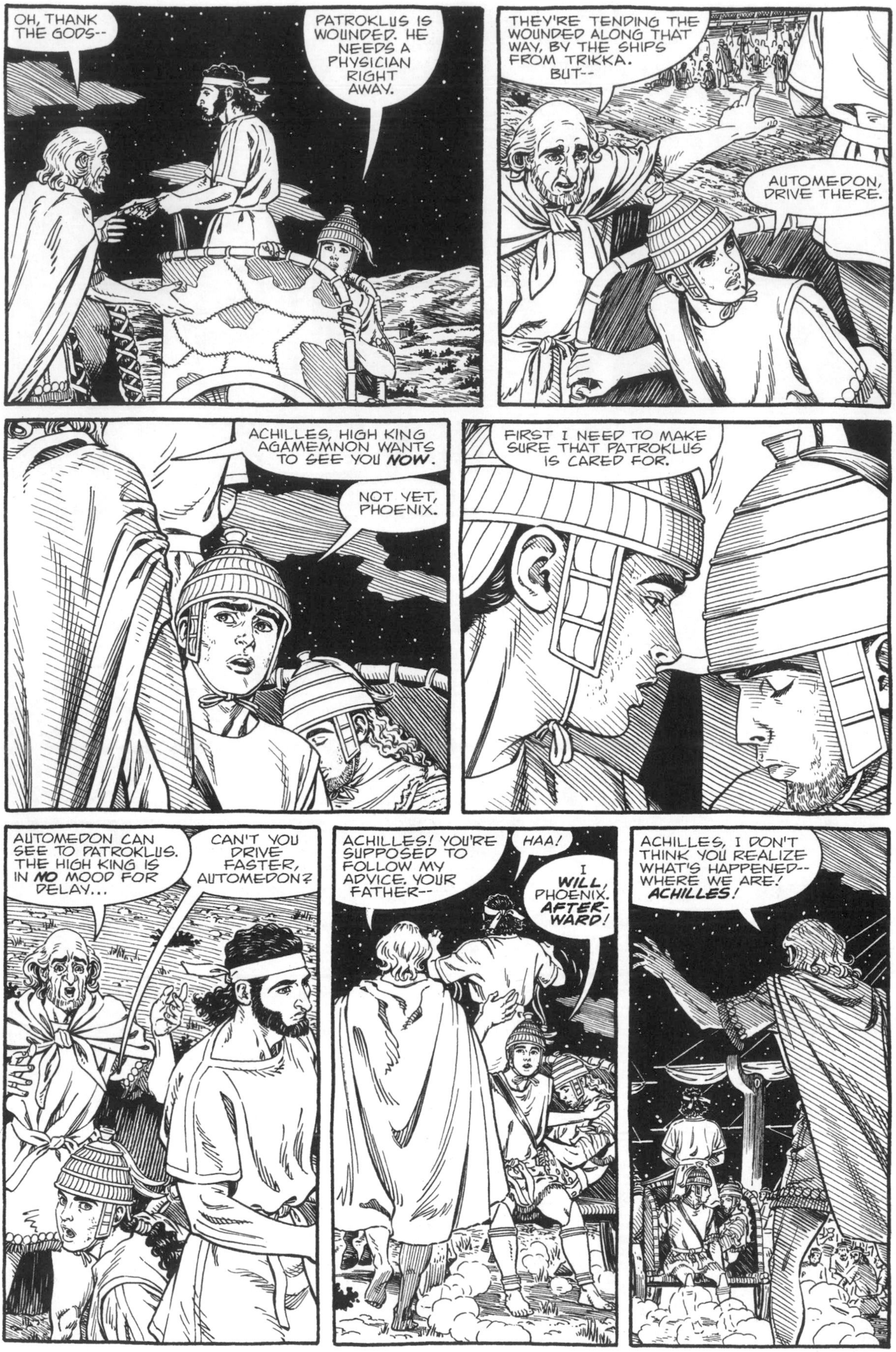
OH, THANK THE GODS--
PATROKLUS IS WOUNDED. HE NEEDS A PHYSICIAN RIGHT AWAY.
THEY'RE TENDING THE WOUNDED ALONG THAT WAY, BY THE SHIPS FROM TRIKKA. BUT--
AUTOMEDON, DRIVE THERE.
ACHILLES, HIGH KING AGAMEMNON WANTS TO SEE YOU NOW.
NOT YET, PHOENIX.
FIRST I NEED TO MAKE SURE THAT PATROKLUS IS CARED FOR.
AUTOMEDON CAN SEE TO PATROKLUS. THE HIGH KING IS IN NO MOOD FOR DELAY...
CAN'T YOU DRIVE FASTER, AUTOMEDON?
ACHILLES! YOU'RE SUPPOSED TO FOLLOW MY ADVICE. YOUR FATHER--
HAA!
I WILL, PHOENIX. AFTERWARD!
ACHILLES, I DON'T THINK YOU REALIZE WHAT'S HAPPENED-- WHERE WE ARE! ACHILLES!

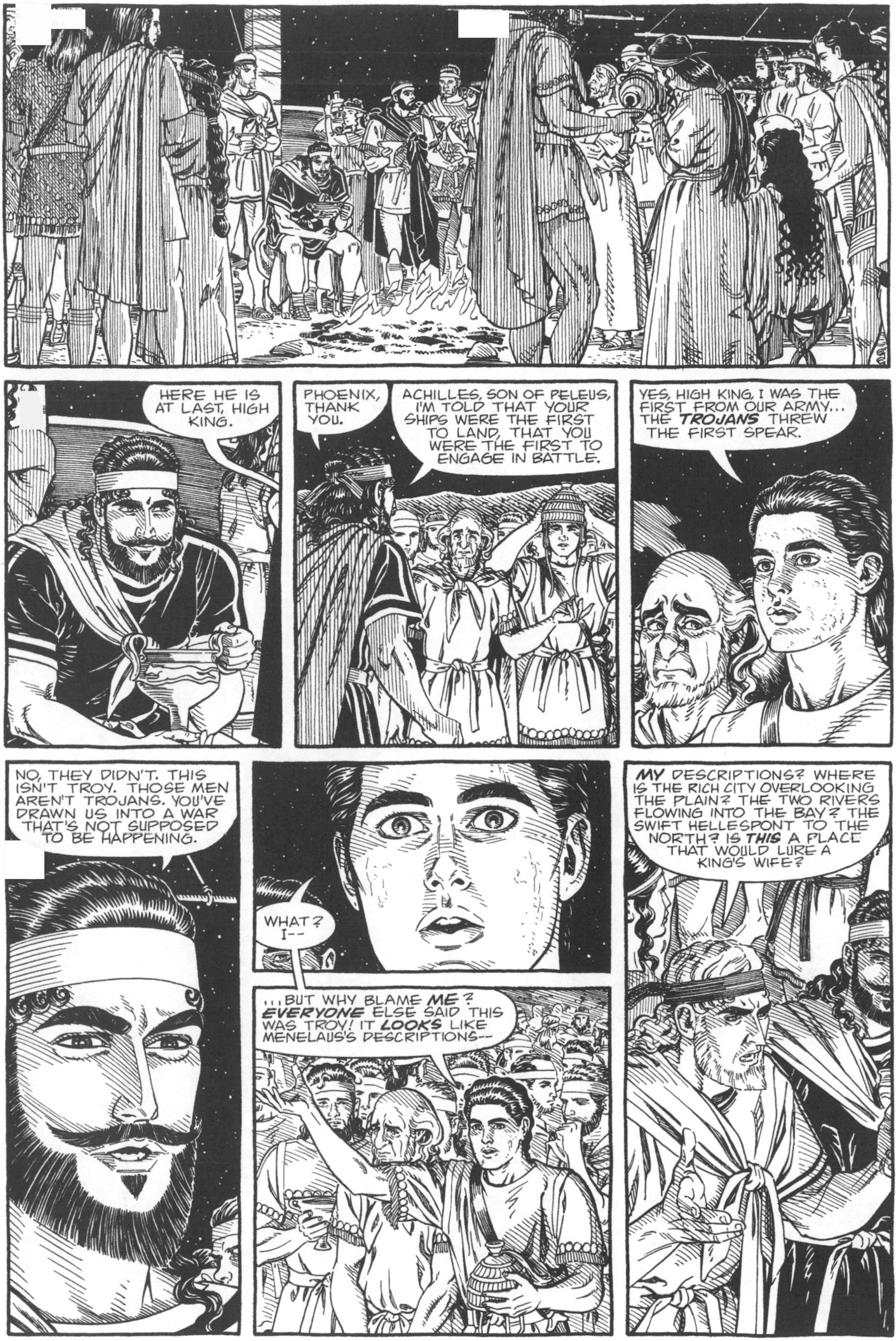
HERE HE IS AT LAST, HIGH KING.
PHOENIX, THANK YOU.
ACHILLES, SON OF PELEUS, I'M TOLD THAT YOUR SHIPS WERE THE FIRST TO LAND, THAT YOU WERE THE FIRST TO ENGAGE IN BATTLE.
YES, HIGH KING, I WAS THE FIRST FROM OUR ARMY... THE **TROJANS** THREW THE FIRST SPEAR.
NO, THEY DIDN'T. THIS ISN'T TROY. THOSE MEN AREN'T TROJANS. YOU'VE DRAWN US INTO A WAR THAT'S NOT SUPPOSED TO BE HAPPENING.
WHAT? I--
...BUT WHY BLAME **ME**? **EVERYONE** ELSE SAID THIS WAS TROY! IT **LOOKS** LIKE MENELAUS'S DESCRIPTIONS--
MY DESCRIPTIONS? WHERE IS THE RICH CITY OVERLOOKING THE PLAIN? THE TWO RIVERS FLOWING INTO THE BAY? THE SWIFT HELLESPONT TO THE NORTH? IS **THIS** A PLACE THAT WOULD LURE A KING'S WIFE?

ENOUGH! *I* LED THE ACHAEANS INTO BATTLE--I ACCEPT RESPONSIBILITY FOR THE MISTAKE. BUT WHAT'S DONE IS DONE. IN THE MORNING, LET'S GET BACK INTO OUR SHIPS AND GO. LET MENELAUS TAKE THE LEAD--OR SOMEONE ELSE WHO'S BEEN TO TROY --SO THAT NO ONE MAKES ANOTHER MISTAKE.

THE FLEET CAN'T SAIL SO QUICKLY. HUNDREDS OF OUR MEN ARE DEAD, AND MANY MORE ARE WOUNDED.

THERSANDER OF THEBES FELL TODAY. HE WAS A GREAT WARRIOR AND KING, SO HE MUST HAVE A FUNERAL AND GAMES.

WE'LL BE DELAYED HERE FOR *DAYS*, RECOVERING--AND THAT'S AS LONG AS THE LOCALS DON'T ATTACK AGAIN!

AND LOOK AT OUR MEN--

--THEY'VE SUFFERED YEARS OF HARDSHIP AND WAITING FOR THIS WAR. WE COAXED THEM WITH TROJAN RICHES, BOUND THEM WITH OATHS, WHIPPED THEM INTO SUBMISSION--

PALAMEDES! THAT'S *ENOUGH!*

--ONLY TO LEAD THEM HERE TO A WAR NO ONE WANTS. WE'RE NOT *LEADING*, WE'RE *BUMBLING--*

AT FIRST LIGHT, I'LL SEND ENVOYS TO THE LOCAL KING TO ARRANGE A TRUCE TO COLLECT AND BURY THE DEAD.

ACHILLES, WE ALL REALIZE YOU'RE YOUNG AND INEXPERIENCED. BUT MISTAKES SUCH AS YOURS TODAY ARE COSTLY. DON'T MAKE ANOTHER.

YES, HIGH KING.

OUR GOAL REMAINS THE SAME--TO TAKE TROY.

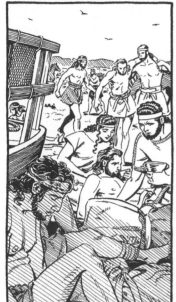

...IT SEEMS SO WRONG TO BURY HIM SO FAR FROM HIS FOREFATHERS, HIGH KING.

EVEN IF YOU SAILED IMMEDIATELY, PENELEOS, THE BODY COULDN'T REACH THEBES BEFORE THE DECAY BECAME SO GREAT--

I KNOW. I KNOW.

BUT LEAVING THERSANDER HERE ON A FOREIGN SHORE --A SHORE WE DON'T EVEN KNOW THE NAME OF...

I THINK WE'LL LEARN THE ANSWER TO THAT RIGHT NOW. MY ENVOYS ARE BACK.

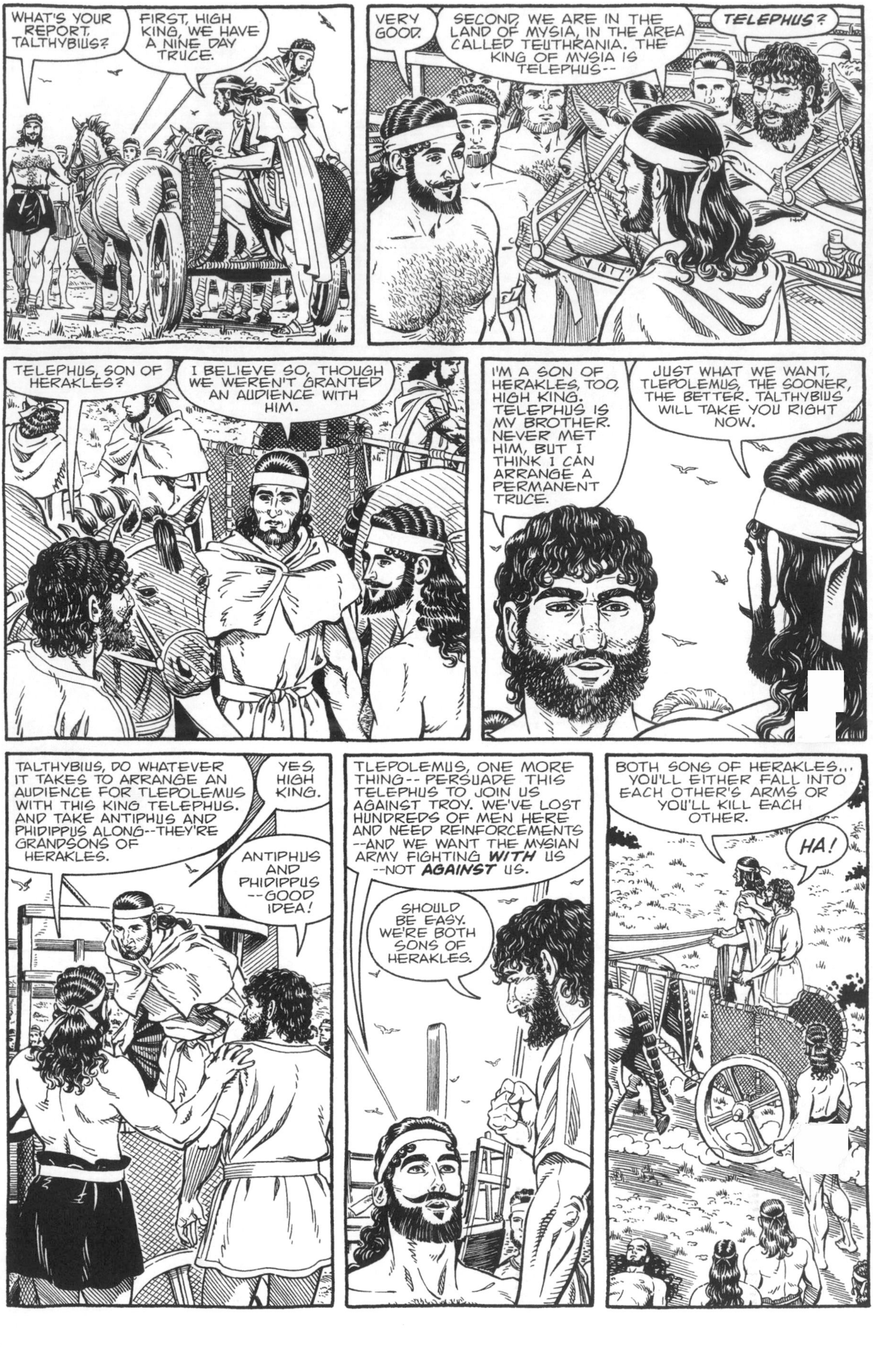
WHAT'S YOUR REPORT, TALTHYBIUS?
FIRST, HIGH KING, WE HAVE A NINE DAY TRUCE.
VERY GOOD.
SECOND, WE ARE IN THE LAND OF MYSIA, IN THE AREA CALLED TEUTHRANIA. THE KING OF MYSIA IS TELEPHUS--
TELEPHUS?
TELEPHUS, SON OF HERAKLES?
I BELIEVE SO, THOUGH WE WEREN'T GRANTED AN AUDIENCE WITH HIM.
I'M A SON OF HERAKLES, TOO, HIGH KING. TELEPHUS IS MY BROTHER. NEVER MET HIM, BUT I THINK I CAN ARRANGE A PERMANENT TRUCE.
JUST WHAT WE WANT, TLEPOLEMUS, THE SOONER, THE BETTER. TALTHYBIUS WILL TAKE YOU RIGHT NOW.
TALTHYBIUS, DO WHATEVER IT TAKES TO ARRANGE AN AUDIENCE FOR TLEPOLEMUS WITH THIS KING TELEPHUS. AND TAKE ANTIPHUS AND PHIDIPPUS ALONG--THEY'RE GRANDSONS OF HERAKLES.
YES, HIGH KING.
ANTIPHUS AND PHIDIPPUS --GOOD IDEA!
TLEPOLEMUS, ONE MORE THING-- PERSUADE THIS TELEPHUS TO JOIN US AGAINST TROY. WE'VE LOST HUNDREDS OF MEN HERE AND NEED REINFORCEMENTS --AND WE WANT THE MYSIAN ARMY FIGHTING **WITH** US --NOT **AGAINST** US.
SHOULD BE EASY. WE'RE BOTH SONS OF HERAKLES.
BOTH SONS OF HERAKLES... YOU'LL EITHER FALL INTO EACH OTHER'S ARMS OR YOU'LL KILL EACH OTHER.
HA!

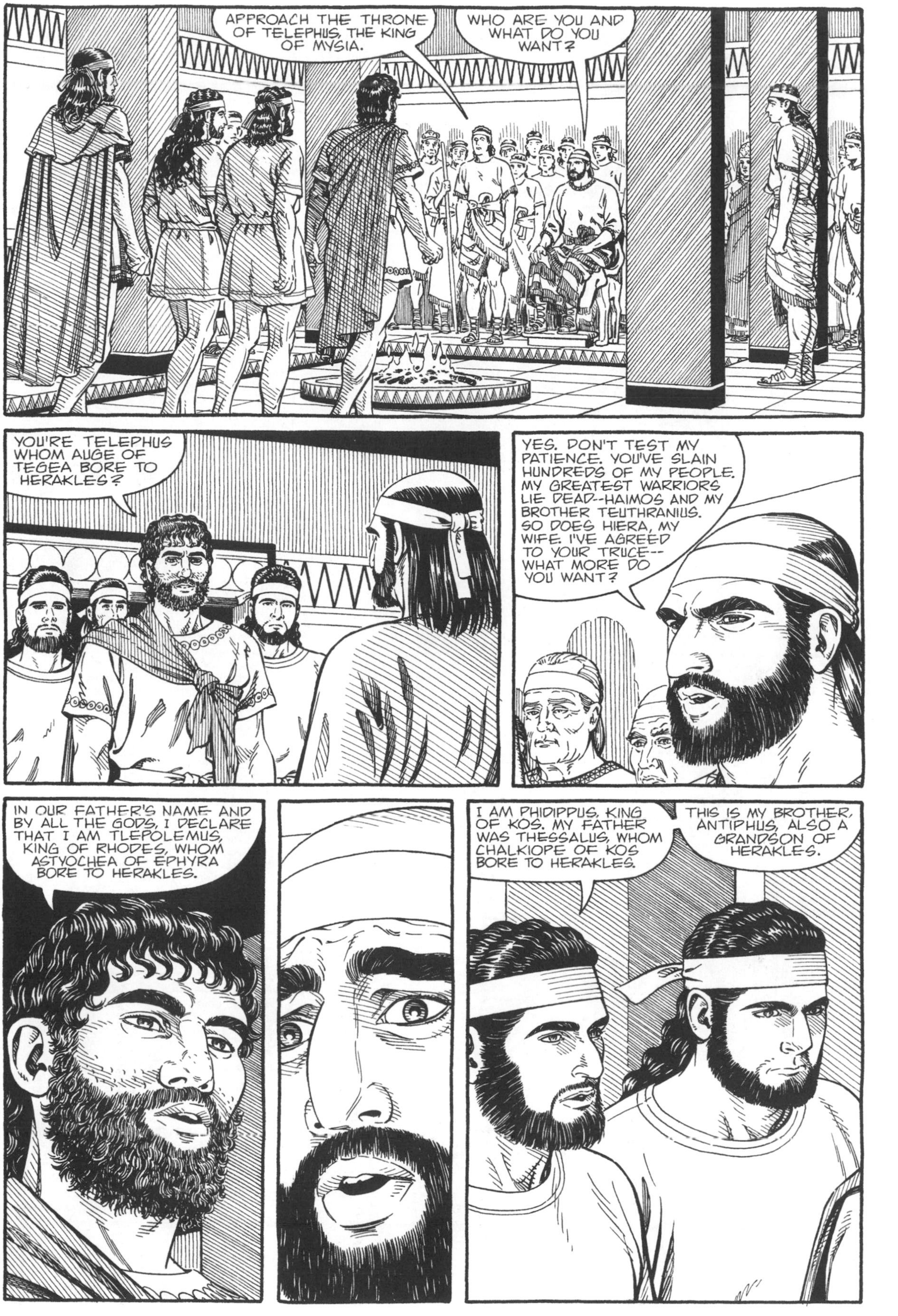
APPROACH THE THRONE OF TELEPHUS, THE KING OF MYSIA.
WHO ARE YOU AND WHAT DO YOU WANT?
YOU'RE TELEPHUS WHOM AUGE OF TEGEA BORE TO HERAKLES?
YES. DON'T TEST MY PATIENCE. YOU'VE SLAIN HUNDREDS OF MY PEOPLE. MY GREATEST WARRIORS LIE DEAD--HAIMOS AND MY BROTHER TEUTHRANIUS. SO DOES HIERA, MY WIFE. I'VE AGREED TO YOUR TRUCE-- WHAT MORE DO YOU WANT?
IN OUR FATHER'S NAME AND BY ALL THE GODS, I DECLARE THAT I AM TLEPOLEMUS, KING OF RHODES, WHOM ASTYOCHEA OF EPHYRA BORE TO HERAKLES.
I AM PHIDIPPUS, KING OF KOS. MY FATHER WAS THESSALUS, WHOM CHALKIOPE OF KOS BORE TO HERAKLES.
THIS IS MY BROTHER, ANTIPHUS, ALSO A GRANDSON OF HERAKLES.

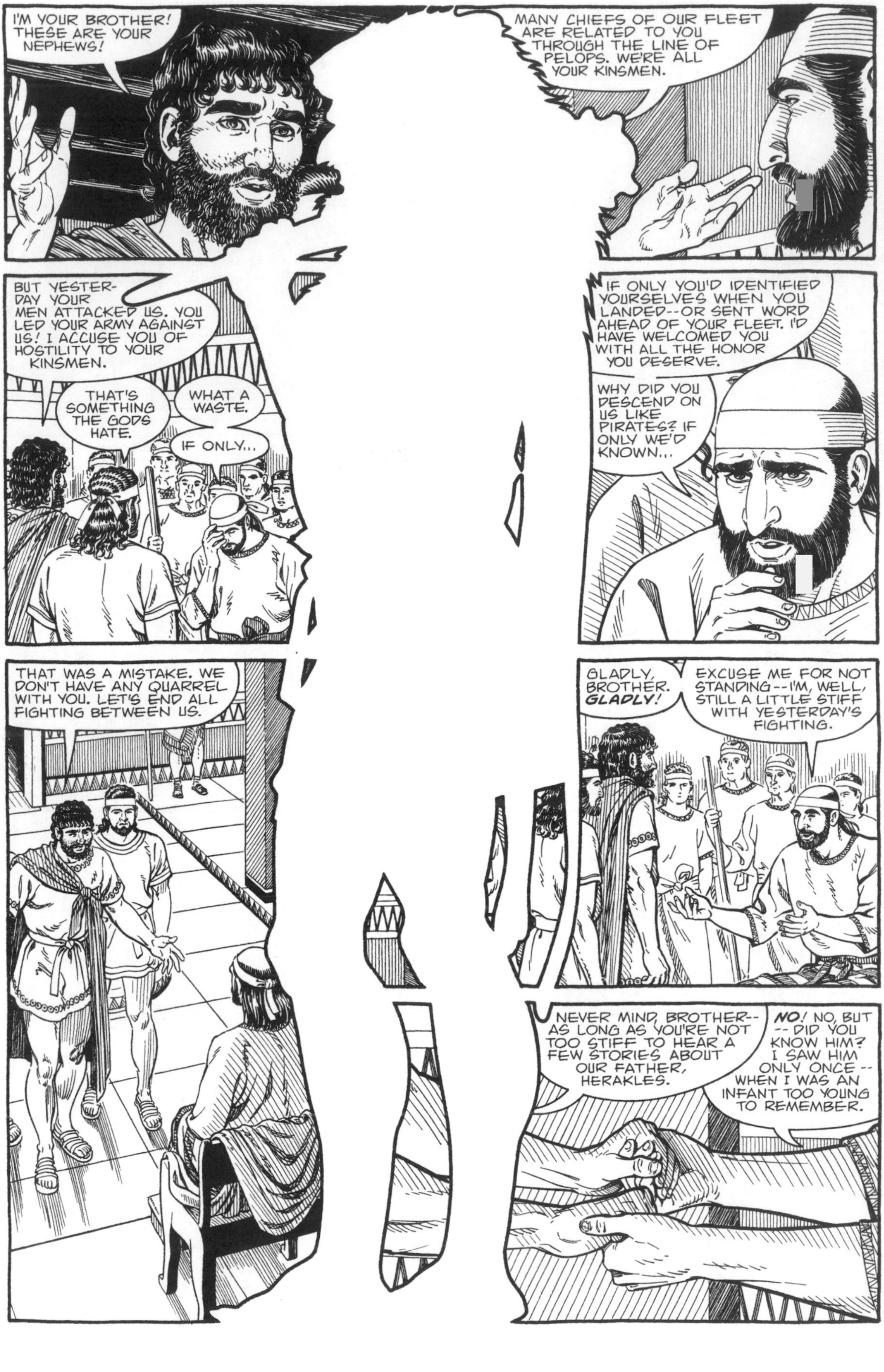
I'M YOUR BROTHER! THESE ARE YOUR NEPHEWS!
MANY CHIEFS OF OUR FLEET ARE RELATED TO YOU THROUGH THE LINE OF PELOPS. WE'RE ALL YOUR KINSMEN.
BUT YESTERDAY YOUR MEN ATTACKED US. YOU LED YOUR ARMY AGAINST US! I ACCUSE YOU OF HOSTILITY TO YOUR KINSMEN.
THAT'S SOMETHING THE GODS HATE.
WHAT A WASTE.
IF ONLY...
IF ONLY YOU'D IDENTIFIED YOURSELVES WHEN YOU LANDED--OR SENT WORD AHEAD OF YOUR FLEET. I'D HAVE WELCOMED YOU WITH ALL THE HONOR YOU DESERVE.
WHY DID YOU DESCEND ON US LIKE PIRATES? IF ONLY WE'D KNOWN...
THAT WAS A MISTAKE. WE DON'T HAVE ANY QUARREL WITH YOU. LET'S END ALL FIGHTING BETWEEN US.
GLADLY, BROTHER. GLADLY!
EXCUSE ME FOR NOT STANDING--I'M, WELL, STILL A LITTLE STIFF WITH YESTERDAY'S FIGHTING.
NEVER MIND, BROTHER-- AS LONG AS YOU'RE NOT TOO STIFF TO HEAR A FEW STORIES ABOUT OUR FATHER, HERAKLES.
NO! NO, BUT --DID YOU KNOW HIM? I SAW HIM ONLY ONCE-- WHEN I WAS AN INFANT TOO YOUNG TO REMEMBER.

YES, I KNEW HIM. I GREW UP IN HIS PALACE AT ARGOS. I SAW HIM MANY TIMES BEFORE HE BECAME A GOD.

BRING SEATS FOR MY GUESTS--AND FOOD AND WINE.

ANTIPHUS AND I DIDN'T KNOW OUR GRANDFATHER, BUT WE NEVER GET TIRED OF HEARING STORIES ABOUT HIM.

YOU SHOULD TALK TO SOME OF THE OTHER ACHAEAN CHIEFS WHO KNEW HIM --PHILOKTETES, NESTOR...

EXCELLENT! IN TWELVE DAYS --AFTER THE FUNERALS-- I INVITE EVERYONE WHO'S KIN TO HERAKLES OR WHO KNEW HIM TO FEAST WITH ME IN MY HALL.

THAT'LL BE A WELCOME CHANGE AFTER OUR SEA JOURNEY AND YESTERDAY'S FIGHTING. YOU KNOW, BROTHER, AS AN ACHAEAN YOURSELF, YOU OUGHT TO JOIN US.

JOIN YOU IN WHAT? PIRATE RAIDS?

NO, IT'S A LONG STORY.

A PRINCE OF TROY NAMED PARIS WAS A GUEST OF MENELAUS OF LAKEDAEMON. BUT THIS PARIS LOOTED MENELAUS'S PALACE AND CARRIED OFF HIS WIFE. YOU MIGHT HAVE HEARD OF HER-- HELEN, DAUGHTER OF TYNDAREUS.

AH, THE BEAUTY BEYOND COMPARE. I REMEMBER ALL OF THE ACHAEAN KINGS TRYING TO OUTDO ONE ANOTHER TO WIN HER. THAT'S ABOUT THE TIME I LEFT TEGEA TO SEARCH FOR MY MOTHER.

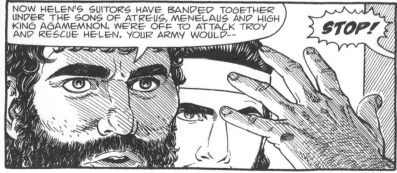

NOW HELEN'S SUITORS HAVE BANDED TOGETHER UNDER THE SONS OF ATREUS, MENELAUS AND HIGH KING AGAMEMNON. WE'RE OFF TO ATTACK TROY AND RESCUE HELEN. YOUR ARMY WOULD--

STOP!

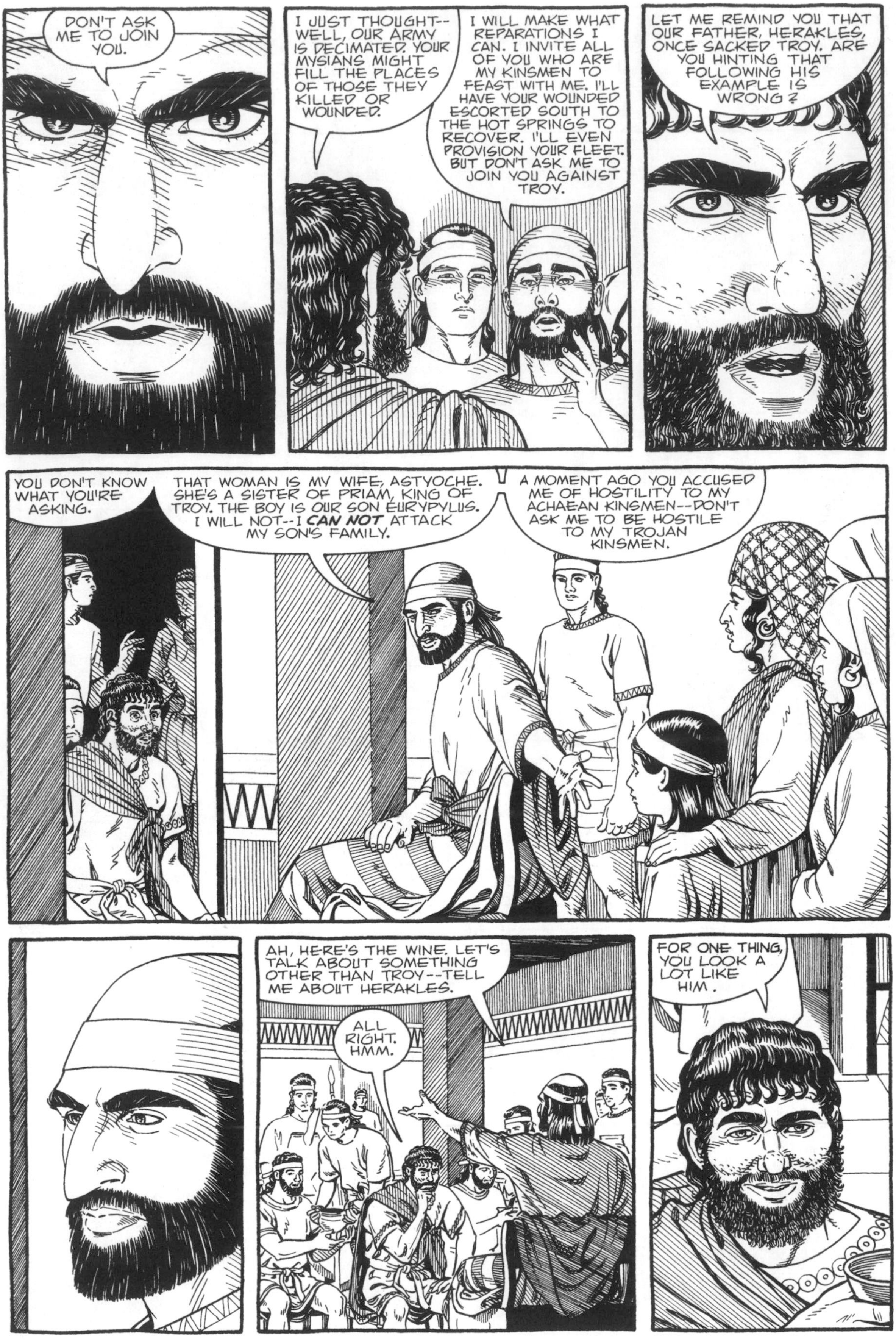
DON'T ASK ME TO JOIN YOU.
I JUST THOUGHT--WELL, OUR ARMY IS DECIMATED. YOUR MYSIANS MIGHT FILL THE PLACES OF THOSE THEY KILLED OR WOUNDED.
I WILL MAKE WHAT REPARATIONS I CAN. I INVITE ALL OF YOU WHO ARE MY KINSMEN TO FEAST WITH ME. I'LL HAVE YOUR WOUNDED ESCORTED SOUTH TO THE HOT SPRINGS TO RECOVER. I'LL EVEN PROVISION YOUR FLEET. BUT DON'T ASK ME TO JOIN YOU AGAINST TROY.
LET ME REMIND YOU THAT OUR FATHER, HERAKLES, ONCE SACKED TROY. ARE YOU HINTING THAT FOLLOWING HIS EXAMPLE IS WRONG?
YOU DON'T KNOW WHAT YOU'RE ASKING.
THAT WOMAN IS MY WIFE, ASTYOCHE. SHE'S A SISTER OF PRIAM, KING OF TROY. THE BOY IS OUR SON EURYPYLUS. I WILL NOT--I ***CAN NOT*** ATTACK MY SON'S FAMILY.
A MOMENT AGO YOU ACCUSED ME OF HOSTILITY TO MY ACHAEAN KINSMEN--DON'T ASK ME TO BE HOSTILE TO MY TROJAN KINSMEN.
AH, HERE'S THE WINE. LET'S TALK ABOUT SOMETHING OTHER THAN TROY--TELL ME ABOUT HERAKLES.
ALL RIGHT. HMM.
FOR ONE THING, YOU LOOK A LOT LIKE HIM.

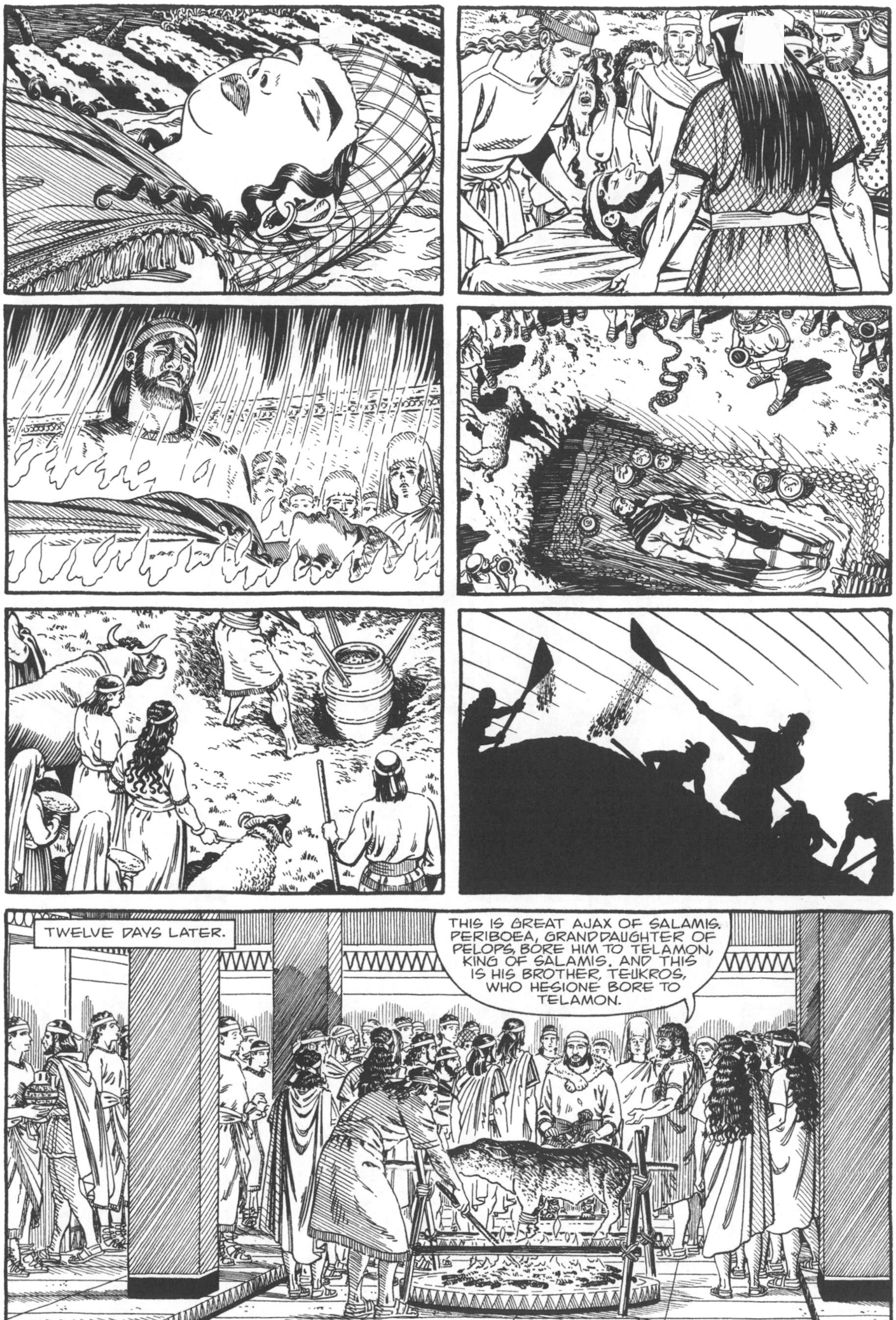
TWELVE DAYS LATER.
THIS IS GREAT AJAX OF SALAMIS. PERIBOEA, GRANDDAUGHTER OF PELOPS, BORE HIM TO TELAMON, KING OF SALAMIS. AND THIS IS HIS BROTHER, TEUKROS, WHO HESIONE BORE TO TELAMON.

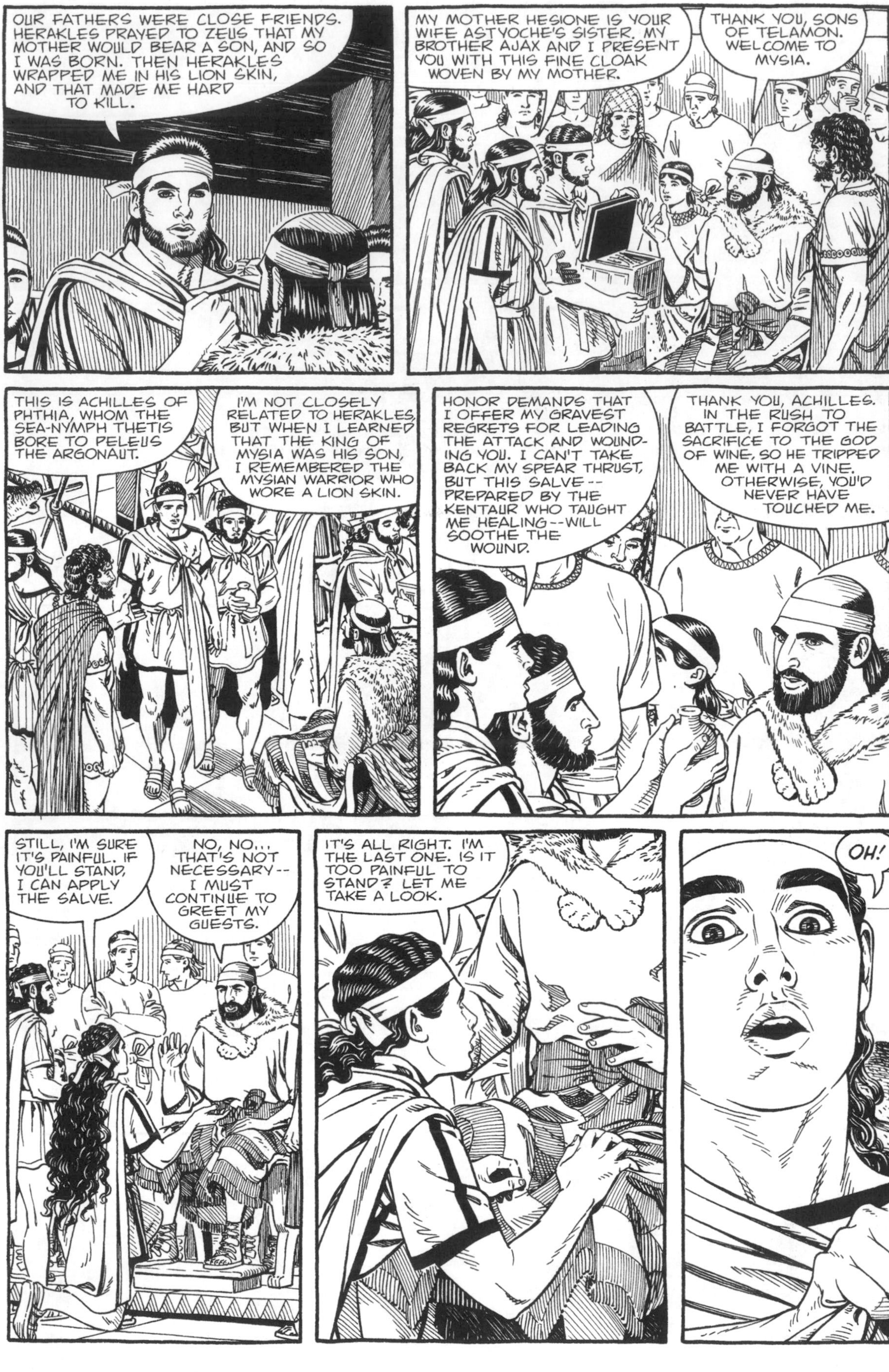
OUR FATHERS WERE CLOSE FRIENDS. HERAKLES PRAYED TO ZEUS THAT MY MOTHER WOULD BEAR A SON, AND SO I WAS BORN. THEN HERAKLES WRAPPED ME IN HIS LION SKIN, AND THAT MADE ME HARD TO KILL.
MY MOTHER HESIONE IS YOUR WIFE ASTYOCHE'S SISTER. MY BROTHER AJAX AND I PRESENT YOU WITH THIS FINE CLOAK WOVEN BY MY MOTHER.
THANK YOU, SONS OF TELAMON. WELCOME TO MYSIA.
THIS IS ACHILLES OF PHTHIA, WHOM THE SEA-NYMPH THETIS BORE TO PELEUS THE ARGONAUT.
I'M NOT CLOSELY RELATED TO HERAKLES, BUT WHEN I LEARNED THAT THE KING OF MYSIA WAS HIS SON, I REMEMBERED THE MYSIAN WARRIOR WHO WORE A LION SKIN.
HONOR DEMANDS THAT I OFFER MY GRAVEST REGRETS FOR LEADING THE ATTACK AND WOUNDING YOU. I CAN'T TAKE BACK MY SPEAR THRUST, BUT THIS SALVE--PREPARED BY THE KENTAUR WHO TAUGHT ME HEALING--WILL SOOTHE THE WOUND.
THANK YOU, ACHILLES. IN THE RUSH TO BATTLE, I FORGOT THE SACRIFICE TO THE GOD OF WINE, SO HE TRIPPED ME WITH A VINE. OTHERWISE, YOU'D NEVER HAVE TOUCHED ME.
STILL, I'M SURE IT'S PAINFUL. IF YOU'LL STAND, I CAN APPLY THE SALVE.
NO, NO... THAT'S NOT NECESSARY--I MUST CONTINUE TO GREET MY GUESTS.
IT'S ALL RIGHT. I'M THE LAST ONE. IS IT TOO PAINFUL TO STAND? LET ME TAKE A LOOK.
OH!

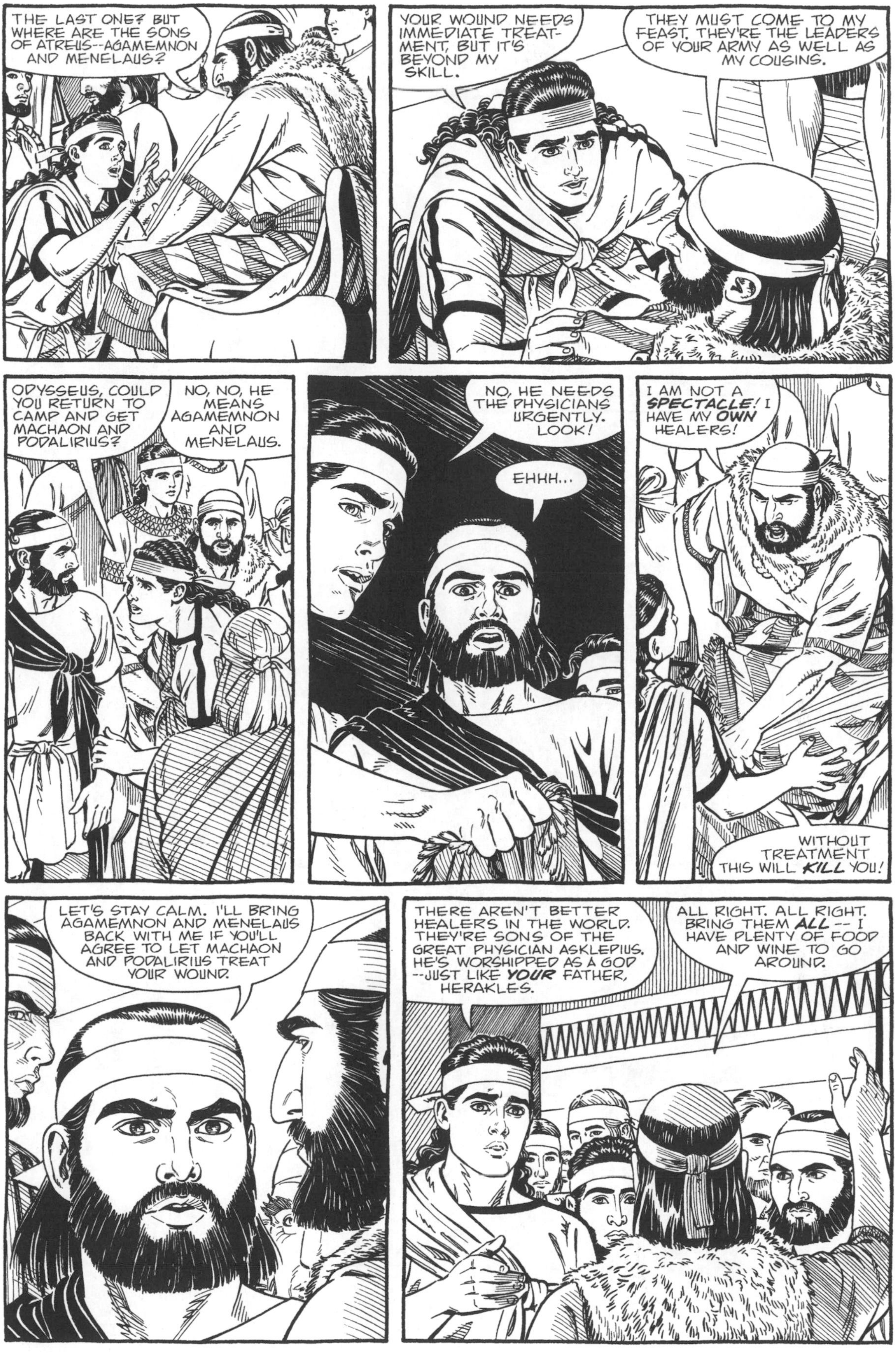
THE LAST ONE? BUT WHERE ARE THE SONS OF ATREUS--AGAMEMNON AND MENELAUS?
YOUR WOUND NEEDS IMMEDIATE TREATMENT, BUT IT'S BEYOND MY SKILL.
THEY MUST COME TO MY FEAST. THEY'RE THE LEADERS OF YOUR ARMY AS WELL AS MY COUSINS.
ODYSSEUS, COULD YOU RETURN TO CAMP AND GET MACHAON AND PODALIRIUS?
NO, NO, HE MEANS AGAMEMNON AND MENELAUS.
NO, HE NEEDS THE PHYSICIANS URGENTLY. LOOK!
EHHH...
I AM NOT A SPECTACLE! I HAVE MY OWN HEALERS!
WITHOUT TREATMENT THIS WILL KILL YOU!
LET'S STAY CALM. I'LL BRING AGAMEMNON AND MENELAUS BACK WITH ME IF YOU'LL AGREE TO LET MACHAON AND PODALIRIUS TREAT YOUR WOUND.
THERE AREN'T BETTER HEALERS IN THE WORLD. THEY'RE SONS OF THE GREAT PHYSICIAN ASKLEPIUS. HE'S WORSHIPPED AS A GOD --JUST LIKE YOUR FATHER, HERAKLES.
ALL RIGHT. ALL RIGHT. BRING THEM ALL -- I HAVE PLENTY OF FOOD AND WINE TO GO AROUND.

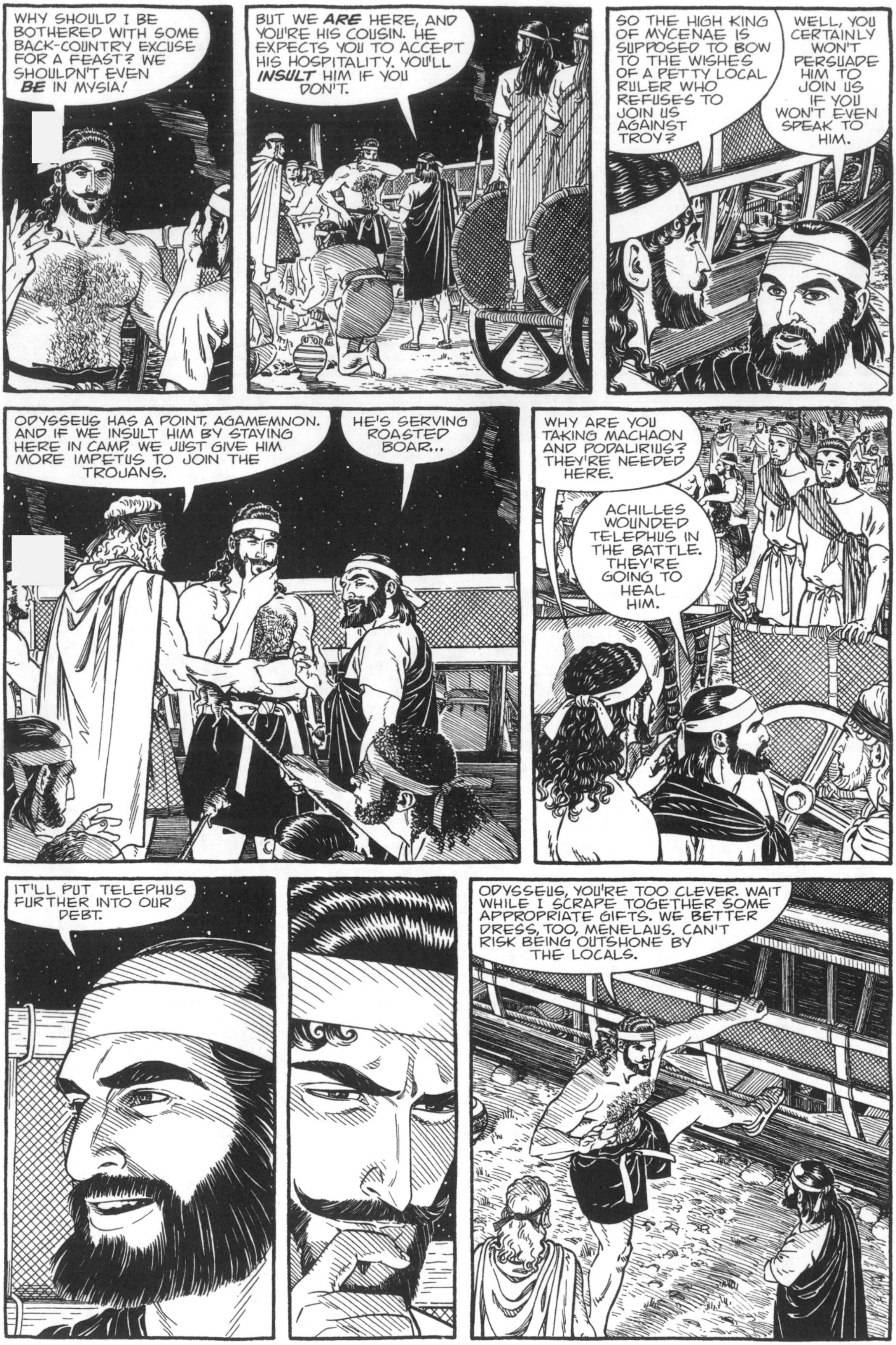

WHY SHOULD I BE BOTHERED WITH SOME BACK-COUNTRY EXCUSE FOR A FEAST? WE SHOULDN'T EVEN BE IN MYSIA!
BUT WE ARE HERE, AND YOU'RE HIS COUSIN. HE EXPECTS YOU TO ACCEPT HIS HOSPITALITY. YOU'LL INSULT HIM IF YOU DON'T.
SO THE HIGH KING OF MYCENAE IS SUPPOSED TO BOW TO THE WISHES OF A PETTY LOCAL RULER WHO REFUSES TO JOIN US AGAINST TROY?
WELL, YOU CERTAINLY WON'T PERSUADE HIM TO JOIN US IF YOU WON'T EVEN SPEAK TO HIM.
ODYSSEUS HAS A POINT, AGAMEMNON. AND IF WE INSULT HIM BY STAYING HERE IN CAMP, WE JUST GIVE HIM MORE IMPETUS TO JOIN THE TROJANS.
HE'S SERVING ROASTED BOAR...
WHY ARE YOU TAKING MACHAON AND PODALIRIUS? THEY'RE NEEDED HERE.
ACHILLES WOUNDED TELEPHUS IN THE BATTLE. THEY'RE GOING TO HEAL HIM.
IT'LL PUT TELEPHUS FURTHER INTO OUR DEBT.
ODYSSEUS, YOU'RE TOO CLEVER. WAIT WHILE I SCRAPE TOGETHER SOME APPROPRIATE GIFTS. WE BETTER DRESS, TOO, MENELAUS. CAN'T RISK BEING OUTSHONE BY THE LOCALS.

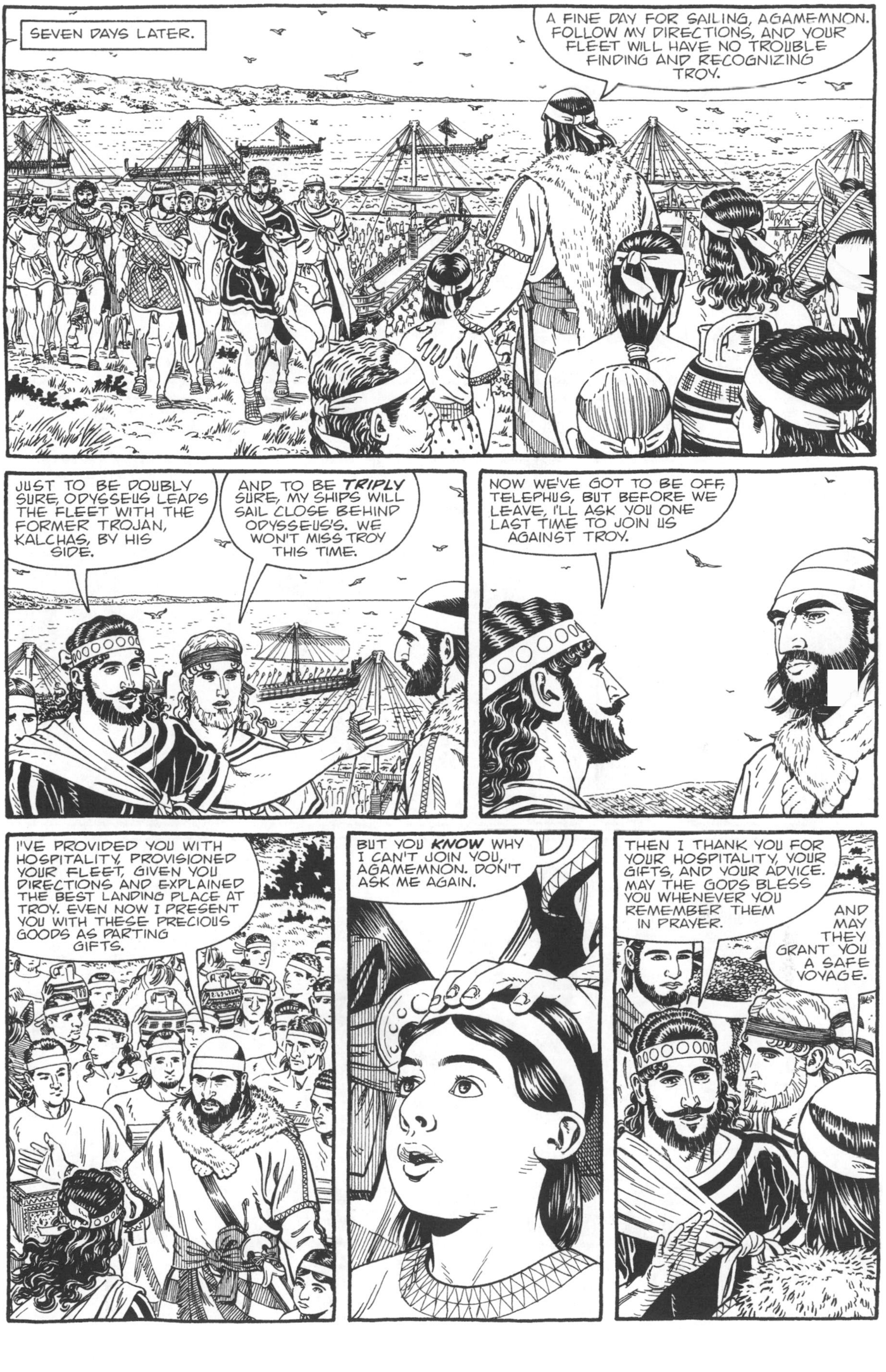
SEVEN DAYS LATER.
A FINE DAY FOR SAILING, AGAMEMNON. FOLLOW MY DIRECTIONS, AND YOUR FLEET WILL HAVE NO TROUBLE FINDING AND RECOGNIZING TROY.
JUST TO BE DOUBLY SURE, ODYSSEUS LEADS THE FLEET WITH THE FORMER TROJAN, KALCHAS, BY HIS SIDE.
AND TO BE *TRIPLY* SURE, MY SHIPS WILL SAIL CLOSE BEHIND ODYSSEUS'S. WE WON'T MISS TROY THIS TIME.
NOW WE'VE GOT TO BE OFF, TELEPHUS, BUT BEFORE WE LEAVE, I'LL ASK YOU ONE LAST TIME TO JOIN US AGAINST TROY.
I'VE PROVIDED YOU WITH HOSPITALITY, PROVISIONED YOUR FLEET, GIVEN YOU DIRECTIONS AND EXPLAINED THE BEST LANDING PLACE AT TROY. EVEN NOW I PRESENT YOU WITH THESE PRECIOUS GOODS AS PARTING GIFTS.
BUT YOU *KNOW* WHY I CAN'T JOIN YOU, AGAMEMNON. DON'T ASK ME AGAIN.
THEN I THANK YOU FOR YOUR HOSPITALITY, YOUR GIFTS, AND YOUR ADVICE. MAY THE GODS BLESS YOU WHENEVER YOU REMEMBER THEM IN PRAYER.
AND MAY THEY GRANT YOU A SAFE VOYAGE.

BEFORE I DEPART, I WANT TO MAKE SURE YOUR WOUND IS HEALING PROPERLY.

YOU SEE ME STANDING, DON'T YOU, MACHAON? YOU AND YOUR BROTHER ARE MARVELOUS.

I WISH THAT WOUND HAD FESTERED AND KILLED HIM.

MACHAON AND PODALIRIUS WOULD *NEVER* HAVE AGREED TO LET THAT HAPPEN.

THAT'S WHY I DIDN'T SUGGEST IT. BUT IT'S ALL I COULD THINK ABOUT THE NIGHT OF THE FEAST.

WELL, IF HE JOINS THE TROJANS, WE'LL JUST SEND TLEPOLEMUS TO CONVINCE HIM OTHERWISE.

TLEPOLEMUS, OF ALL THE THINGS YOUR FLEET CARRIED HERE TO TEUTHRANIA, I'M MOST GRATEFUL FOR THE FAMILY I NEVER KNEW BEFORE, PARTICULARLY YOU, MY NEW BROTHER.

AND I'M GRATEFUL THAT THE GODS BROUGHT ME HERE TO YOU, TELEPHUS. I JUST WISH IT HADN'T BEEN AT THE EXPENSE OF SO MANY OTHERS --TEUTHRANIUS, HIERA...

YES, TOO MANY LOSSES ON BOTH SIDES. I SEE A CEMETARY HAS SPRUNG UP HERE AT THE MOUTH OF THE KAIKOS RIVER WHERE DAYS AGO ONLY SCRUBBY BRUSH GREW.

AND WHO'S BURIAL MOUND IS THAT? ANYONE WITH EYES WILL SEE IT FROM FAR AWAY ON BOTH LAND AND WATER.

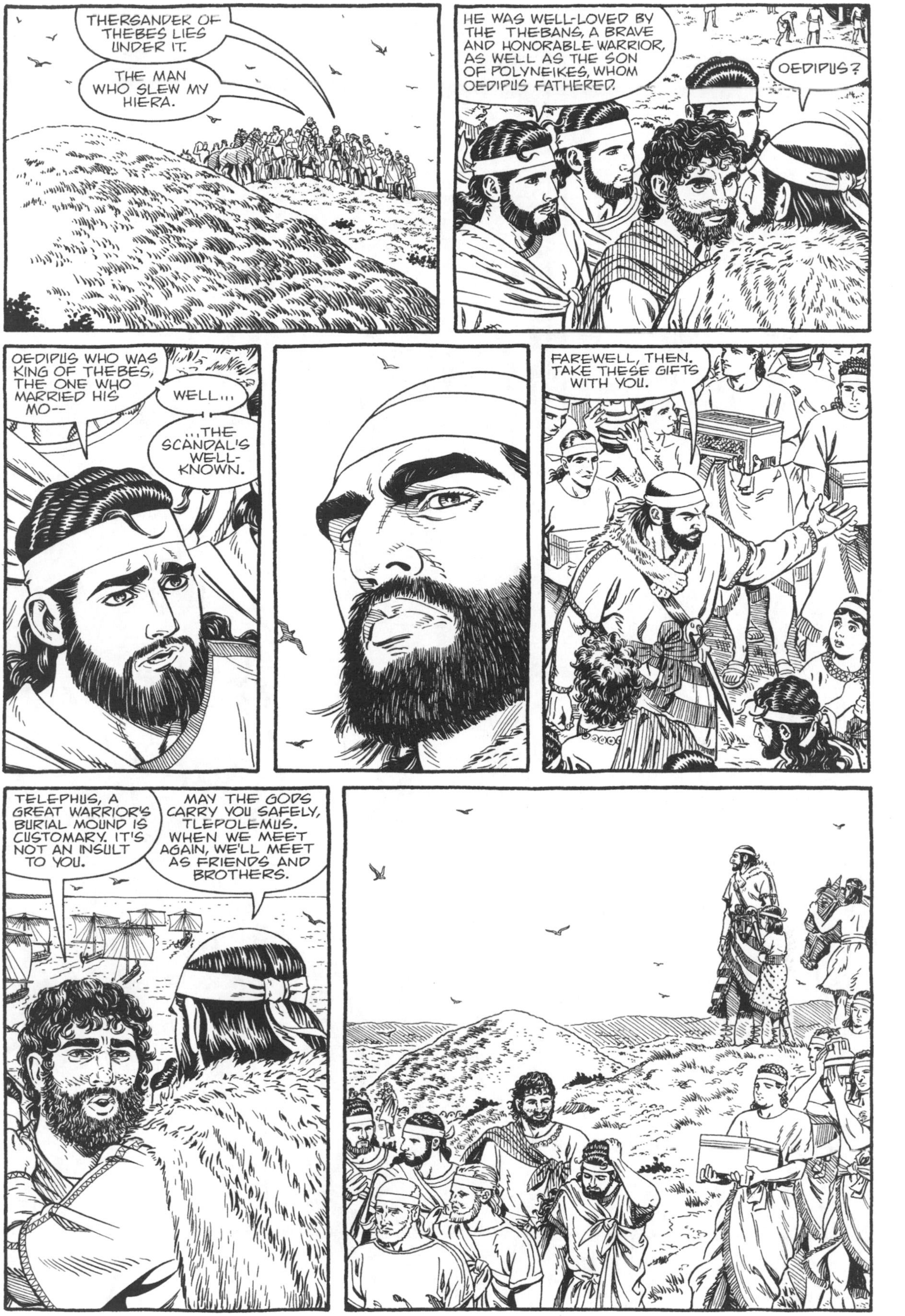
THERSANDER OF THEBES LIES UNDER IT.
THE MAN WHO SLEW MY HIERA.
HE WAS WELL-LOVED BY THE THEBANS, A BRAVE AND HONORABLE WARRIOR, AS WELL AS THE SON OF POLYNEIKES, WHOM OEDIPUS FATHERED.
OEDIPUS?
OEDIPUS WHO WAS KING OF THEBES, THE ONE WHO MARRIED HIS MO--
WELL...
...THE SCANDAL'S WELL-KNOWN.
FAREWELL, THEN. TAKE THESE GIFTS WITH YOU.
TELEPHUS, A GREAT WARRIOR'S BURIAL MOUND IS CUSTOMARY. IT'S NOT AN INSULT TO YOU.
MAY THE GODS CARRY YOU SAFELY, TLEPOLEMUS. WHEN WE MEET AGAIN, WE'LL MEET AS FRIENDS AND BROTHERS.

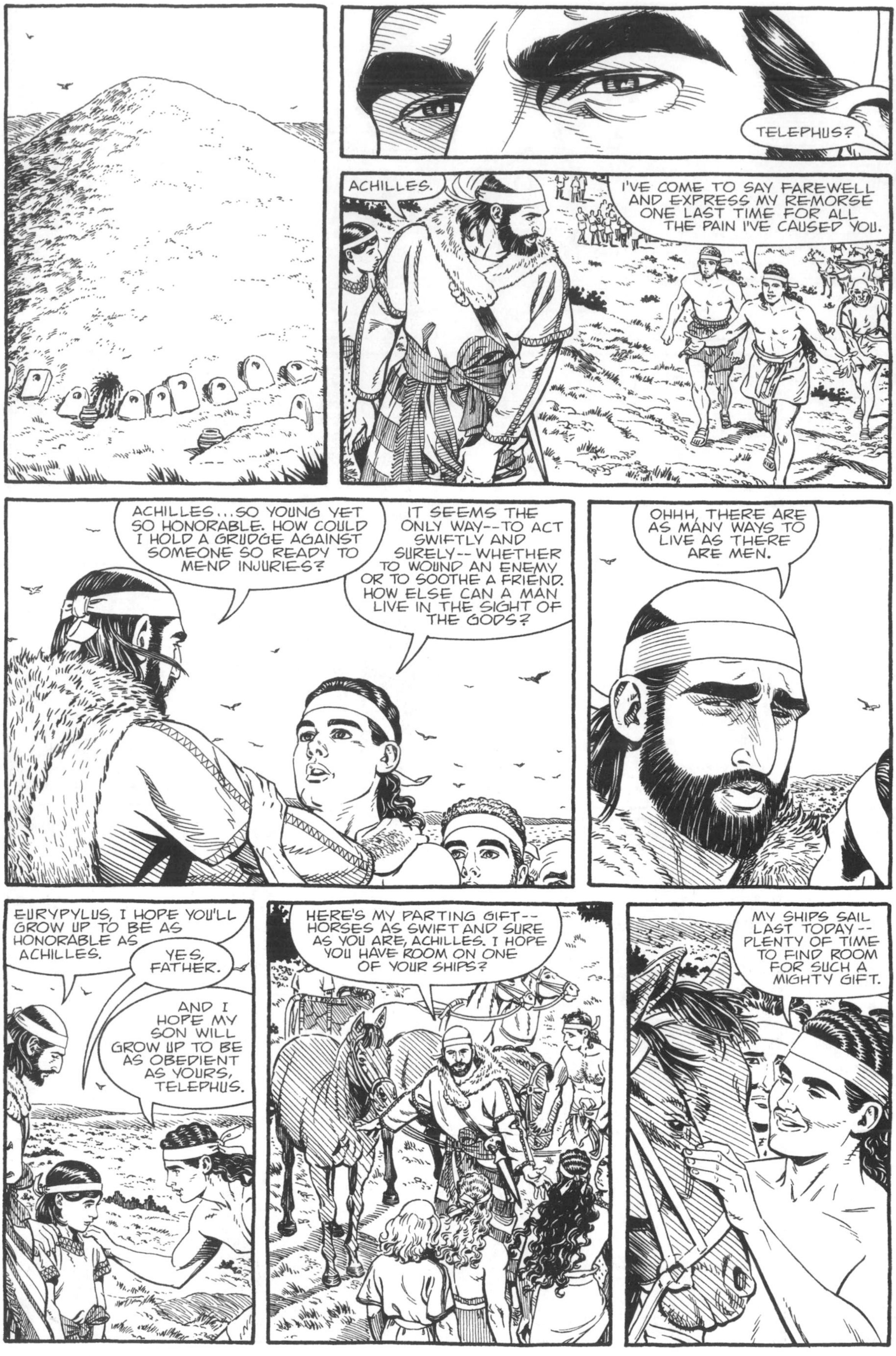
TELEPHUS?
ACHILLES.
I'VE COME TO SAY FAREWELL AND EXPRESS MY REMORSE ONE LAST TIME FOR ALL THE PAIN I'VE CAUSED YOU.
ACHILLES...SO YOUNG YET SO HONORABLE. HOW COULD I HOLD A GRUDGE AGAINST SOMEONE SO READY TO MEND INJURIES?
IT SEEMS THE ONLY WAY--TO ACT SWIFTLY AND SURELY--WHETHER TO WOUND AN ENEMY OR TO SOOTHE A FRIEND. HOW ELSE CAN A MAN LIVE IN THE SIGHT OF THE GODS?
OHHH, THERE ARE AS MANY WAYS TO LIVE AS THERE ARE MEN.
EURYPYLUS, I HOPE YOU'LL GROW UP TO BE AS HONORABLE AS ACHILLES.
YES, FATHER.
AND I HOPE MY SON WILL GROW UP TO BE AS OBEDIENT AS YOURS, TELEPHUS.
HERE'S MY PARTING GIFT--HORSES AS SWIFT AND SURE AS YOU ARE, ACHILLES. I HOPE YOU HAVE ROOM ON ONE OF YOUR SHIPS?
MY SHIPS SAIL LAST TODAY--PLENTY OF TIME TO FIND ROOM FOR SUCH A MIGHTY GIFT.

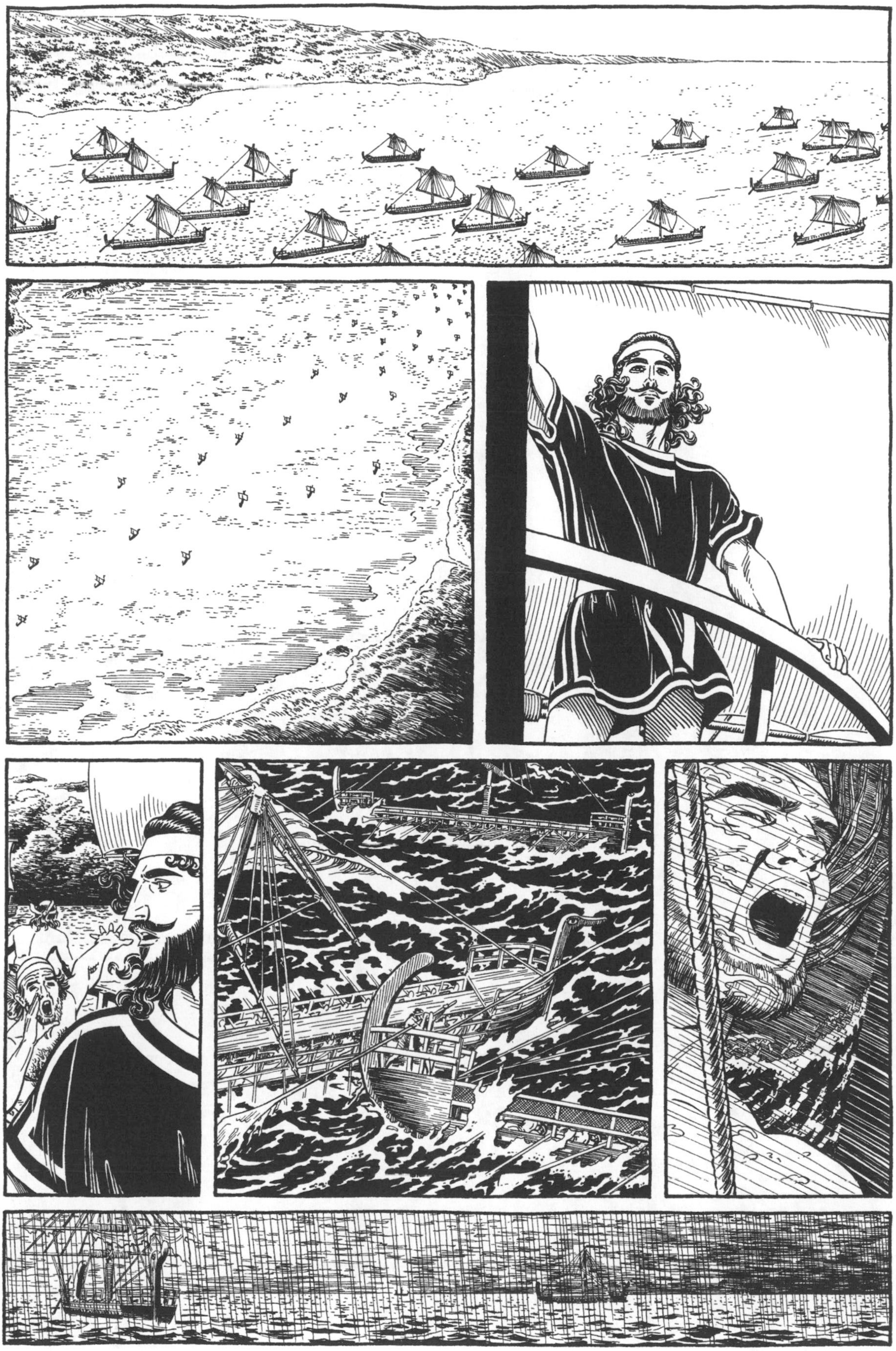

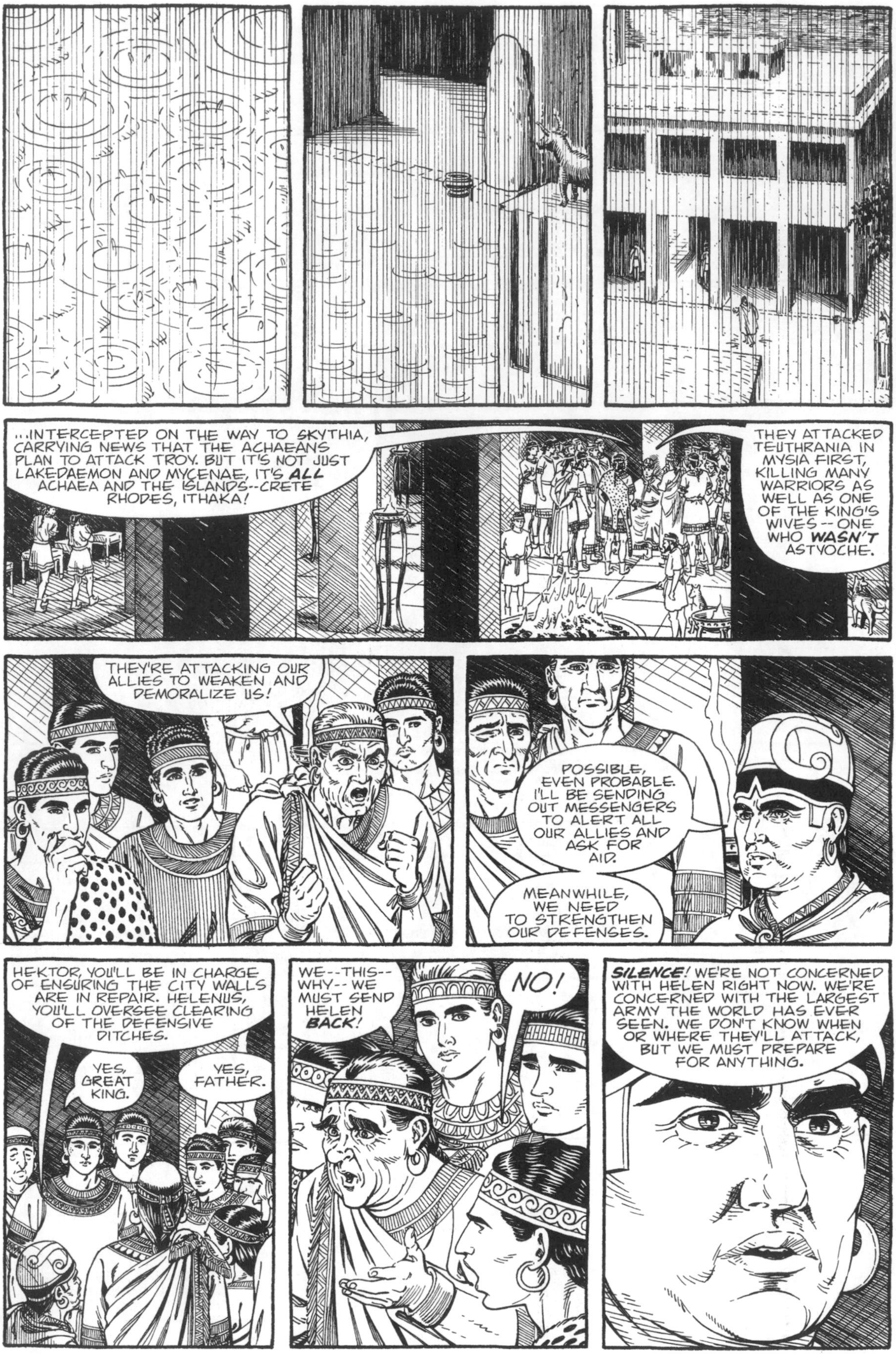
...INTERCEPTED ON THE WAY TO SKYTHIA, CARRYING NEWS THAT THE ACHAEANS PLAN TO ATTACK TROY. BUT IT'S NOT JUST LAKEDAEMON AND MYCENAE, IT'S **ALL** ACHAEA AND THE ISLANDS--CRETE RHODES, ITHAKA!
THEY ATTACKED TEUTHRANIA IN MYSIA FIRST, KILLING MANY WARRIORS AS WELL AS ONE OF THE KING'S WIVES--ONE WHO **WASN'T** ASTYOCHE.
THEY'RE ATTACKING OUR ALLIES TO WEAKEN AND DEMORALIZE US!
POSSIBLE, EVEN PROBABLE. I'LL BE SENDING OUT MESSENGERS TO ALERT ALL OUR ALLIES AND ASK FOR AID.
MEANWHILE, WE NEED TO STRENGTHEN OUR DEFENSES.
HEKTOR, YOU'LL BE IN CHARGE OF ENSURING THE CITY WALLS ARE IN REPAIR. HELENUS, YOU'LL OVERSEE CLEARING OF THE DEFENSIVE DITCHES.
YES, GREAT KING.
YES, FATHER.
WE--THIS--WHY--WE MUST SEND HELEN **BACK**!
NO!
SILENCE! WE'RE NOT CONCERNED WITH HELEN RIGHT NOW. WE'RE CONCERNED WITH THE LARGEST ARMY THE WORLD HAS EVER SEEN. WE DON'T KNOW WHEN OR WHERE THEY'LL ATTACK, BUT WE MUST PREPARE FOR ANYTHING.

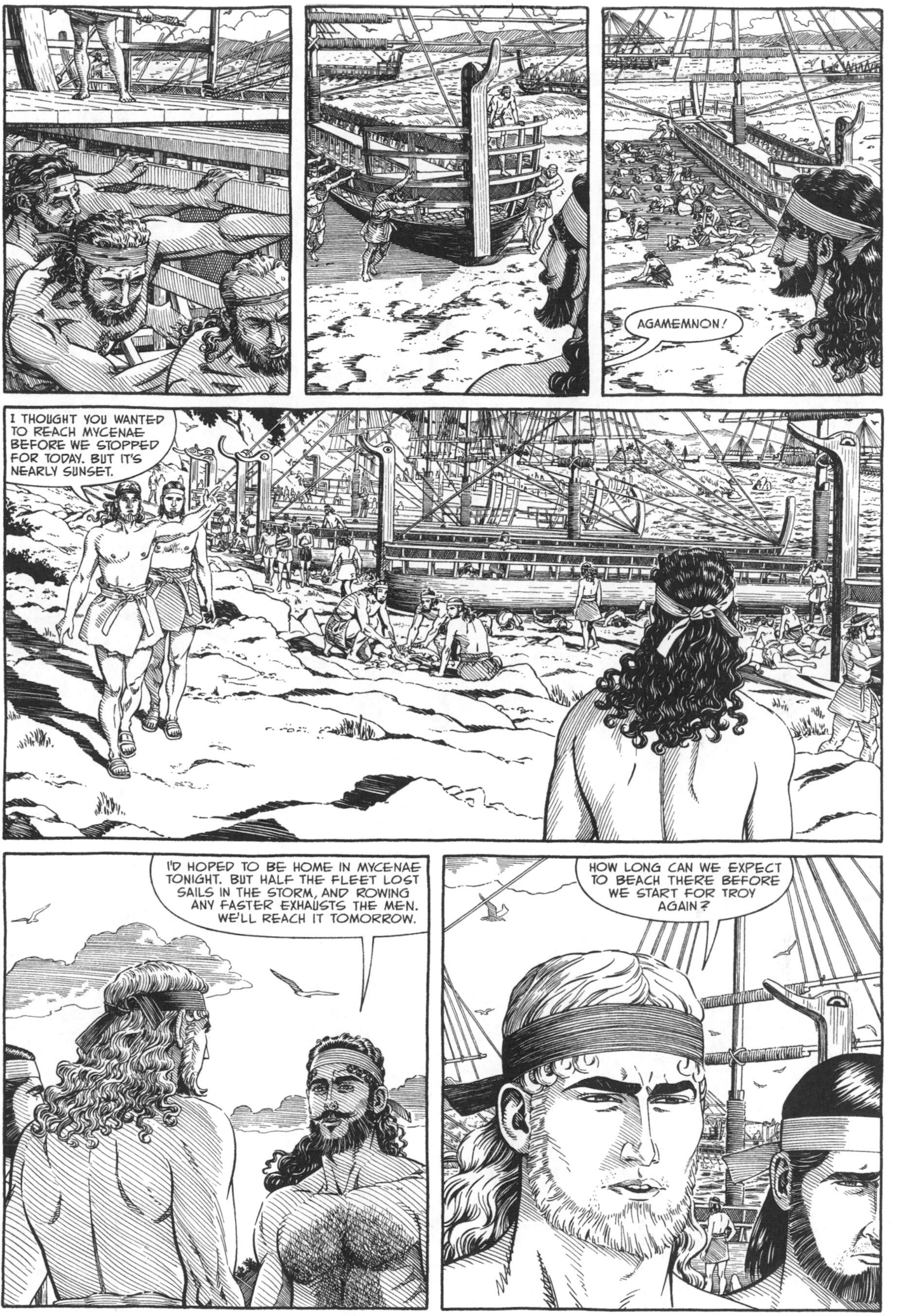
AGAMEMNON!
I THOUGHT YOU WANTED TO REACH MYCENAE BEFORE WE STOPPED FOR TODAY. BUT IT'S NEARLY SUNSET.
I'D HOPED TO BE HOME IN MYCENAE TONIGHT. BUT HALF THE FLEET LOST SAILS IN THE STORM, AND ROWING ANY FASTER EXHAUSTS THE MEN. WE'LL REACH IT TOMORROW.
HOW LONG CAN WE EXPECT TO BEACH THERE BEFORE WE START FOR TROY AGAIN?

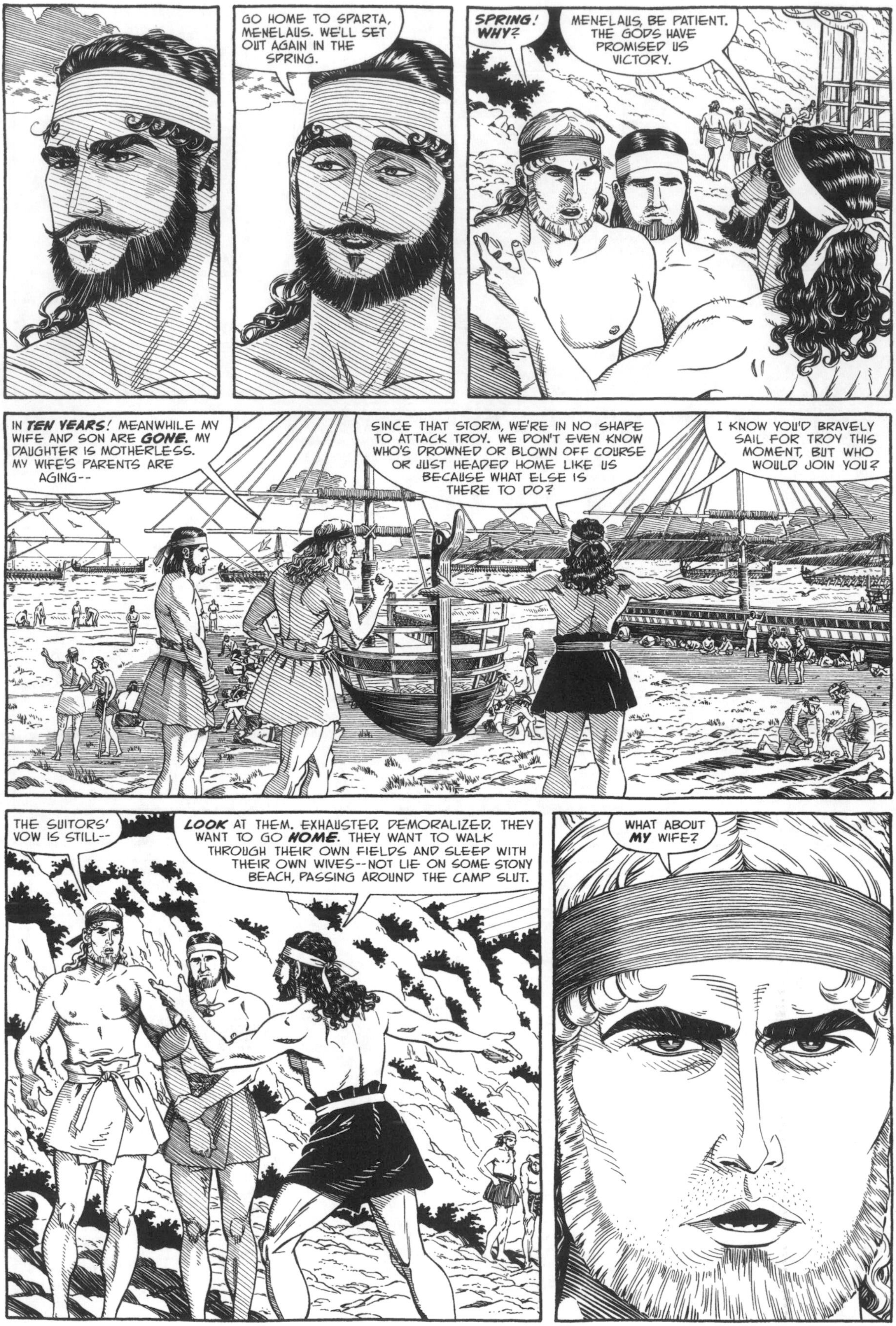
GO HOME TO SPARTA, MENELAUS. WE'LL SET OUT AGAIN IN THE SPRING.
SPRING! WHY?
MENELAUS, BE PATIENT. THE GODS HAVE PROMISED US VICTORY.
IN TEN YEARS! MEANWHILE MY WIFE AND SON ARE GONE. MY DAUGHTER IS MOTHERLESS. MY WIFE'S PARENTS ARE AGING--
SINCE THAT STORM, WE'RE IN NO SHAPE TO ATTACK TROY. WE DON'T EVEN KNOW WHO'S DROWNED OR BLOWN OFF COURSE OR JUST HEADED HOME LIKE US BECAUSE WHAT ELSE IS THERE TO DO?
I KNOW YOU'D BRAVELY SAIL FOR TROY THIS MOMENT, BUT WHO WOULD JOIN YOU?
THE SUITORS' VOW IS STILL--
LOOK AT THEM. EXHAUSTED. DEMORALIZED. THEY WANT TO GO HOME. THEY WANT TO WALK THROUGH THEIR OWN FIELDS AND SLEEP WITH THEIR OWN WIVES--NOT LIE ON SOME STONY BEACH, PASSING AROUND THE CAMP SLUT.
WHAT ABOUT MY WIFE?

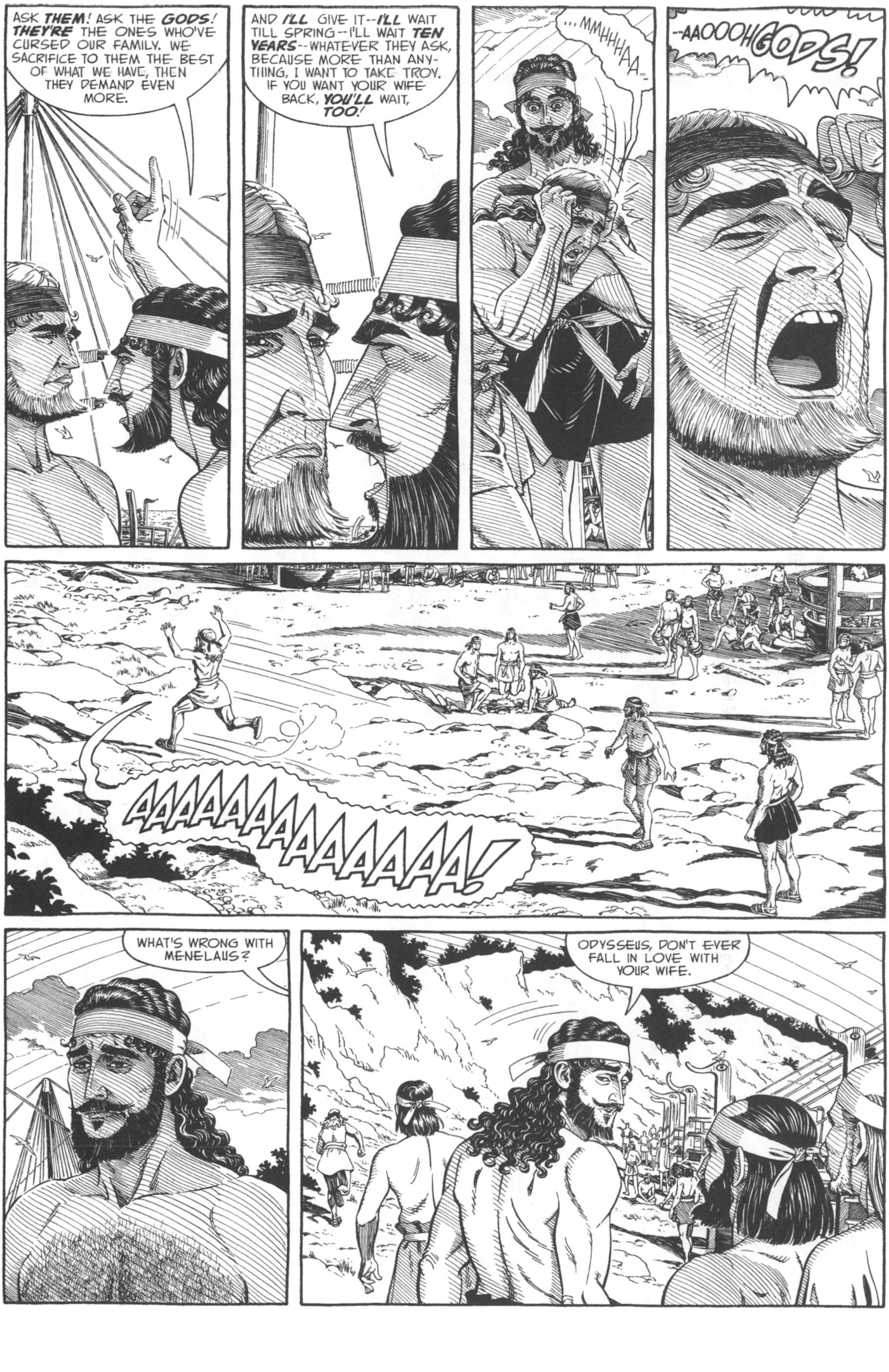
ASK THEM! ASK THE GODS! THEY'RE THE ONES WHO'VE CURSED OUR FAMILY. WE SACRIFICE TO THEM THE BEST OF WHAT WE HAVE, THEN THEY DEMAND EVEN MORE.
AND I'LL GIVE IT--I'LL WAIT TILL SPRING--I'LL WAIT TEN YEARS--WHATEVER THEY ASK, BECAUSE MORE THAN ANYTHING, I WANT TO TAKE TROY. IF YOU WANT YOUR WIFE BACK, YOU'LL WAIT, TOO!
...MMHHHAA--
--AAOOOH GODS!
AAAAAAAAAAAAAAAA!
WHAT'S WRONG WITH MENELAUS?
ODYSSEUS, DON'T EVER FALL IN LOVE WITH YOUR WIFE.

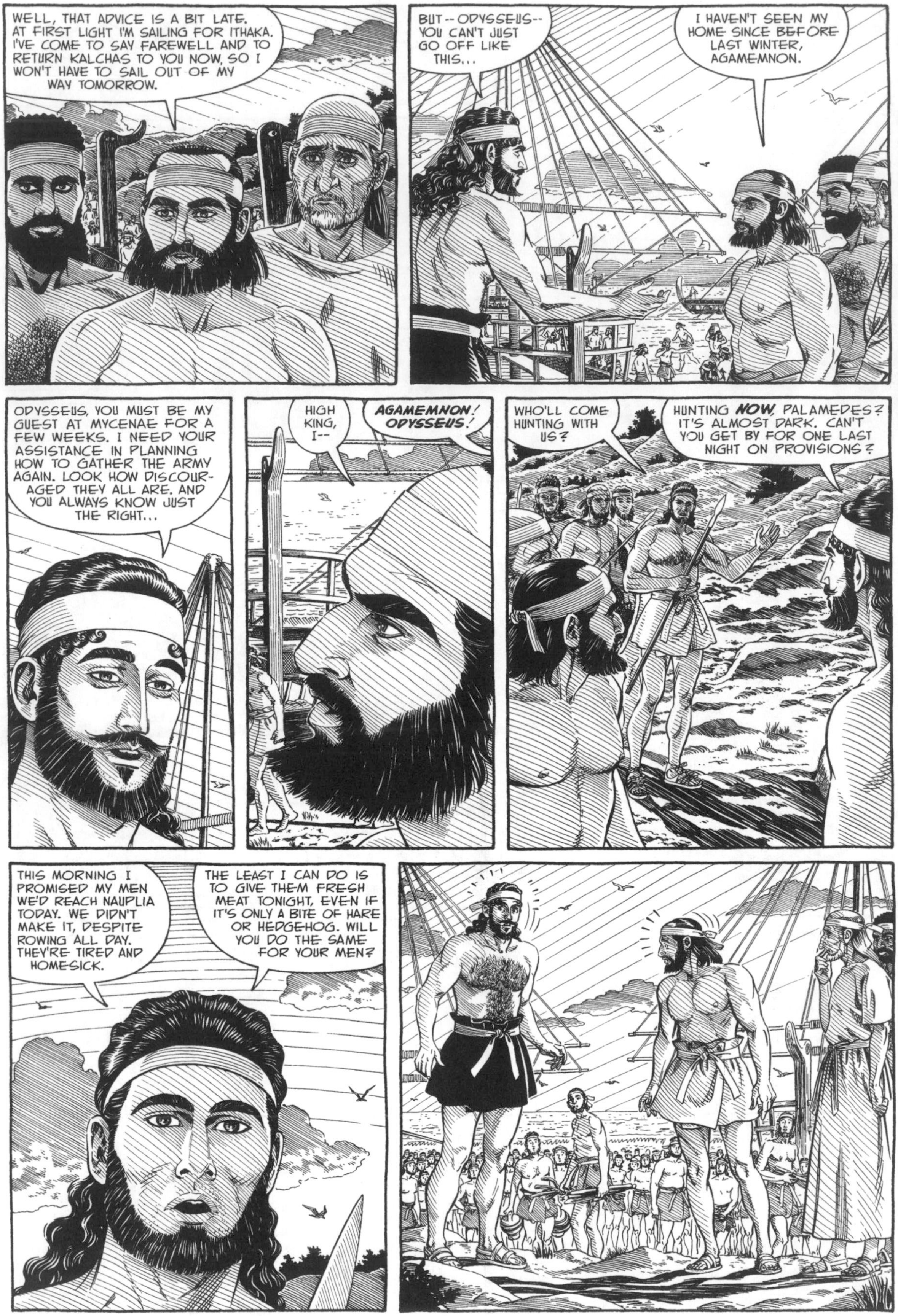

WELL, THAT ADVICE IS A BIT LATE. AT FIRST LIGHT I'M SAILING FOR ITHAKA. I'VE COME TO SAY FAREWELL AND TO RETURN KALCHAS TO YOU NOW, SO I WON'T HAVE TO SAIL OUT OF MY WAY TOMORROW.
BUT -- ODYSSEUS -- YOU CAN'T JUST GO OFF LIKE THIS...
I HAVEN'T SEEN MY HOME SINCE BEFORE LAST WINTER, AGAMEMNON.
ODYSSEUS, YOU MUST BE MY GUEST AT MYCENAE FOR A FEW WEEKS. I NEED YOUR ASSISTANCE IN PLANNING HOW TO GATHER THE ARMY AGAIN. LOOK HOW DISCOURAGED THEY ALL ARE. AND YOU ALWAYS KNOW JUST THE RIGHT...
HIGH KING, I--
AGAMEMNON! ODYSSEUS!
WHO'LL COME HUNTING WITH US?
HUNTING NOW, PALAMEDES? IT'S ALMOST DARK. CAN'T YOU GET BY FOR ONE LAST NIGHT ON PROVISIONS?
THIS MORNING I PROMISED MY MEN WE'D REACH NAUPLIA TODAY. WE DIDN'T MAKE IT, DESPITE ROWING ALL DAY. THEY'RE TIRED AND HOMESICK.
THE LEAST I CAN DO IS TO GIVE THEM FRESH MEAT TONIGHT, EVEN IF IT'S ONLY A BITE OF HARE OR HEDGEHOG. WILL YOU DO THE SAME FOR YOUR MEN?

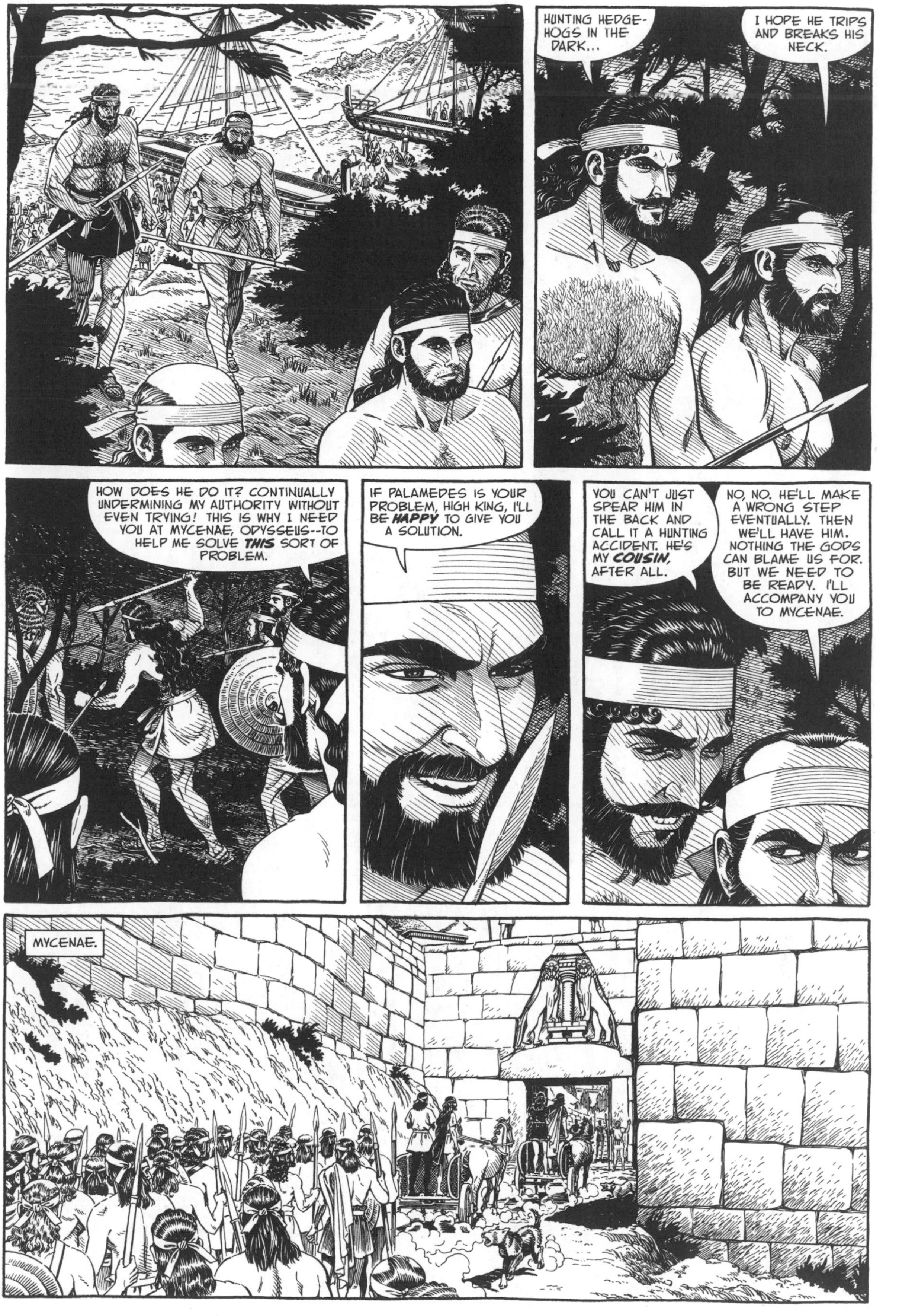
HUNTING HEDGE-HOGS IN THE DARK...
I HOPE HE TRIPS AND BREAKS HIS NECK.
HOW DOES HE DO IT? CONTINUALLY UNDERMINING MY AUTHORITY WITHOUT EVEN TRYING! THIS IS WHY I NEED YOU AT MYCENAE, ODYSSEUS--TO HELP ME SOLVE **THIS** SORT OF PROBLEM.
IF PALAMEDES IS YOUR PROBLEM, HIGH KING, I'LL BE **HAPPY** TO GIVE YOU A SOLUTION.
YOU CAN'T JUST SPEAR HIM IN THE BACK AND CALL IT A HUNTING ACCIDENT. HE'S MY **COUSIN,** AFTER ALL.
NO, NO. HE'LL MAKE A WRONG STEP EVENTUALLY. THEN WE'LL HAVE HIM. NOTHING THE GODS CAN BLAME US FOR. BUT WE NEED TO BE READY. I'LL ACCOMPANY YOU TO MYCENAE.
MYCENAE.

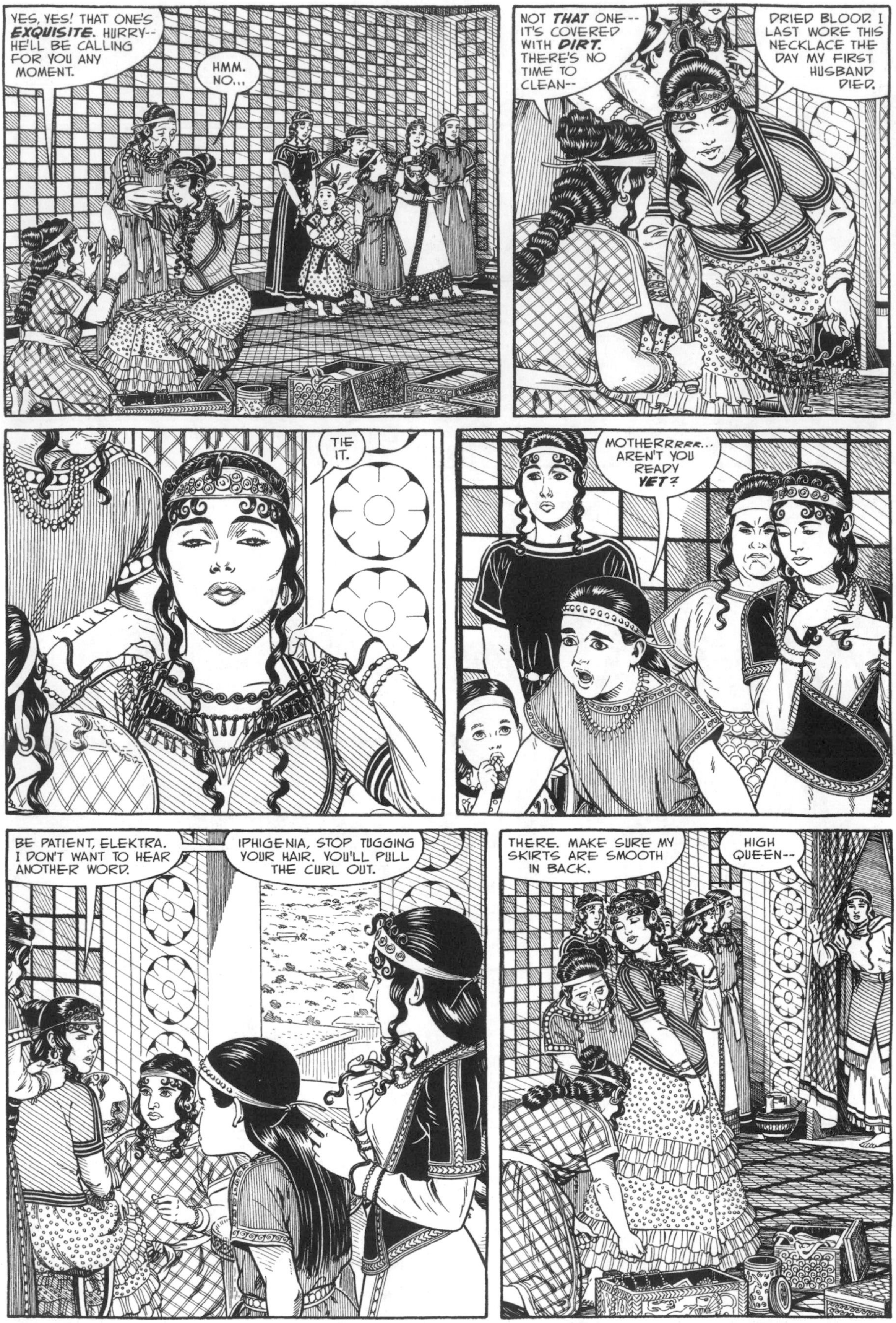

YES, YES! THAT ONE'S **EXQUISITE**. HURRY-- HE'LL BE CALLING FOR YOU ANY MOMENT.
HMM. NO...
NOT **THAT** ONE-- IT'S COVERED WITH **DIRT**. THERE'S NO TIME TO CLEAN--
DRIED BLOOD. I LAST WORE THIS NECKLACE THE DAY MY FIRST HUSBAND DIED.
TIE IT.
MOTHERRRRR... AREN'T YOU READY **YET**?
BE PATIENT, ELEKTRA. I DON'T WANT TO HEAR ANOTHER WORD.
IPHIGENIA, STOP TUGGING YOUR HAIR. YOU'LL PULL THE CURL OUT.
THERE. MAKE SURE MY SKIRTS ARE SMOOTH IN BACK.
HIGH QUEEN--

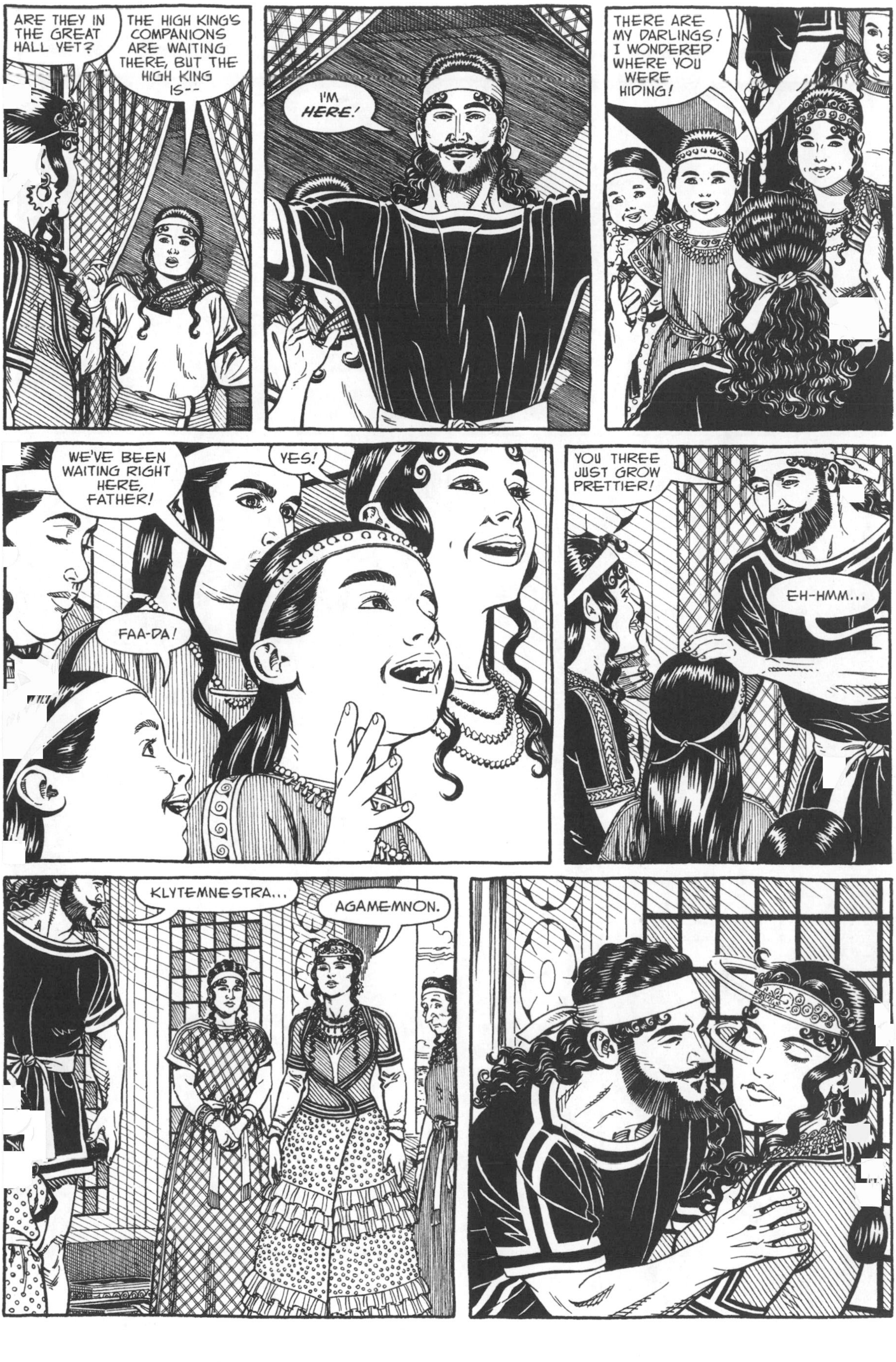
ARE THEY IN THE GREAT HALL YET?
THE HIGH KING'S COMPANIONS ARE WAITING THERE, BUT THE HIGH KING IS--
I'M *HERE!*
THERE ARE MY DARLINGS! I WONDERED WHERE YOU WERE HIDING!
WE'VE BEEN WAITING RIGHT HERE, FATHER!
YES!
FAA-DA!
YOU THREE JUST GROW PRETTIER!
EH-HMM...
KLYTEMNESTRA...
AGAMEMNON.

HOW DO YOU EXPECT ME TO GREET YOUR GUESTS IF YOU SPOIL MY HAIR AND MAKE-UP?

THERE'S *PLENTY* OF TIME. ODYSSEUS OF ITHAKA SHOULD BE STAYING FOR *QUITE* AWHILE IF I HAVE MY WAY.

YOU'RE NOT HAVING YOUR WAY *NOW.*

WHAT'S THE MATTER WITH YOU?

YOU--YOU *KNOW* I'M WITH CHILD...

THEN ONE OF THE SERVANT GIRLS WILL HAVE TO DO.

FATHER? I DON'T KNOW WHAT YOU NEED DONE, BUT I'D BE HAPPY TO DO IT FOR YOU--

IPHIGENIA! GO TO YOUR ROOM *AT ONCE!* TAKE YOUR SISTERS WITH YOU!

YES, MOTHER.

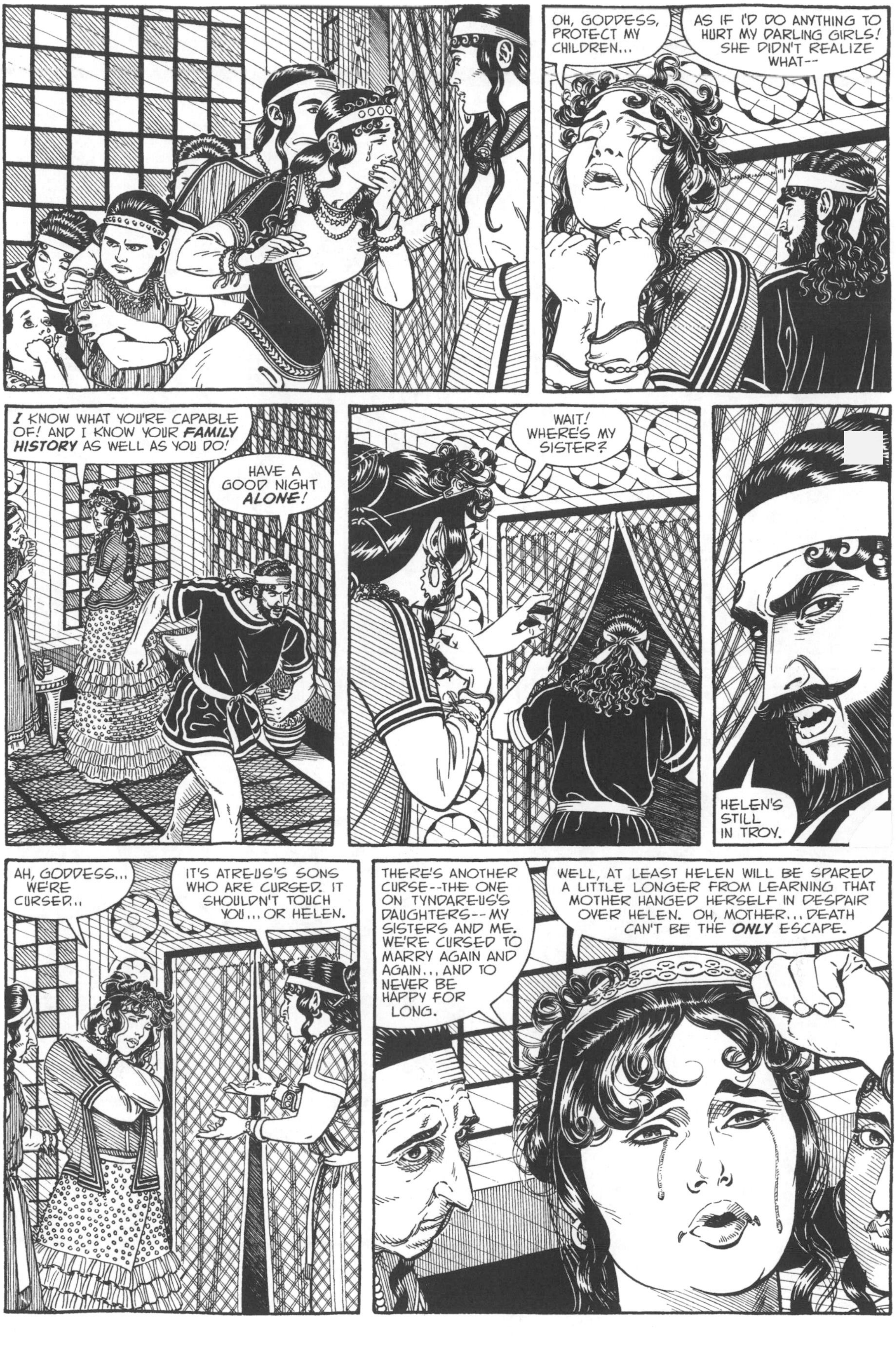
OH, GODDESS, PROTECT MY CHILDREN...
AS IF I'D DO ANYTHING TO HURT MY DARLING GIRLS! SHE DIDN'T REALIZE WHAT--
I KNOW WHAT YOU'RE CAPABLE OF! AND I KNOW YOUR FAMILY HISTORY AS WELL AS YOU DO!
HAVE A GOOD NIGHT ALONE!
WAIT! WHERE'S MY SISTER?
HELEN'S STILL IN TROY.
AH, GODDESS... WE'RE CURSED...
IT'S ATREUS'S SONS WHO ARE CURSED. IT SHOULDN'T TOUCH YOU... OR HELEN.
THERE'S ANOTHER CURSE--THE ONE ON TYNDAREUS'S DAUGHTERS--MY SISTERS AND ME. WE'RE CURSED TO MARRY AGAIN AND AGAIN... AND TO NEVER BE HAPPY FOR LONG.
WELL, AT LEAST HELEN WILL BE SPARED A LITTLE LONGER FROM LEARNING THAT MOTHER HANGED HERSELF IN DESPAIR OVER HELEN. OH, MOTHER... DEATH CAN'T BE THE ONLY ESCAPE.

SKYROS.

PYRRHA!

PYRRHA'S BACK!

ACHILLES!

ACHILLES IS HOME!

PYRRHA!

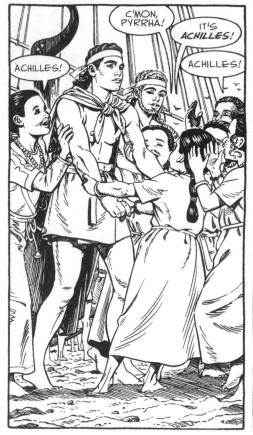

ACHILLES!

C'MON, PYRRHA!

IT'S *ACHILLES!*

ACHILLES!

LYKOMEDES-- FATHER--WE'VE RETURNED.

ACHILLES, WE HAVEN'T HEARD EVEN ONE WORD OF NEWS ABOUT TROY'S FALL. DON'T TELL US YOU'VE RETURNED TO SKYROS WITHOUT GAINING THE GLORY YOU SOUGHT.

WE WERE...UNSUCCESSFUL. I LOST MEN. BOTH SKYRIANS AND MVRMIDONS FELL IN BATTLE AT MYSIA. THEN A STORM SANK ONE OF THE SHIPS YOU ENTRUSTED TO ME.

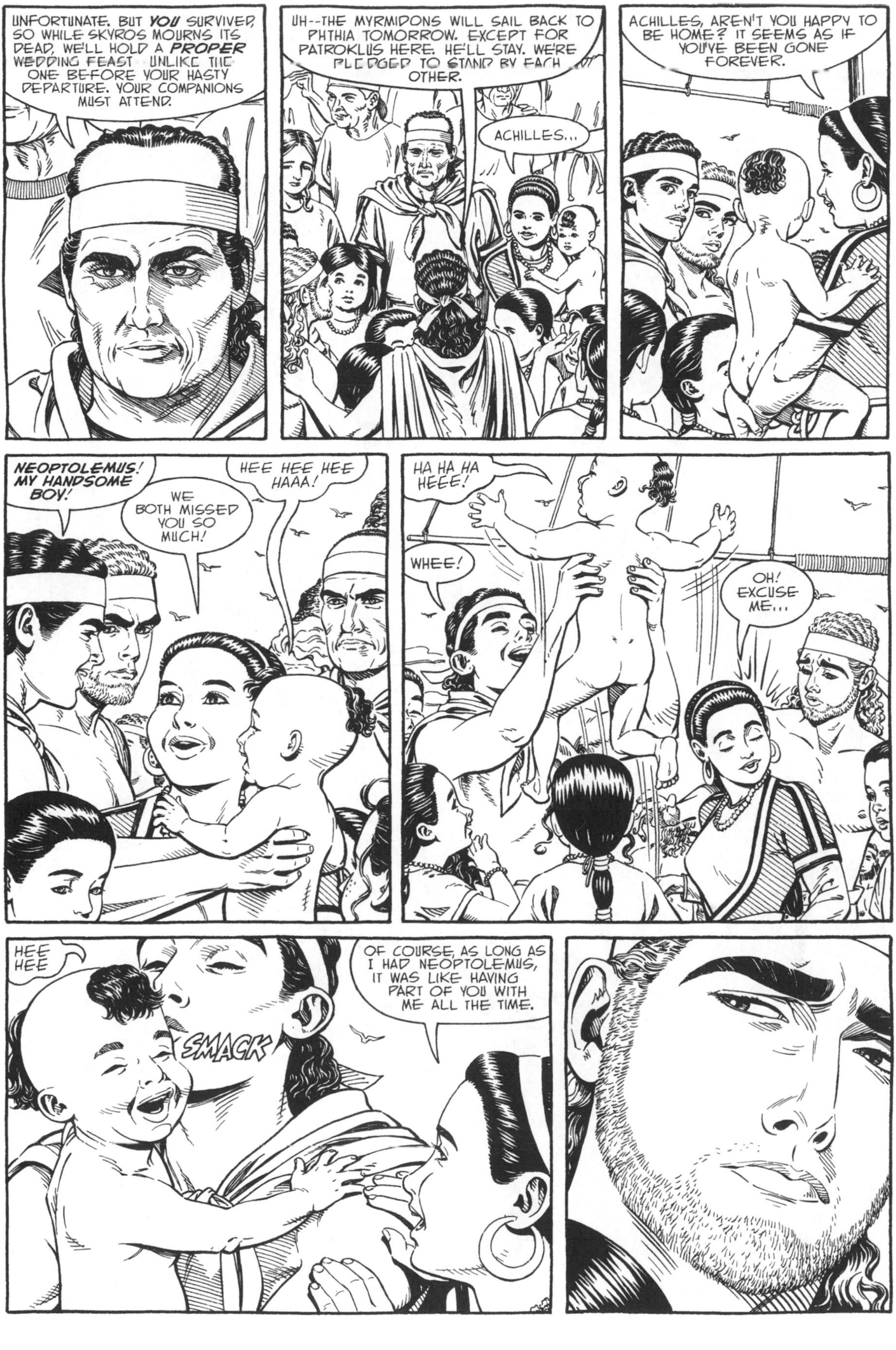
UNFORTUNATE. BUT *YOU* SURVIVED, SO WHILE SKYROS MOURNS ITS DEAD, WE'LL HOLD A *PROPER* WEDDING FEAST. UNLIKE THE ONE BEFORE YOUR HASTY DEPARTURE. YOUR COMPANIONS MUST ATTEND.
UH--THE MYRMIDONS WILL SAIL BACK TO PHTHIA TOMORROW. EXCEPT FOR PATROKLUS HERE. HE'LL STAY. WE'RE PLEDGED TO STAND BY EACH OTHER.
ACHILLES...
ACHILLES, AREN'T YOU HAPPY TO BE HOME? IT SEEMS AS IF YOU'VE BEEN GONE FOREVER.
NEOPTOLEMUS! MY HANDSOME BOY!
WE BOTH MISSED YOU SO MUCH!
HEE HEE HEE HAAA!
HA HA HA HEEE!
WHEE!
OH! EXCUSE ME...
HEE HEE
SMACK
OF COURSE, AS LONG AS I HAD NEOPTOLEMUS, IT WAS LIKE HAVING PART OF YOU WITH ME ALL THE TIME.

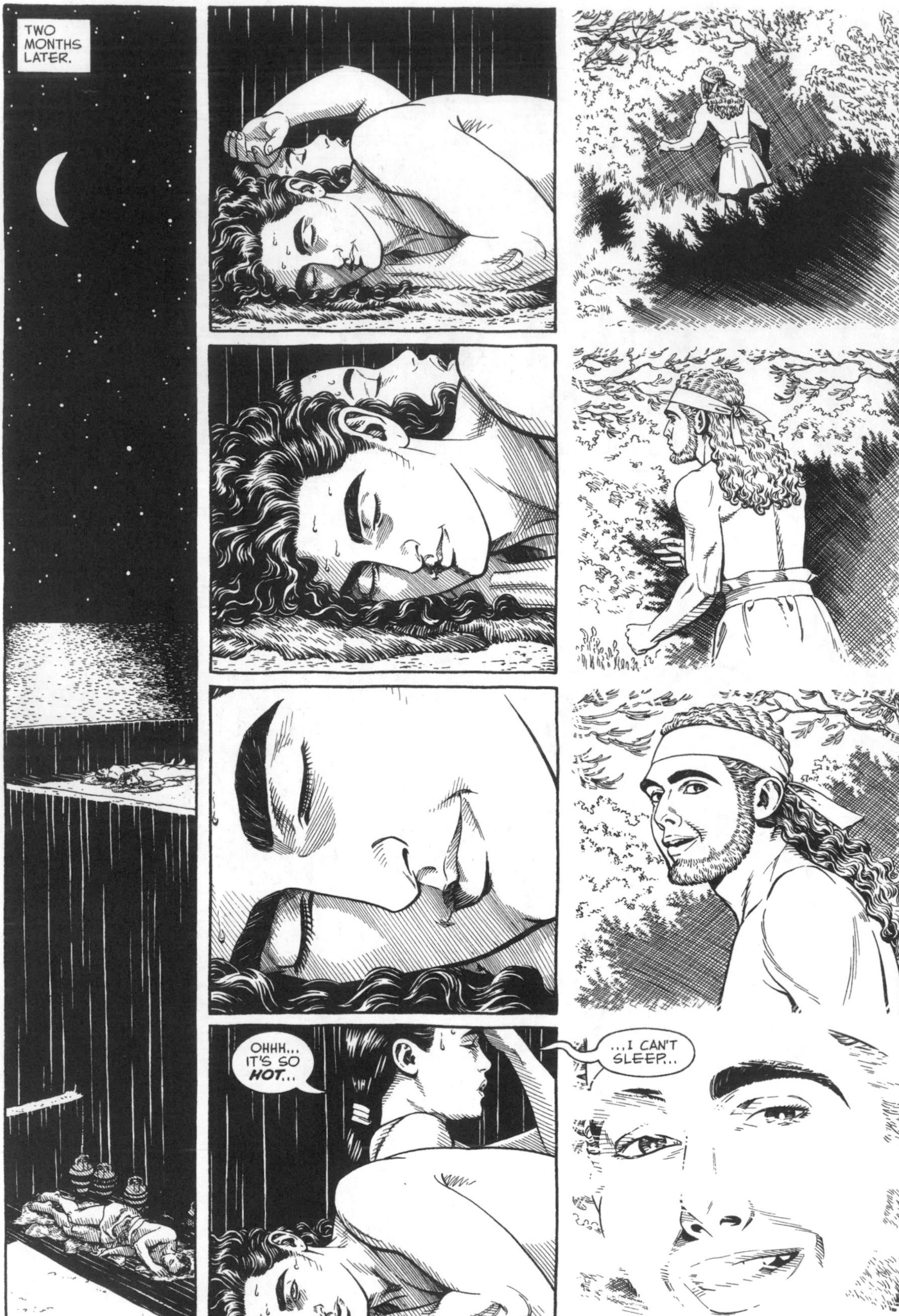
TWO MONTHS LATER.
OHHH... IT'S SO **HOT**...
...I CAN'T SLEEP...

HEH...REMEMBER HOW ON NIGHTS LIKE THIS WE'D ALL COME UP TO THE ROOF TO SLEEP, BUT YOU'D STAY DOWN IN BED UNDER BLANKETS? YOU MUST HAVE SWELTERED.

ACHILLES? ARE YOU AWAKE?

OOO...

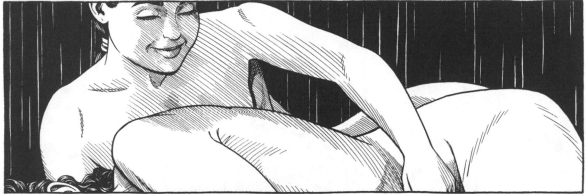

IT'S TOO *HOT*, DEIDAMIA.

IT'S *ALWAYS* TOO HOT--OR YOU'RE TOO *TIRED*. I DON'T KNOW *WHY* YOU'RE SO TIRED. ALL YOU DO IS GO HUNTING ALL DAY WITH PATROKLUS WHILE *I* HAVE TO MILK THE GOATS OR SPIN WOOL OR MAKE CHEESE.

YOU WERE NICER WHEN YOU WERE A GIRL.
WHAT'S WRONG? I'M SORRY--
WHAT HAVE I DONE WRONG?
NOTHING.
WHAT-- DO YOU SEE SOME-THING?
ACHILLES, IS SOMEONE THERE?

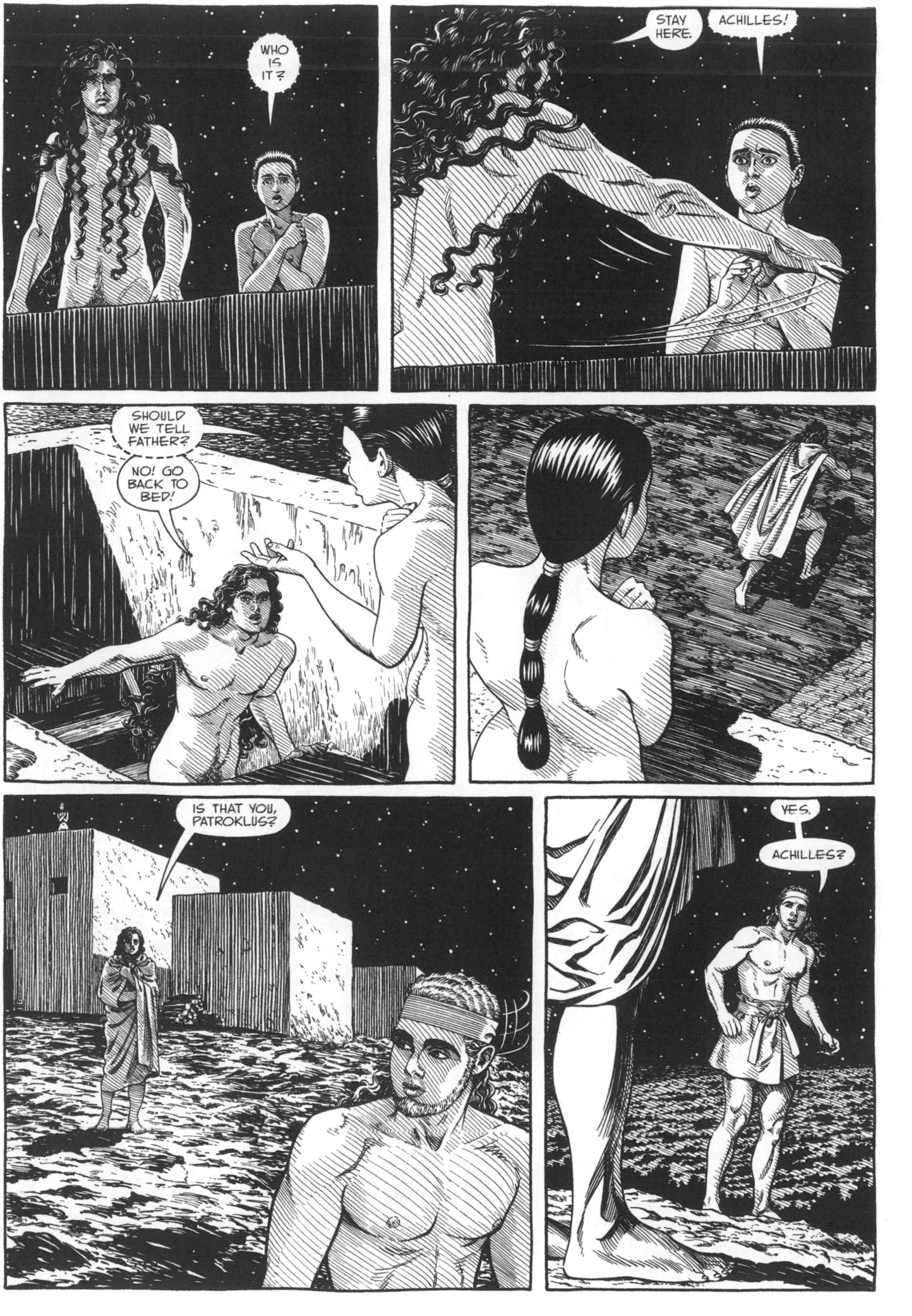
WHO IS IT?
STAY HERE.
ACHILLES!
SHOULD WE TELL FATHER?
NO! GO BACK TO BED!
IS THAT YOU, PATROKLUS?
YES.
ACHILLES?

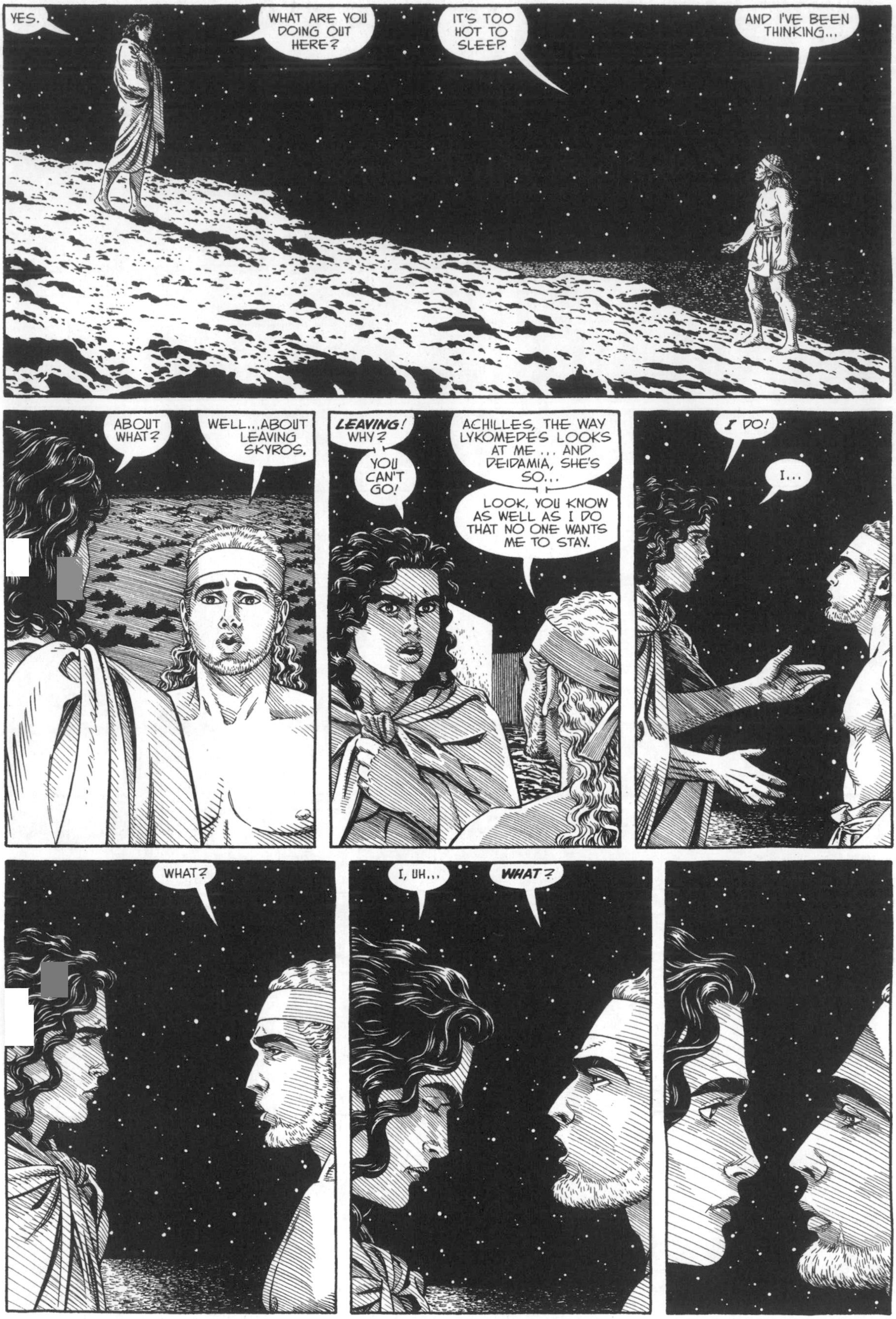
YES.
WHAT ARE YOU DOING OUT HERE?
IT'S TOO HOT TO SLEEP.
AND I'VE BEEN THINKING...
ABOUT WHAT?
WELL...ABOUT LEAVING SKYROS.
LEAVING! WHY?
YOU CAN'T GO!
ACHILLES, THE WAY LYKOMEDES LOOKS AT ME ... AND DEIDAMIA, SHE'S SO...
LOOK, YOU KNOW AS WELL AS I DO THAT NO ONE WANTS ME TO STAY.
I DO!
I...
WHAT?
I, UH...
WHAT?

ACHILLES...

I DON'T WANT YOU TO GO... NOT EVER...

ACHILLES, COME WITH ME.

YES, YES! I'LL LEAVE SKYROS WITH YOU...

NO--I MEAN **YES!** I MEAN **NOW**-- COME WITH ME DOWN THE HILL-- I KNOW A PLACE WE CAN BE ALONE TOGETHER.

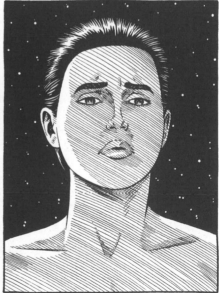

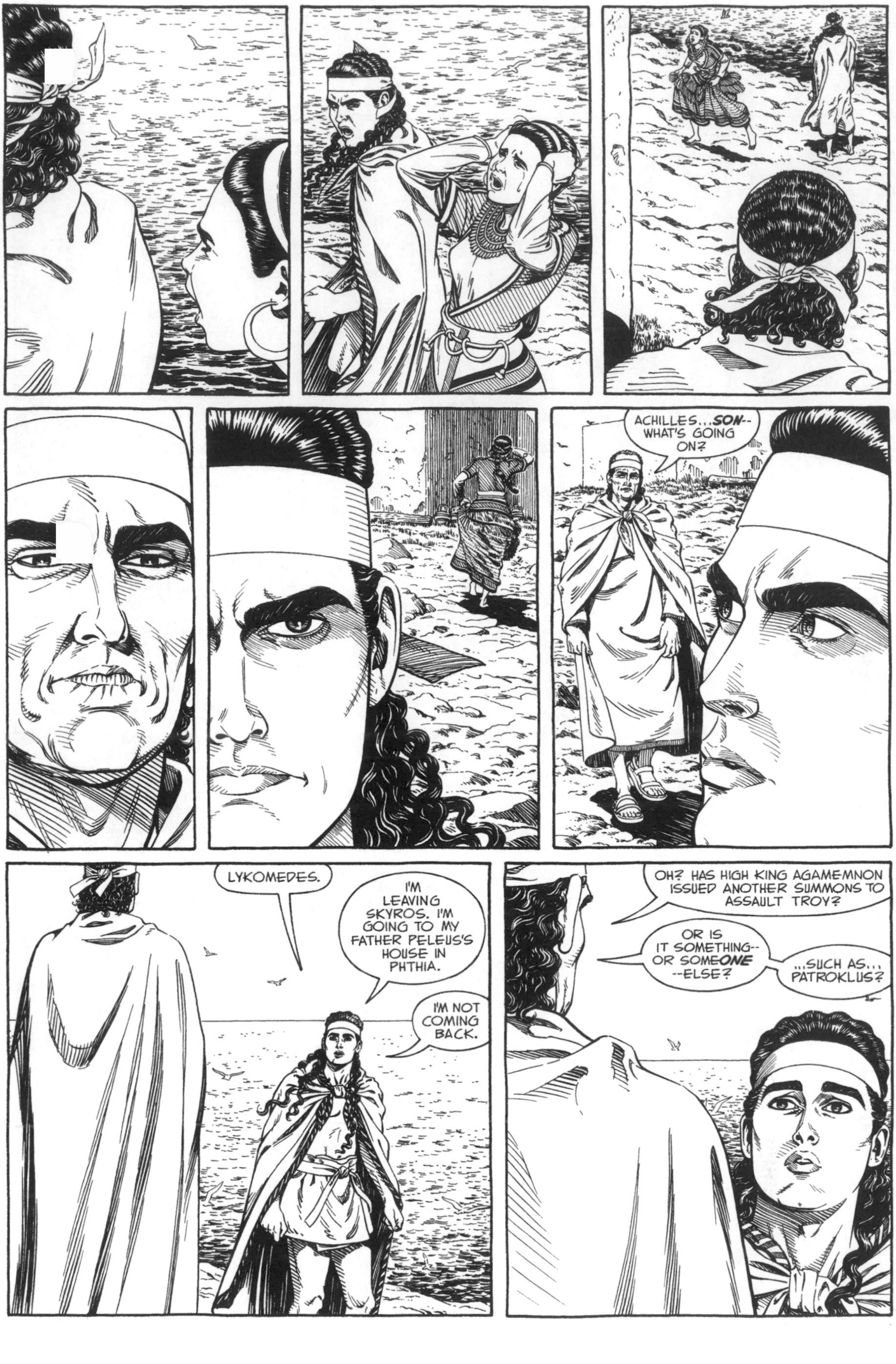
ACHILLES...SON--
WHAT'S GOING ON?
LYKOMEDES.
I'M LEAVING SKYROS. I'M GOING TO MY FATHER PELEUS'S HOUSE IN PHTHIA.
I'M NOT COMING BACK.
OH? HAS HIGH KING AGAMEMNON ISSUED ANOTHER SUMMONS TO ASSAULT TROY?
OR IS IT SOMETHING-- OR SOMEONE --ELSE?
...SUCH AS... PATROKLUS?

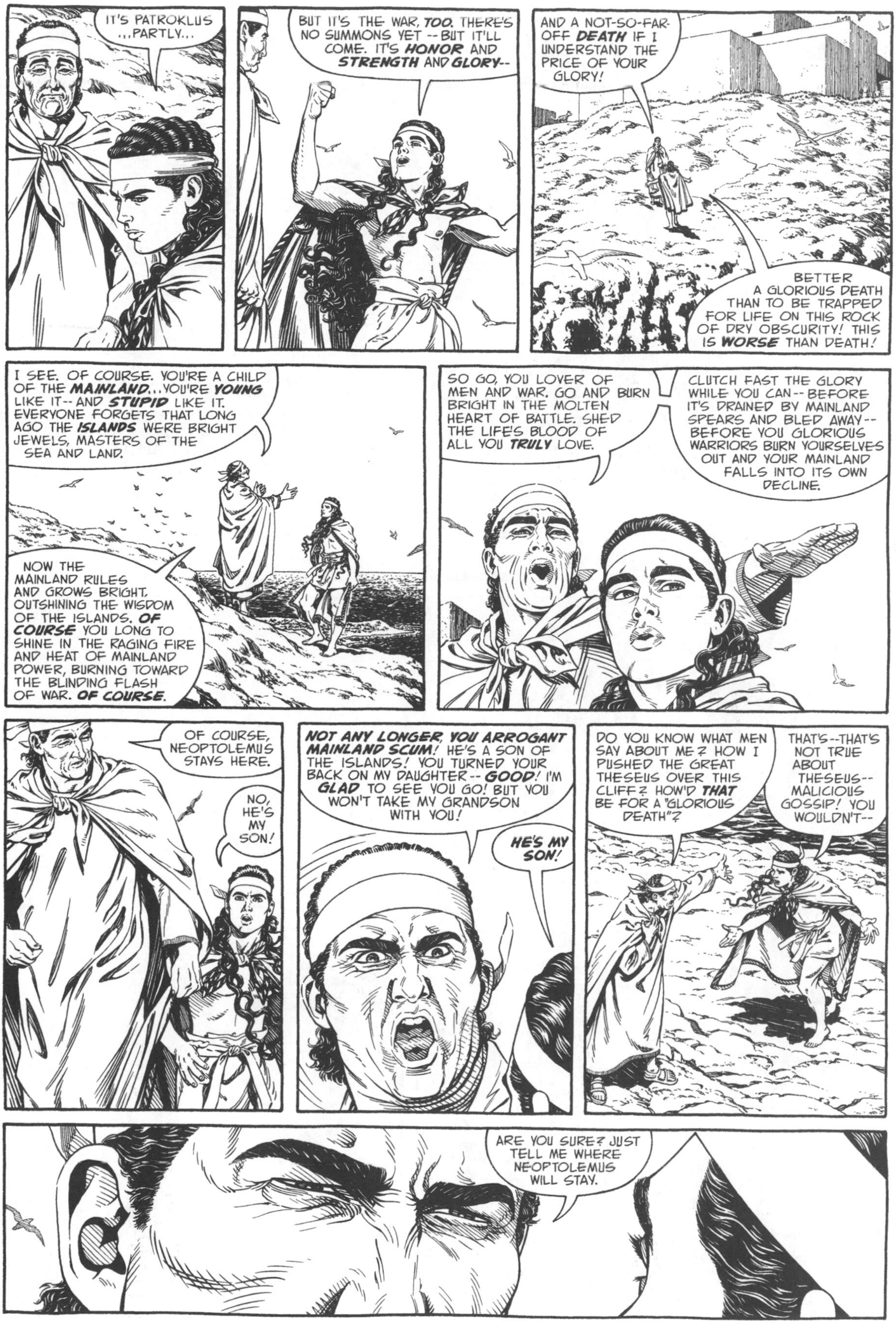

IT'S PATROKLUS ...PARTLY...
BUT IT'S THE WAR, TOO. THERE'S NO SUMMONS YET -- BUT IT'LL COME. IT'S HONOR AND STRENGTH AND GLORY--
AND A NOT-SO-FAR-OFF DEATH IF I UNDERSTAND THE PRICE OF YOUR GLORY!
BETTER A GLORIOUS DEATH THAN TO BE TRAPPED FOR LIFE ON THIS ROCK OF DRY OBSCURITY! THIS IS WORSE THAN DEATH!
I SEE. OF COURSE. YOU'RE A CHILD OF THE MAINLAND...YOU'RE YOUNG LIKE IT-- AND STUPID LIKE IT. EVERYONE FORGETS THAT LONG AGO THE ISLANDS WERE BRIGHT JEWELS, MASTERS OF THE SEA AND LAND.
NOW THE MAINLAND RULES AND GROWS BRIGHT, OUTSHINING THE WISDOM OF THE ISLANDS. OF COURSE YOU LONG TO SHINE IN THE RAGING FIRE AND HEAT OF MAINLAND POWER, BURNING TOWARD THE BLINDING FLASH OF WAR. OF COURSE.
SO GO, YOU LOVER OF MEN AND WAR. GO AND BURN BRIGHT IN THE MOLTEN HEART OF BATTLE. SHED THE LIFE'S BLOOD OF ALL YOU TRULY LOVE.
CLUTCH FAST THE GLORY WHILE YOU CAN -- BEFORE IT'S DRAINED BY MAINLAND SPEARS AND BLED AWAY -- BEFORE YOU GLORIOUS WARRIORS BURN YOURSELVES OUT AND YOUR MAINLAND FALLS INTO ITS OWN DECLINE.
OF COURSE, NEOPTOLEMUS STAYS HERE.
NO, HE'S MY SON!
NOT ANY LONGER, YOU ARROGANT MAINLAND SCUM! HE'S A SON OF THE ISLANDS! YOU TURNED YOUR BACK ON MY DAUGHTER -- GOOD! I'M GLAD TO SEE YOU GO! BUT YOU WON'T TAKE MY GRANDSON WITH YOU!
HE'S MY SON!
DO YOU KNOW WHAT MEN SAY ABOUT ME? HOW I PUSHED THE GREAT THESEUS OVER THIS CLIFF? HOW'D THAT BE FOR A "GLORIOUS DEATH"?
THAT'S--THAT'S NOT TRUE ABOUT THESEUS-- MALICIOUS GOSSIP! YOU WOULDN'T--
ARE YOU SURE? JUST TELL ME WHERE NEOPTOLEMUS WILL STAY.

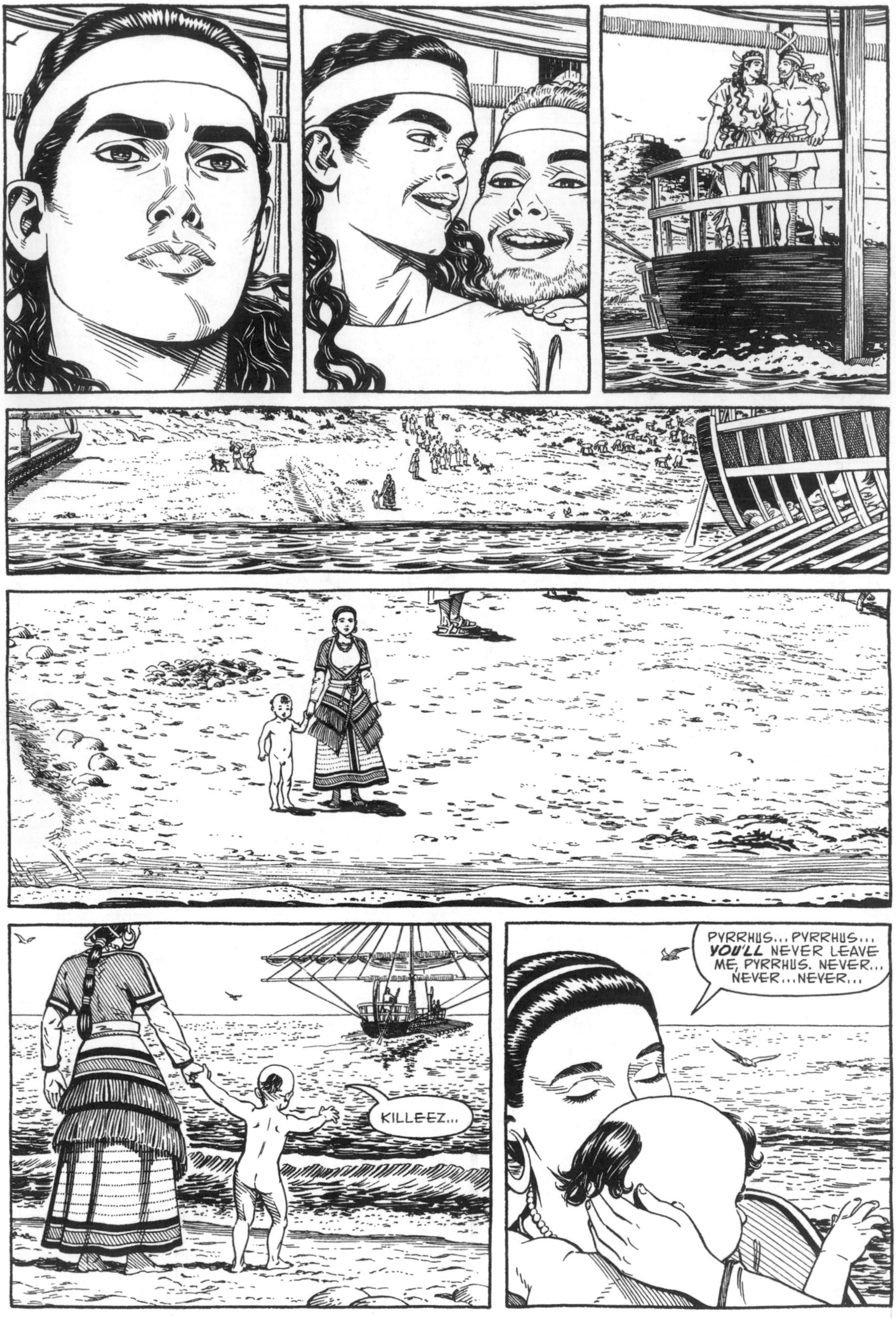
KILLEEZ...
PYRRHUS... PYRRHUS... YOU'LL NEVER LEAVE ME, PYRRHUS. NEVER... NEVER... NEVER...

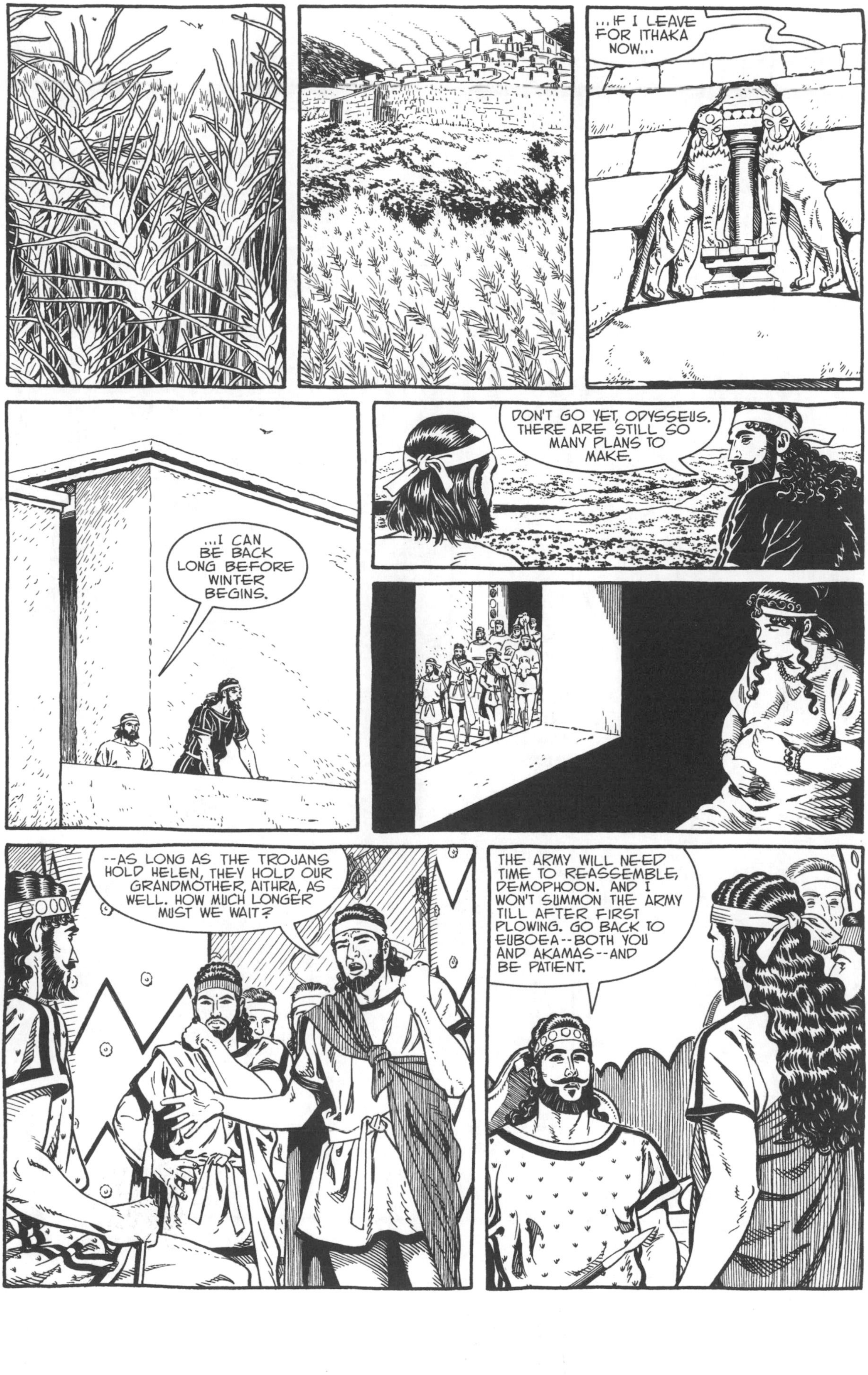
...IF I LEAVE FOR ITHAKA NOW...
...I CAN BE BACK LONG BEFORE WINTER BEGINS.
DON'T GO YET, ODYSSEUS. THERE ARE STILL SO MANY PLANS TO MAKE.
--AS LONG AS THE TROJANS HOLD HELEN, THEY HOLD OUR GRANDMOTHER, AITHRA, AS WELL. HOW MUCH LONGER MUST WE WAIT?
THE ARMY WILL NEED TIME TO REASSEMBLE, DEMOPHOON. AND I WON'T SUMMON THE ARMY TILL AFTER FIRST PLOWING. GO BACK TO EUBOEA--BOTH YOU AND AKAMAS--AND BE PATIENT.

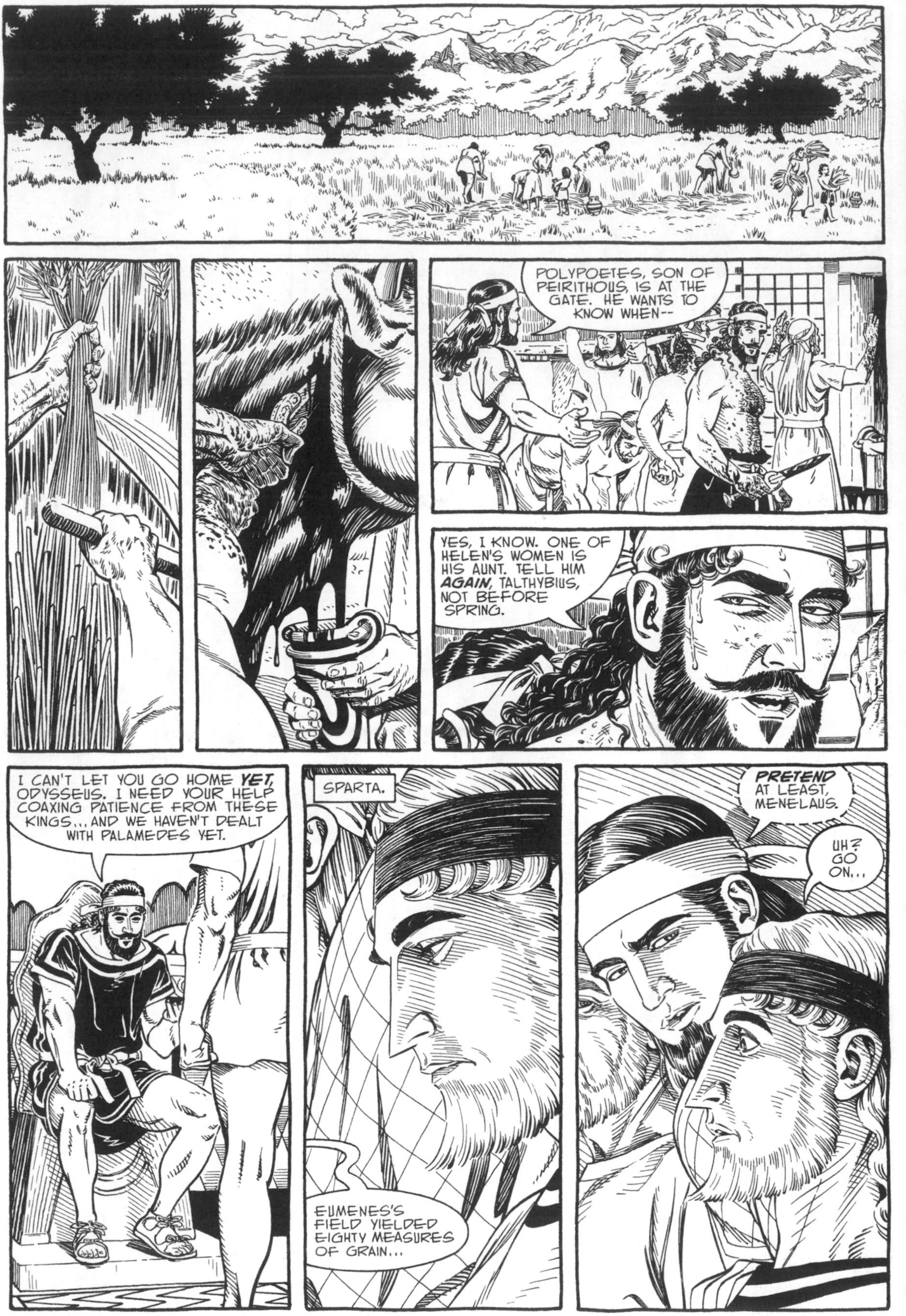
POLYPOETES, SON OF PEIRITHOUS, IS AT THE GATE. HE WANTS TO KNOW WHEN--
YES, I KNOW. ONE OF HELEN'S WOMEN IS HIS AUNT. TELL HIM AGAIN, TALTHYBIUS, NOT BEFORE SPRING.
I CAN'T LET YOU GO HOME YET, ODYSSEUS. I NEED YOUR HELP COAXING PATIENCE FROM THESE KINGS... AND WE HAVEN'T DEALT WITH PALAMEDES YET.
SPARTA.
EUMENES'S FIELD YIELDED EIGHTY MEASURES OF GRAIN...
PRETEND AT LEAST, MENELAUS.
UH? GO ON...

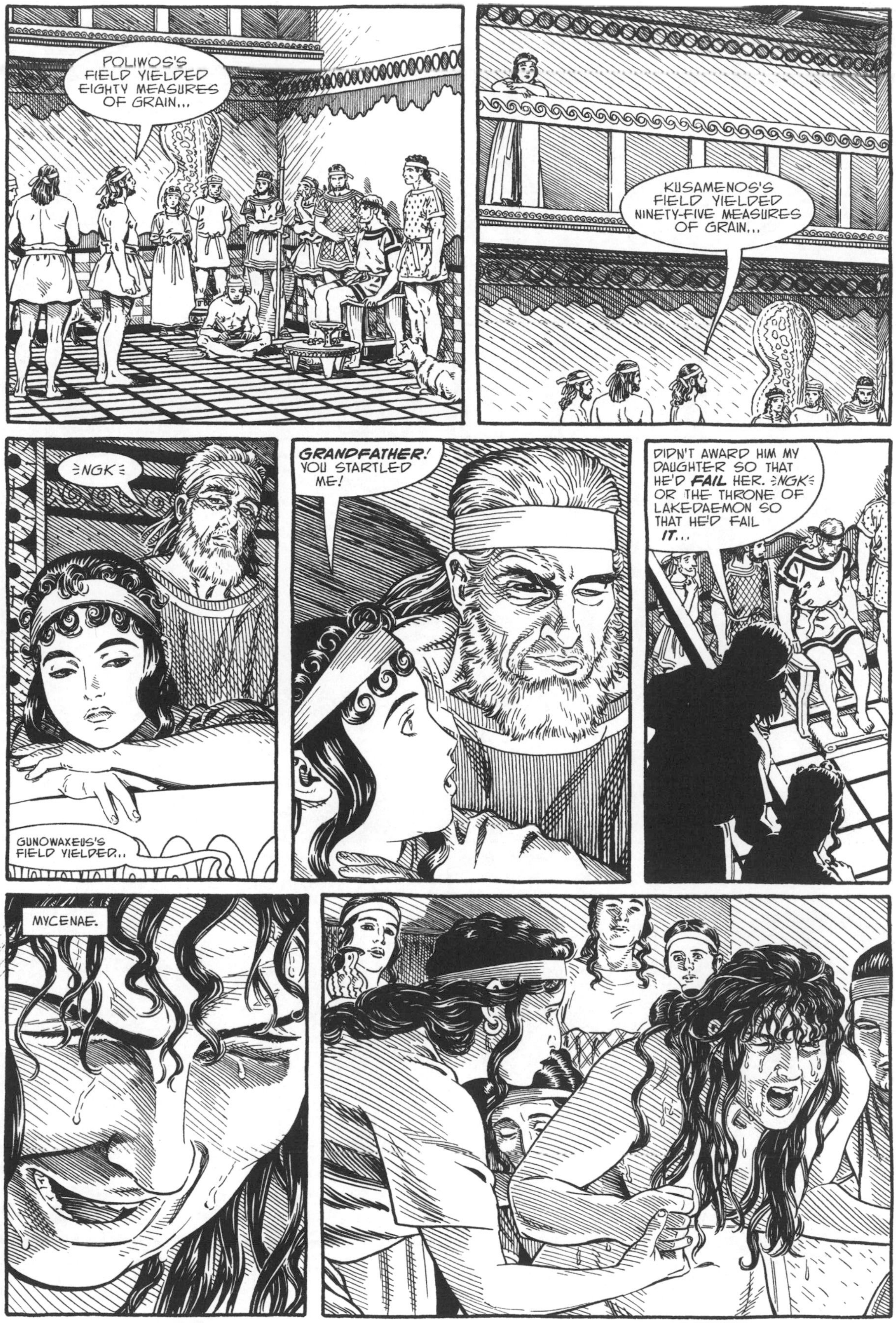
POLIWOS'S FIELD YIELDED EIGHTY MEASURES OF GRAIN...
KUSAMENOS'S FIELD YIELDED NINETY-FIVE MEASURES OF GRAIN...
NGK
GUNOWAXEUS'S FIELD YIELDED...
GRANDFATHER! YOU STARTLED ME!
DIDN'T AWARD HIM MY DAUGHTER SO THAT HE'D FAIL HER. NGK OR THE THRONE OF LAKEDAEMON SO THAT HE'D FAIL IT...
MYCENAE.

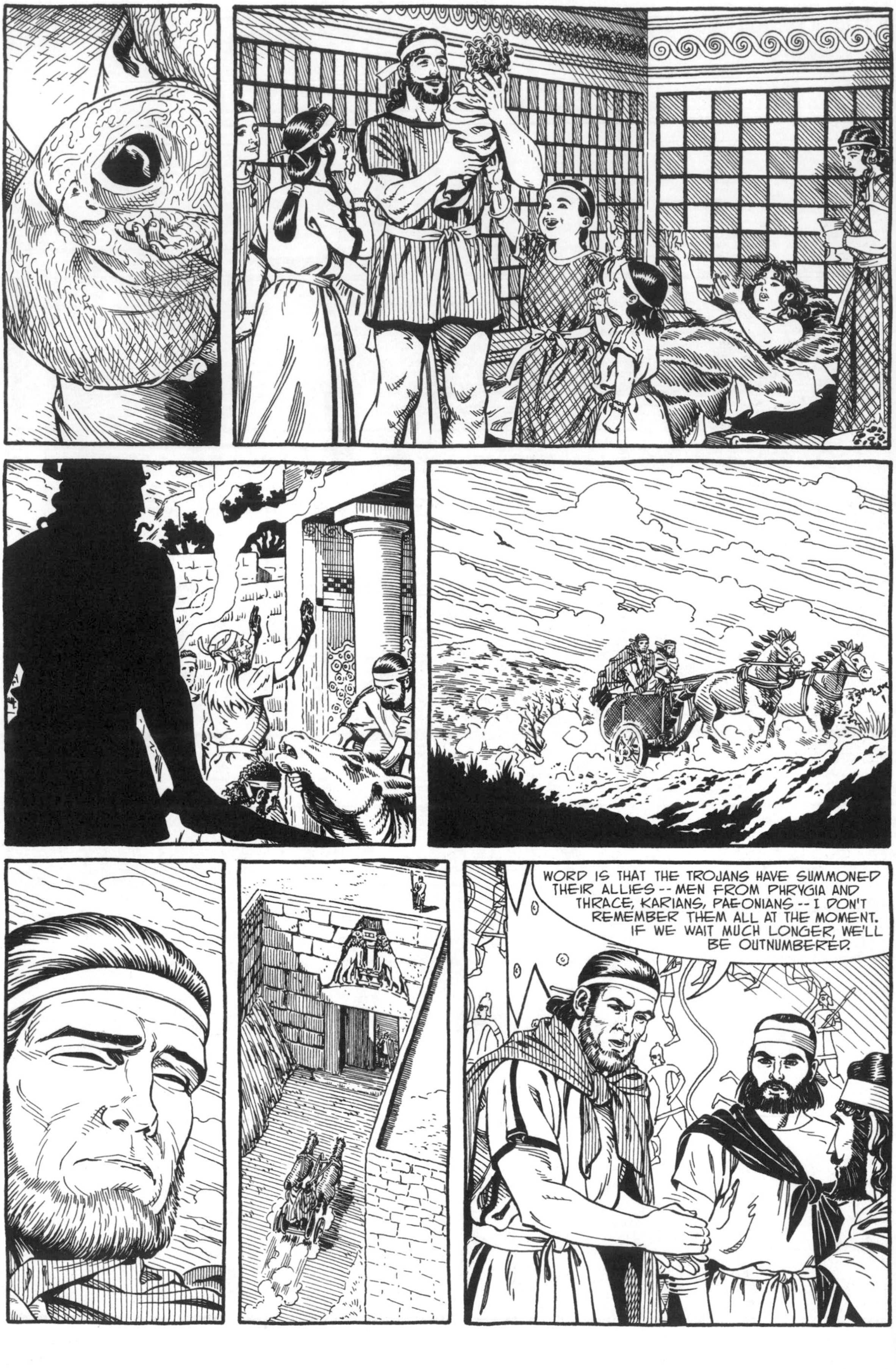
WORD IS THAT THE TROJANS HAVE SUMMONED THEIR ALLIES -- MEN FROM PHRYGIA AND THRACE, KARIANS, PAEONIANS -- I DON'T REMEMBER THEM ALL AT THE MOMENT. IF WE WAIT MUCH LONGER, WE'LL BE OUTNUMBERED.

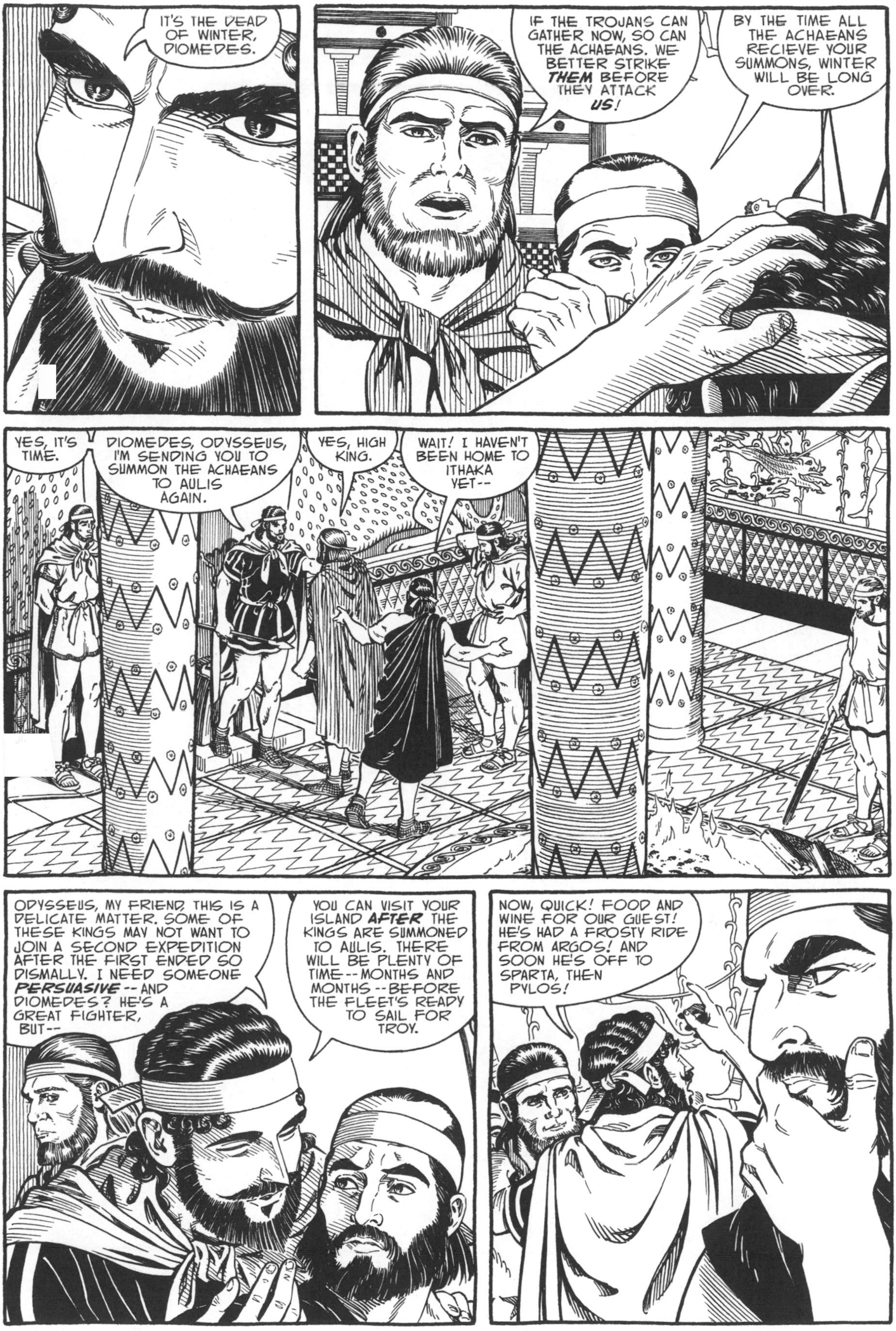

IT'S THE DEAD OF WINTER, DIOMEDES.
IF THE TROJANS CAN GATHER NOW, SO CAN THE ACHAEANS. WE BETTER STRIKE **THEM** BEFORE THEY ATTACK **US**!
BY THE TIME ALL THE ACHAEANS RECIEVE YOUR SUMMONS, WINTER WILL BE LONG OVER.
YES, IT'S TIME.
DIOMEDES, ODYSSEUS, I'M SENDING YOU TO SUMMON THE ACHAEANS TO AULIS AGAIN.
YES, HIGH KING.
WAIT! I HAVEN'T BEEN HOME TO ITHAKA YET--
ODYSSEUS, MY FRIEND, THIS IS A DELICATE MATTER. SOME OF THESE KINGS MAY NOT WANT TO JOIN A SECOND EXPEDITION AFTER THE FIRST ENDED SO DISMALLY. I NEED SOMEONE **PERSUASIVE**-- AND DIOMEDES? HE'S A GREAT FIGHTER, BUT--
YOU CAN VISIT YOUR ISLAND **AFTER** THE KINGS ARE SUMMONED TO AULIS. THERE WILL BE PLENTY OF TIME-- MONTHS AND MONTHS-- BEFORE THE FLEET'S READY TO SAIL FOR TROY.
NOW, QUICK! FOOD AND WINE FOR OUR GUEST! HE'S HAD A FROSTY RIDE FROM ARGOS! AND SOON HE'S OFF TO SPARTA, THEN PYLOS!

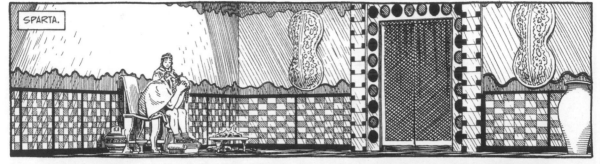

SPARTA.

ODYSSEUS OF ITHAKA AND DIOMEDES OF ARGOS.

MENELAUS, SON OF ATREUS! WE'VE BROUGHT YOU SUMMONS FROM AGAMEMNON!

SUMMONS?

TO AULIS! BRING YOUR SHIPS AND MEN! WE'RE OFF TO ATTACK TROY!

PRAISE THE GODS! AT LAST!

NESTOR OF PYLOS.

OF COURSE I'LL JOIN THE ARMY AGAIN. BUT I SUSPECT THAT MANY OF THE ACHAEANS WON'T BE SO WILLING. AGAMEMNON'S TIMING IS FAR FROM CONVENIENT. THE HARVEST WAS LATE AND LEAN... WINTER'S BEEN HARD...

LET ME COME WITH YOU TO THE OTHER KINGS.

IF ANY KING PROVES A RELUCTANT WARRIOR, I'LL GLADLY RECOUNT A TALE TO REMIND HIM HOW EAGERLY HIS FATHER HEEDED ANY CALL TO ARMS.

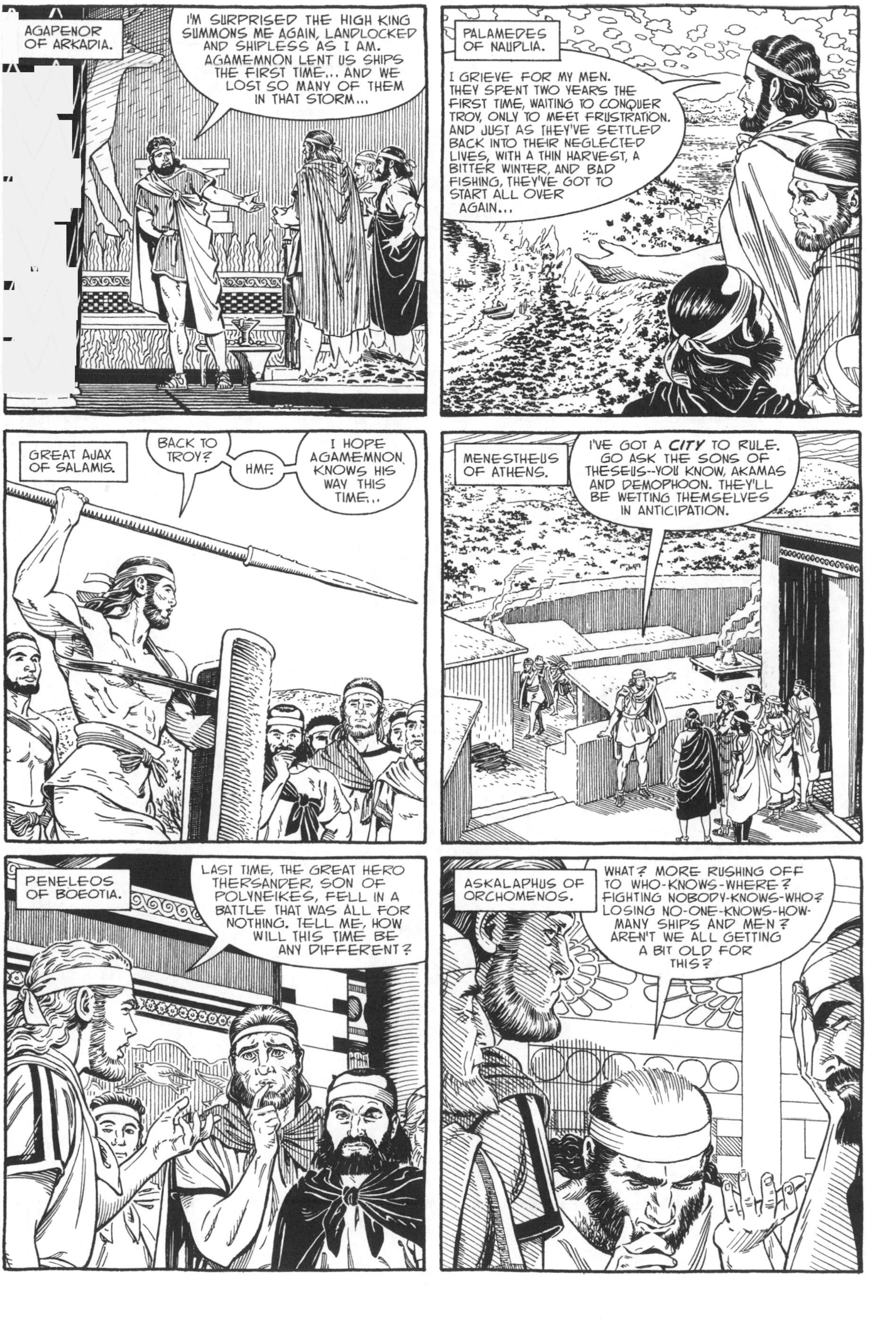

AGAPENOR OF ARKADIA.
I'M SURPRISED THE HIGH KING SUMMONS ME AGAIN, LANDLOCKED AND SHIPLESS AS I AM. AGAMEMNON LENT US SHIPS THE FIRST TIME... AND WE LOST SO MANY OF THEM IN THAT STORM...
PALAMEDES OF NAUPLIA.
I GRIEVE FOR MY MEN. THEY SPENT TWO YEARS THE FIRST TIME, WAITING TO CONQUER TROY, ONLY TO MEET FRUSTRATION. AND JUST AS THEY'VE SETTLED BACK INTO THEIR NEGLECTED LIVES, WITH A THIN HARVEST, A BITTER WINTER, AND BAD FISHING, THEY'VE GOT TO START ALL OVER AGAIN...
GREAT AJAX OF SALAMIS.
BACK TO TROY?
HMF.
I HOPE AGAMEMNON KNOWS HIS WAY THIS TIME...
MENESTHEUS OF ATHENS.
I'VE GOT A CITY TO RULE. GO ASK THE SONS OF THESEUS--YOU KNOW, AKAMAS AND DEMOPHOON. THEY'LL BE WETTING THEMSELVES IN ANTICIPATION.
PENELEOS OF BOEOTIA.
LAST TIME, THE GREAT HERO THERSANDER, SON OF POLYNEIKES, FELL IN A BATTLE THAT WAS ALL FOR NOTHING. TELL ME, HOW WILL THIS TIME BE ANY DIFFERENT?
ASKALAPHUS OF ORCHOMENOS.
WHAT? MORE RUSHING OFF TO WHO-KNOWS-WHERE? FIGHTING NOBODY-KNOWS-WHO? LOSING NO-ONE-KNOWS-HOW-MANY SHIPS AND MEN? AREN'T WE ALL GETTING A BIT OLD FOR THIS?

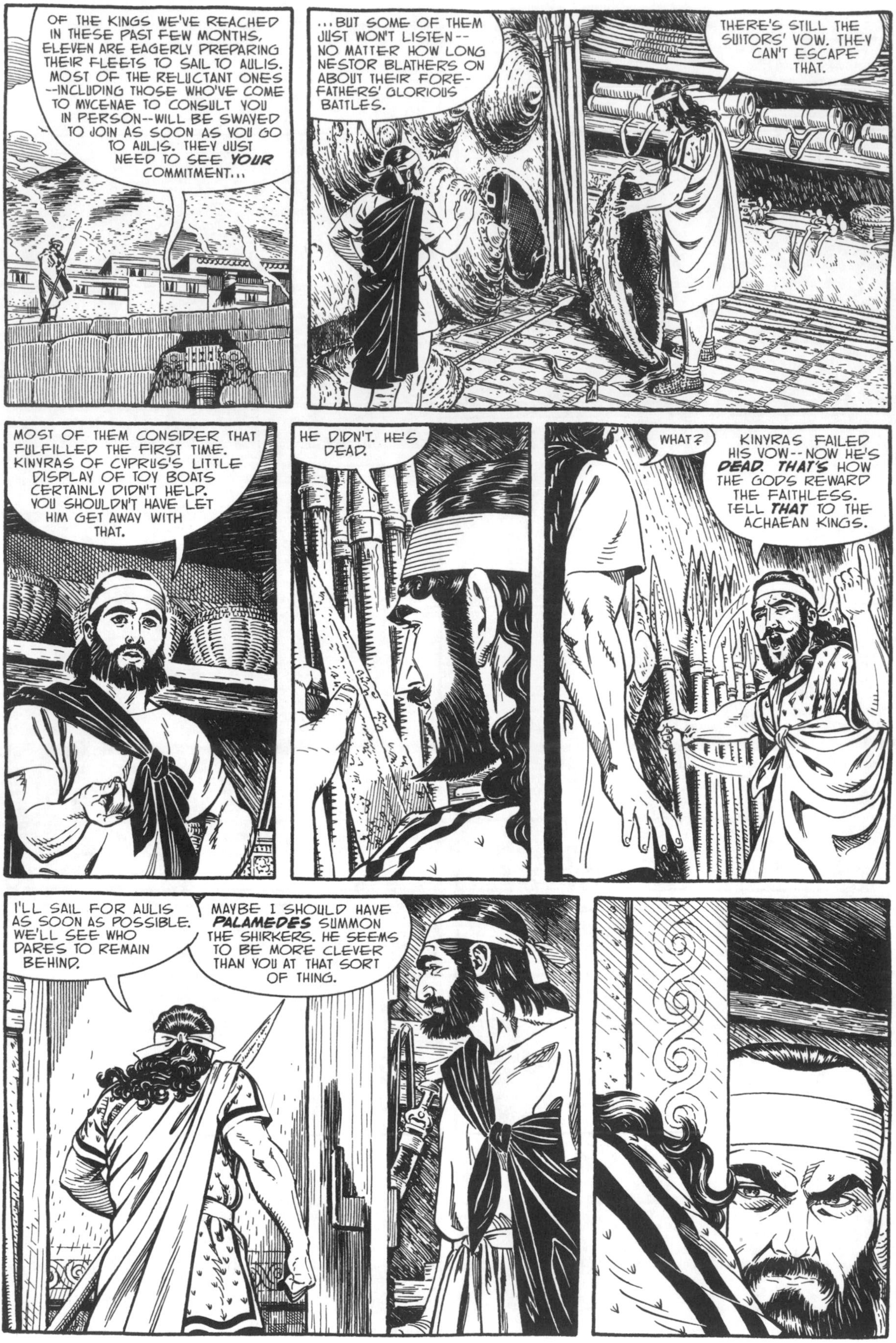
OF THE KINGS WE'VE REACHED IN THESE PAST FEW MONTHS, ELEVEN ARE EAGERLY PREPARING THEIR FLEETS TO SAIL TO AULIS. MOST OF THE RELUCTANT ONES --INCLUDING THOSE WHO'VE COME TO MYCENAE TO CONSULT YOU IN PERSON--WILL BE SWAYED TO JOIN AS SOON AS YOU GO TO AULIS. THEY JUST NEED TO SEE YOUR COMMITMENT...
...BUT SOME OF THEM JUST WON'T LISTEN-- NO MATTER HOW LONG NESTOR BLATHERS ON ABOUT THEIR FORE-FATHERS' GLORIOUS BATTLES.
THERE'S STILL THE SUITORS' VOW. THEY CAN'T ESCAPE THAT.
MOST OF THEM CONSIDER THAT FULFILLED THE FIRST TIME. KINYRAS OF CYPRUS'S LITTLE DISPLAY OF TOY BOATS CERTAINLY DIDN'T HELP. YOU SHOULDN'T HAVE LET HIM GET AWAY WITH THAT.
HE DIDN'T. HE'S DEAD.
WHAT?
KINYRAS FAILED HIS VOW--NOW HE'S DEAD. THAT'S HOW THE GODS REWARD THE FAITHLESS. TELL THAT TO THE ACHAEAN KINGS.
I'LL SAIL FOR AULIS AS SOON AS POSSIBLE. WE'LL SEE WHO DARES TO REMAIN BEHIND.
MAYBE I SHOULD HAVE PALAMEDES SUMMON THE SHIRKERS. HE SEEMS TO BE MORE CLEVER THAN YOU AT THAT SORT OF THING.

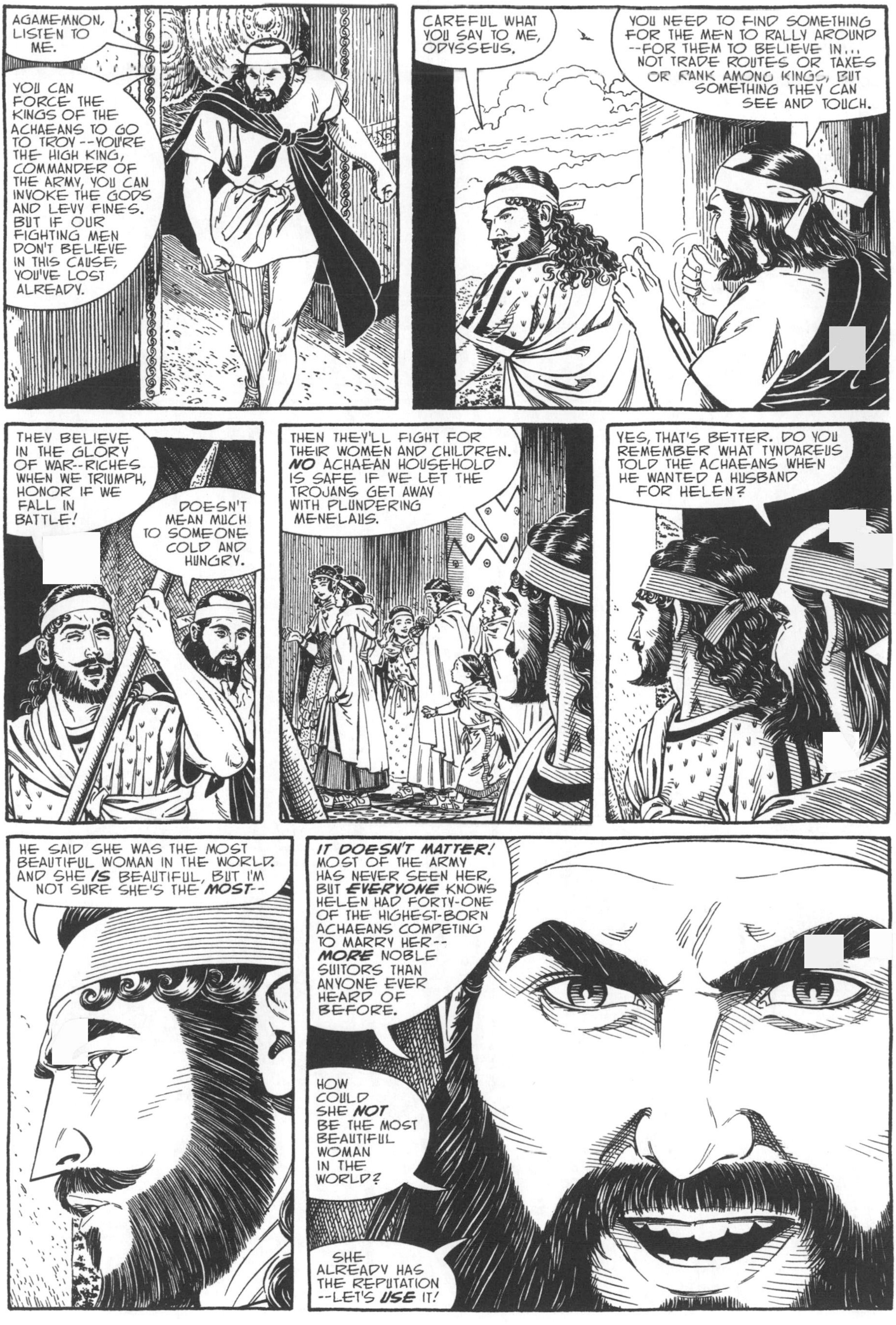
AGAMEMNON, LISTEN TO ME.
YOU CAN FORCE THE KINGS OF THE ACHAEANS TO GO TO TROY--YOU'RE THE HIGH KING, COMMANDER OF THE ARMY, YOU CAN INVOKE THE GODS AND LEVY FINES. BUT IF OUR FIGHTING MEN DON'T BELIEVE IN THIS CAUSE, YOU'VE LOST ALREADY.
CAREFUL WHAT YOU SAY TO ME, ODYSSEUS.
YOU NEED TO FIND SOMETHING FOR THE MEN TO RALLY AROUND --FOR THEM TO BELIEVE IN... NOT TRADE ROUTES OR TAXES OR RANK AMONG KINGS, BUT SOMETHING THEY CAN SEE AND TOUCH.
THEY BELIEVE IN THE GLORY OF WAR--RICHES WHEN WE TRIUMPH, HONOR IF WE FALL IN BATTLE!
DOESN'T MEAN MUCH TO SOMEONE COLD AND HUNGRY.
THEN THEY'LL FIGHT FOR THEIR WOMEN AND CHILDREN. NO ACHAEAN HOUSEHOLD IS SAFE IF WE LET THE TROJANS GET AWAY WITH PLUNDERING MENELAUS.
YES, THAT'S BETTER. DO YOU REMEMBER WHAT TYNDAREUS TOLD THE ACHAEANS WHEN HE WANTED A HUSBAND FOR HELEN?
HE SAID SHE WAS THE MOST BEAUTIFUL WOMAN IN THE WORLD. AND SHE IS BEAUTIFUL, BUT I'M NOT SURE SHE'S THE MOST--
IT DOESN'T MATTER! MOST OF THE ARMY HAS NEVER SEEN HER, BUT EVERYONE KNOWS HELEN HAD FORTY-ONE OF THE HIGHEST-BORN ACHAEANS COMPETING TO MARRY HER--MORE NOBLE SUITORS THAN ANYONE EVER HEARD OF BEFORE.
HOW COULD SHE NOT BE THE MOST BEAUTIFUL WOMAN IN THE WORLD?
SHE ALREADY HAS THE REPUTATION --LET'S USE IT!

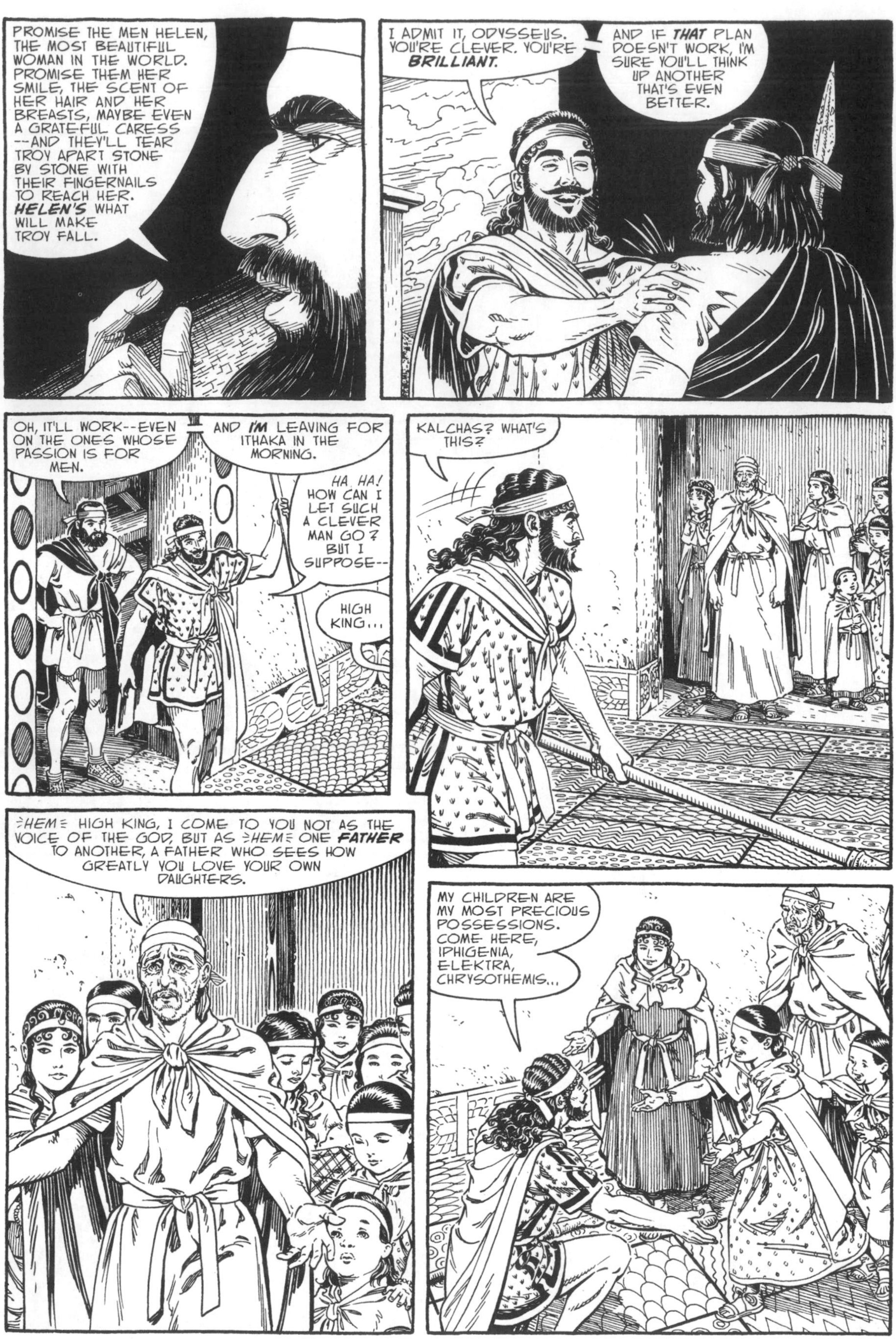
PROMISE THE MEN HELEN, THE MOST BEAUTIFUL WOMAN IN THE WORLD. PROMISE THEM HER SMILE, THE SCENT OF HER HAIR AND HER BREASTS, MAYBE EVEN A GRATEFUL CARESS --AND THEY'LL TEAR TROY APART STONE BY STONE WITH THEIR FINGERNAILS TO REACH HER. HELEN'S WHAT WILL MAKE TROY FALL.
I ADMIT IT, ODYSSEUS. YOU'RE CLEVER. YOU'RE BRILLIANT.
AND IF THAT PLAN DOESN'T WORK, I'M SURE YOU'LL THINK UP ANOTHER THAT'S EVEN BETTER.
OH, IT'LL WORK--EVEN ON THE ONES WHOSE PASSION IS FOR MEN.
AND I'M LEAVING FOR ITHAKA IN THE MORNING.
HA HA! HOW CAN I LET SUCH A CLEVER MAN GO? BUT I SUPPOSE--
HIGH KING...
KALCHAS? WHAT'S THIS?
=HEM= HIGH KING, I COME TO YOU NOT AS THE VOICE OF THE GOD, BUT AS =HEM= ONE FATHER TO ANOTHER, A FATHER WHO SEES HOW GREATLY YOU LOVE YOUR OWN DAUGHTERS.
MY CHILDREN ARE MY MOST PRECIOUS POSSESSIONS. COME HERE, IPHIGENIA, ELEKTRA, CHRYSOTHEMIS...

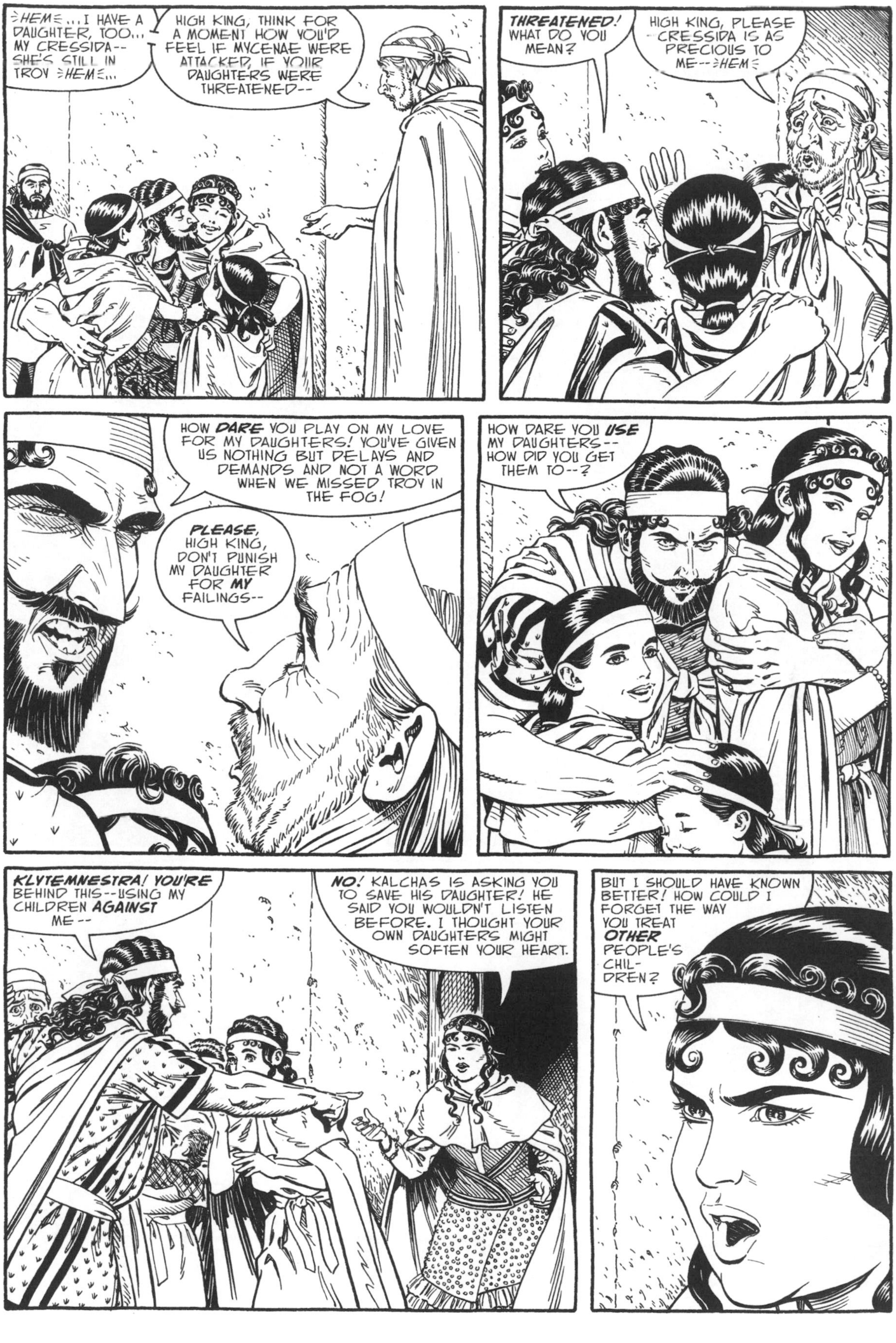

HEM... I HAVE A DAUGHTER, TOO... MY CRESSIDA-- SHE'S STILL IN TROY HEM...
HIGH KING, THINK FOR A MOMENT HOW YOU'D FEEL IF MYCENAE WERE ATTACKED, IF YOUR DAUGHTERS WERE THREATENED--
THREATENED! WHAT DO YOU MEAN?
HIGH KING, PLEASE --CRESSIDA IS AS PRECIOUS TO ME-- HEM
HOW DARE YOU PLAY ON MY LOVE FOR MY DAUGHTERS! YOU'VE GIVEN US NOTHING BUT DELAYS AND DEMANDS AND NOT A WORD WHEN WE MISSED TROY IN THE FOG!
PLEASE, HIGH KING, DON'T PUNISH MY DAUGHTER FOR MY FAILINGS--
HOW DARE YOU USE MY DAUGHTERS-- HOW DID YOU GET THEM TO--?
KLYTEMNESTRA! YOU'RE BEHIND THIS--USING MY CHILDREN AGAINST ME--
NO! KALCHAS IS ASKING YOU TO SAVE HIS DAUGHTER! HE SAID YOU WOULDN'T LISTEN BEFORE. I THOUGHT YOUR OWN DAUGHTERS MIGHT SOFTEN YOUR HEART.
BUT I SHOULD HAVE KNOWN BETTER! HOW COULD I FORGET THE WAY YOU TREAT OTHER PEOPLE'S CHIL-DREN?

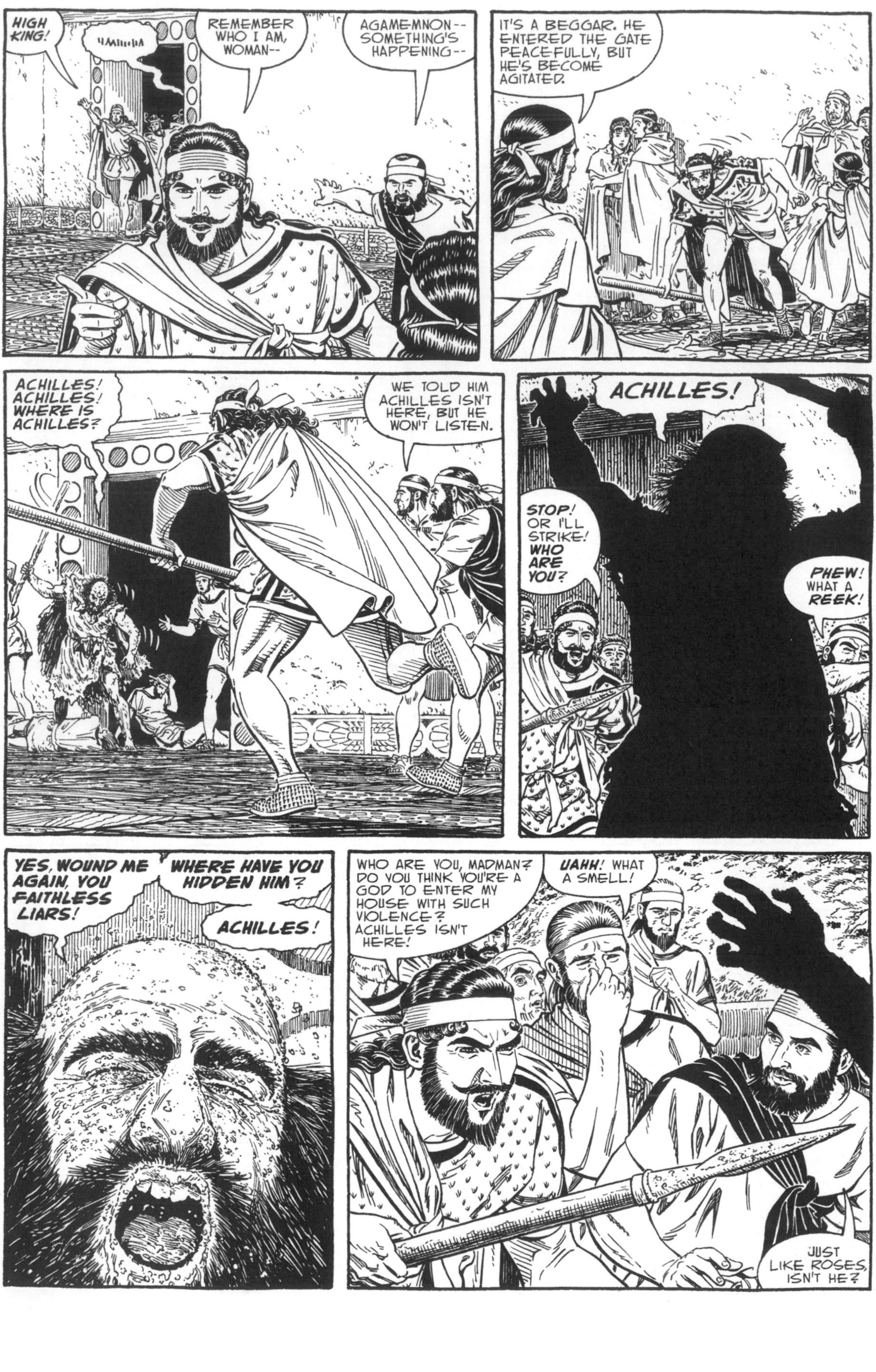
HIGH KING!
REMEMBER WHO I AM, WOMAN--
AGAMEMNON-- SOMETHING'S HAPPENING--
IT'S A BEGGAR. HE ENTERED THE GATE PEACEFULLY, BUT HE'S BECOME AGITATED.
ACHILLES! ACHILLES! WHERE IS ACHILLES?
WE TOLD HIM ACHILLES ISN'T HERE, BUT HE WON'T LISTEN.
ACHILLES!
STOP! OR I'LL STRIKE! WHO ARE YOU?
PHEW! WHAT A REEK!
YES, WOUND ME AGAIN, YOU FAITHLESS LIARS!
WHERE HAVE YOU HIDDEN HIM?
ACHILLES!
WHO ARE YOU, MADMAN? DO YOU THINK YOU'RE A GOD TO ENTER MY HOUSE WITH SUCH VIOLENCE? ACHILLES ISN'T HERE!
UAHH! WHAT A SMELL!
JUST LIKE ROSES, ISN'T HE?

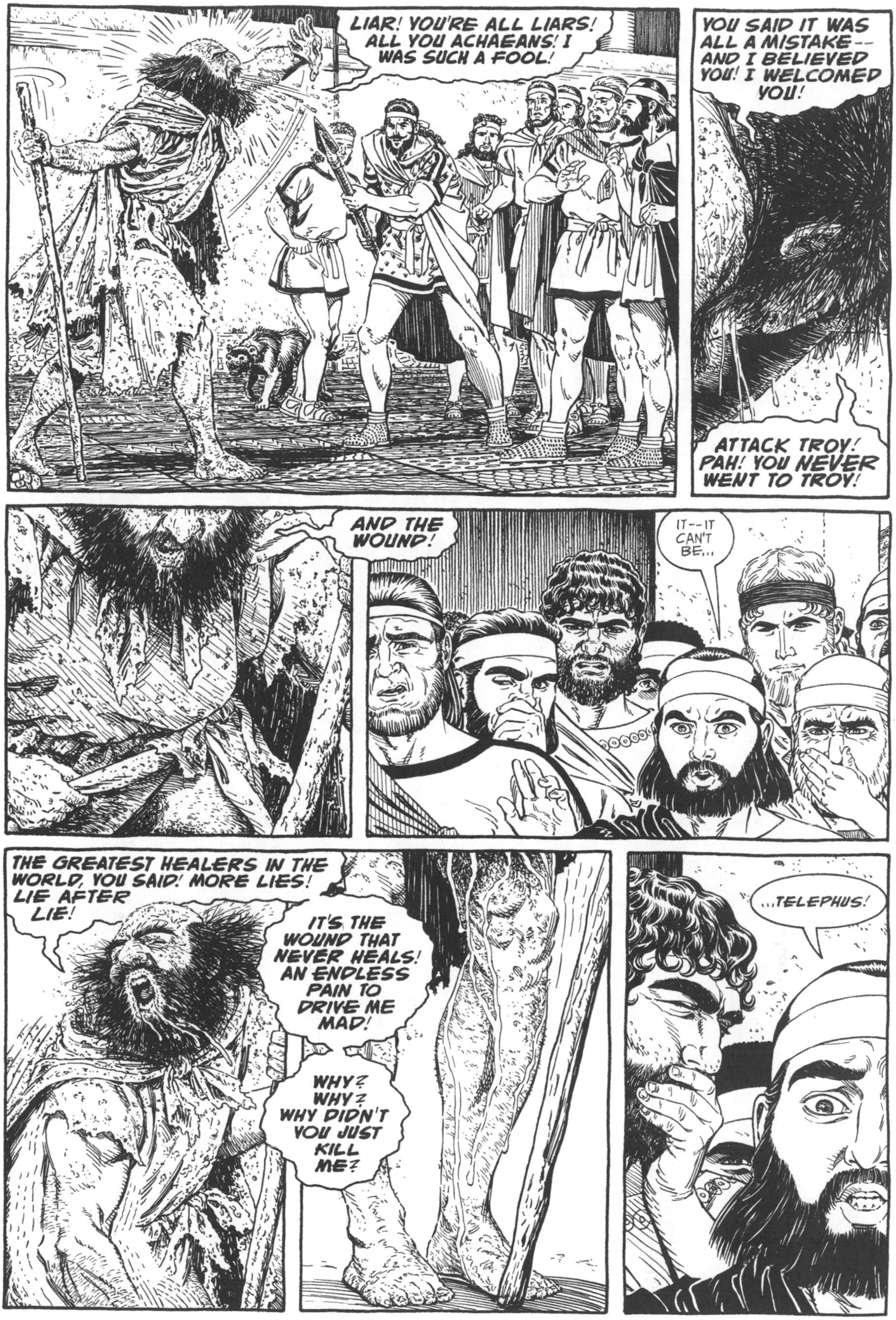
LIAR! YOU'RE ALL LIARS! ALL YOU ACHAEANS! I WAS SUCH A FOOL!
YOU SAID IT WAS ALL A MISTAKE-- AND I BELIEVED YOU! I WELCOMED YOU!
ATTACK TROY! PAH! YOU NEVER WENT TO TROY!
AND THE WOUND!
IT--IT CAN'T BE...
THE GREATEST HEALERS IN THE WORLD, YOU SAID! MORE LIES! LIE AFTER LIE!
IT'S THE WOUND THAT NEVER HEALS! AN ENDLESS PAIN TO DRIVE ME MAD!
WHY? WHY? WHY DIDN'T YOU JUST KILL ME?
...TELEPHUS!

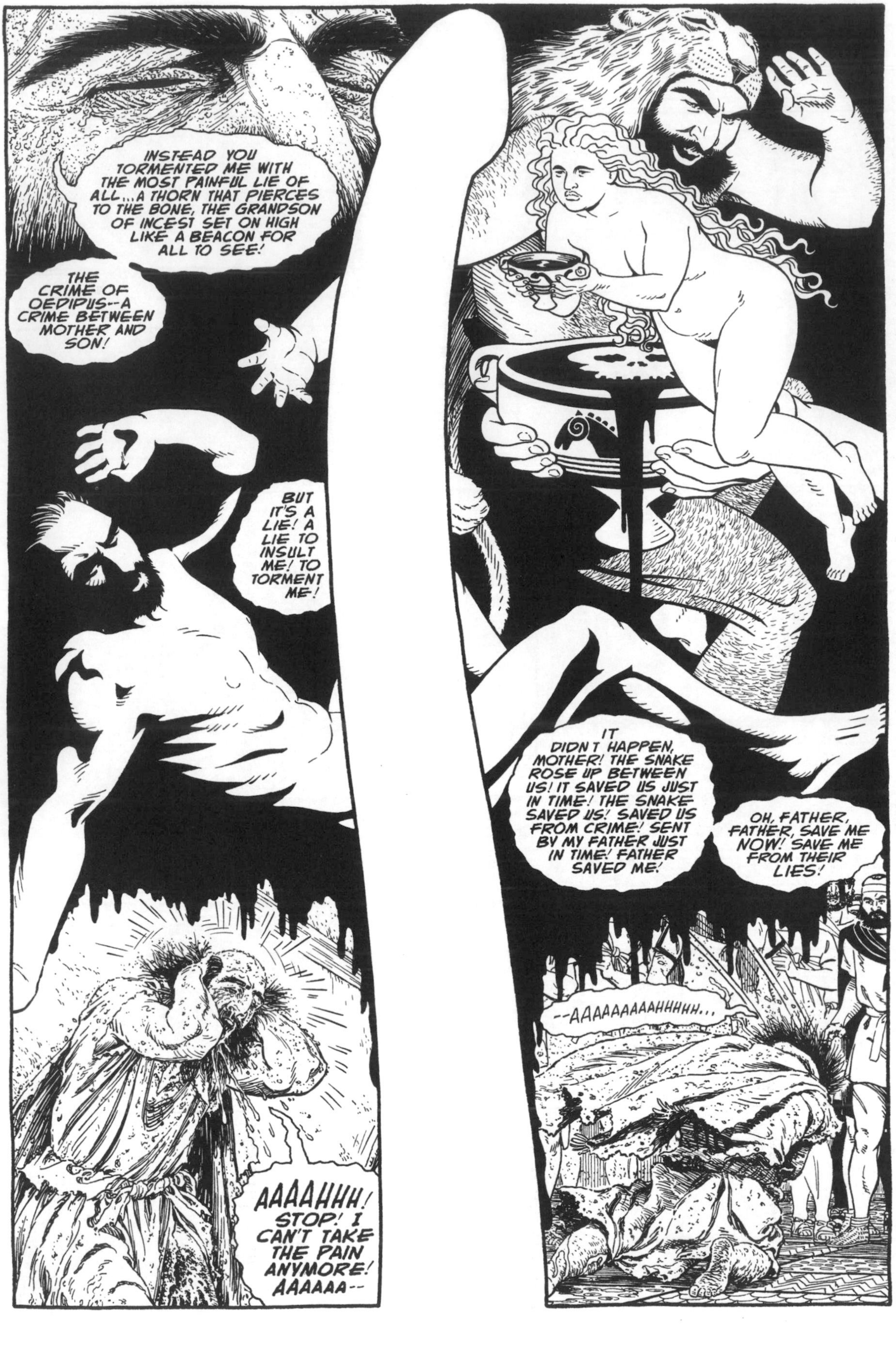
INSTEAD YOU TORMENTED ME WITH THE MOST PAINFUL LIE OF ALL...A THORN THAT PIERCES TO THE BONE, THE GRANDSON OF INCEST SET ON HIGH LIKE A BEACON FOR ALL TO SEE!
THE CRIME OF OEDIPUS--A CRIME BETWEEN MOTHER AND SON!
BUT IT'S A LIE! A LIE TO INSULT ME! TO TORMENT ME!
AAAAHHH! STOP! I CAN'T TAKE THE PAIN ANYMORE! AAAAAA--
IT DIDN'T HAPPEN, MOTHER! THE SNAKE ROSE UP BETWEEN US! IT SAVED US JUST IN TIME! THE SNAKE SAVED US! SAVED US FROM CRIME! SENT BY MY FATHER JUST IN TIME! FATHER SAVED ME!
OH, FATHER, FATHER, SAVE ME NOW! SAVE ME FROM THEIR LIES!
--AAAAAAAAAHHHHH...

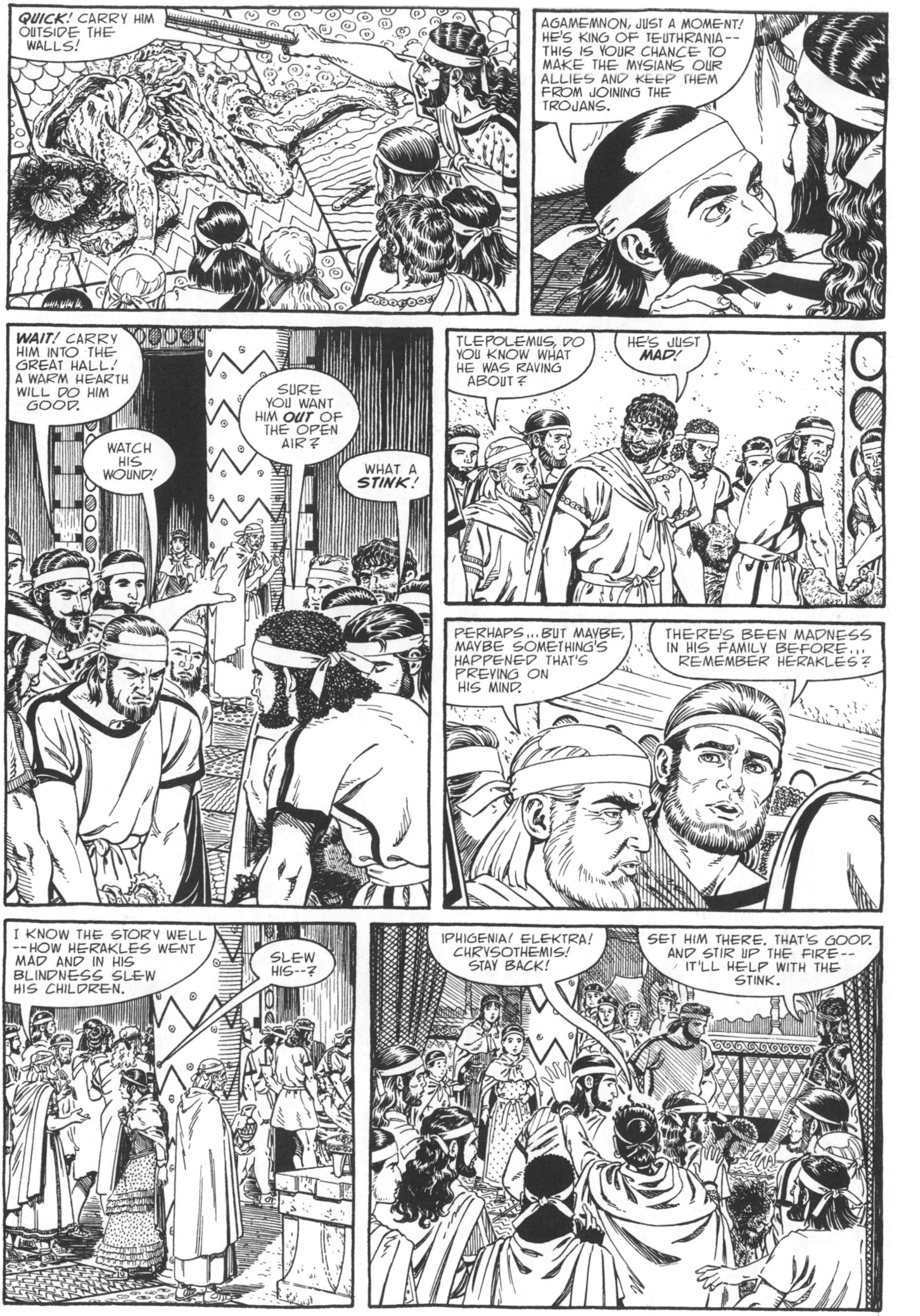
QUICK! CARRY HIM OUTSIDE THE WALLS!
AGAMEMNON, JUST A MOMENT! HE'S KING OF TEUTHRANIA-- THIS IS YOUR CHANCE TO MAKE THE MYSIANS OUR ALLIES AND KEEP THEM FROM JOINING THE TROJANS.
WAIT! CARRY HIM INTO THE GREAT HALL! A WARM HEARTH WILL DO HIM GOOD.
WATCH HIS WOUND!
SURE YOU WANT HIM OUT OF THE OPEN AIR?
WHAT A STINK!
TLEPOLEMUS, DO YOU KNOW WHAT HE WAS RAVING ABOUT?
HE'S JUST MAD!
PERHAPS... BUT MAYBE, MAYBE SOMETHING'S HAPPENED THAT'S PREYING ON HIS MIND.
THERE'S BEEN MADNESS IN HIS FAMILY BEFORE... REMEMBER HERAKLES?
I KNOW THE STORY WELL --HOW HERAKLES WENT MAD AND IN HIS BLINDNESS SLEW HIS CHILDREN.
SLEW HIS--?
IPHIGENIA! ELEKTRA! CHRYSOTHEMIS! STAY BACK!
SET HIM THERE. THAT'S GOOD. AND STIR UP THE FIRE-- IT'LL HELP WITH THE STINK.

ELEKTRA! COME BACK!
NO! I WANNA SEE!
I'LL GET HER!
uhhh...
KILISSA, NO! DON'T TAKE ORESTES ANY CLOSER!
ELEKTRA!
GIVE ORESTES TO ME!
OH!
EW! HE'S STINKY!
TAKE MY CHILDREN OUT OF HERE --NOW!
LOOK!
CAREFUL!
WHAT'S HE--?
LEMME GO, KILISSA!
OH, PRAISE THE MOTHER--
AAAH!
AAAAH!
AAAAH!
BRING ACHILLES TO ME OR I'LL RIP THIS CHILD APART!
--AAAAA--

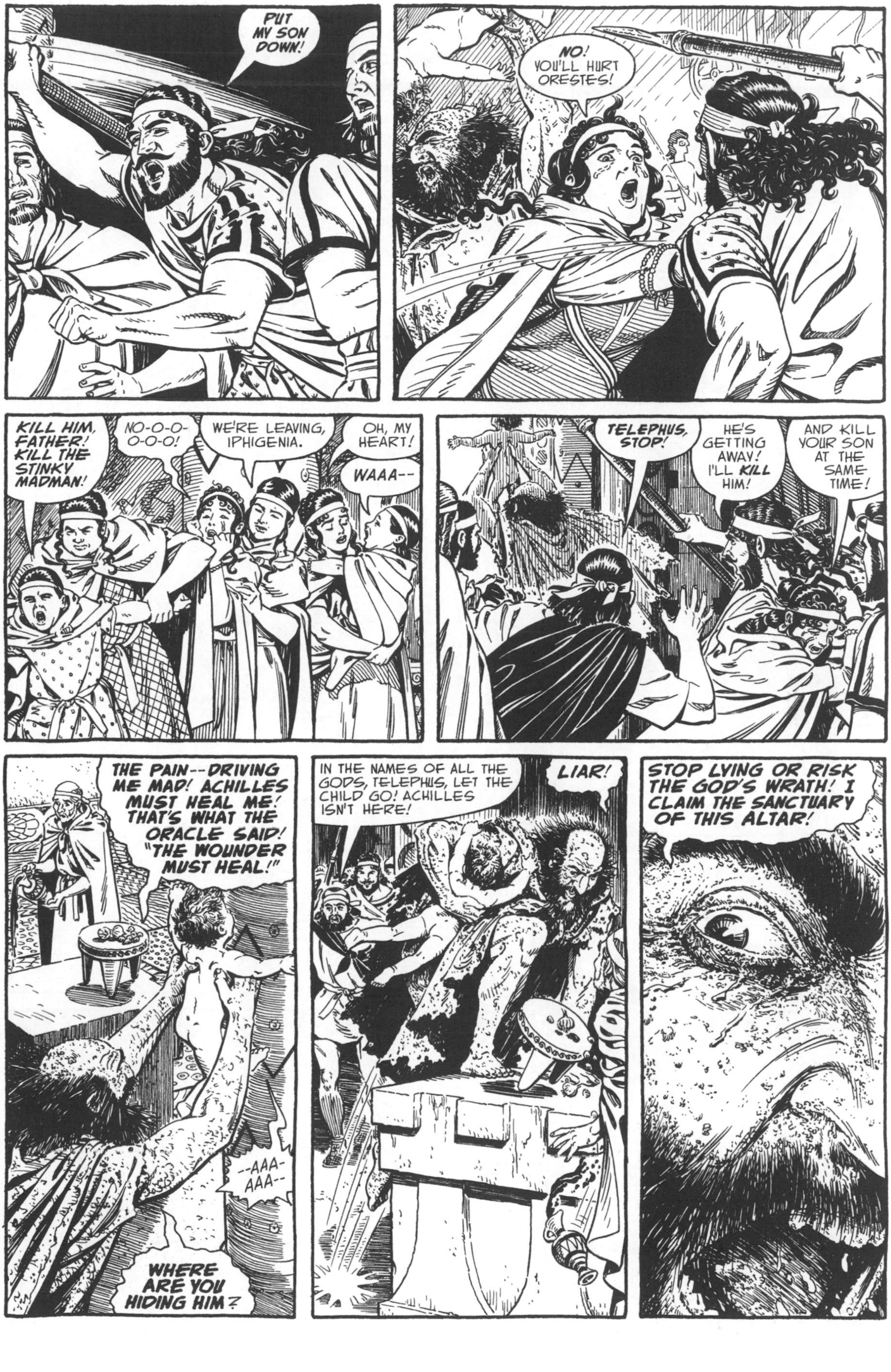
PUT MY SON DOWN!
NO! YOU'LL HURT ORESTES!
KILL HIM, FATHER! KILL THE STINKY MADMAN!
NO-O-O-O-O-O!
WE'RE LEAVING, IPHIGENIA.
OH, MY HEART!
WAAA--
TELEPHUS, STOP!
HE'S GETTING AWAY! I'LL KILL HIM!
AND KILL YOUR SON AT THE SAME TIME!
THE PAIN--DRIVING ME MAD! ACHILLES MUST HEAL ME! THAT'S WHAT THE ORACLE SAID! "THE WOUNDER MUST HEAL!"
--AAA-AAA--
WHERE ARE YOU HIDING HIM?
IN THE NAMES OF ALL THE GODS, TELEPHUS, LET THE CHILD GO! ACHILLES ISN'T HERE!
LIAR!
STOP LYING OR RISK THE GOD'S WRATH! I CLAIM THE SANCTUARY OF THIS ALTAR!

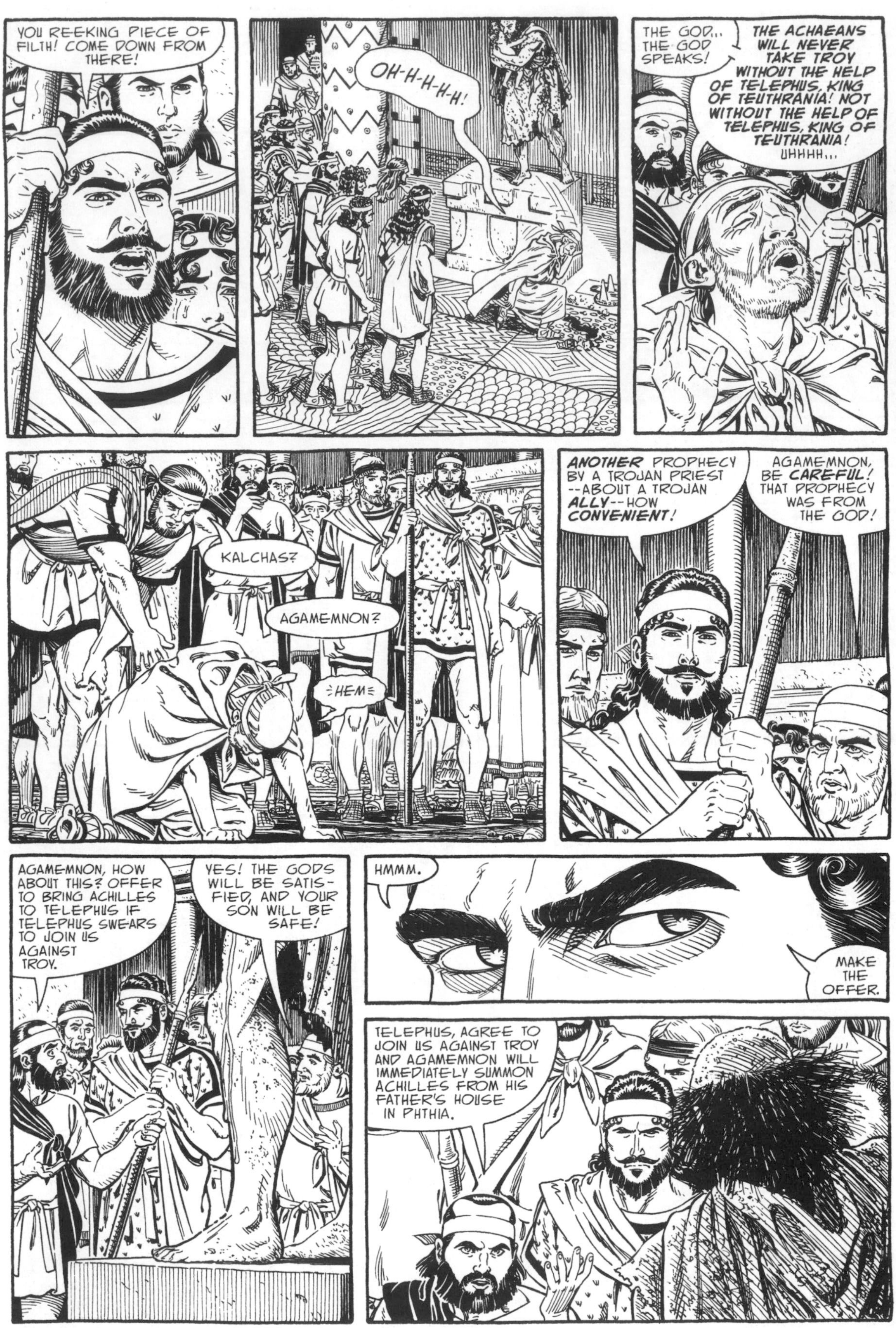
YOU REEKING PIECE OF FILTH! COME DOWN FROM THERE!
OH-H-H-H-H!
THE GOD... THE GOD SPEAKS!
THE ACHAEANS WILL NEVER TAKE TROY WITHOUT THE HELP OF TELEPHUS, KING OF TEUTHRANIA! NOT WITHOUT THE HELP OF TELEPHUS, KING OF TEUTHRANIA! UHHHH...
KALCHAS?
AGAMEMNON?
HEM
ANOTHER PROPHECY BY A TROJAN PRIEST --ABOUT A TROJAN ALLY--HOW CONVENIENT!
AGAMEMNON, BE CAREFUL! THAT PROPHECY WAS FROM THE GOD!
AGAMEMNON, HOW ABOUT THIS? OFFER TO BRING ACHILLES TO TELEPHUS IF TELEPHUS SWEARS TO JOIN US AGAINST TROY.
YES! THE GODS WILL BE SATISFIED, AND YOUR SON WILL BE SAFE!
HMMM.
MAKE THE OFFER.
TELEPHUS, AGREE TO JOIN US AGAINST TROY AND AGAMEMNON WILL IMMEDIATELY SUMMON ACHILLES FROM HIS FATHER'S HOUSE IN PHTHIA.

NO! I'LL NEVER JOIN SUCH LIARS AND TORMENTERS AGAINST MY SON'S FAMILY!

YOU ALL HEARD HIM REFUSE! HE CAN'T STAY UP THERE FOREVER. WHEN HE STEPS DOWN, HE DIES!

ORESTES!

NO! WE NEED HIM IN ORDER TO TAKE TROY!

WAIT!

TELEPHUS, WE WON'T ASK YOU TO FIGHT THE TROJANS. JUST PROMISE NOT TO AID THEM. AND YOU MUST SHOW US THE WAY TO TROY -- GUIDE OUR FLEET THERE.

FATHER, GUIDE ME...

I...

I'LL DO THAT MUCH. BRING ACHILLES TO HEAL ME AND I'LL DENY AID TO TROY...

...AND I'LL GUIDE YOU THERE... IF THAT'S WHERE YOU TRULY WISH TO GO.

I SWEAR UPON THIS ALTAR.

GOOD, GOOD. NOW WHY DON'T YOU STEP DOWN?

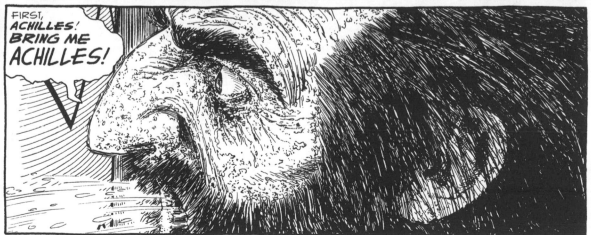

FIRST, ACHILLES! BRING ME ACHILLES!

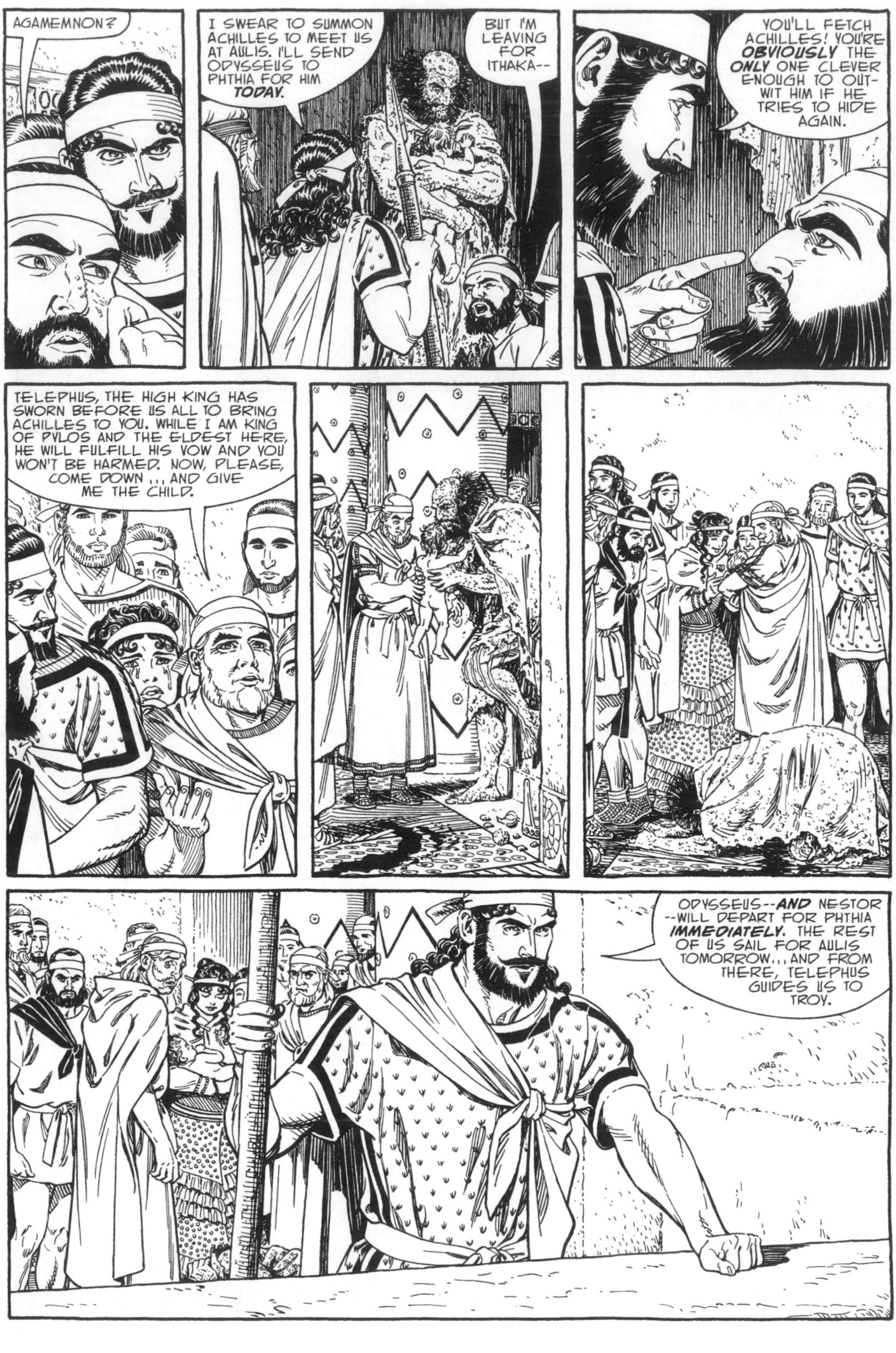
AGAMEMNON?
I SWEAR TO SUMMON ACHILLES TO MEET US AT AULIS. I'LL SEND ODYSSEUS TO PHTHIA FOR HIM TODAY.
BUT I'M LEAVING FOR ITHAKA--
YOU'LL FETCH ACHILLES! YOU'RE OBVIOUSLY THE ONLY ONE CLEVER ENOUGH TO OUT-WIT HIM IF HE TRIES TO HIDE AGAIN.
TELEPHUS, THE HIGH KING HAS SWORN BEFORE US ALL TO BRING ACHILLES TO YOU. WHILE I AM KING OF PYLOS AND THE ELDEST HERE, HE WILL FULFILL HIS VOW AND YOU WON'T BE HARMED. NOW, PLEASE, COME DOWN... AND GIVE ME THE CHILD.
ODYSSEUS--AND NESTOR--WILL DEPART FOR PHTHIA IMMEDIATELY. THE REST OF US SAIL FOR AULIS TOMORROW... AND FROM THERE, TELEPHUS GUIDES US TO TROY.

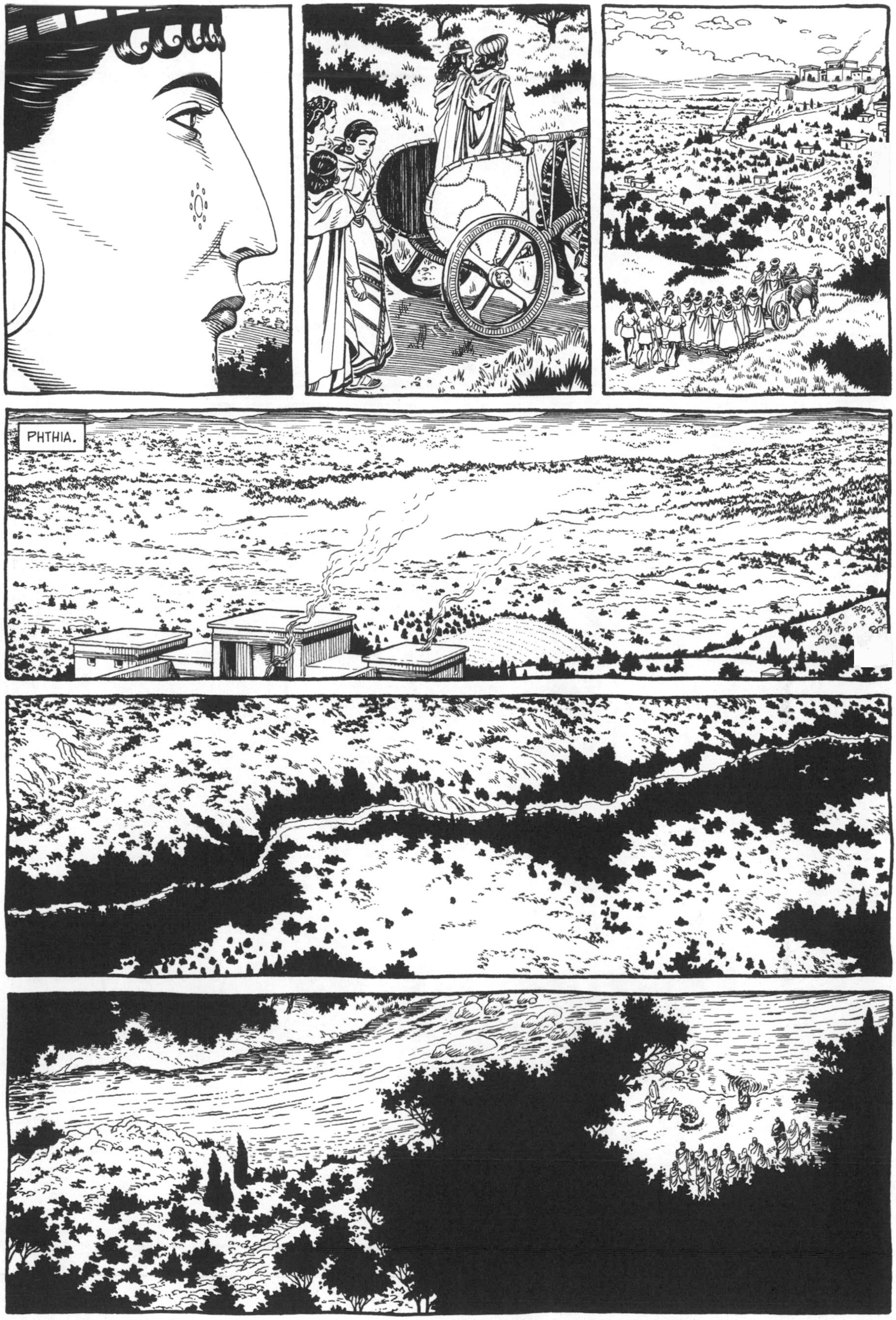
PHTHIA.

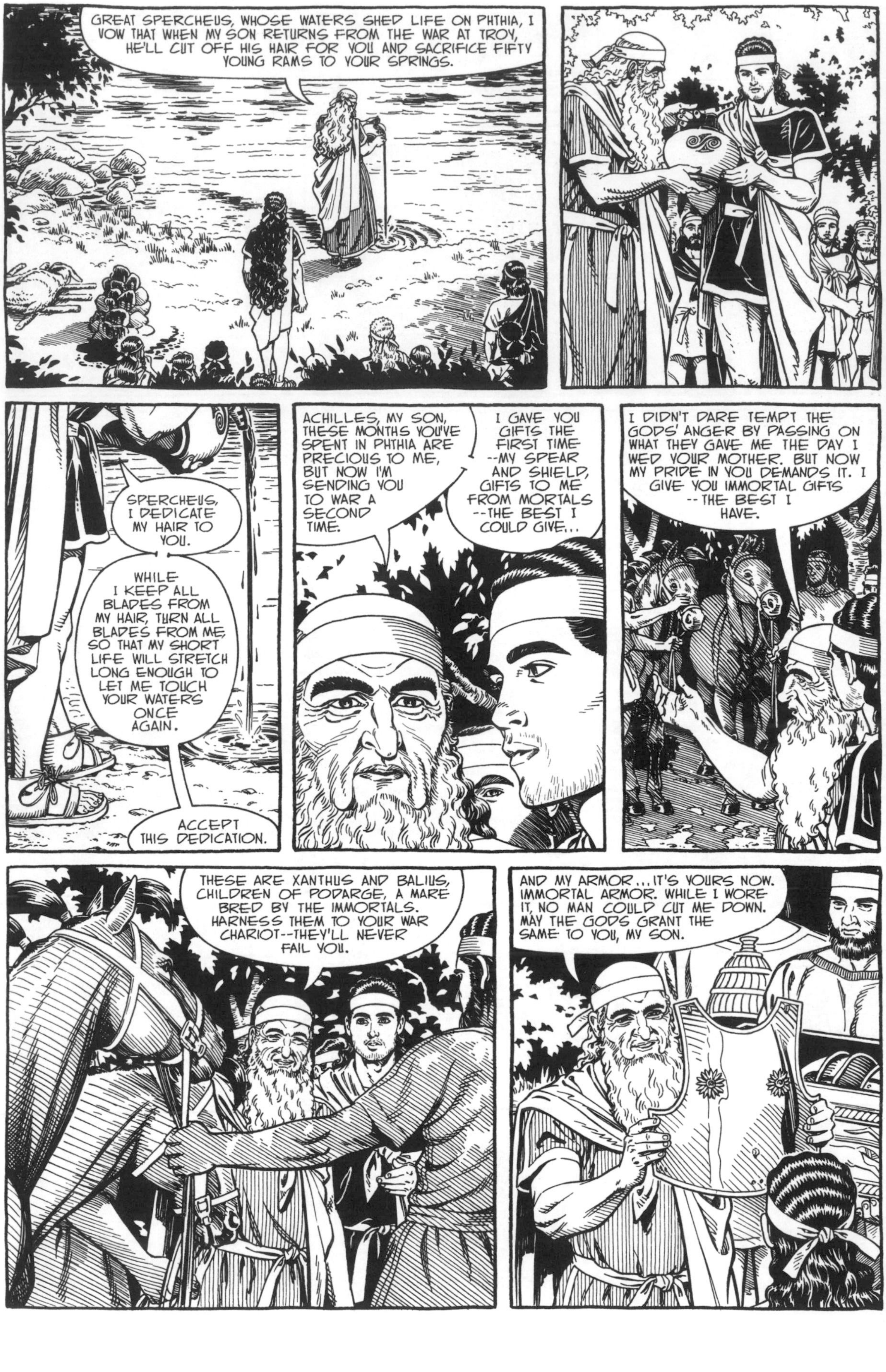
GREAT SPERCHEUS, WHOSE WATERS SHED LIFE ON PHTHIA, I VOW THAT WHEN MY SON RETURNS FROM THE WAR AT TROY, HE'LL CUT OFF HIS HAIR FOR YOU AND SACRIFICE FIFTY YOUNG RAMS TO YOUR SPRINGS.
SPERCHEUS, I DEDICATE MY HAIR TO YOU.
WHILE I KEEP ALL BLADES FROM MY HAIR, TURN ALL BLADES FROM ME, SO THAT MY SHORT LIFE WILL STRETCH LONG ENOUGH TO LET ME TOUCH YOUR WATERS ONCE AGAIN.
ACCEPT THIS DEDICATION.
ACHILLES, MY SON, THESE MONTHS YOU'VE SPENT IN PHTHIA ARE PRECIOUS TO ME, BUT NOW I'M SENDING YOU TO WAR A SECOND TIME.
I GAVE YOU GIFTS THE FIRST TIME --MY SPEAR AND SHIELD, GIFTS TO ME FROM MORTALS --THE BEST I COULD GIVE...
I DIDN'T DARE TEMPT THE GODS' ANGER BY PASSING ON WHAT THEY GAVE ME THE DAY I WED YOUR MOTHER. BUT NOW MY PRIDE IN YOU DEMANDS IT. I GIVE YOU IMMORTAL GIFTS --THE BEST I HAVE.
THESE ARE XANTHUS AND BALIUS, CHILDREN OF PODARGE, A MARE BRED BY THE IMMORTALS. HARNESS THEM TO YOUR WAR CHARIOT--THEY'LL NEVER FAIL YOU.
AND MY ARMOR...IT'S YOURS NOW. IMMORTAL ARMOR. WHILE I WORE IT, NO MAN COULD CUT ME DOWN. MAY THE GODS GRANT THE SAME TO YOU, MY SON.

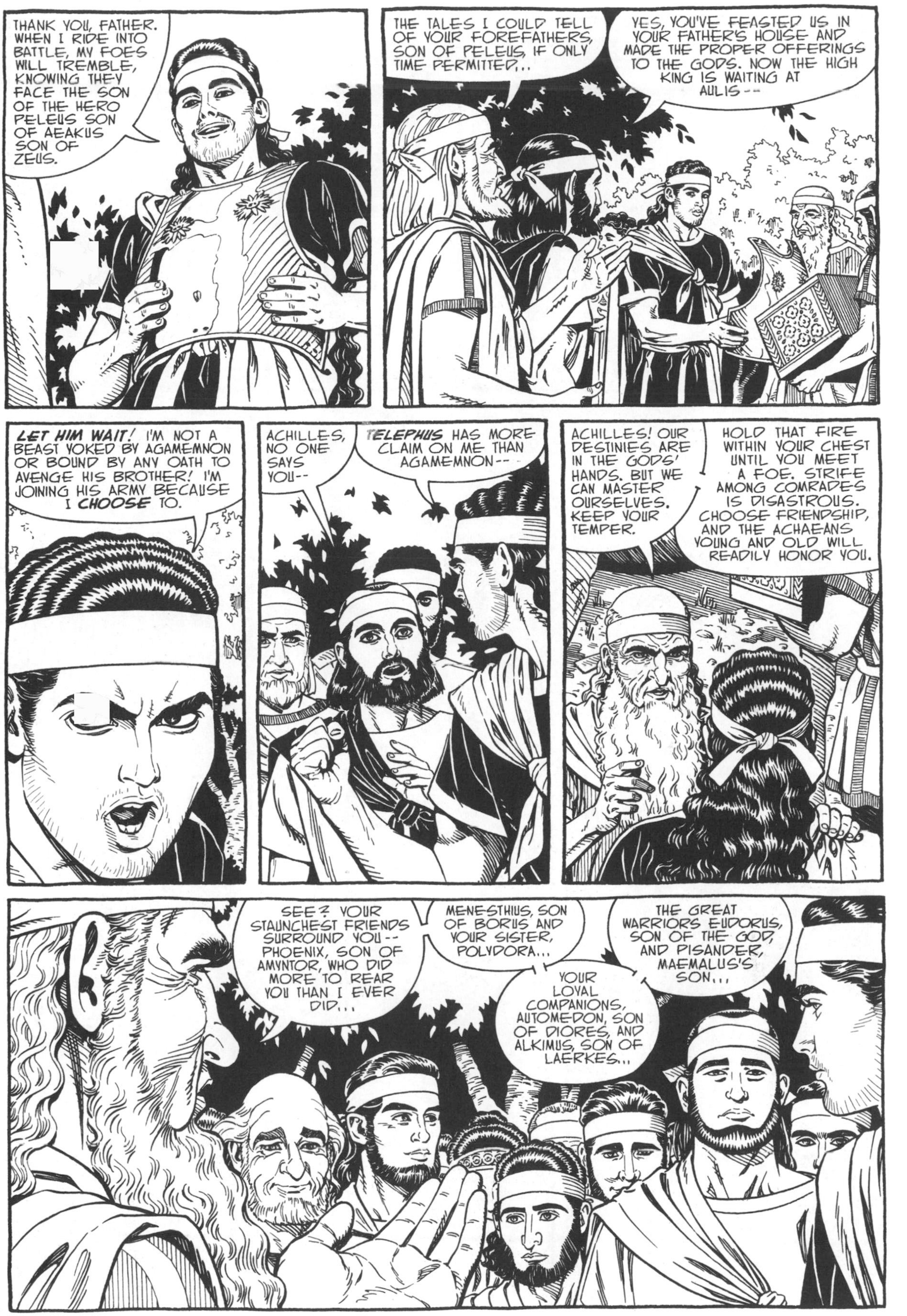

THANK YOU, FATHER. WHEN I RIDE INTO BATTLE, MY FOES WILL TREMBLE, KNOWING THEY FACE THE SON OF THE HERO PELEUS SON OF AEAKUS SON OF ZEUS.
THE TALES I COULD TELL OF YOUR FOREFATHERS, SON OF PELEUS, IF ONLY TIME PERMITTED...
YES, YOU'VE FEASTED US IN YOUR FATHER'S HOUSE AND MADE THE PROPER OFFERINGS TO THE GODS. NOW THE HIGH KING IS WAITING AT AULIS--
LET HIM WAIT! I'M NOT A BEAST YOKED BY AGAMEMNON OR BOUND BY ANY OATH TO AVENGE HIS BROTHER! I'M JOINING HIS ARMY BECAUSE I CHOOSE TO.
ACHILLES, NO ONE SAYS YOU--
TELEPHUS HAS MORE CLAIM ON ME THAN AGAMEMNON--
ACHILLES! OUR DESTINIES ARE IN THE GODS' HANDS. BUT WE CAN MASTER OURSELVES. KEEP YOUR TEMPER.
HOLD THAT FIRE WITHIN YOUR CHEST UNTIL YOU MEET A FOE. STRIFE AMONG COMRADES IS DISASTROUS. CHOOSE FRIENDSHIP, AND THE ACHAEANS YOUNG AND OLD WILL READILY HONOR YOU.
SEE? YOUR STAUNCHEST FRIENDS SURROUND YOU--PHOENIX, SON OF AMYNTOR, WHO DID MORE TO REAR YOU THAN I EVER DID...
MENESTHIUS, SON OF BORUS AND YOUR SISTER, POLYDORA...
YOUR LOYAL COMPANIONS, AUTOMEDON, SON OF DIORES, AND ALKIMUS, SON OF LAERKES...
THE GREAT WARRIORS EUDORUS, SON OF THE GOD, AND PISANDER, MAEMALUS'S SON...

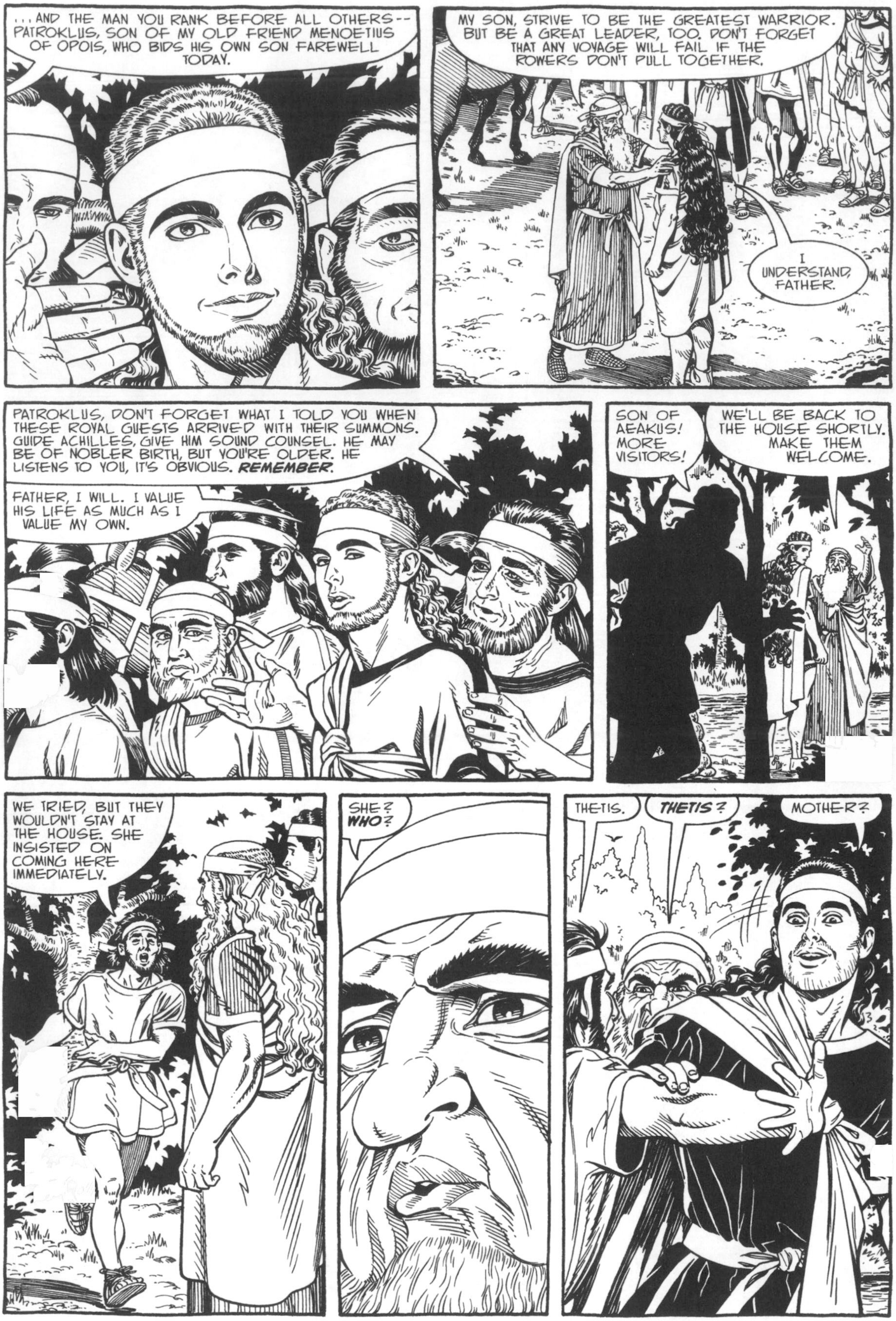
...AND THE MAN YOU RANK BEFORE ALL OTHERS--PATROKLUS, SON OF MY OLD FRIEND MENOETIUS OF OPOIS, WHO BIDS HIS OWN SON FAREWELL TODAY.
MY SON, STRIVE TO BE THE GREATEST WARRIOR. BUT BE A GREAT LEADER, TOO. DON'T FORGET THAT ANY VOYAGE WILL FAIL IF THE ROWERS DON'T PULL TOGETHER.
I UNDERSTAND, FATHER.
PATROKLUS, DON'T FORGET WHAT I TOLD YOU WHEN THESE ROYAL GUESTS ARRIVED WITH THEIR SUMMONS. GUIDE ACHILLES, GIVE HIM SOUND COUNSEL. HE MAY BE OF NOBLER BIRTH, BUT YOU'RE OLDER. HE LISTENS TO YOU, IT'S OBVIOUS. REMEMBER.
FATHER, I WILL. I VALUE HIS LIFE AS MUCH AS I VALUE MY OWN.
SON OF AEAKUS! MORE VISITORS!
WE'LL BE BACK TO THE HOUSE SHORTLY. MAKE THEM WELCOME.
WE TRIED, BUT THEY WOULDN'T STAY AT THE HOUSE. SHE INSISTED ON COMING HERE IMMEDIATELY.
SHE? WHO?
THE-TIS.
THETIS?
MOTHER?

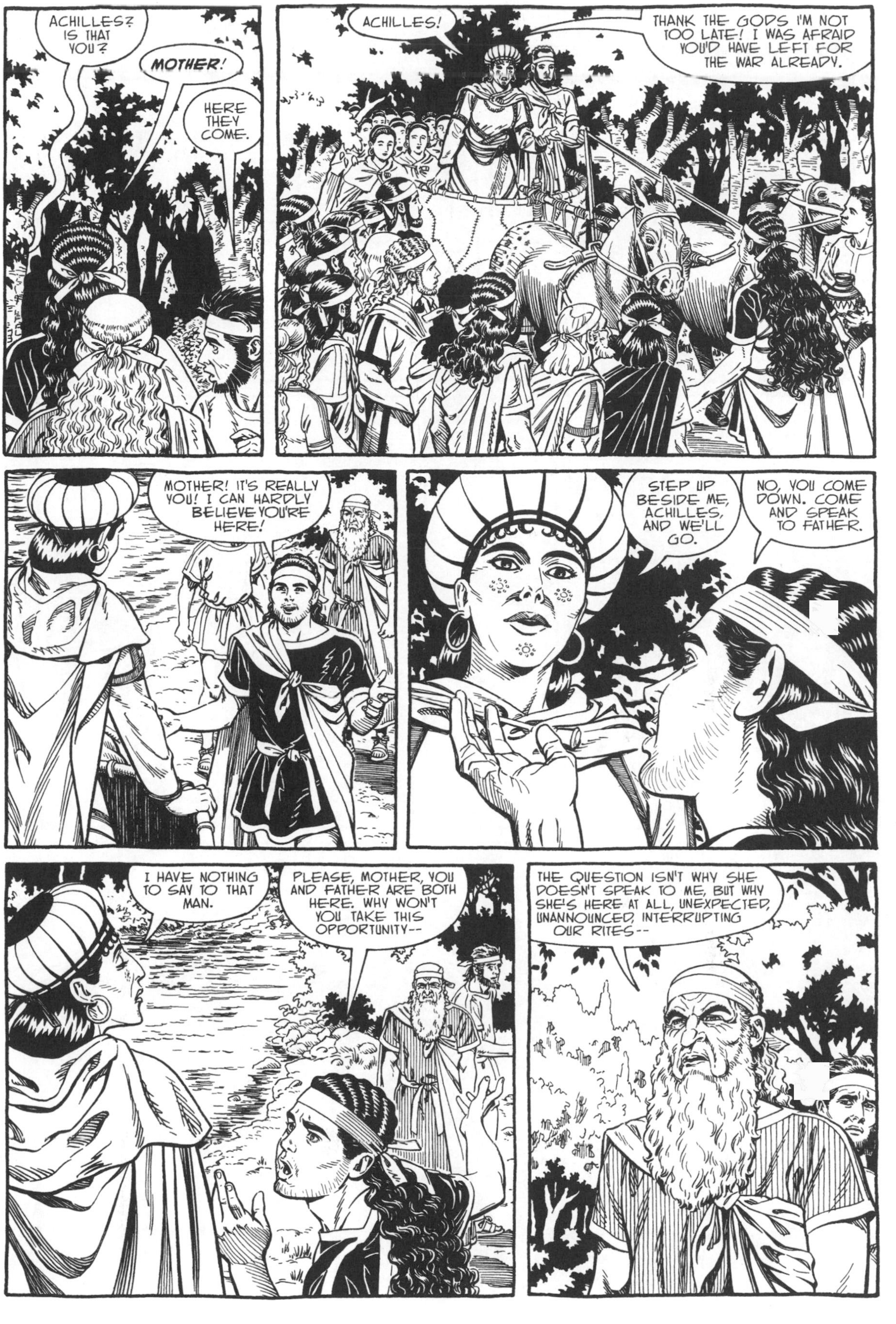
ACHILLES? IS THAT YOU?
MOTHER!
HERE THEY COME.
ACHILLES!
THANK THE GODS I'M NOT TOO LATE! I WAS AFRAID YOU'D HAVE LEFT FOR THE WAR ALREADY.
MOTHER! IT'S REALLY YOU! I CAN HARDLY BELIEVE YOU'RE HERE!
STEP UP BESIDE ME, ACHILLES, AND WE'LL GO.
NO, YOU COME DOWN. COME AND SPEAK TO FATHER.
I HAVE NOTHING TO SAY TO THAT MAN.
PLEASE, MOTHER, YOU AND FATHER ARE BOTH HERE. WHY WON'T YOU TAKE THIS OPPORTUNITY--
THE QUESTION ISN'T WHY SHE DOESN'T SPEAK TO ME, BUT WHY SHE'S HERE AT ALL, UNEXPECTED, UNANNOUNCED, INTERRUPTING OUR RITES--

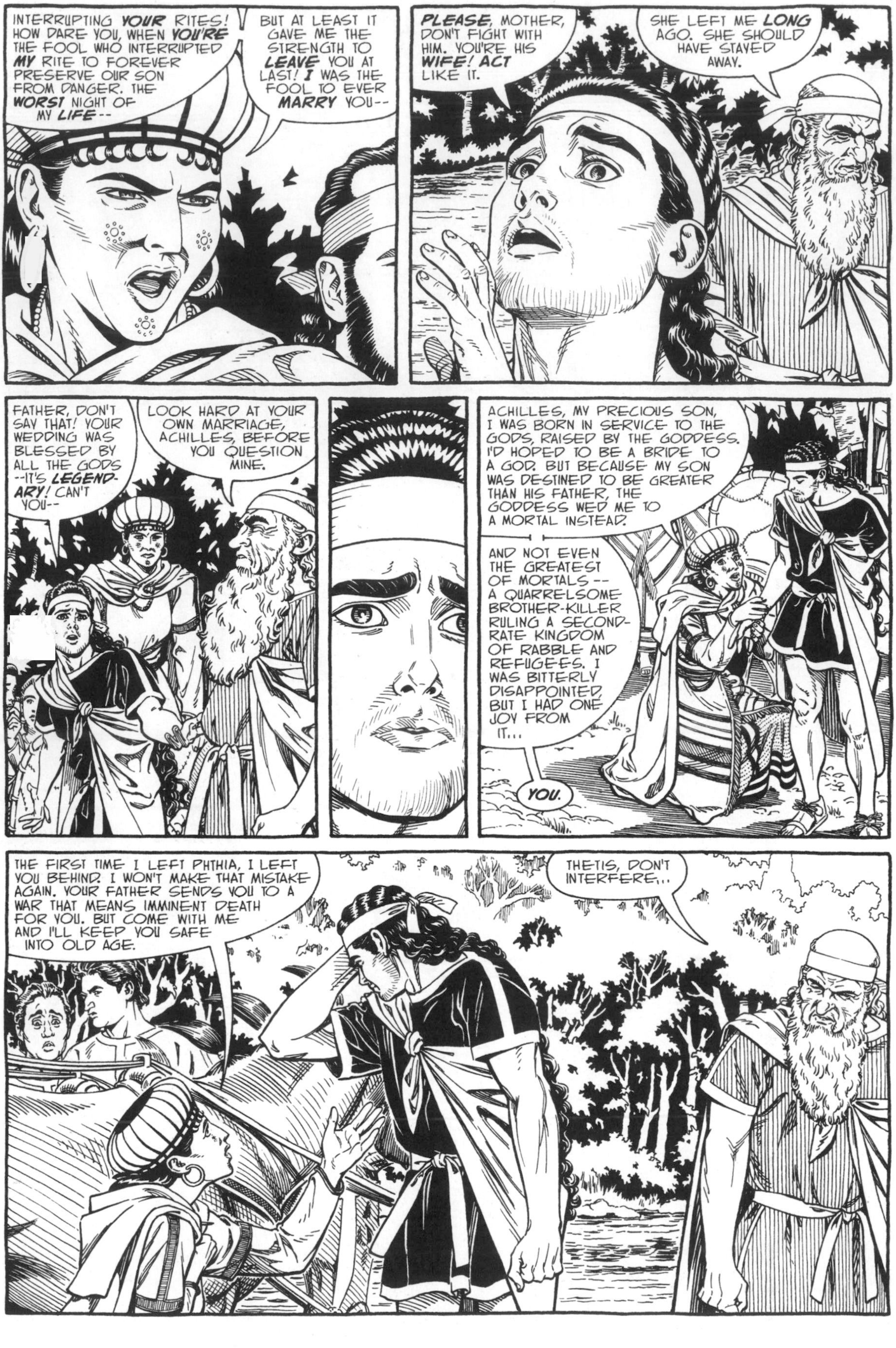
INTERRUPTING YOUR RITES! HOW DARE YOU, WHEN YOU'RE THE FOOL WHO INTERRUPTED MY RITE TO FOREVER PRESERVE OUR SON FROM DANGER. THE WORST NIGHT OF MY LIFE--
BUT AT LEAST IT GAVE ME THE STRENGTH TO LEAVE YOU AT LAST! I WAS THE FOOL TO EVER MARRY YOU--
PLEASE, MOTHER, DON'T FIGHT WITH HIM. YOU'RE HIS WIFE! ACT LIKE IT.
SHE LEFT ME LONG AGO. SHE SHOULD HAVE STAYED AWAY.
FATHER, DON'T SAY THAT! YOUR WEDDING WAS BLESSED BY ALL THE GODS --IT'S LEGENDARY! CAN'T YOU--
LOOK HARD AT YOUR OWN MARRIAGE, ACHILLES, BEFORE YOU QUESTION MINE.
ACHILLES, MY PRECIOUS SON, I WAS BORN IN SERVICE TO THE GODS, RAISED BY THE GODDESS. I'D HOPED TO BE A BRIDE TO A GOD. BUT BECAUSE MY SON WAS DESTINED TO BE GREATER THAN HIS FATHER, THE GODDESS WED ME TO A MORTAL INSTEAD.
AND NOT EVEN THE GREATEST OF MORTALS -- A QUARRELSOME BROTHER-KILLER RULING A SECOND-RATE KINGDOM OF RABBLE AND REFUGEES. I WAS BITTERLY DISAPPOINTED, BUT I HAD ONE JOY FROM IT...
YOU.
THE FIRST TIME I LEFT PHTHIA, I LEFT YOU BEHIND. I WON'T MAKE THAT MISTAKE AGAIN. YOUR FATHER SENDS YOU TO A WAR THAT MEANS IMMINENT DEATH FOR YOU. BUT COME WITH ME AND I'LL KEEP YOU SAFE INTO OLD AGE.
THETIS, DON'T INTERFERE...

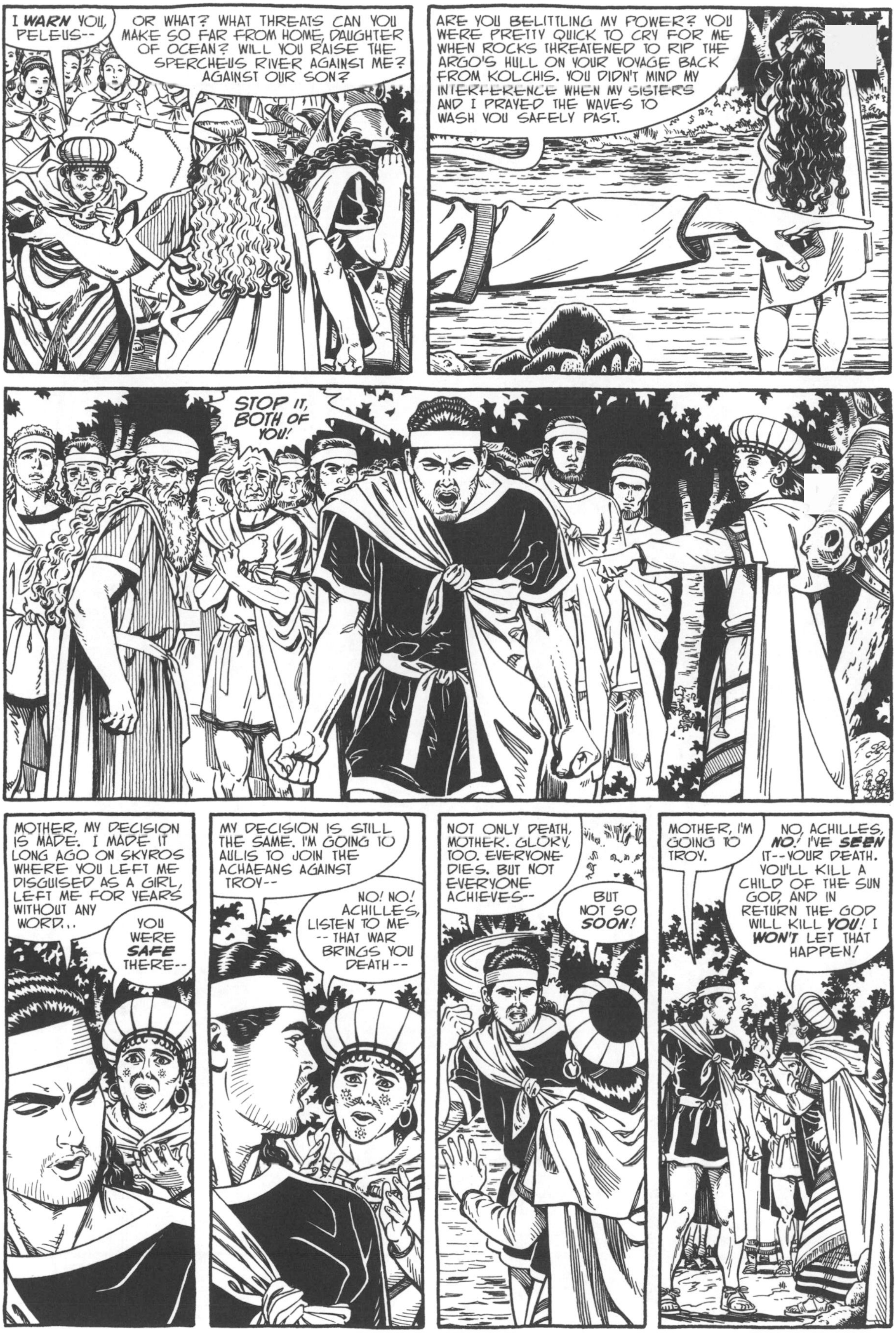
I WARN YOU, PELEUS--
OR WHAT? WHAT THREATS CAN YOU MAKE SO FAR FROM HOME, DAUGHTER OF OCEAN? WILL YOU RAISE THE SPERCHEUS RIVER AGAINST ME? AGAINST OUR SON?
ARE YOU BELITTLING MY POWER? YOU WERE PRETTY QUICK TO CRY FOR ME WHEN ROCKS THREATENED TO RIP THE ARGO'S HULL ON YOUR VOYAGE BACK FROM KOLCHIS. YOU DIDN'T MIND MY INTERFERENCE WHEN MY SISTERS AND I PRAYED THE WAVES TO WASH YOU SAFELY PAST.
STOP IT, BOTH OF YOU!
MOTHER, MY DECISION IS MADE. I MADE IT LONG AGO ON SKYROS WHERE YOU LEFT ME DISGUISED AS A GIRL, LEFT ME FOR YEARS WITHOUT ANY WORD..
YOU WERE SAFE THERE--
MY DECISION IS STILL THE SAME. I'M GOING TO AULIS TO JOIN THE ACHAEANS AGAINST TROY--
NO! NO! ACHILLES, LISTEN TO ME -- THAT WAR BRINGS YOU DEATH --
NOT ONLY DEATH, MOTHER. GLORY, TOO. EVERYONE DIES. BUT NOT EVERYONE ACHIEVES--
BUT NOT SO SOON!
MOTHER, I'M GOING TO TROY.
NO, ACHILLES, NO! I'VE SEEN IT--YOUR DEATH. YOU'LL KILL A CHILD OF THE SUN GOD, AND IN RETURN THE GOD WILL KILL YOU! I WON'T LET THAT HAPPEN!

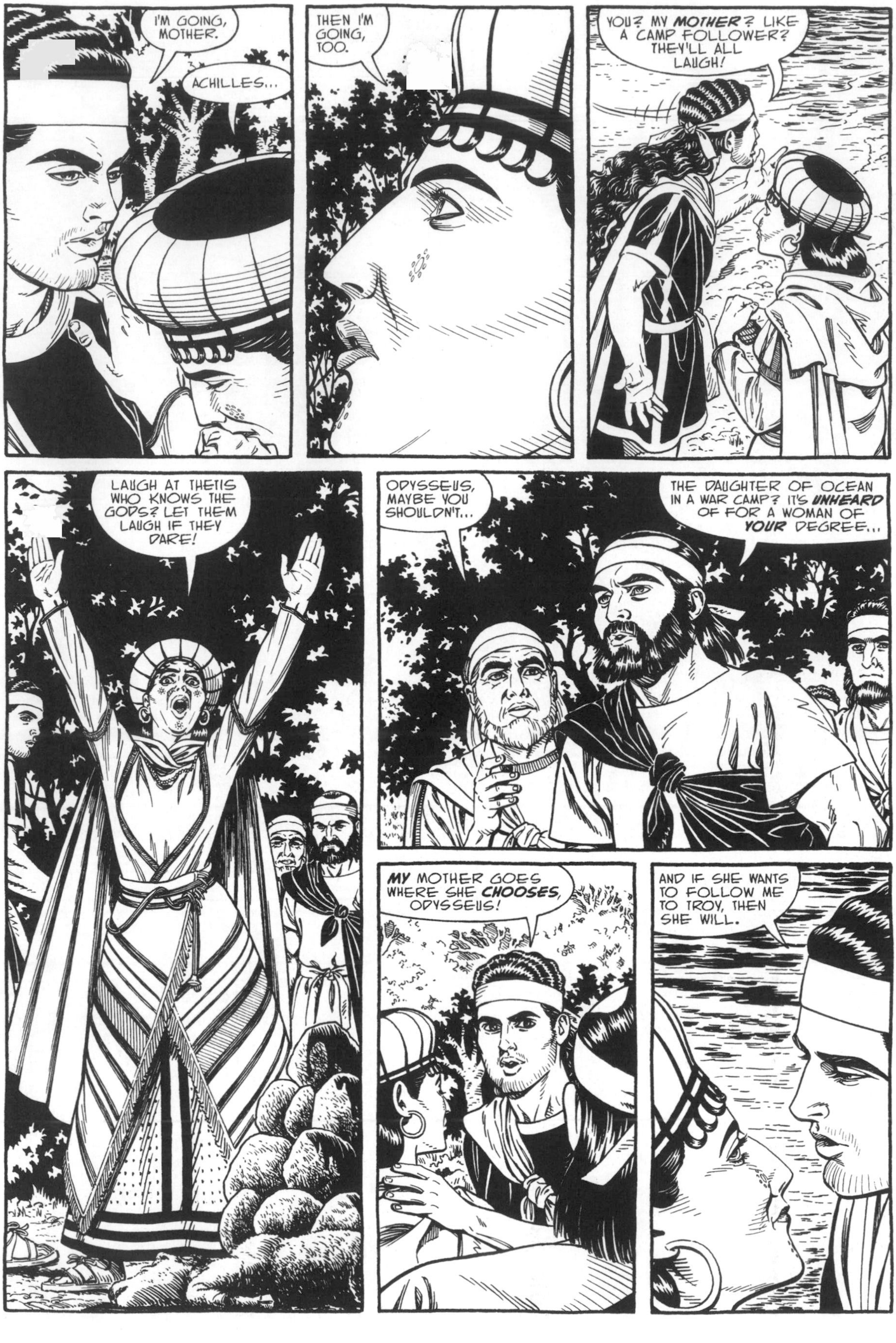
I'M GOING, MOTHER.
ACHILLES...
THEN I'M GOING, TOO.
YOU? MY **MOTHER**? LIKE A CAMP FOLLOWER? THEY'LL ALL LAUGH!
LAUGH AT THETIS WHO KNOWS THE GODS? LET THEM LAUGH IF THEY DARE!
ODYSSEUS, MAYBE YOU SHOULDN'T...
THE DAUGHTER OF OCEAN IN A WAR CAMP? IT'S **UNHEARD** OF FOR A WOMAN OF **YOUR** DEGREE...
MY MOTHER GOES WHERE SHE **CHOOSES**, ODYSSEUS!
AND IF SHE WANTS TO FOLLOW ME TO TROY, THEN SHE WILL.

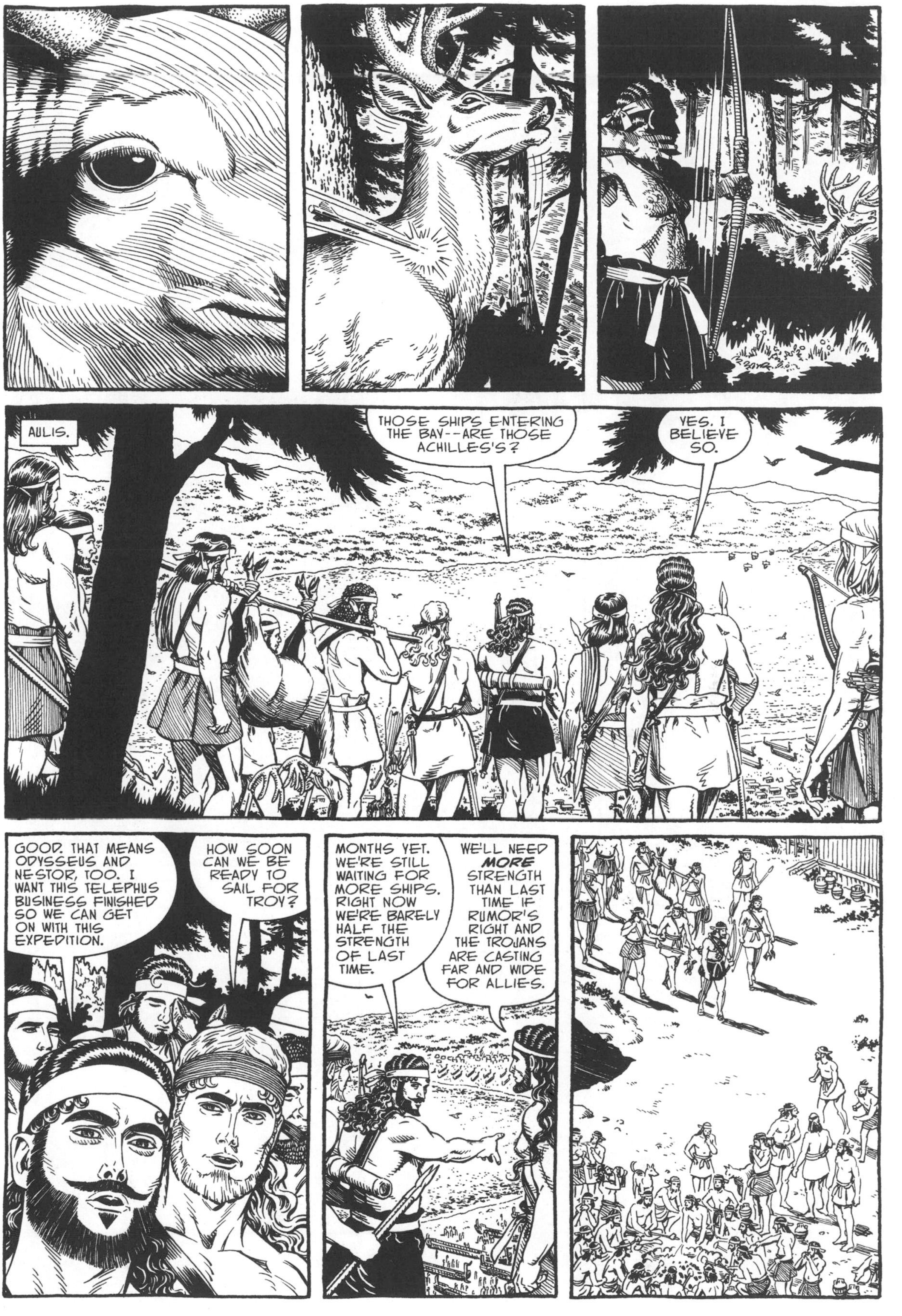
AULIS.
THOSE SHIPS ENTERING THE BAY--ARE THOSE ACHILLES'S?
YES. I BELIEVE SO.
GOOD. THAT MEANS ODYSSEUS AND NESTOR, TOO. I WANT THIS TELEPHUS BUSINESS FINISHED SO WE CAN GET ON WITH THIS EXPEDITION.
HOW SOON CAN WE BE READY TO SAIL FOR TROY?
MONTHS YET. WE'RE STILL WAITING FOR MORE SHIPS. RIGHT NOW WE'RE BARELY HALF THE STRENGTH OF LAST TIME.
WE'LL NEED MORE STRENGTH THAN LAST TIME IF RUMOR'S RIGHT AND THE TROJANS ARE CASTING FAR AND WIDE FOR ALLIES.

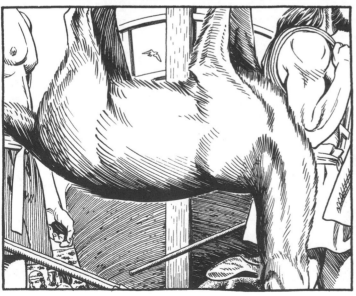

I THINK IT'S THE DEER, AGAMEMNON. NONE OF THEM IS GETTING FOOD HALF SO--

WHAT DO THEY EXPECT? THEY GET *PLENTY* OF GRAIN, OIL, AND WINE FROM DELOS. I CAN'T SHARE ONE DEER AMONG HUNDREDS OF MEN. IF THEY WANT VENISON, THEY SHOULD *HUNT!*

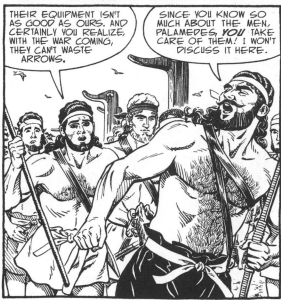

THEIR EQUIPMENT ISN'T AS GOOD AS OURS. AND CERTAINLY YOU REALIZE, WITH THE WAR COMING, THEY CAN'T WASTE ARROWS.

SINCE YOU KNOW SO MUCH ABOUT THE MEN, PALAMEDES, *YOU* TAKE CARE OF THEM! I WON'T DISCUSS IT HERE.

HE JUST SHOT A DEER--WHY IS *HE* IN A BAD MOOD?

YOU NEVER KNOW WHEN TO STOP, DO YOU, PALAMEDES?

WHAT?

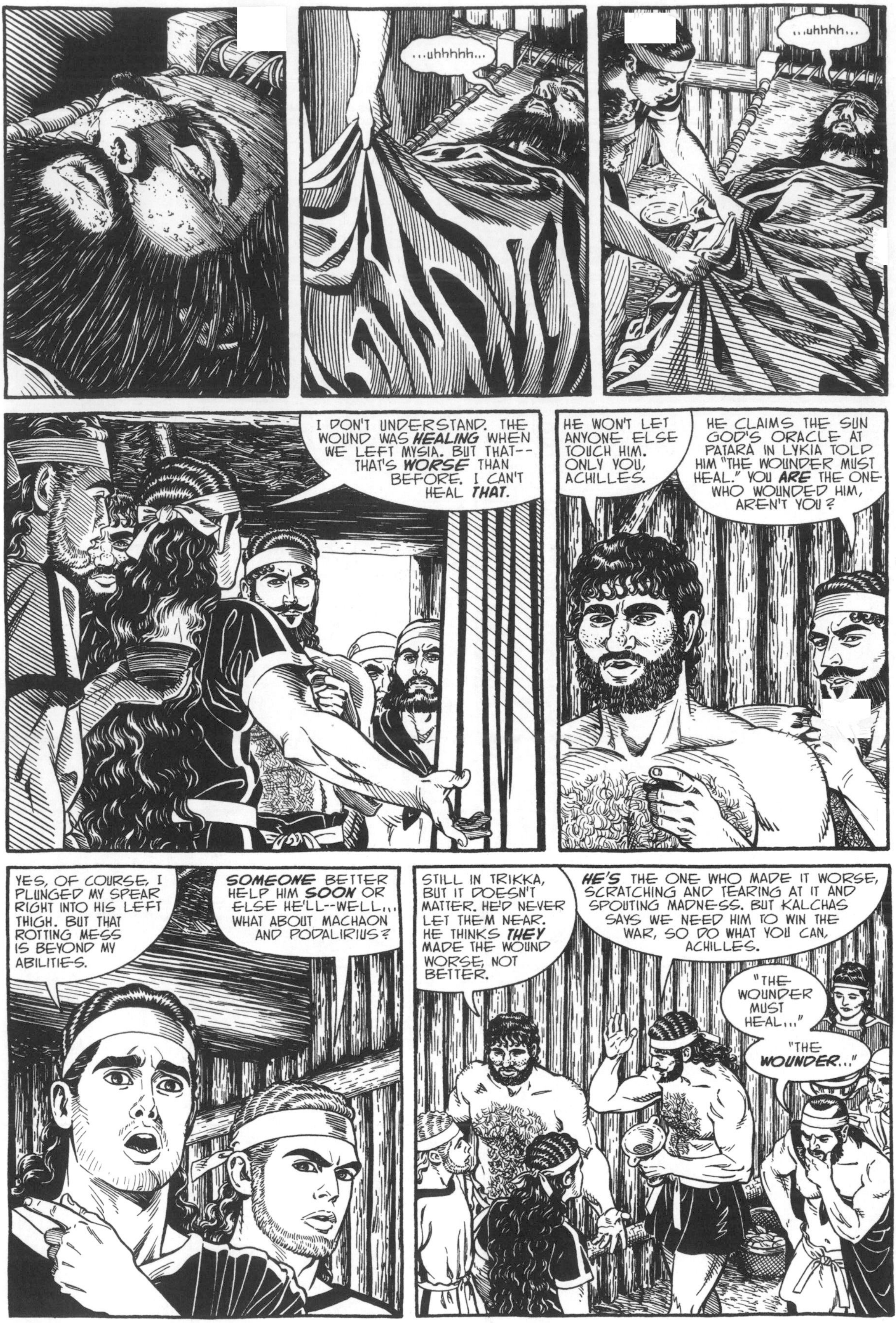
...uhhhhh...
...uhhhh...
I DON'T UNDERSTAND. THE WOUND WAS HEALING WHEN WE LEFT MYSIA. BUT THAT-- THAT'S WORSE THAN BEFORE. I CAN'T HEAL THAT.
HE WON'T LET ANYONE ELSE TOUCH HIM. ONLY YOU, ACHILLES.
HE CLAIMS THE SUN GOD'S ORACLE AT PATARA IN LYKIA TOLD HIM "THE WOUNDER MUST HEAL." YOU ARE THE ONE WHO WOUNDED HIM, AREN'T YOU?
YES, OF COURSE, I PLUNGED MY SPEAR RIGHT INTO HIS LEFT THIGH. BUT THAT ROTTING MESS IS BEYOND MY ABILITIES.
SOMEONE BETTER HELP HIM SOON OR ELSE HE'LL--WELL... WHAT ABOUT MACHAON AND PODALIRIUS?
STILL IN TRIKKA, BUT IT DOESN'T MATTER. HE'D NEVER LET THEM NEAR. HE THINKS THEY MADE THE WOUND WORSE, NOT BETTER.
HE'S THE ONE WHO MADE IT WORSE, SCRATCHING AND TEARING AT IT AND SPOUTING MADNESS. BUT KALCHAS SAYS WE NEED HIM TO WIN THE WAR, SO DO WHAT YOU CAN, ACHILLES.
"THE WOUNDER MUST HEAL..."
"THE WOUNDER..."

THE SPEAR! IT'S ACHILLES'S **SPEAR!** THE SUN GOD'S ORACLE SAID "THE **WOUNDER** MUST HEAL." THE SPEAR IS THE **ACTUAL** WOUNDER.

ARE **YOU** MAD, TOO, ODYSSEUS? HOW CAN A SPEAR HEAL **ANYTHING?**

THERE'S PRECEDENT--MY COUSIN MELAMPUS CURED IPHIKLUS'S IMPOTENCE USING THE KNIFE THAT CAUSED IT. OF COURSE, THAT WAS MORE A WOUND OF THE MIND THAN THE FLESH.

IS THIS ANY DIFFERENT? TELEPHUS WOULDN'T TEAR AT HIS WOUND IF HE WEREN'T **MAD.**

KALCHAS, YOU'RE A PRIEST OF THE SUN GOD. WILL ACHILLES'S SPEAR HEAL TELEPHUS?

OH! UH--≥HEM≤ IF THE ORACLE SAID SO, IT MUST BE TRUE... ≥HEM≤

FINE. I'LL FETCH MY SPEAR, BUT I WANT **YOU** TO FETCH MACHAON AND PODALIRIUS FROM TRIKKA. TELEPHUS MAY NOT WANT THEIR HELP, BUT **I** WANT IT. AND THE **ARMY** WILL NEED THEM AT TROY.

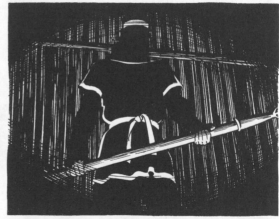

...uhh...

TELEPHUS?

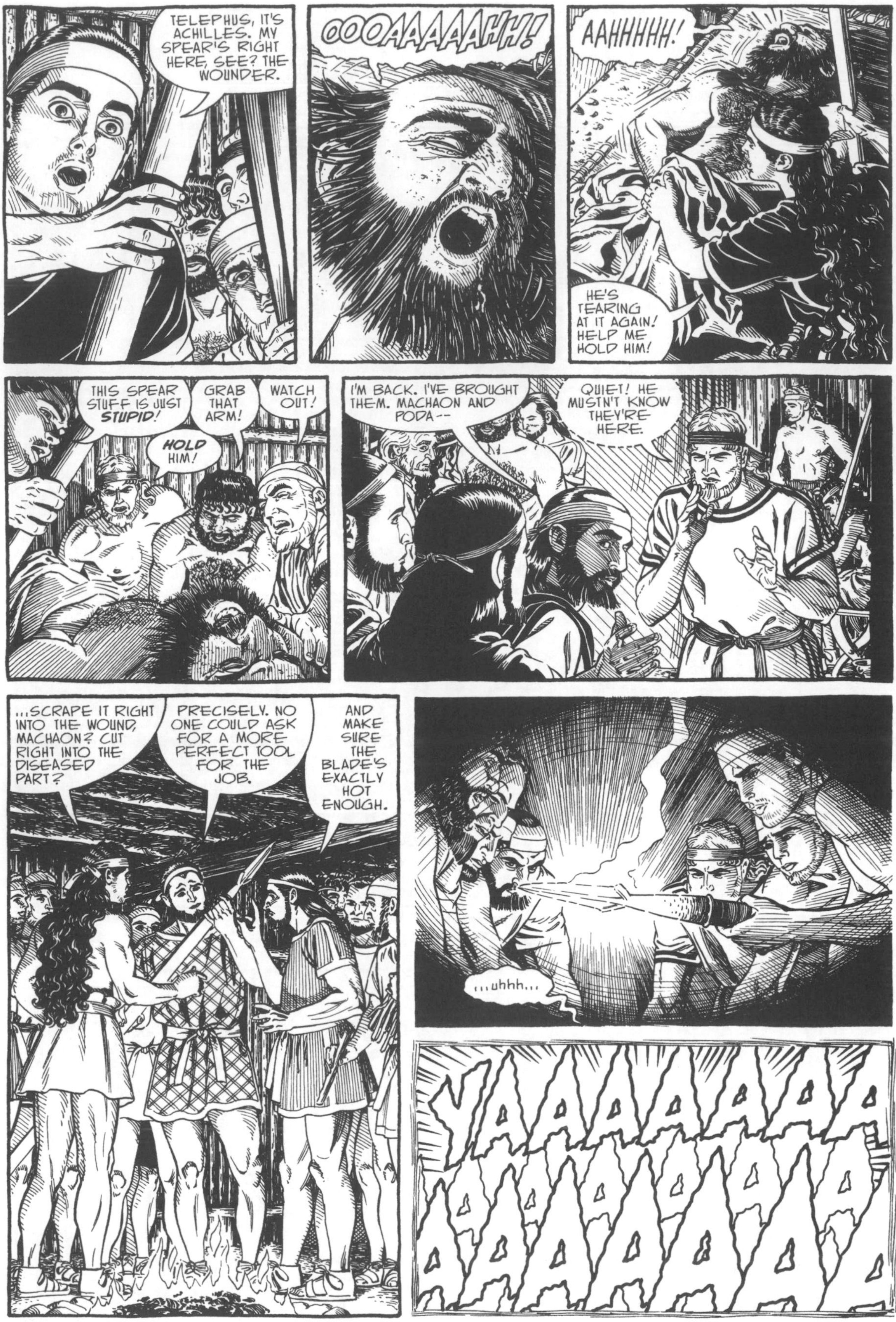
TELEPHUS, IT'S ACHILLES. MY SPEAR'S RIGHT HERE, SEE? THE WOUNDER.
OOOAAAAAAHH!
AAHHHHH!
HE'S TEARING AT IT AGAIN! HELP ME HOLD HIM!
THIS SPEAR STUFF IS JUST STUPID!
GRAB THAT ARM!
WATCH OUT!
HOLD HIM!
I'M BACK. I'VE BROUGHT THEM. MACHAON AND PODA--
QUIET! HE MUSTN'T KNOW THEY'RE HERE.
...SCRAPE IT RIGHT INTO THE WOUND, MACHAON? CUT RIGHT INTO THE DISEASED PART?
PRECISELY. NO ONE COULD ASK FOR A MORE PERFECT TOOL FOR THE JOB.
AND MAKE SURE THE BLADE'S EXACTLY HOT ENOUGH.
...uhhh...
YAAAAAAAAAAAAAAAAAAA

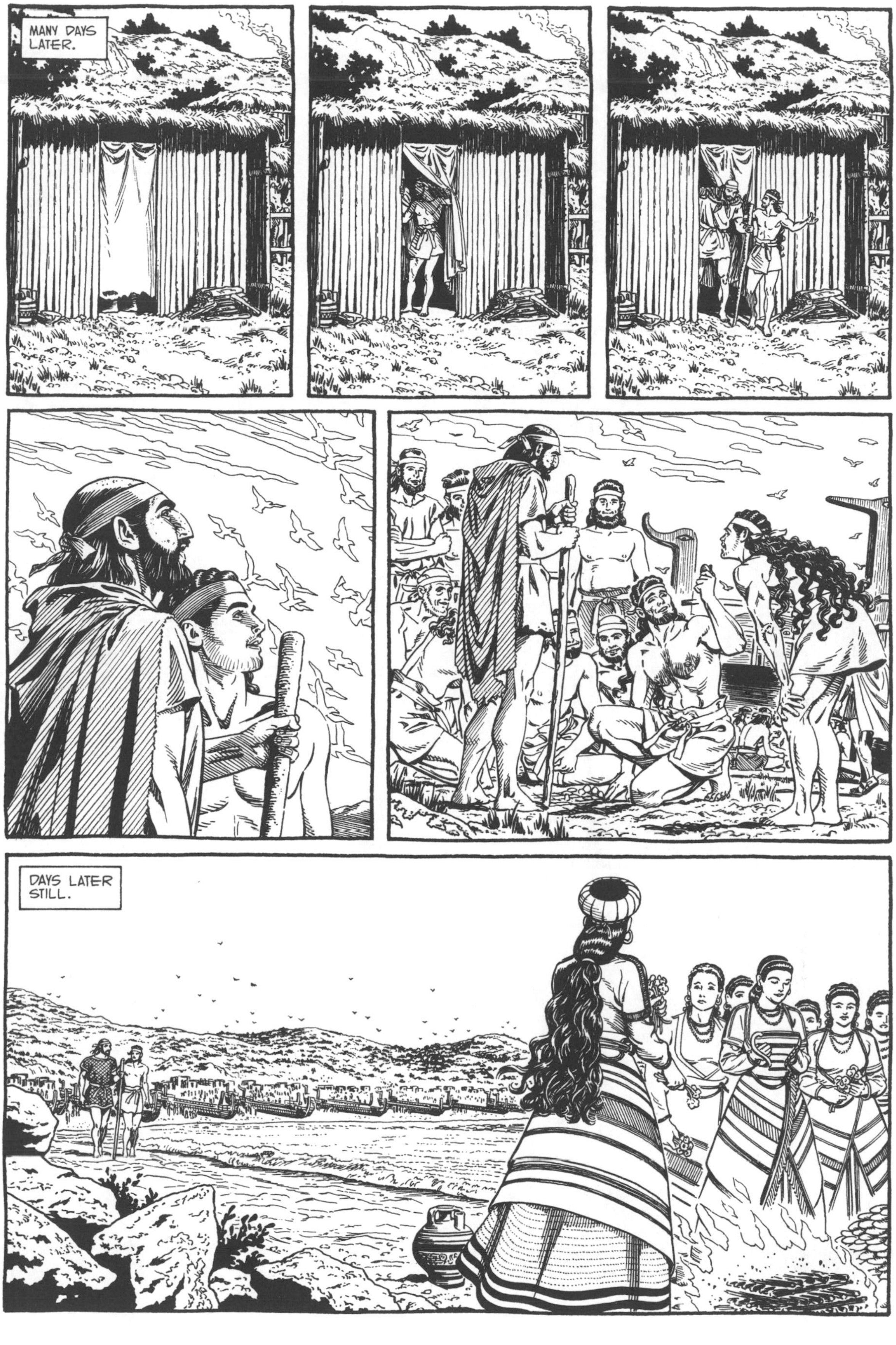
MANY DAYS LATER.
DAYS LATER STILL.

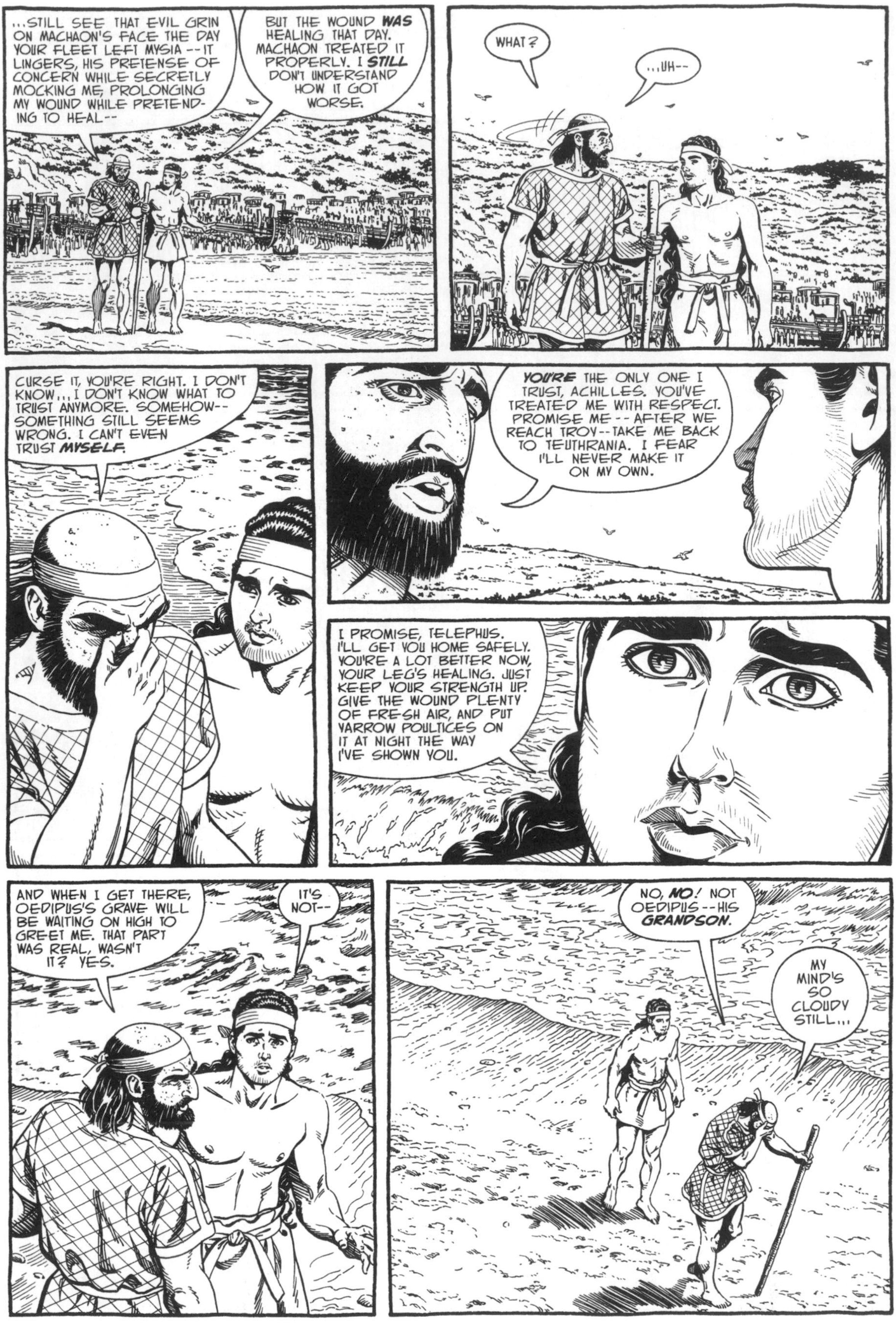
...STILL SEE THAT EVIL GRIN ON MACHAON'S FACE THE DAY YOUR FLEET LEFT MYSIA -- IT LINGERS, HIS PRETENSE OF CONCERN WHILE SECRETLY MOCKING ME, PROLONGING MY WOUND WHILE PRETENDING TO HEAL--
BUT THE WOUND **WAS** HEALING THAT DAY. MACHAON TREATED IT PROPERLY. I **STILL** DON'T UNDERSTAND HOW IT GOT WORSE.
WHAT?
...UH--
CURSE IT, YOU'RE RIGHT. I DON'T KNOW... I DON'T KNOW WHAT TO TRUST ANYMORE. SOMEHOW-- SOMETHING STILL SEEMS WRONG. I CAN'T EVEN TRUST **MYSELF**.
YOU'RE THE ONLY ONE I TRUST, ACHILLES. YOU'VE TREATED ME WITH RESPECT. PROMISE ME -- AFTER WE REACH TROY--TAKE ME BACK TO TEUTHRANIA. I FEAR I'LL NEVER MAKE IT ON MY OWN.
I PROMISE, TELEPHUS. I'LL GET YOU HOME SAFELY. YOU'RE A LOT BETTER NOW, YOUR LEG'S HEALING. JUST KEEP YOUR STRENGTH UP. GIVE THE WOUND PLENTY OF FRESH AIR, AND PUT YARROW POULTICES ON IT AT NIGHT THE WAY I'VE SHOWN YOU.
AND WHEN I GET THERE, OEDIPUS'S GRAVE WILL BE WAITING ON HIGH TO GREET ME. THAT PART WAS REAL, WASN'T IT? YES.
IT'S NOT--
NO, **NO!** NOT OEDIPUS--HIS **GRANDSON**.
MY MIND'S SO CLOUDY STILL...

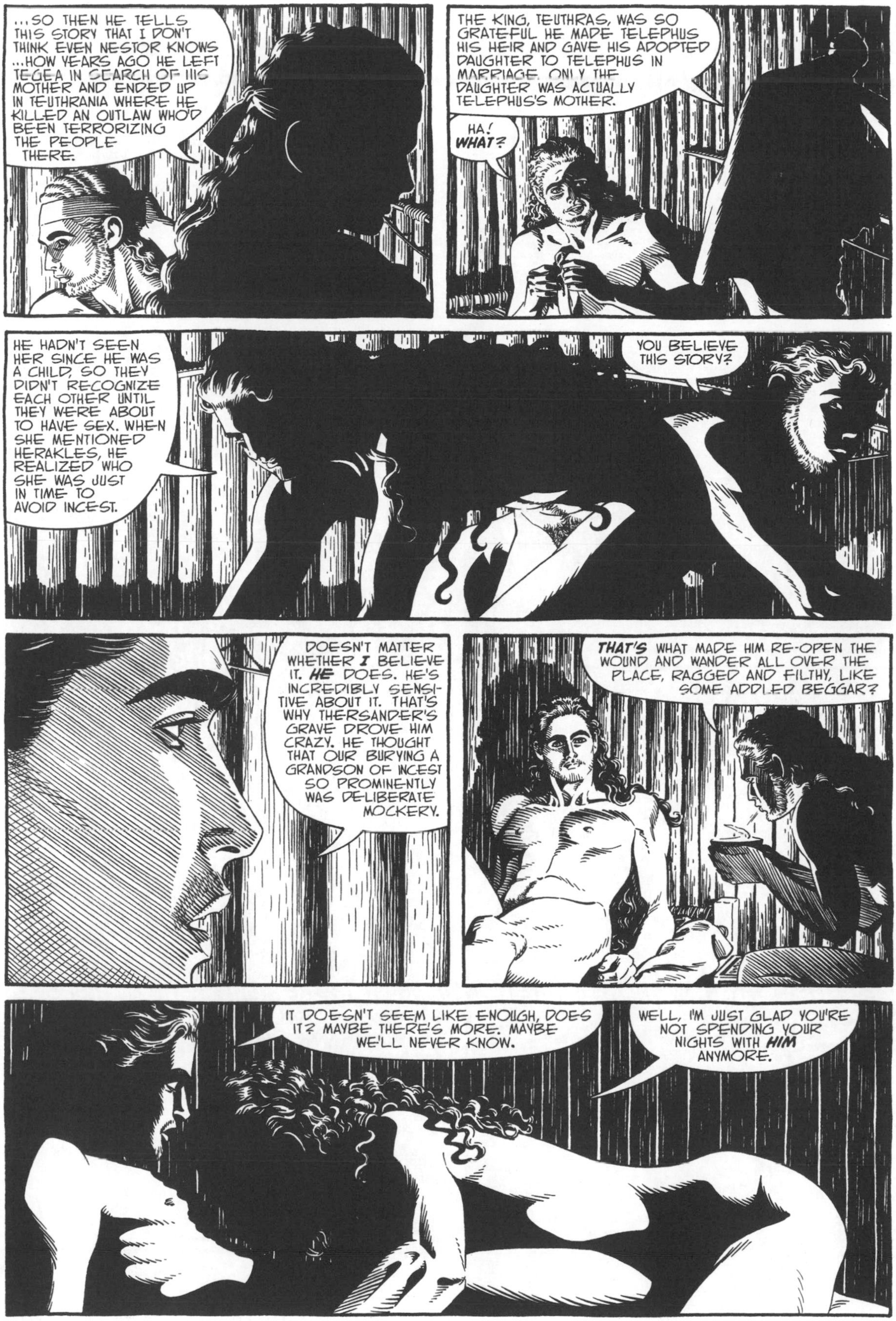

...SO THEN HE TELLS THIS STORY THAT I DON'T THINK EVEN NESTOR KNOWS ...HOW YEARS AGO HE LEFT TEGEA IN SEARCH OF HIS MOTHER AND ENDED UP IN TEUTHRANIA WHERE HE KILLED AN OUTLAW WHO'D BEEN TERRORIZING THE PEOPLE THERE.
THE KING, TEUTHRAS, WAS SO GRATEFUL HE MADE TELEPHUS HIS HEIR AND GAVE HIS ADOPTED DAUGHTER TO TELEPHUS IN MARRIAGE. ONLY THE DAUGHTER WAS ACTUALLY TELEPHUS'S MOTHER.
HA! WHAT?
HE HADN'T SEEN HER SINCE HE WAS A CHILD, SO THEY DIDN'T RECOGNIZE EACH OTHER UNTIL THEY WERE ABOUT TO HAVE SEX. WHEN SHE MENTIONED HERAKLES, HE REALIZED WHO SHE WAS JUST IN TIME TO AVOID INCEST.
YOU BELIEVE THIS STORY?
DOESN'T MATTER WHETHER I BELIEVE IT. HE DOES. HE'S INCREDIBLY SENSITIVE ABOUT IT. THAT'S WHY THERSANDER'S GRAVE DROVE HIM CRAZY. HE THOUGHT THAT OUR BURYING A GRANDSON OF INCEST SO PROMINENTLY WAS DELIBERATE MOCKERY.
THAT'S WHAT MADE HIM RE-OPEN THE WOUND AND WANDER ALL OVER THE PLACE, RAGGED AND FILTHY, LIKE SOME ADDLED BEGGAR?
IT DOESN'T SEEM LIKE ENOUGH, DOES IT? MAYBE THERE'S MORE. MAYBE WE'LL NEVER KNOW.
WELL, I'M JUST GLAD YOU'RE NOT SPENDING YOUR NIGHTS WITH HIM ANYMORE.

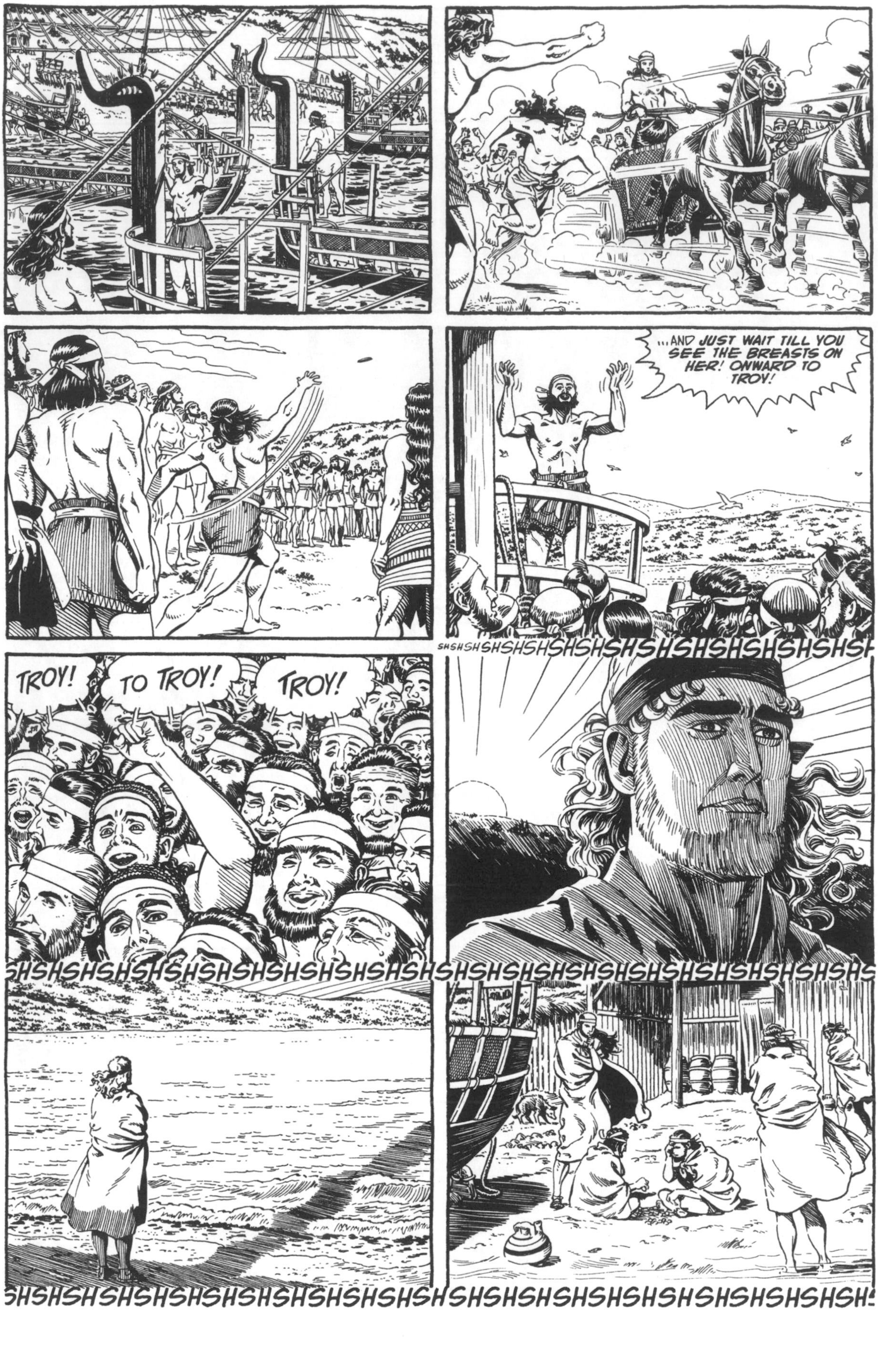
...AND JUST WAIT TILL YOU SEE THE BREASTS ON HER! ONWARD TO TROY!
SHSHSHSHSHSHSHSHSHSHSHSHSHSHSHSHSHSHSHSHSH
TROY!
TO TROY!
TROY!
SHSHSHSHSHSHSHSHSHSHSHSHSHSHSHSHSHSHSHSHSHSHSHSHSHSHSHSHSH
SHSHSHSHSHSHSHSHSHSHSHSHSHSHSHSHSHSHSHSHSHSHSHSHSHSHSHSHSH

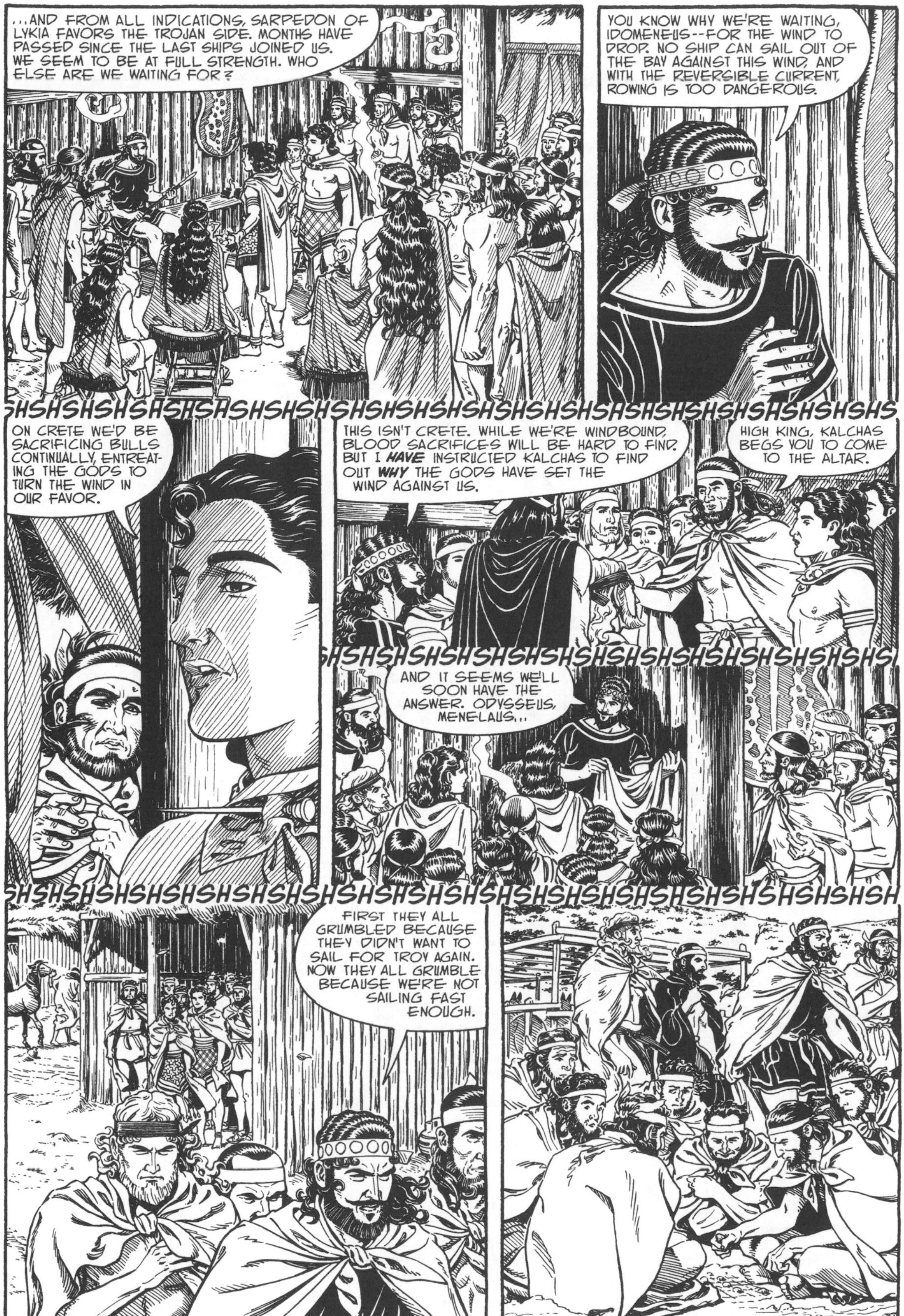
...AND FROM ALL INDICATIONS, SARPEDON OF LYKIA FAVORS THE TROJAN SIDE. MONTHS HAVE PASSED SINCE THE LAST SHIPS JOINED US. WE SEEM TO BE AT FULL STRENGTH. WHO ELSE ARE WE WAITING FOR?
YOU KNOW WHY WE'RE WAITING, IDOMENEUS--FOR THE WIND TO DROP. NO SHIP CAN SAIL OUT OF THE BAY AGAINST THIS WIND, AND WITH THE REVERSIBLE CURRENT, ROWING IS TOO DANGEROUS.
SHSHSHSHSHSHSHSHSHSHSHSHSHSHSHSHSHSHSHSHSHS
ON CRETE WE'D BE SACRIFICING BULLS CONTINUALLY, ENTREATING THE GODS TO TURN THE WIND IN OUR FAVOR.
THIS ISN'T CRETE. WHILE WE'RE WINDBOUND, BLOOD SACRIFICES WILL BE HARD TO FIND. BUT I HAVE INSTRUCTED KALCHAS TO FIND OUT WHY THE GODS HAVE SET THE WIND AGAINST US.
HIGH KING, KALCHAS BEGS YOU TO COME TO THE ALTAR.
AND IT SEEMS WE'LL SOON HAVE THE ANSWER. ODYSSEUS, MENELAUS...
FIRST THEY ALL GRUMBLED BECAUSE THEY DIDN'T WANT TO SAIL FOR TROY AGAIN. NOW THEY ALL GRUMBLE BECAUSE WE'RE NOT SAILING FAST ENOUGH.

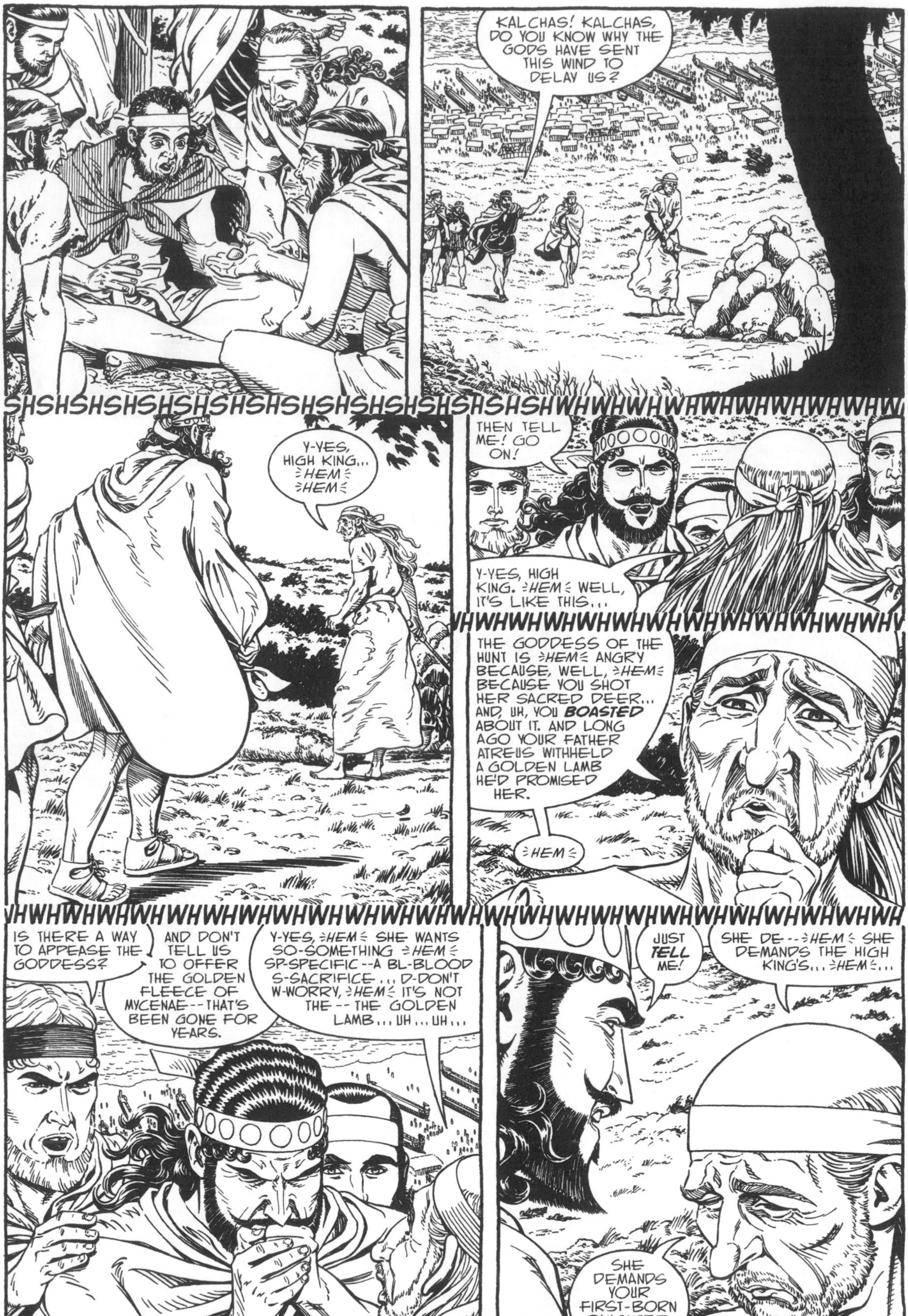
KALCHAS! KALCHAS, DO YOU KNOW WHY THE GODS HAVE SENT THIS WIND TO DELAY US?
SHSHSHSHSHSHSHSHSHSHSHSHSHSHSHSHWHWHWHWHWHWHWHWH
Y-YES, HIGH KING... HEM HEM
THEN TELL ME! GO ON!
Y-YES, HIGH KING. HEM WELL, IT'S LIKE THIS...
THE GODDESS OF THE HUNT IS HEM ANGRY BECAUSE, WELL, HEM BECAUSE YOU SHOT HER SACRED DEER... AND, UH, YOU BOASTED ABOUT IT. AND LONG AGO YOUR FATHER ATREUS WITHHELD A GOLDEN LAMB HE'D PROMISED HER.
HEM
IS THERE A WAY TO APPEASE THE GODDESS?
AND DON'T TELL US TO OFFER THE GOLDEN FLEECE OF MYCENAE--THAT'S BEEN GONE FOR YEARS.
Y-YES, HEM SHE WANTS SO-SOMETHING HEM SP-SPECIFIC--A BL-BLOOD S-SACRIFICE... D-DON'T W-WORRY, HEM IT'S NOT THE--THE GOLDEN LAMB... UH... UH...
JUST TELL ME!
SHE DE--HEM SHE DEMANDS THE HIGH KING'S... HEM...
SHE DEMANDS YOUR FIRST-BORN DAUGHTER.

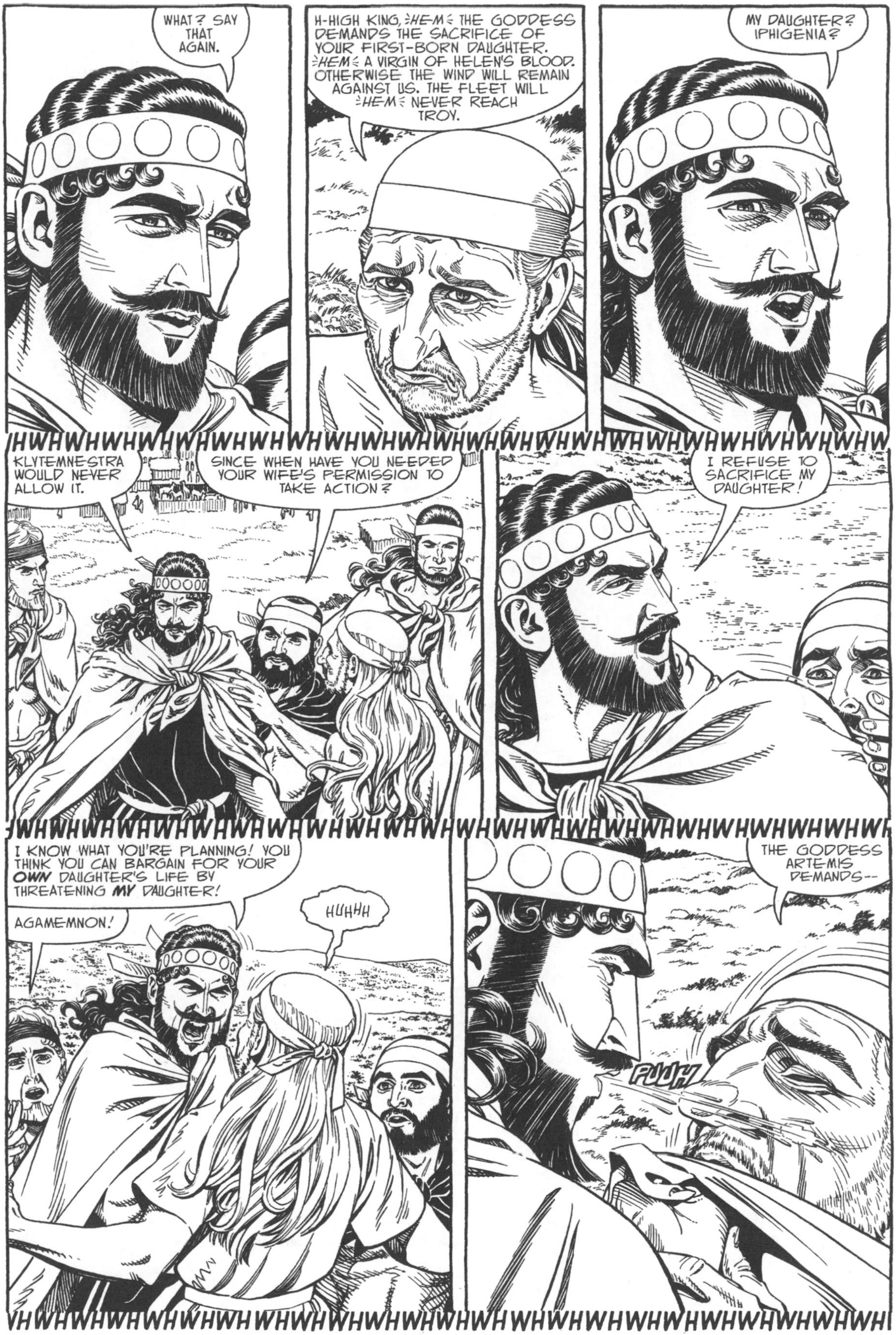
WHAT? SAY THAT AGAIN.
H-HIGH KING, *HEM* THE GODDESS DEMANDS THE SACRIFICE OF YOUR FIRST-BORN DAUGHTER. *HEM* A VIRGIN OF HELEN'S BLOOD. OTHERWISE THE WIND WILL REMAIN AGAINST US. THE FLEET WILL *HEM* NEVER REACH TROY.
MY DAUGHTER? IPHIGENIA?
WHWHWHWHWHWHWHWHWHWHWHWHWHWHWHWHWHWHWHWHW
KLYTEMNESTRA WOULD NEVER ALLOW IT.
SINCE WHEN HAVE YOU NEEDED YOUR WIFE'S PERMISSION TO TAKE ACTION?
I REFUSE TO SACRIFICE MY DAUGHTER!
WHWHWHWHWHWHWHWHWHWHWHWHWHWHWHWHWHWHWHWHW
I KNOW WHAT YOU'RE PLANNING! YOU THINK YOU CAN BARGAIN FOR YOUR **OWN** DAUGHTER'S LIFE BY THREATENING **MY** DAUGHTER!
AGAMEMNON!
HUHHH
THE GODDESS ARTEMIS DEMANDS--
PUUH
WHWHWHWHWHWHWHWHWHWHWHWHWHWHWHWHWHWHWHWHW

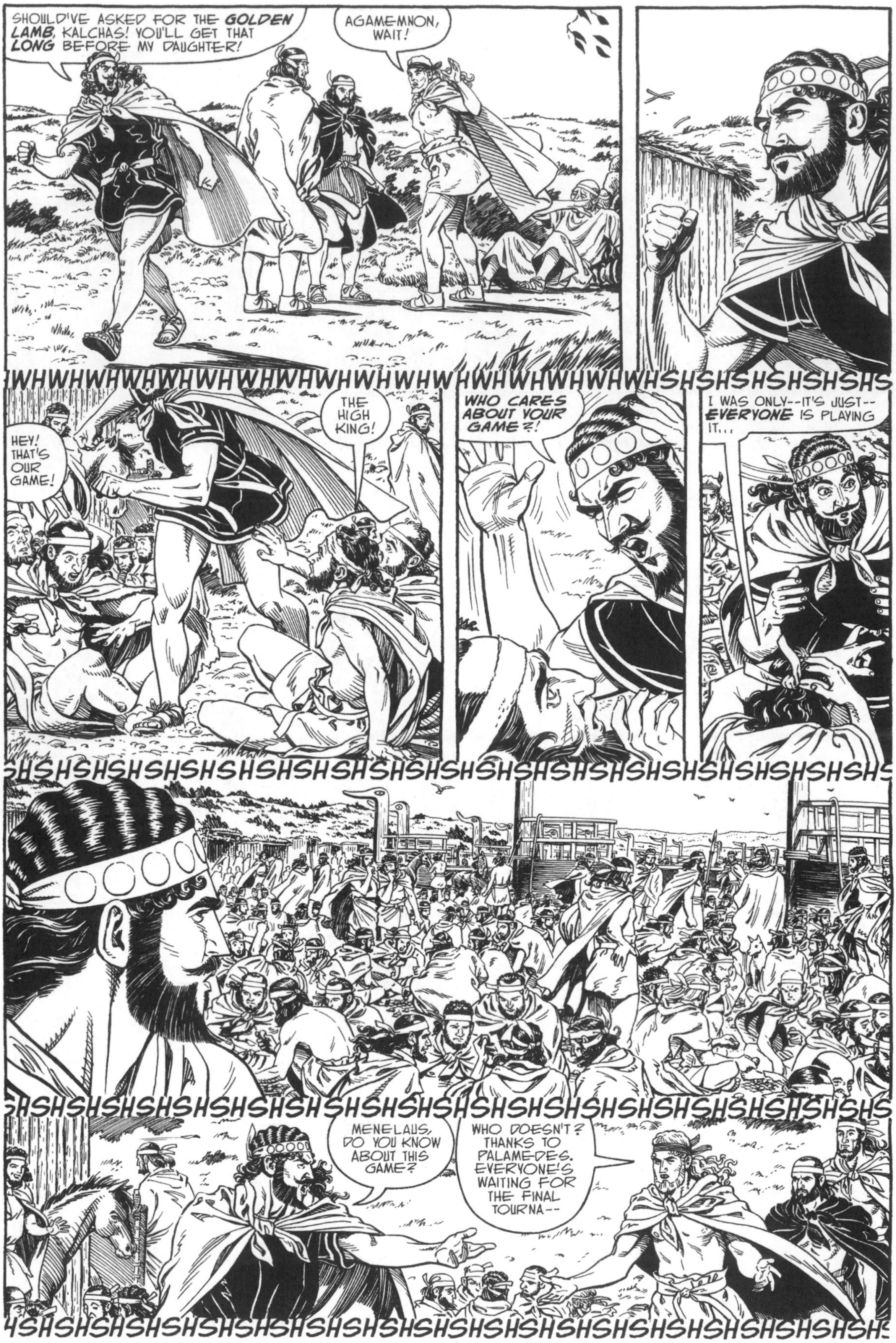
SHOULD'VE ASKED FOR THE GOLDEN LAMB, KALCHAS! YOU'LL GET THAT LONG BEFORE MY DAUGHTER!
AGAMEMNON, WAIT!
WHWHWHWHWHWHWHWHWHWHWHWHWHW
HEY! THAT'S OUR GAME!
THE HIGH KING!
WHO CARES ABOUT YOUR GAME?!
I WAS ONLY--IT'S JUST-- EVERYONE IS PLAYING IT...
SHSHSHSHSHSHSHSHSHSHSHSHSHSH
MENELAUS, DO YOU KNOW ABOUT THIS GAME?
WHO DOESN'T? THANKS TO PALAMEDES. EVERYONE'S WAITING FOR THE FINAL TOURNA--

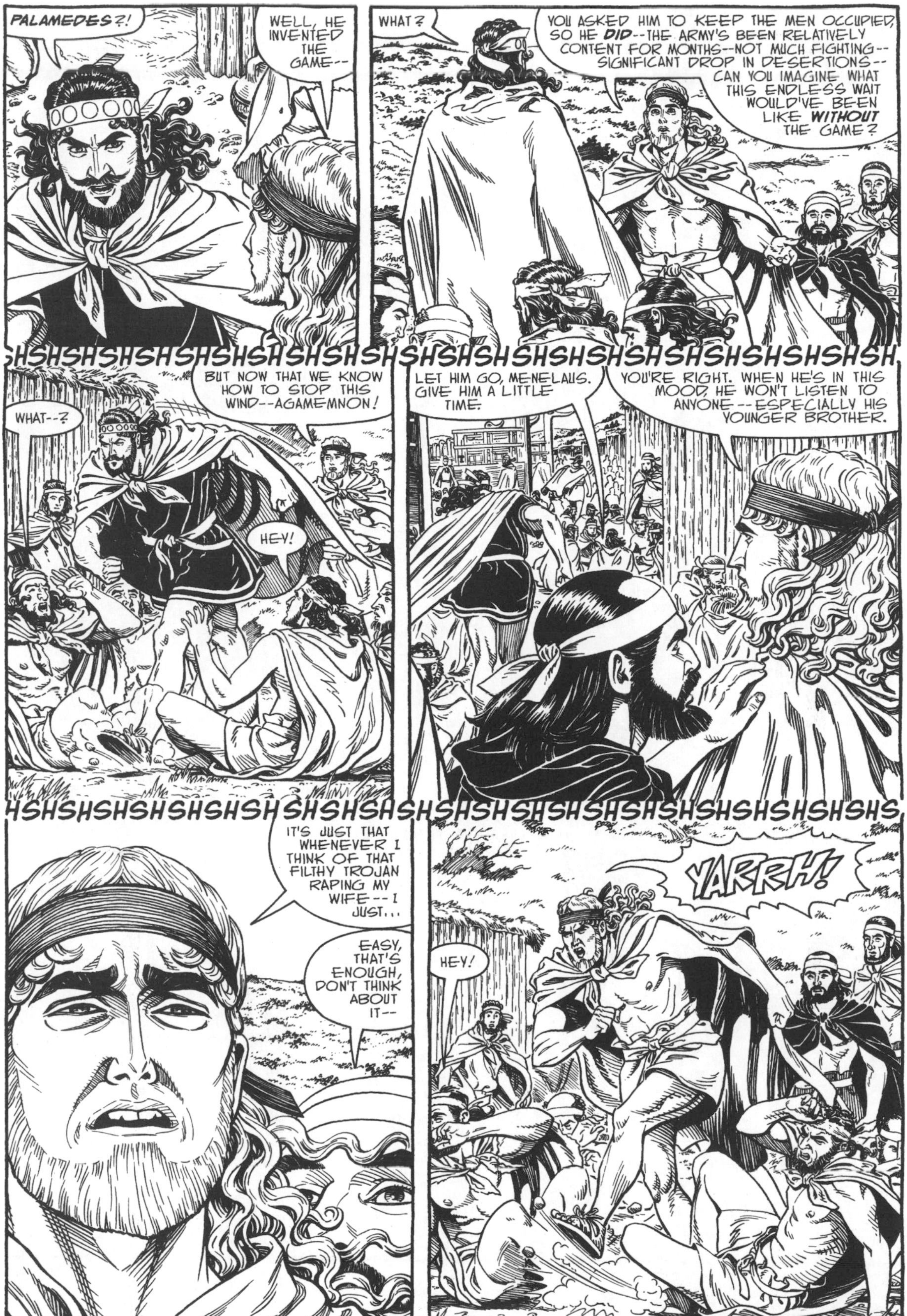
PALAMEDES?!
WELL, HE INVENTED THE GAME--
WHAT?
YOU ASKED HIM TO KEEP THE MEN OCCUPIED, SO HE DID--THE ARMY'S BEEN RELATIVELY CONTENT FOR MONTHS--NOT MUCH FIGHTING--SIGNIFICANT DROP IN DESERTIONS--CAN YOU IMAGINE WHAT THIS ENDLESS WAIT WOULD'VE BEEN LIKE WITHOUT THE GAME?
SHSHSHSHSHSHSHSHSHSHSHSHSHSHSHSHSHSHSHSH
WHAT--?
BUT NOW THAT WE KNOW HOW TO STOP THIS WIND--AGAMEMNON!
HEY!
LET HIM GO, MENELAUS. GIVE HIM A LITTLE TIME.
YOU'RE RIGHT. WHEN HE'S IN THIS MOOD, HE WON'T LISTEN TO ANYONE--ESPECIALLY HIS YOUNGER BROTHER.
SHSHSHSHSHSHSHSHSHSHSHSHSHSHSHSHSHSHSHSHS
IT'S JUST THAT WHENEVER I THINK OF THAT FILTHY TROJAN RAPING MY WIFE--I JUST...
EASY, THAT'S ENOUGH, DON'T THINK ABOUT IT--
YARRH!
HEY!
SHSHSHSHSHSHSHSHSHSHSHSHSHSHSHSHSHSHSHSHS

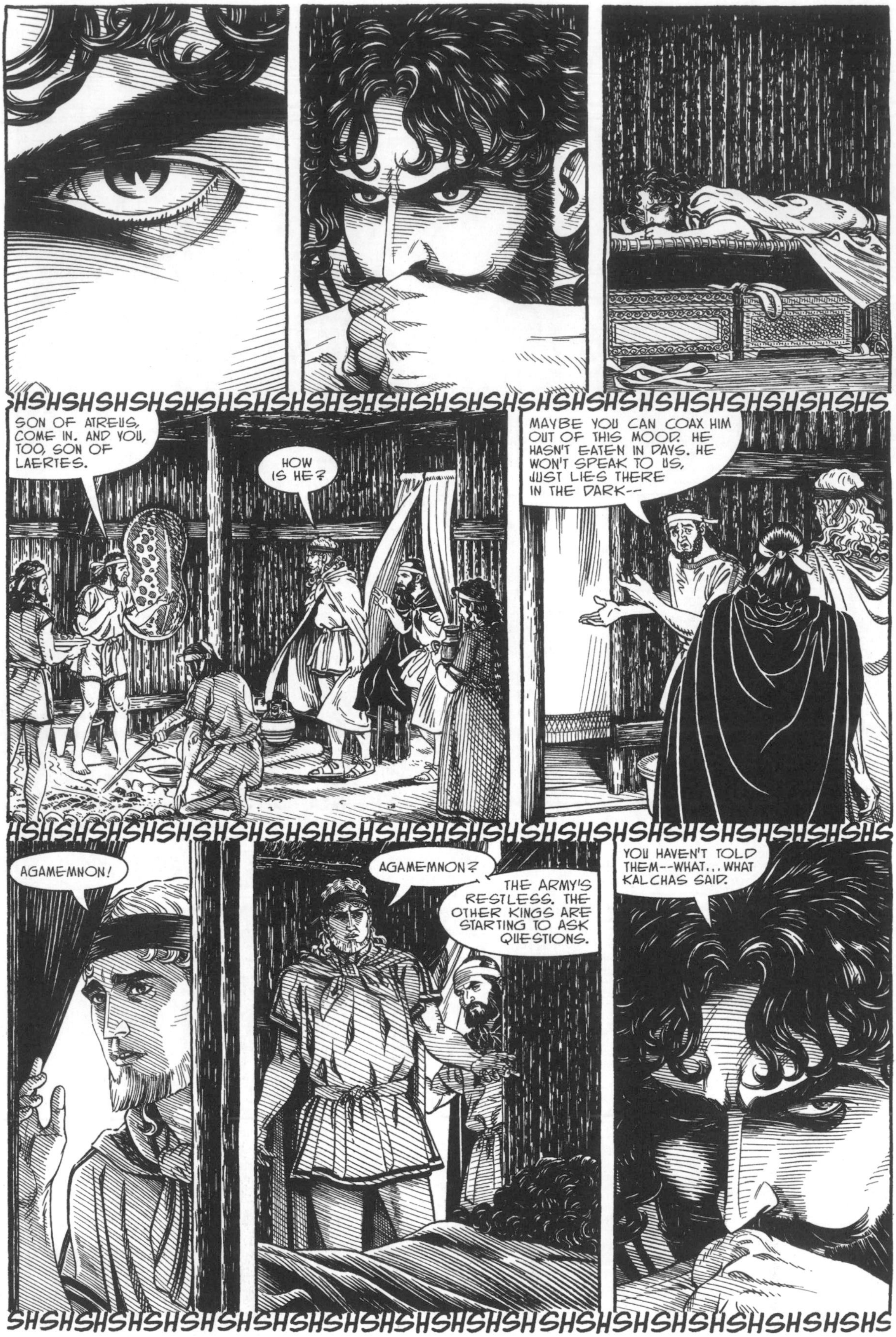
SHSHSHSHSHSHSHSHSHSHSHSHSHSHSHSHSHSHSHS
SON OF ATREUS, COME IN. AND YOU, TOO, SON OF LAERTES.
HOW IS HE?
MAYBE YOU CAN COAX HIM OUT OF THIS MOOD. HE HASN'T EATEN IN DAYS. HE WON'T SPEAK TO US, JUST LIES THERE IN THE DARK--
SHSHSHSHSHSHSHSHSHSHSHSHSHSHSHSHSHSHSHS
AGAMEMNON!
AGAMEMNON?
THE ARMY'S RESTLESS. THE OTHER KINGS ARE STARTING TO ASK QUESTIONS.
YOU HAVEN'T TOLD THEM--WHAT... WHAT KALCHAS SAID.
SHSHSHSHSHSHSHSHSHSHSHSHSHSHSHSHSHSHSHS

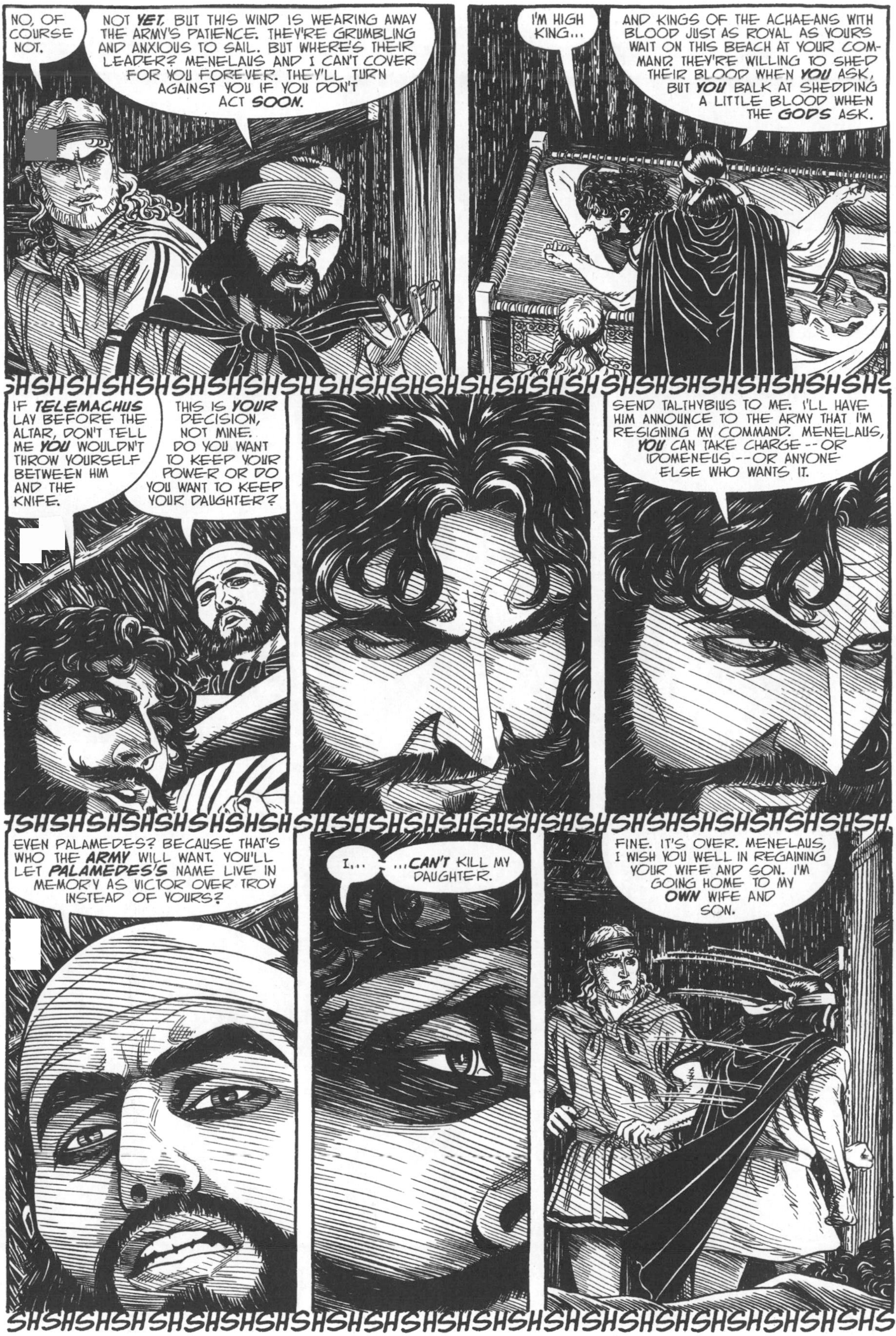
NO, OF COURSE NOT.
NOT YET. BUT THIS WIND IS WEARING AWAY THE ARMY'S PATIENCE. THEY'RE GRUMBLING AND ANXIOUS TO SAIL. BUT WHERE'S THEIR LEADER? MENELAUS AND I CAN'T COVER FOR YOU FOREVER. THEY'LL TURN AGAINST YOU IF YOU DON'T ACT SOON.
I'M HIGH KING...
AND KINGS OF THE ACHAEANS WITH BLOOD JUST AS ROYAL AS YOURS WAIT ON THIS BEACH AT YOUR COMMAND. THEY'RE WILLING TO SHED THEIR BLOOD WHEN YOU ASK, BUT YOU BALK AT SHEDDING A LITTLE BLOOD WHEN THE GODS ASK.
IF TELEMACHUS LAY BEFORE THE ALTAR, DON'T TELL ME YOU WOULDN'T THROW YOURSELF BETWEEN HIM AND THE KNIFE.
THIS IS YOUR DECISION, NOT MINE. DO YOU WANT TO KEEP YOUR POWER OR DO YOU WANT TO KEEP YOUR DAUGHTER?
SEND TALTHYBIUS TO ME. I'LL HAVE HIM ANNOUNCE TO THE ARMY THAT I'M RESIGNING MY COMMAND. MENELAUS, YOU CAN TAKE CHARGE --OR IDOMENEUS --OR ANYONE ELSE WHO WANTS IT.
EVEN PALAMEDES? BECAUSE THAT'S WHO THE ARMY WILL WANT. YOU'LL LET PALAMEDES'S NAME LIVE IN MEMORY AS VICTOR OVER TROY INSTEAD OF YOURS?
I...
...CAN'T KILL MY DAUGHTER.
FINE. IT'S OVER. MENELAUS, I WISH YOU WELL IN REGAINING YOUR WIFE AND SON. I'M GOING HOME TO MY OWN WIFE AND SON.

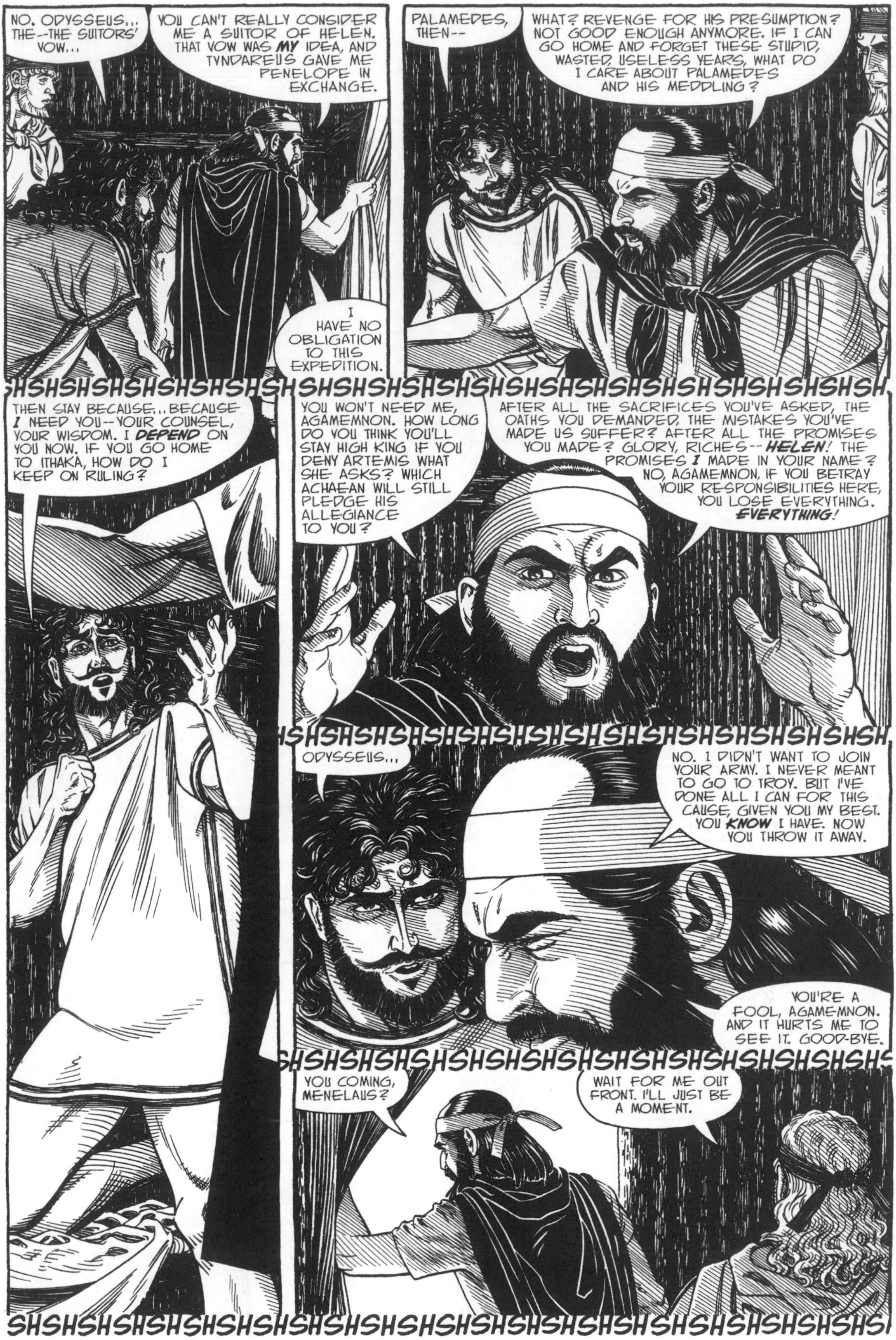
NO. ODYSSEUS... THE--THE SUITORS' VOW...
YOU CAN'T REALLY CONSIDER ME A SUITOR OF HELEN. THAT VOW WAS MY IDEA, AND TYNDAREUS GAVE ME PENELOPE IN EXCHANGE.
I HAVE NO OBLIGATION TO THIS EXPEDITION.
PALAMEDES, THEN--
WHAT? REVENGE FOR HIS PRESUMPTION? NOT GOOD ENOUGH ANYMORE. IF I CAN GO HOME AND FORGET THESE STUPID, WASTED, USELESS YEARS, WHAT DO I CARE ABOUT PALAMEDES AND HIS MEDDLING?
SHSHSHSHSHSHSHSHSHSHSHSHSHSHSHSHSHSHSHSHSHSHSH
THEN STAY BECAUSE... BECAUSE I NEED YOU--YOUR COUNSEL, YOUR WISDOM. I DEPEND ON YOU NOW. IF YOU GO HOME TO ITHAKA, HOW DO I KEEP ON RULING?
YOU WON'T NEED ME, AGAMEMNON. HOW LONG DO YOU THINK YOU'LL STAY HIGH KING IF YOU DENY ARTEMIS WHAT SHE ASKS? WHICH ACHAEAN WILL STILL PLEDGE HIS ALLEGIANCE TO YOU?
AFTER ALL THE SACRIFICES YOU'VE ASKED, THE OATHS YOU DEMANDED, THE MISTAKES YOU'VE MADE US SUFFER? AFTER ALL THE PROMISES YOU MADE? GLORY, RICHES--HELEN! THE PROMISES I MADE IN YOUR NAME? NO, AGAMEMNON, IF YOU BETRAY YOUR RESPONSIBILITIES HERE, YOU LOSE EVERYTHING. EVERYTHING!
SHSHSHSHSHSHSHSHSHSHSHSHSHSHSHSH
ODYSSEUS...
NO. I DIDN'T WANT TO JOIN YOUR ARMY. I NEVER MEANT TO GO TO TROY. BUT I'VE DONE ALL I CAN FOR THIS CAUSE, GIVEN YOU MY BEST. YOU KNOW I HAVE. NOW YOU THROW IT AWAY.
YOU'RE A FOOL, AGAMEMNON. AND IT HURTS ME TO SEE IT. GOOD-BYE.
SHSHSHSHSHSHSHSHSHSHSHSHSHSHSHSHS
YOU COMING, MENELAUS?
WAIT FOR ME OUT FRONT. I'LL JUST BE A MOMENT.
SHSHSHSHSHSHSHSHSHSHSHSHSHSHSHSHSHSHSHSHSHSHSHSHSHSHSHSHSHSHSHSHSHSHSHSHSHSHSHSHSHSHSHSHSHSHSHSHSHSHSHSHSHSHSHSHSHSHSHSHS

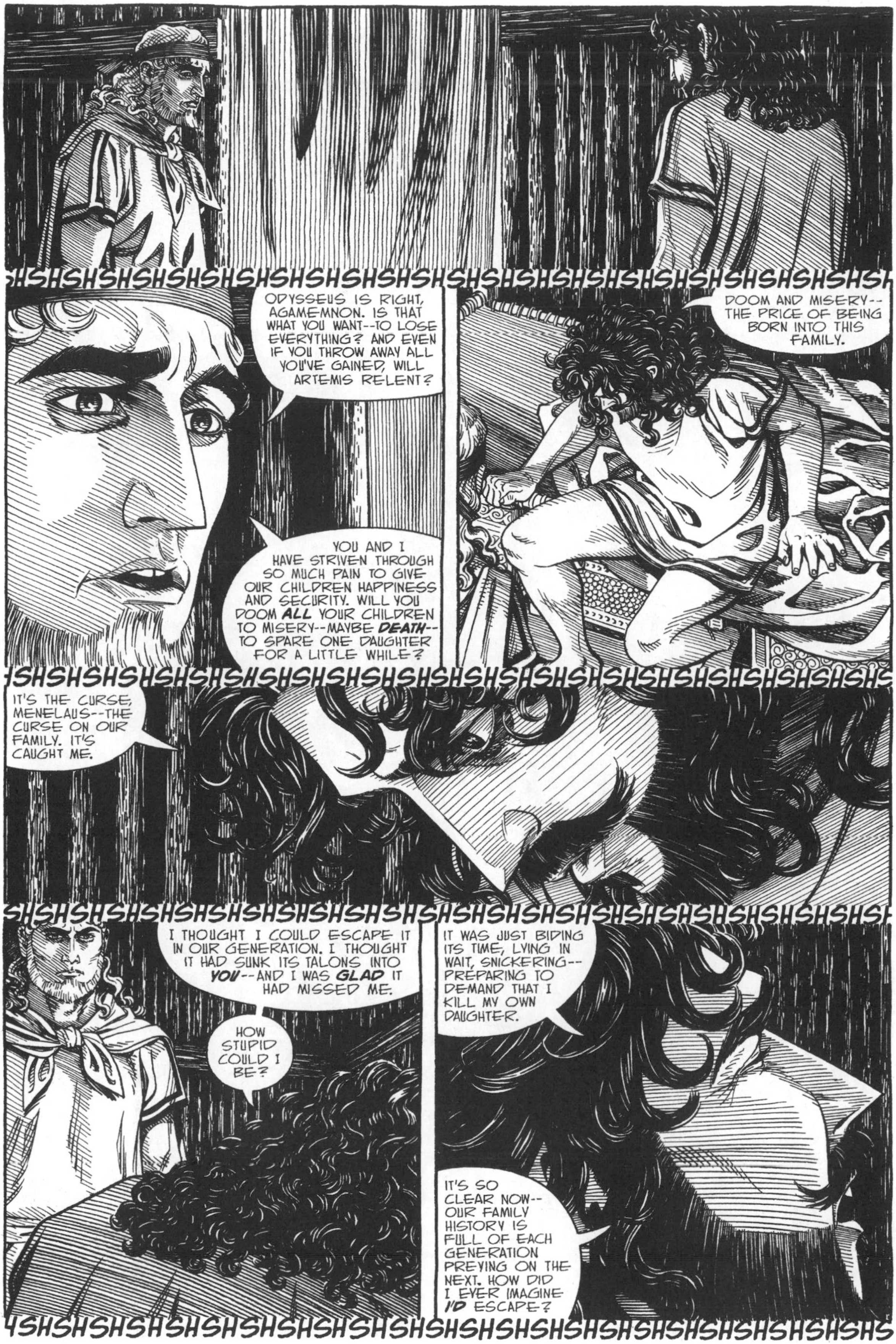
SHSHSHSHSHSHSHSHSHSHSHSHSHSHSHSHSHSHSHSHSHSHSHSHSHSHSH
ODYSSEUS IS RIGHT, AGAMEMNON. IS THAT WHAT YOU WANT--TO LOSE EVERYTHING? AND EVEN IF YOU THROW AWAY ALL YOU'VE GAINED, WILL ARTEMIS RELENT?
YOU AND I HAVE STRIVEN THROUGH SO MUCH PAIN TO GIVE OUR CHILDREN HAPPINESS AND SECURITY. WILL YOU DOOM ALL YOUR CHILDREN TO MISERY--MAYBE DEATH--TO SPARE ONE DAUGHTER FOR A LITTLE WHILE?
DOOM AND MISERY--THE PRICE OF BEING BORN INTO THIS FAMILY.
SHSHSHSHSHSHSHSHSHSHSHSHSHSHSHSHSHSHSHSHSHSHSHSHSHSHSH
IT'S THE CURSE, MENELAUS--THE CURSE ON OUR FAMILY. IT'S CAUGHT ME.
SHSHSHSHSHSHSHSHSHSHSHSHSHSHSHSHSHSHSHSHSHSHSHSHSHSHSH
I THOUGHT I COULD ESCAPE IT IN OUR GENERATION. I THOUGHT IT HAD SUNK ITS TALONS INTO YOU--AND I WAS GLAD IT HAD MISSED ME.
HOW STUPID COULD I BE?
IT WAS JUST BIDING ITS TIME, LYING IN WAIT, SNICKERING--PREPARING TO DEMAND THAT I KILL MY OWN DAUGHTER.
IT'S SO CLEAR NOW--OUR FAMILY HISTORY IS FULL OF EACH GENERATION PREYING ON THE NEXT. HOW DID I EVER IMAGINE I'D ESCAPE?
SHSHSHSHSHSHSHSHSHSHSHSHSHSHSHSHSHSHSHSHSHSHSHSHSHSHSH

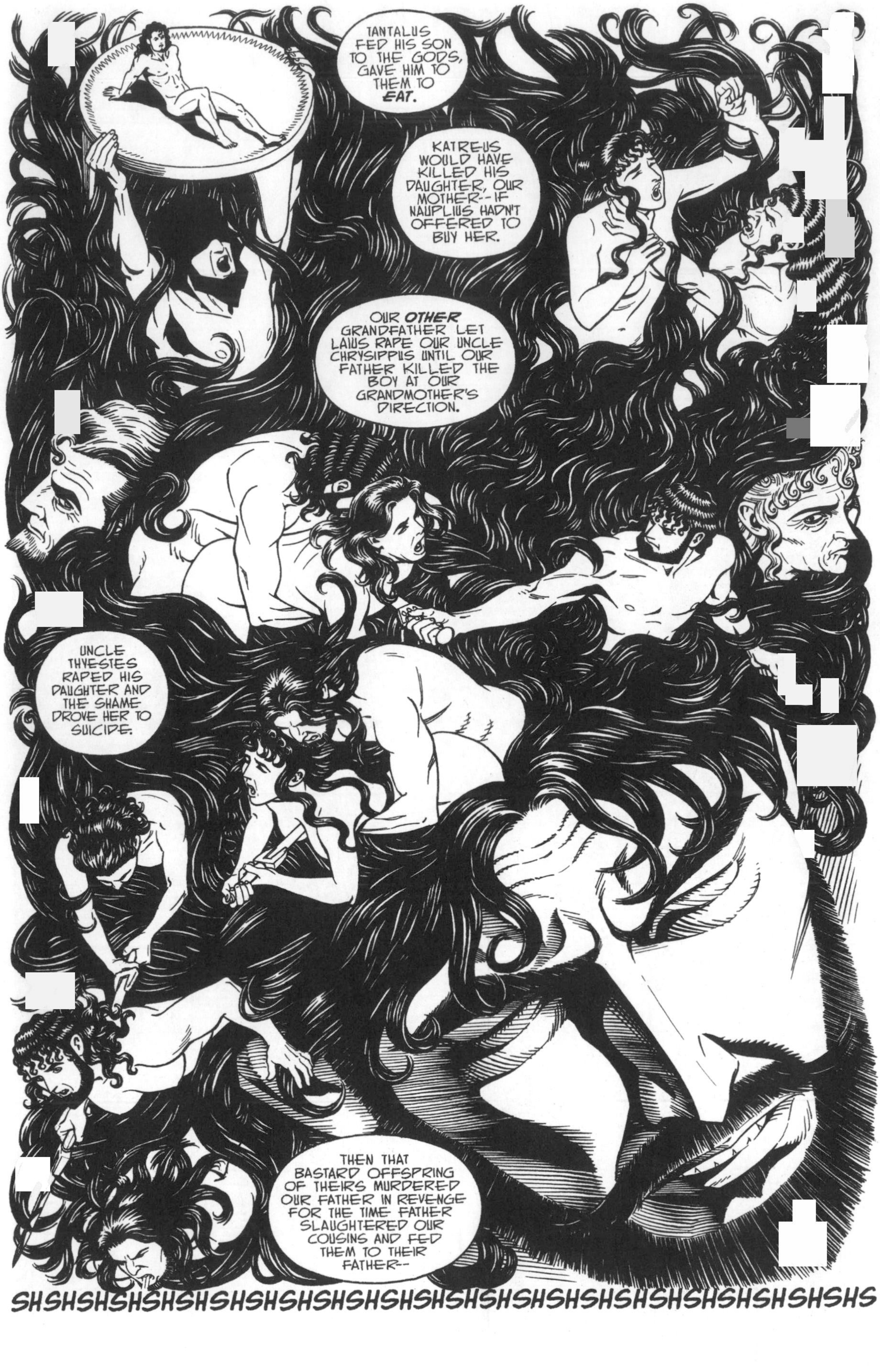
TANTALUS FED HIS SON TO THE GODS, GAVE HIM TO THEM TO EAT.
KATREUS WOULD HAVE KILLED HIS DAUGHTER, OUR MOTHER-- IF NAUPLIUS HADN'T OFFERED TO BUY HER.
OUR OTHER GRANDFATHER LET LAIUS RAPE OUR UNCLE CHRYSIPPUS UNTIL OUR FATHER KILLED THE BOY AT OUR GRANDMOTHER'S DIRECTION.
UNCLE THYESTES RAPED HIS DAUGHTER AND THE SHAME DROVE HER TO SUICIDE.
THEN THAT BASTARD OFFSPRING OF THEIRS MURDERED OUR FATHER IN REVENGE FOR THE TIME FATHER SLAUGHTERED OUR COUSINS AND FED THEM TO THEIR FATHER--
SHSHSHSHSHSHSHSHSHSHSHSHSHSHSHSHSHSHSHSHSHSHSHSHSHSHSHSHS

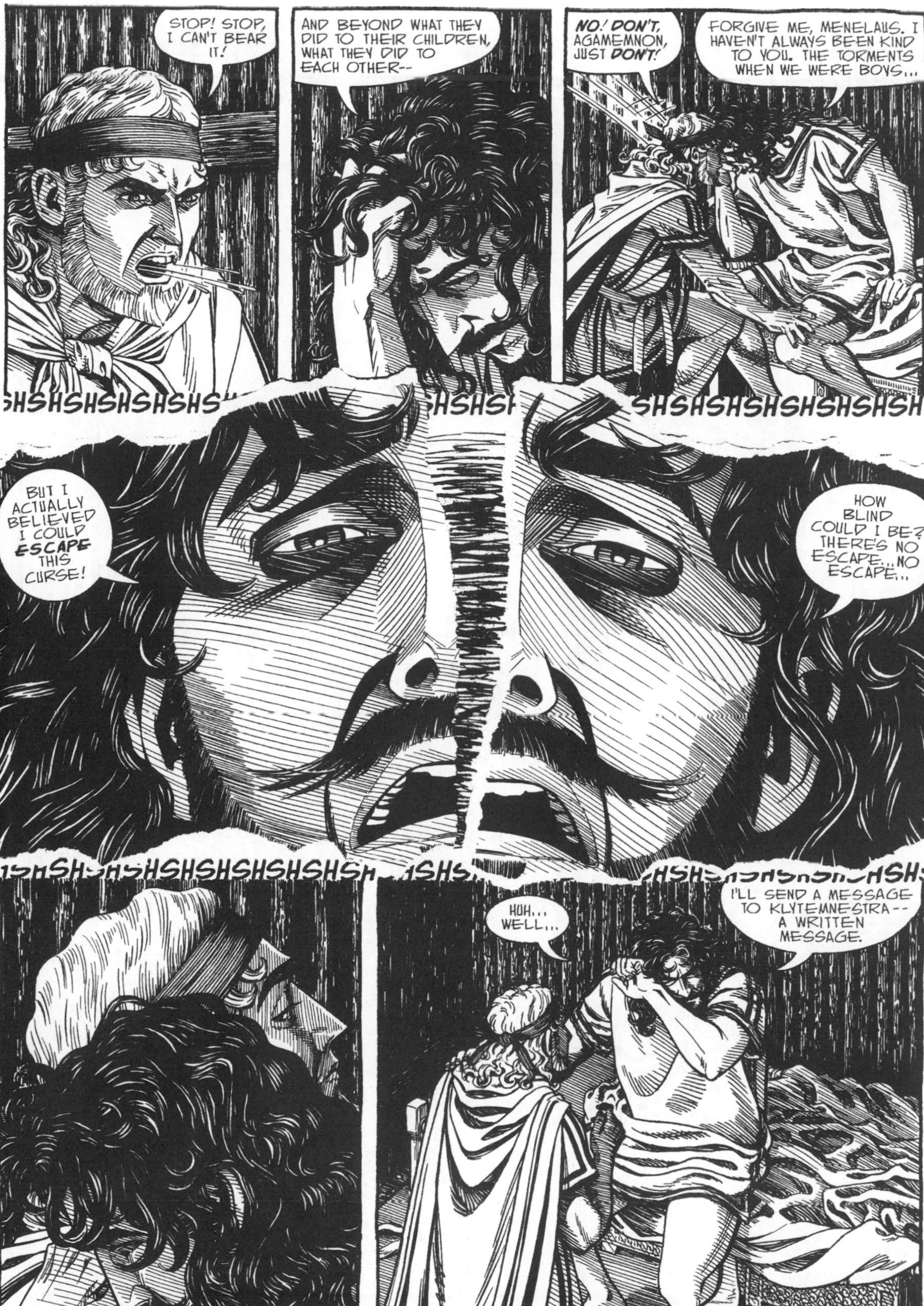
STOP! STOP, I CAN'T BEAR IT!
AND BEYOND WHAT THEY DID TO THEIR CHILDREN, WHAT THEY DID TO EACH OTHER--
NO! DON'T, AGAMEMNON, JUST DON'T!
FORGIVE ME, MENELAUS. I HAVEN'T ALWAYS BEEN KIND TO YOU. THE TORMENTS WHEN WE WERE BOYS...
SHSHSHSHSHSHSHSHSHSHSHSHSHSHSHSH
BUT I ACTUALLY BELIEVED I COULD ESCAPE THIS CURSE!
HOW BLIND COULD I BE? THERE'S NO ESCAPE... NO ESCAPE...
SHSHSHSHSHSHSHSHSHSHSHSHSHSH
HUH... WELL...
I'LL SEND A MESSAGE TO KLYTEMNESTRA-- A WRITTEN MESSAGE.
SHSHSHSHSHSHSHSHSHSHSHSHSHSHSHSHSHSHSH

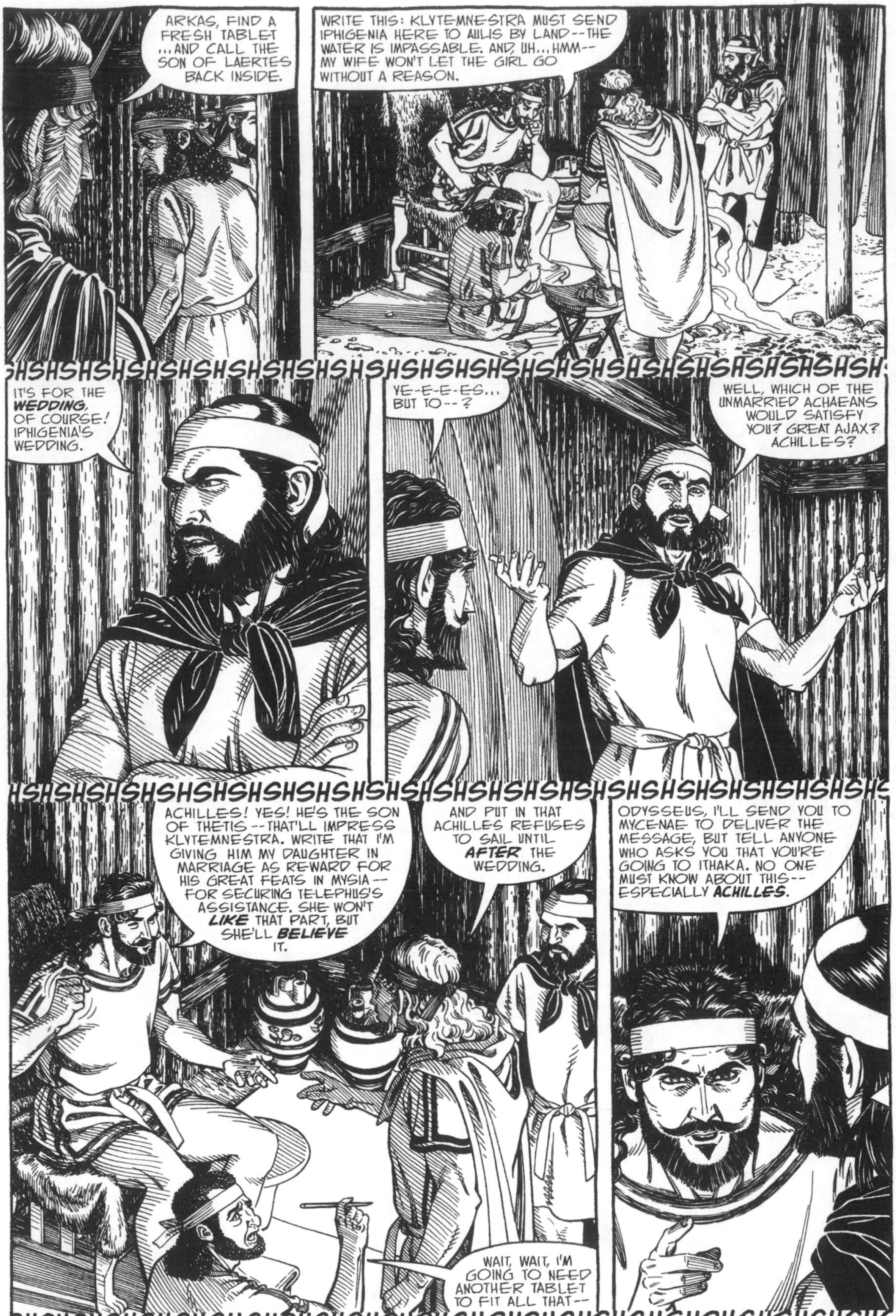

ARKAS, FIND A FRESH TABLET ...AND CALL THE SON OF LAERTES BACK INSIDE.
WRITE THIS: KLYTEMNESTRA MUST SEND IPHIGENIA HERE TO AULIS BY LAND--THE WATER IS IMPASSABLE. AND, UH...HMM-- MY WIFE WON'T LET THE GIRL GO WITHOUT A REASON.
SHSHSHSHSHSHSHSHSHSHSHSHSHSHSHSHSHSH
IT'S FOR THE WEDDING, OF COURSE! IPHIGENIA'S WEDDING.
YE-E-E-ES... BUT TO--?
WELL, WHICH OF THE UNMARRIED ACHAEANS WOULD SATISFY YOU? GREAT AJAX? ACHILLES?
SHSHSHSHSHSHSHSHSHSHSHSHSHSHSHSHSHSHS
ACHILLES! YES! HE'S THE SON OF THETIS--THAT'LL IMPRESS KLYTEMNESTRA. WRITE THAT I'M GIVING HIM MY DAUGHTER IN MARRIAGE AS REWARD FOR HIS GREAT FEATS IN MYSIA-- FOR SECURING TELEPHUS'S ASSISTANCE. SHE WON'T LIKE THAT PART, BUT SHE'LL BELIEVE IT.
AND PUT IN THAT ACHILLES REFUSES TO SAIL UNTIL AFTER THE WEDDING.
WAIT, WAIT, I'M GOING TO NEED ANOTHER TABLET TO FIT ALL THAT--
ODYSSEUS, I'LL SEND YOU TO MYCENAE TO DELIVER THE MESSAGE, BUT TELL ANYONE WHO ASKS YOU THAT YOU'RE GOING TO ITHAKA. NO ONE MUST KNOW ABOUT THIS-- ESPECIALLY ACHILLES.
SHSHSHSHSHSHSHSHSHSHSHSHSHSHSHSHSHSHS

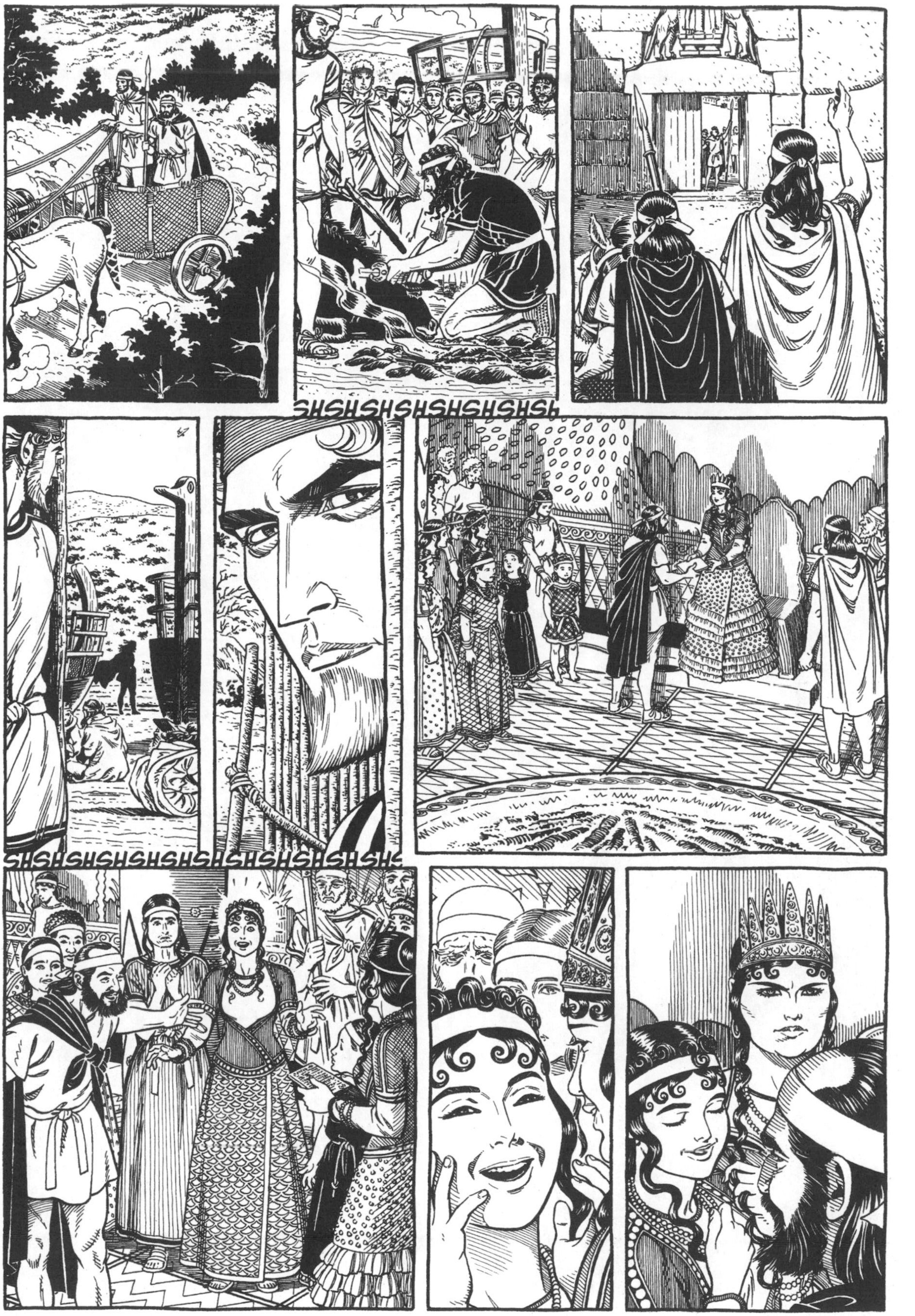
SHSHSHSHSHSHSHSHSHSH
SHSHSHSHSHSHSHSHSHSHSHSHSH

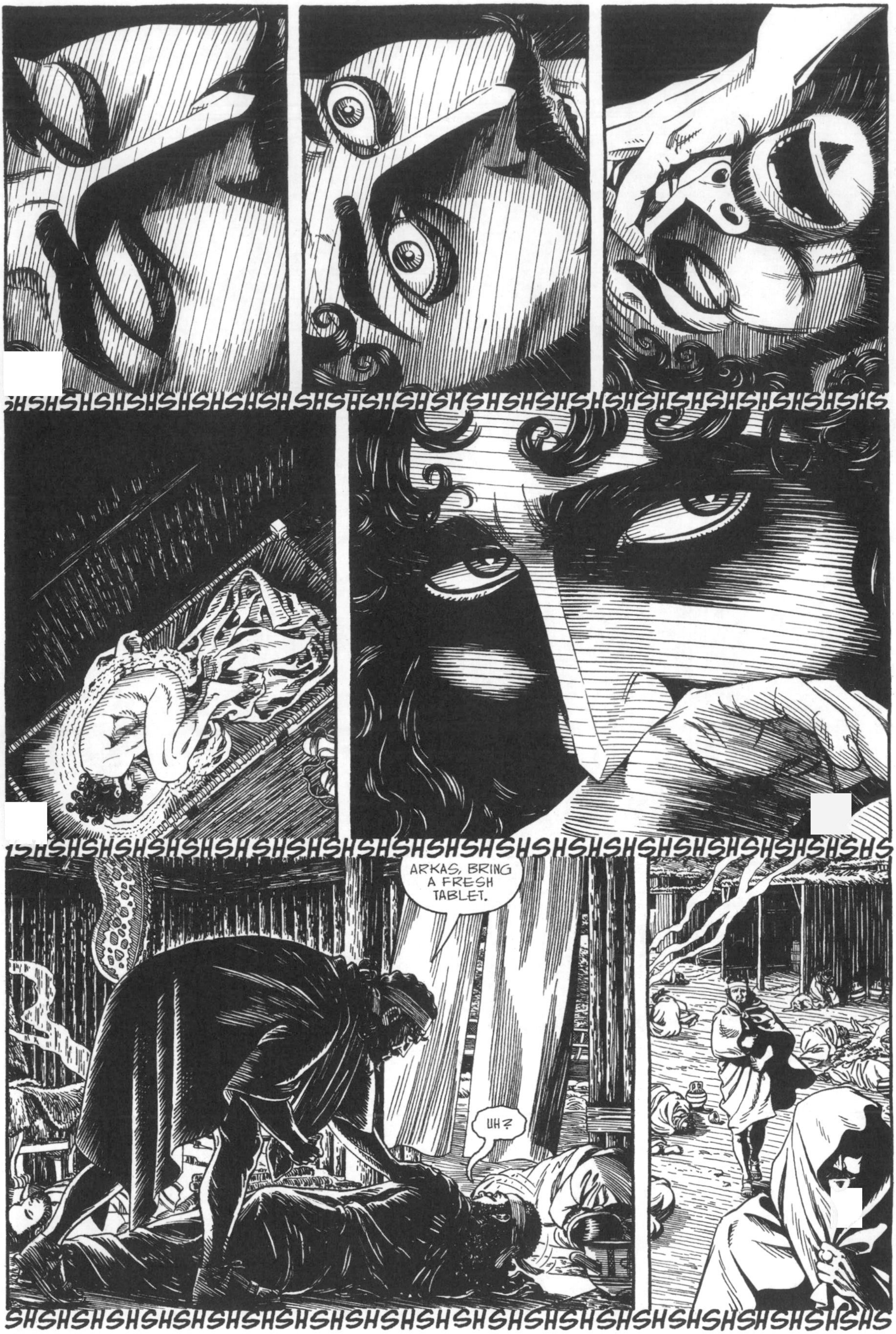
SHSHSHSHSHSHSHSHSHSHSHSHSHSHSHSHSHSHSHSHSHSHS
SHSHSHSHSHSHSHSHSHSHSHSHSHSHSHSHSHSHSHSHSHS
ARKAS, BRING A FRESH TABLET.
UH?
SHSHSHSHSHSHSHSHSHSHSHSHSHSHSHSHSHSHSHSHSHS

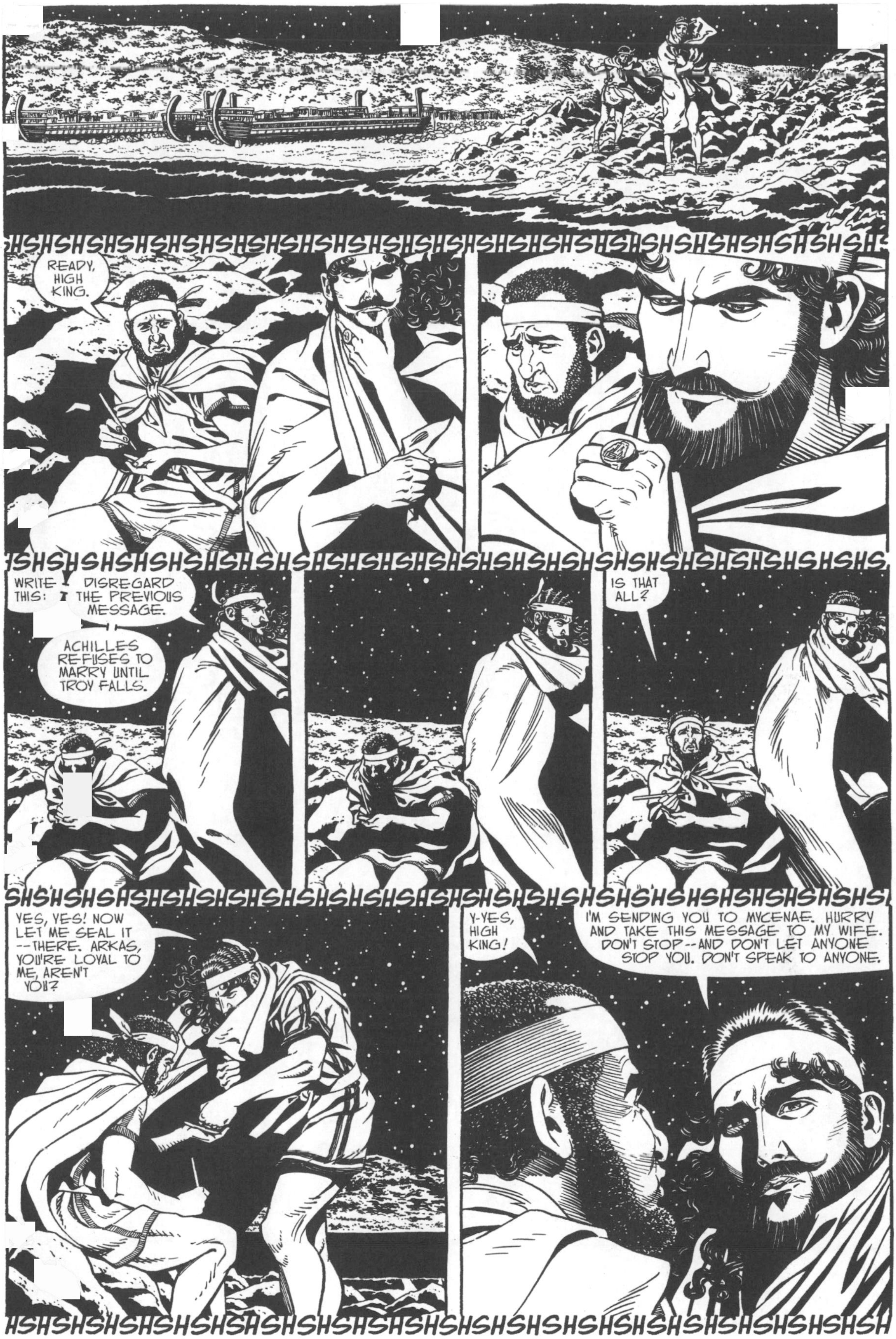
SHSHSHSHSHSHSHSHSHSHSHSHSHSHSHSHSHSHSHSH
READY, HIGH KING.
SHSHSHSHSHSHSHSHSHSHSHSHSHSHSHSHSHSHSHSH
WRITE THIS:
DISREGARD THE PREVIOUS MESSAGE.
ACHILLES REFUSES TO MARRY UNTIL TROY FALLS.
IS THAT ALL?
SHSHSHSHSHSHSHSHSHSHSHSHSHSHSHSHSHSHSHSH
YES, YES! NOW LET ME SEAL IT --THERE. ARKAS, YOU'RE LOYAL TO ME, AREN'T YOU?
Y-YES, HIGH KING!
I'M SENDING YOU TO MYCENAE. HURRY AND TAKE THIS MESSAGE TO MY WIFE. DON'T STOP--AND DON'T LET ANYONE STOP YOU. DON'T SPEAK TO ANYONE.
SHSHSHSHSHSHSHSHSHSHSHSHSHSHSHSHSHSHSHSH

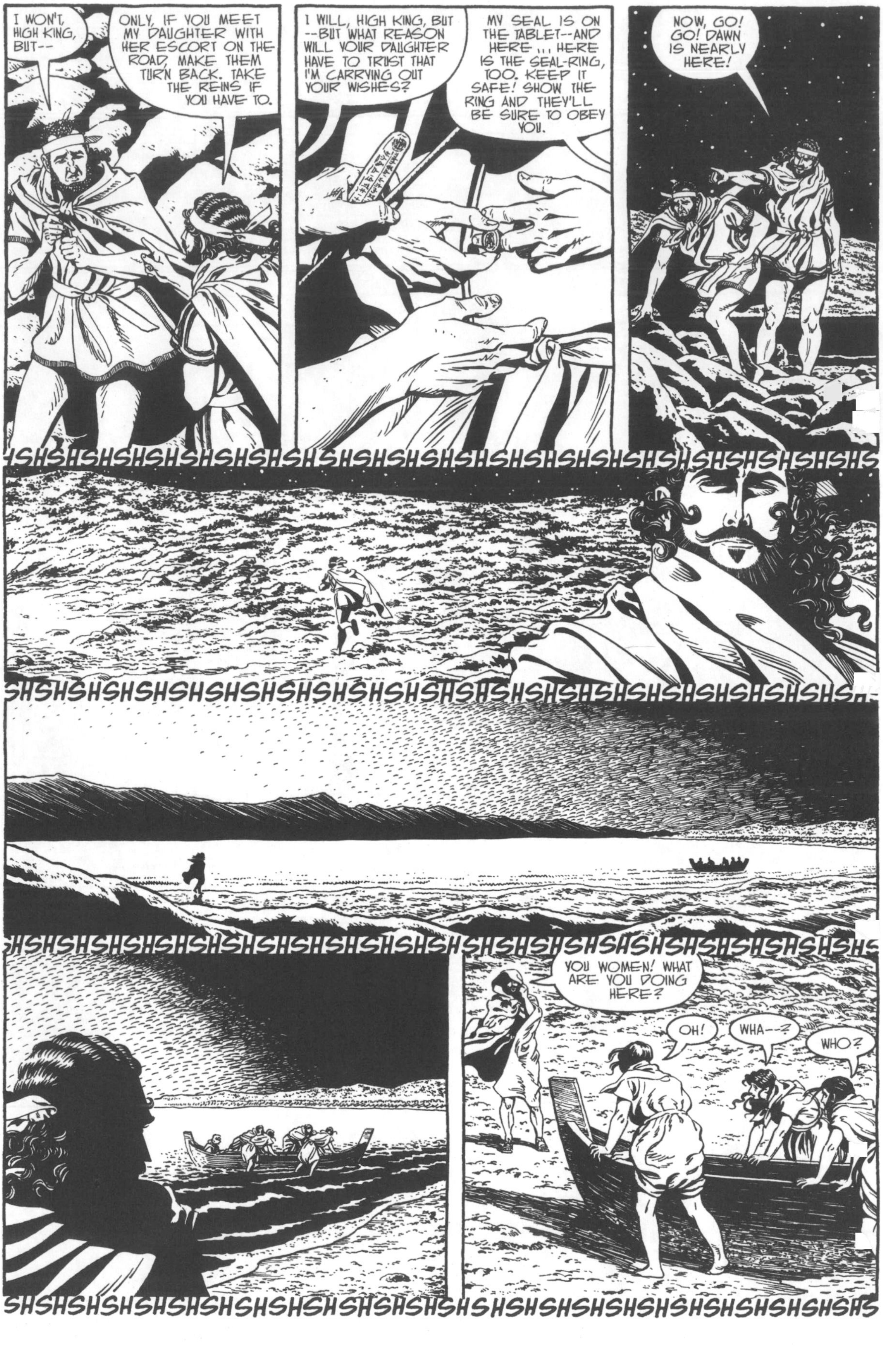
I WON'T, HIGH KING, BUT--
ONLY, IF YOU MEET MY DAUGHTER WITH HER ESCORT ON THE ROAD, MAKE THEM TURN BACK. TAKE THE REINS IF YOU HAVE TO.
I WILL, HIGH KING, BUT --BUT WHAT REASON WILL YOUR DAUGHTER HAVE TO TRUST THAT I'M CARRYING OUT YOUR WISHES?
MY SEAL IS ON THE TABLET--AND HERE ... HERE IS THE SEAL-RING, TOO. KEEP IT SAFE! SHOW THE RING AND THEY'LL BE SURE TO OBEY YOU.
NOW, GO! GO! DAWN IS NEARLY HERE!
SHSHSHSHSHSHSHSHSHSHSHSHSHSHSHSHSHSHSHSHSHSHS
SHSHSHSHSHSHSHSHSHSHSHSHSHSHSHSHSHSHSHSHSHSHS
SHSHSHSHSHSHSHSHSHSHSHSHSHSHSHSHSHSHSHSHSHSHS
YOU WOMEN! WHAT ARE YOU DOING HERE?
OH!
WHA--?
WHO?
SHSHSHSHSHSHSHSHSHSHSHSHSHSHSHSHSHSHSHSHSHSHS

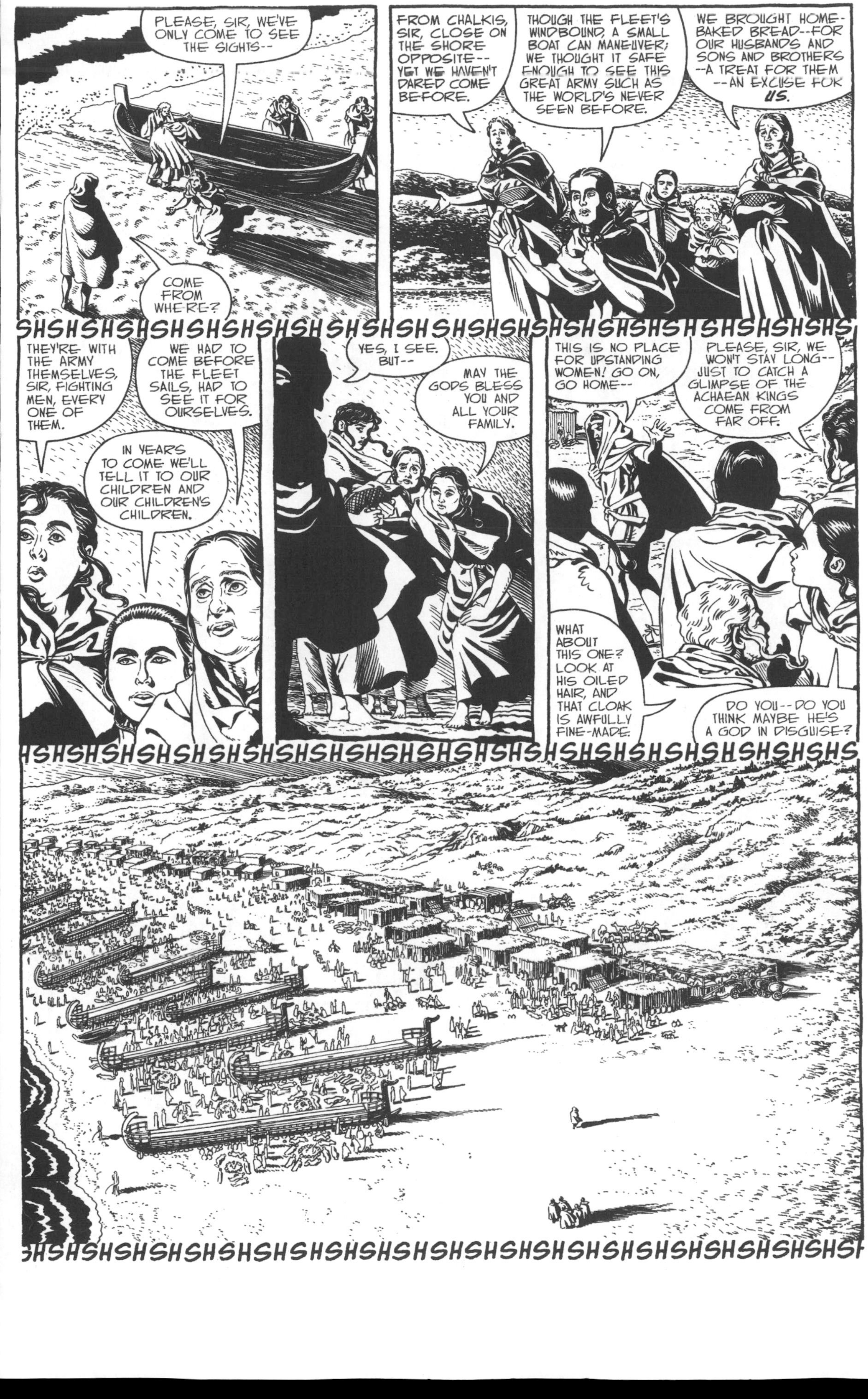
PLEASE, SIR, WE'VE ONLY COME TO SEE THE SIGHTS--
COME FROM WHERE?
FROM CHALKIS, SIR, CLOSE ON THE SHORE OPPOSITE-- YET WE HAVEN'T DARED COME BEFORE.
THOUGH THE FLEET'S WINDBOUND, A SMALL BOAT CAN MANEUVER; WE THOUGHT IT SAFE ENOUGH TO SEE THIS GREAT ARMY SUCH AS THE WORLD'S NEVER SEEN BEFORE.
WE BROUGHT HOME-BAKED BREAD--FOR OUR HUSBANDS AND SONS AND BROTHERS --A TREAT FOR THEM --AN EXCUSE FOR US.
SHSHSHSHSHSHSHSHSHSHSHSHSHSHSHSHSHSHS
THEY'RE WITH THE ARMY THEMSELVES, SIR, FIGHTING MEN, EVERY ONE OF THEM.
WE HAD TO COME BEFORE THE FLEET SAILS, HAD TO SEE IT FOR OURSELVES.
IN YEARS TO COME WE'LL TELL IT TO OUR CHILDREN AND OUR CHILDREN'S CHILDREN.
YES, I SEE. BUT--
MAY THE GODS BLESS YOU AND ALL YOUR FAMILY.
THIS IS NO PLACE FOR UPSTANDING WOMEN! GO ON, GO HOME--
PLEASE, SIR, WE WON'T STAY LONG-- JUST TO CATCH A GLIMPSE OF THE ACHAEAN KINGS COME FROM FAR OFF.
WHAT ABOUT THIS ONE? LOOK AT HIS OILED HAIR, AND THAT CLOAK IS AWFULLY FINE-MADE.
DO YOU--DO YOU THINK MAYBE HE'S A GOD IN DISGUISE?
SHSHSHSHSHSHSHSHSHSHSHSHSHSHSHSHSHSHS
SHSHSHSHSHSHSHSHSHSHSHSHSHSHSHSHSHSHS

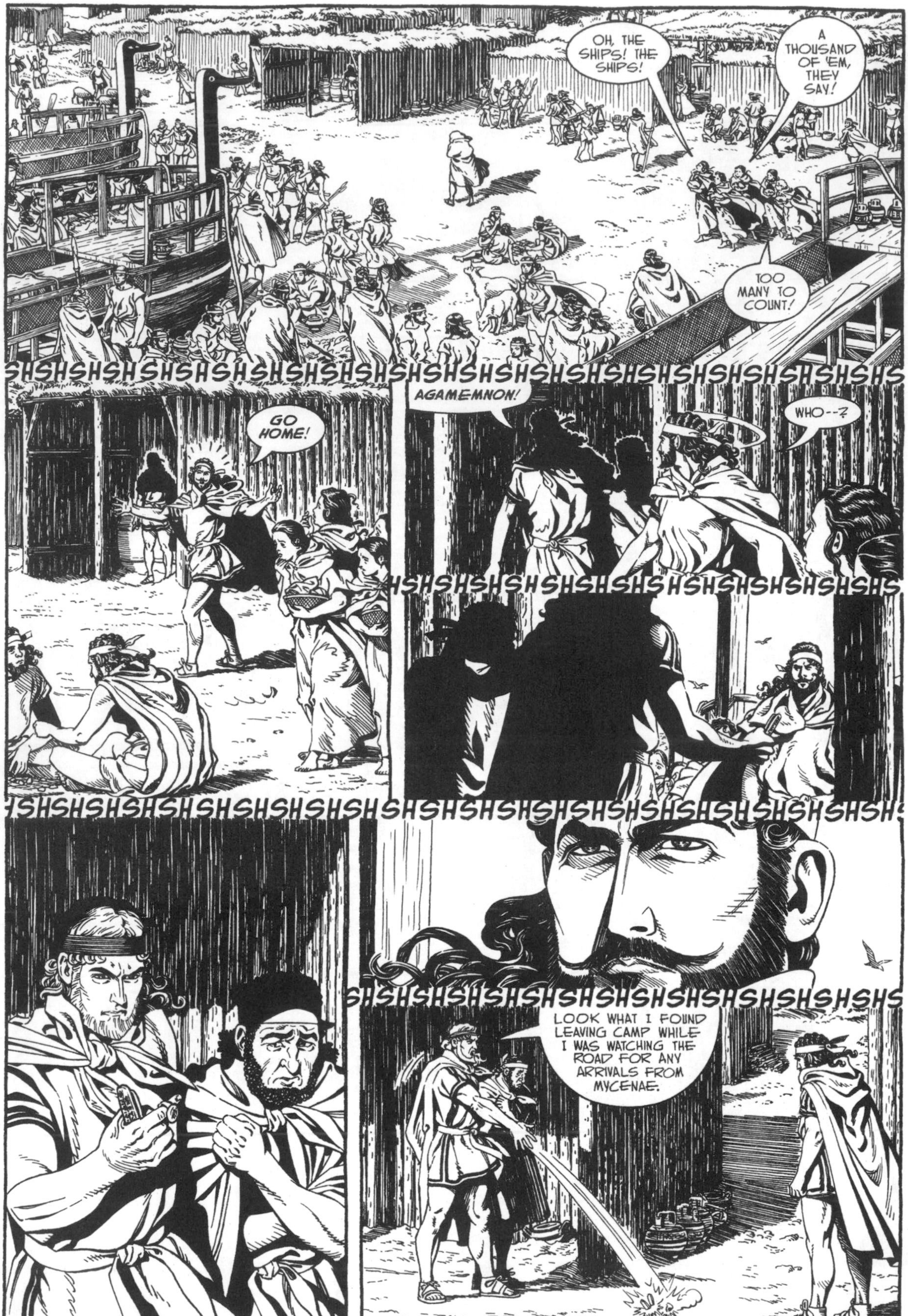
OH, THE SHIPS! THE SHIPS!
A THOUSAND OF 'EM, THEY SAY!
TOO MANY TO COUNT!
GO HOME!
AGAMEMNON!
WHO--?
LOOK WHAT I FOUND LEAVING CAMP WHILE I WAS WATCHING THE ROAD FOR ANY ARRIVALS FROM MYCENAE.

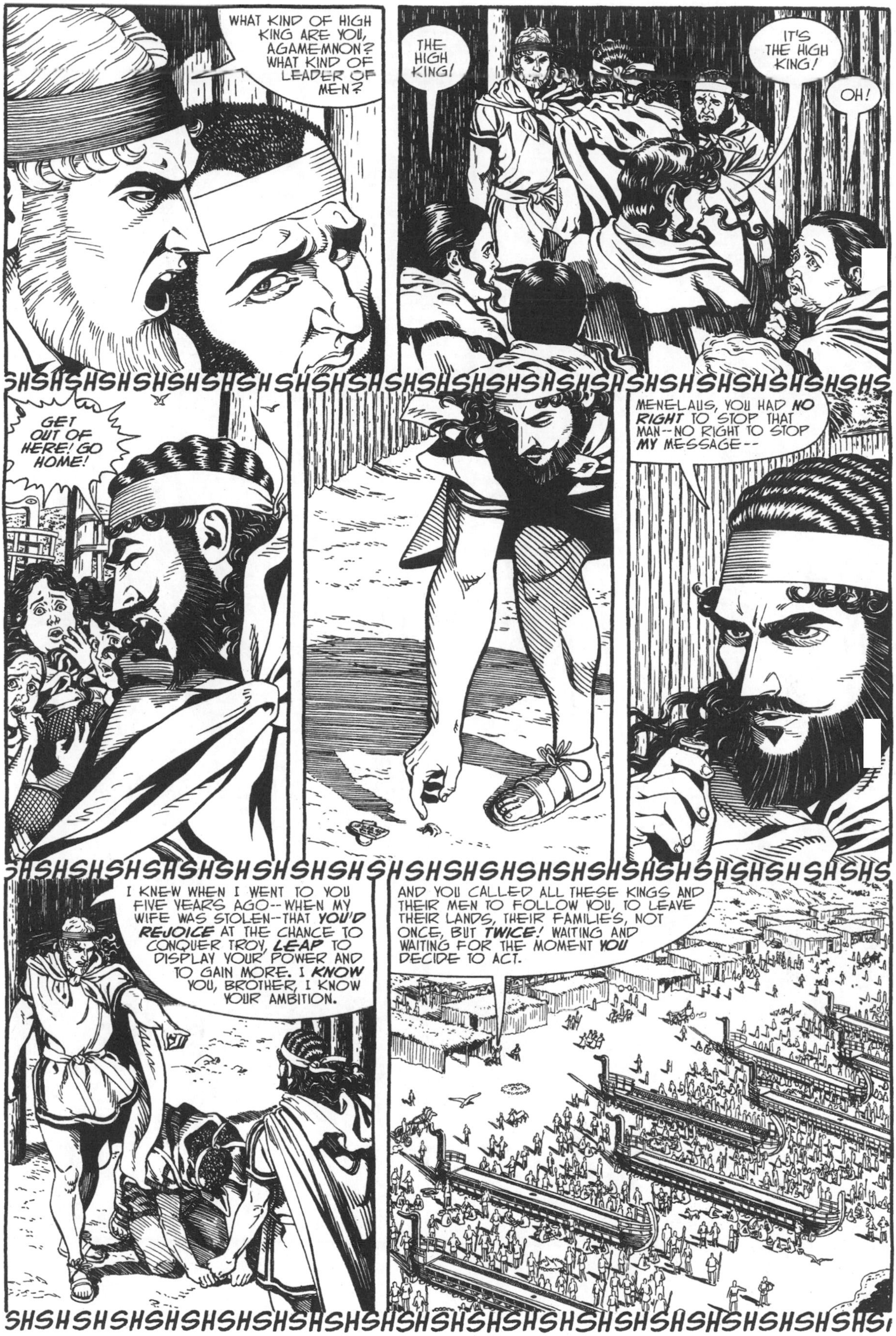
WHAT KIND OF HIGH KING ARE YOU, AGAMEMNON? WHAT KIND OF LEADER OF MEN?
THE HIGH KING!
IT'S THE HIGH KING!
OH!
SHSHSHSHSHSHSHSHSHSHSHSHSHSHSHSHSHSHSHSHSHS
GET OUT OF HERE! GO HOME!
MENELAUS, YOU HAD NO RIGHT TO STOP THAT MAN--NO RIGHT TO STOP MY MESSAGE--
SHSHSHSHSHSHSHSHSHSHSHSHSHSHSHSHSHSHSHSHSHS
I KNEW WHEN I WENT TO YOU FIVE YEARS AGO--WHEN MY WIFE WAS STOLEN--THAT YOU'D REJOICE AT THE CHANCE TO CONQUER TROY, LEAP TO DISPLAY YOUR POWER AND TO GAIN MORE. I KNOW YOU, BROTHER, I KNOW YOUR AMBITION.
AND YOU CALLED ALL THESE KINGS AND THEIR MEN TO FOLLOW YOU, TO LEAVE THEIR LANDS, THEIR FAMILIES, NOT ONCE, BUT TWICE! WAITING AND WAITING FOR THE MOMENT YOU DECIDE TO ACT.
SHSHSHSHSHSHSHSHSHSHSHSHSHSHSHSHSHSHSHSHSHS

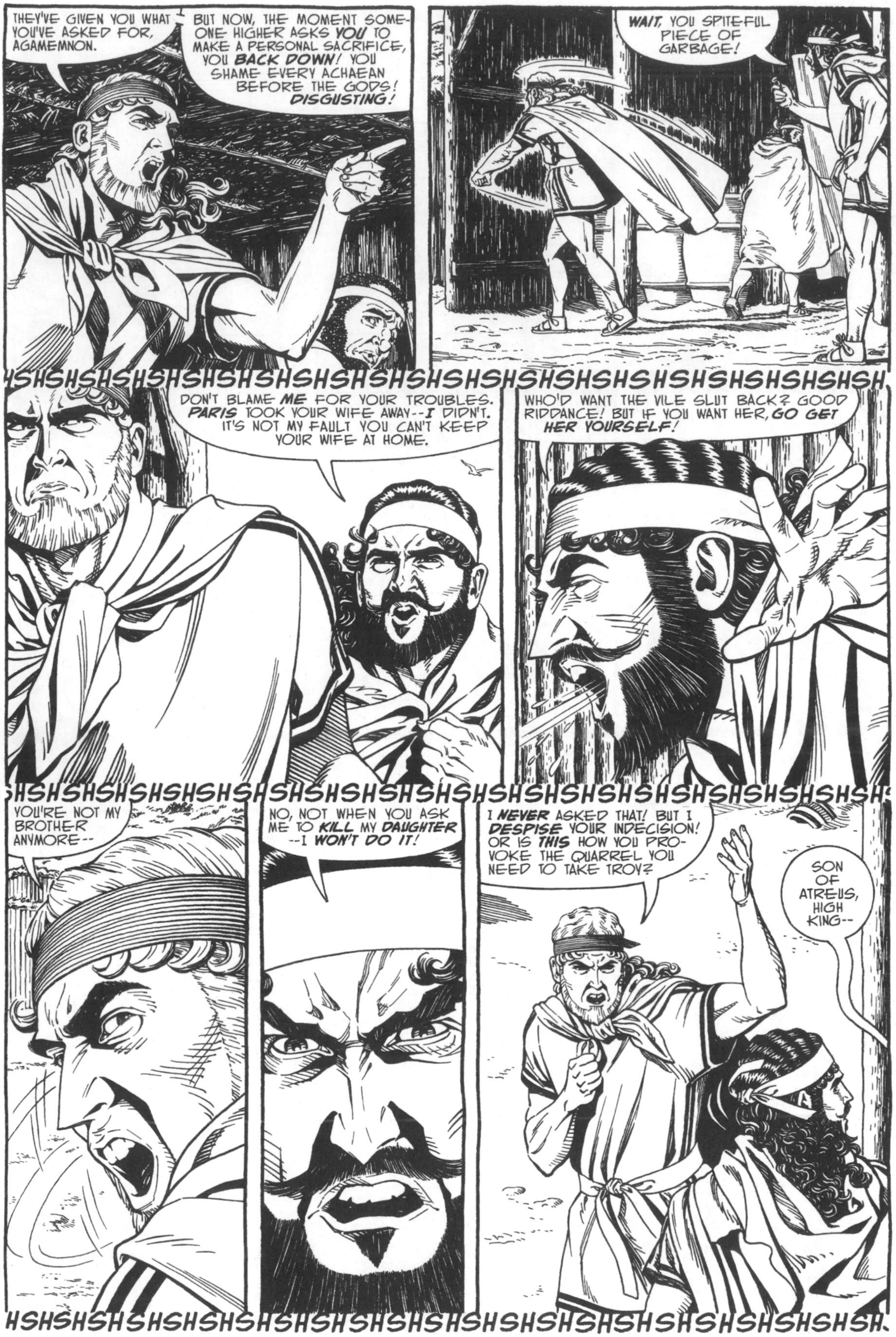
THEY'VE GIVEN YOU WHAT YOU'VE ASKED FOR, AGAMEMNON.
BUT NOW, THE MOMENT SOME-ONE HIGHER ASKS YOU TO MAKE A PERSONAL SACRIFICE, YOU BACK DOWN! YOU SHAME EVERY ACHAEAN BEFORE THE GODS! DISGUSTING!
WAIT, YOU SPITEFUL PIECE OF GARBAGE!
HSHSHSHSHSHSHSHSHSHSHSHSHSHSHSHSHSHSHSHSHSH
DON'T BLAME ME FOR YOUR TROUBLES. PARIS TOOK YOUR WIFE AWAY--I DIDN'T. IT'S NOT MY FAULT YOU CAN'T KEEP YOUR WIFE AT HOME.
WHO'D WANT THE VILE SLUT BACK? GOOD RIDDANCE! BUT IF YOU WANT HER, GO GET HER YOURSELF!
HSHSHSHSHSHSHSHSHSHSHSHSHSHSHSHSHSHSHSHSHSH
YOU'RE NOT MY BROTHER ANYMORE--
NO, NOT WHEN YOU ASK ME TO KILL MY DAUGHTER --I WON'T DO IT!
I NEVER ASKED THAT! BUT I DESPISE YOUR INDECISION! OR IS THIS HOW YOU PROVOKE THE QUARREL YOU NEED TO TAKE TROY?
SON OF ATREUS, HIGH KING--
HSHSHSHSHSHSHSHSHSHSHSHSHSHSHSHSHSHSHSHSHSH

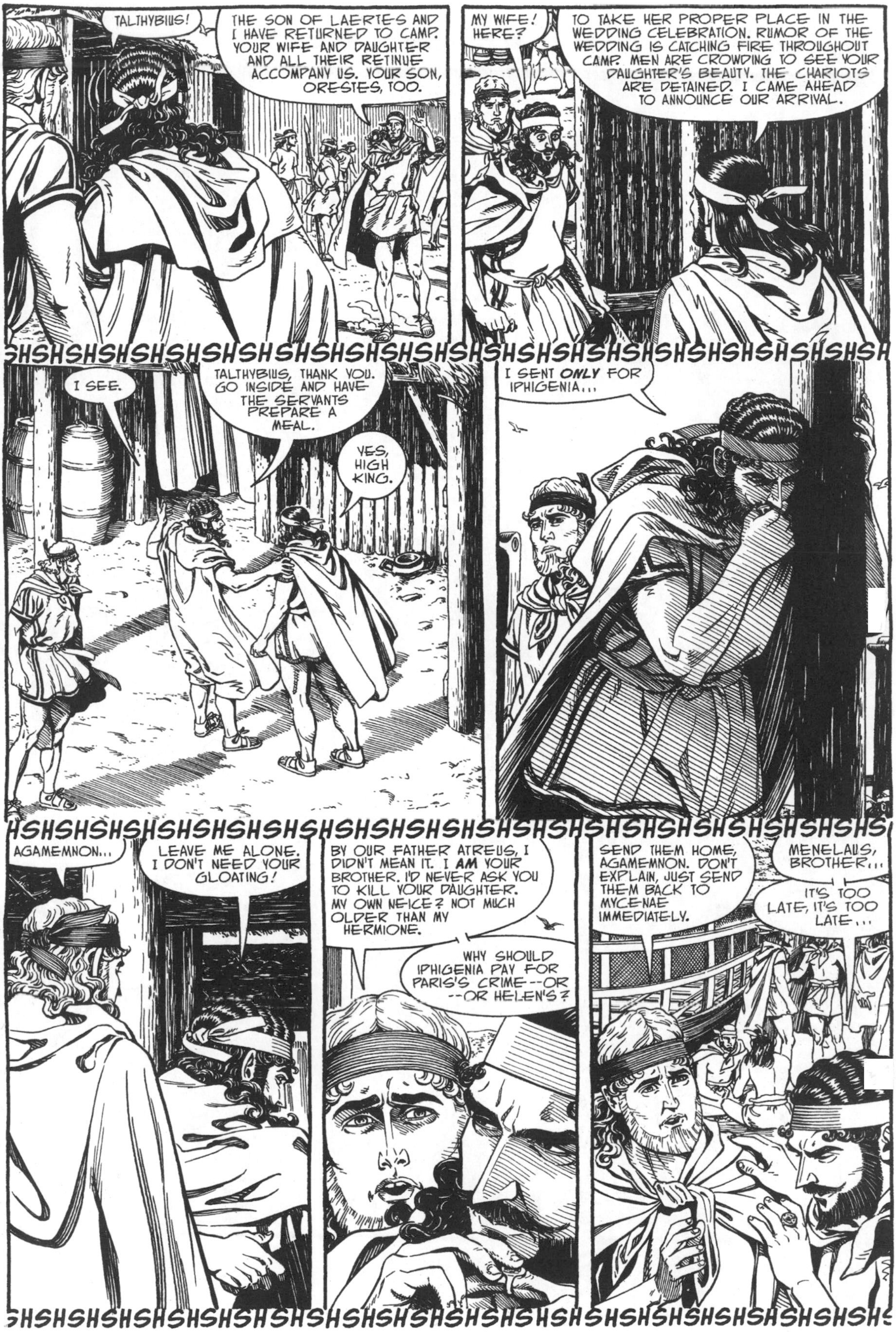

TALTHYBIUS!
THE SON OF LAERTES AND I HAVE RETURNED TO CAMP. YOUR WIFE AND DAUGHTER AND ALL THEIR RETINUE ACCOMPANY US. YOUR SON, ORESTES, TOO.
MY WIFE! HERE?
TO TAKE HER PROPER PLACE IN THE WEDDING CELEBRATION. RUMOR OF THE WEDDING IS CATCHING FIRE THROUGHOUT CAMP. MEN ARE CROWDING TO SEE YOUR DAUGHTER'S BEAUTY. THE CHARIOTS ARE DETAINED. I CAME AHEAD TO ANNOUNCE OUR ARRIVAL.
I SEE.
TALTHYBIUS, THANK YOU. GO INSIDE AND HAVE THE SERVANTS PREPARE A MEAL.
YES, HIGH KING.
I SENT ONLY FOR IPHIGENIA...
AGAMEMNON...
LEAVE ME ALONE. I DON'T NEED YOUR GLOATING!
BY OUR FATHER ATREUS, I DIDN'T MEAN IT. I AM YOUR BROTHER. I'D NEVER ASK YOU TO KILL YOUR DAUGHTER. MY OWN NEICE? NOT MUCH OLDER THAN MY HERMIONE.
WHY SHOULD IPHIGENIA PAY FOR PARIS'S CRIME--OR --OR HELEN'S?
SEND THEM HOME, AGAMEMNON. DON'T EXPLAIN, JUST SEND THEM BACK TO MYCENAE IMMEDIATELY.
MENELAUS, BROTHER...
IT'S TOO LATE, IT'S TOO LATE...

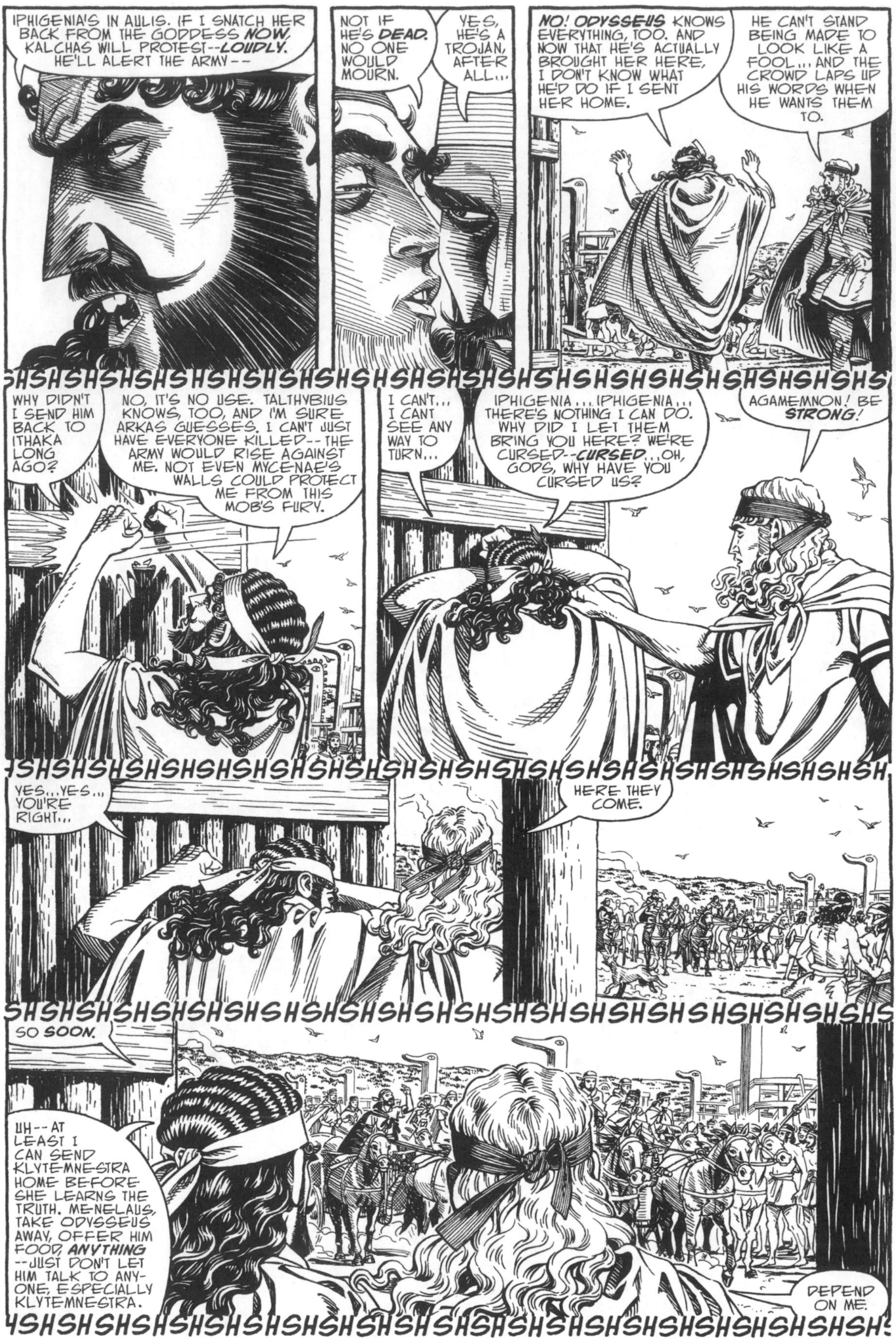

IPHIGENIA'S IN AULIS. IF I SNATCH HER BACK FROM THE GODDESS **NOW**, KALCHAS WILL PROTEST--**LOUDLY**. HE'LL ALERT THE ARMY--
NOT IF HE'S **DEAD**. NO ONE WOULD MOURN.
YES, HE'S A TROJAN, AFTER ALL...
NO! ODYSSEUS KNOWS EVERYTHING, TOO. AND NOW THAT HE'S ACTUALLY BROUGHT HER HERE, I DON'T KNOW WHAT HE'D DO IF I SENT HER HOME.
HE CAN'T STAND BEING MADE TO LOOK LIKE A FOOL... AND THE CROWD LAPS UP HIS WORDS WHEN HE WANTS THEM TO.
SHSHSHSHSHSHSHSHSHSHSHSHSHSHSHSHSHSHS
WHY DIDN'T I SEND HIM BACK TO ITHAKA LONG AGO?
NO, IT'S NO USE. TALTHYBIUS KNOWS, TOO, AND I'M SURE ARKAS GUESSES. I CAN'T JUST HAVE EVERYONE KILLED--THE ARMY WOULD RISE AGAINST ME. NOT EVEN MYCENAE'S WALLS COULD PROTECT ME FROM THIS MOB'S FURY.
I CAN'T... I CAN'T SEE ANY WAY TO TURN...
IPHIGENIA... IPHIGENIA... THERE'S NOTHING I CAN DO. WHY DID I LET THEM BRING YOU HERE? WE'RE CURSED--**CURSED**... OH, GODS, WHY HAVE YOU CURSED US?
AGAMEMNON! BE **STRONG**!
SHSHSHSHSHSHSHSHSHSHSHSHSHSHSHSHSHSH
YES... YES... YOU'RE RIGHT...
HERE THEY COME.
SHSHSHSHSHSHSHSHSHSHSHSHSHSHSHSHSHS
SO **SOON**.
UH--AT LEAST I CAN SEND KLYTEMNESTRA HOME BEFORE SHE LEARNS THE TRUTH. MENELAUS, TAKE ODYSSEUS AWAY, OFFER HIM FOOD, **ANYTHING** --JUST DON'T LET HIM TALK TO ANYONE, ESPECIALLY KLYTEMNESTRA.
DEPEND ON ME.
SHSHSHSHSHSHSHSHSHSHSHSHSHSHSHSHSHSHS

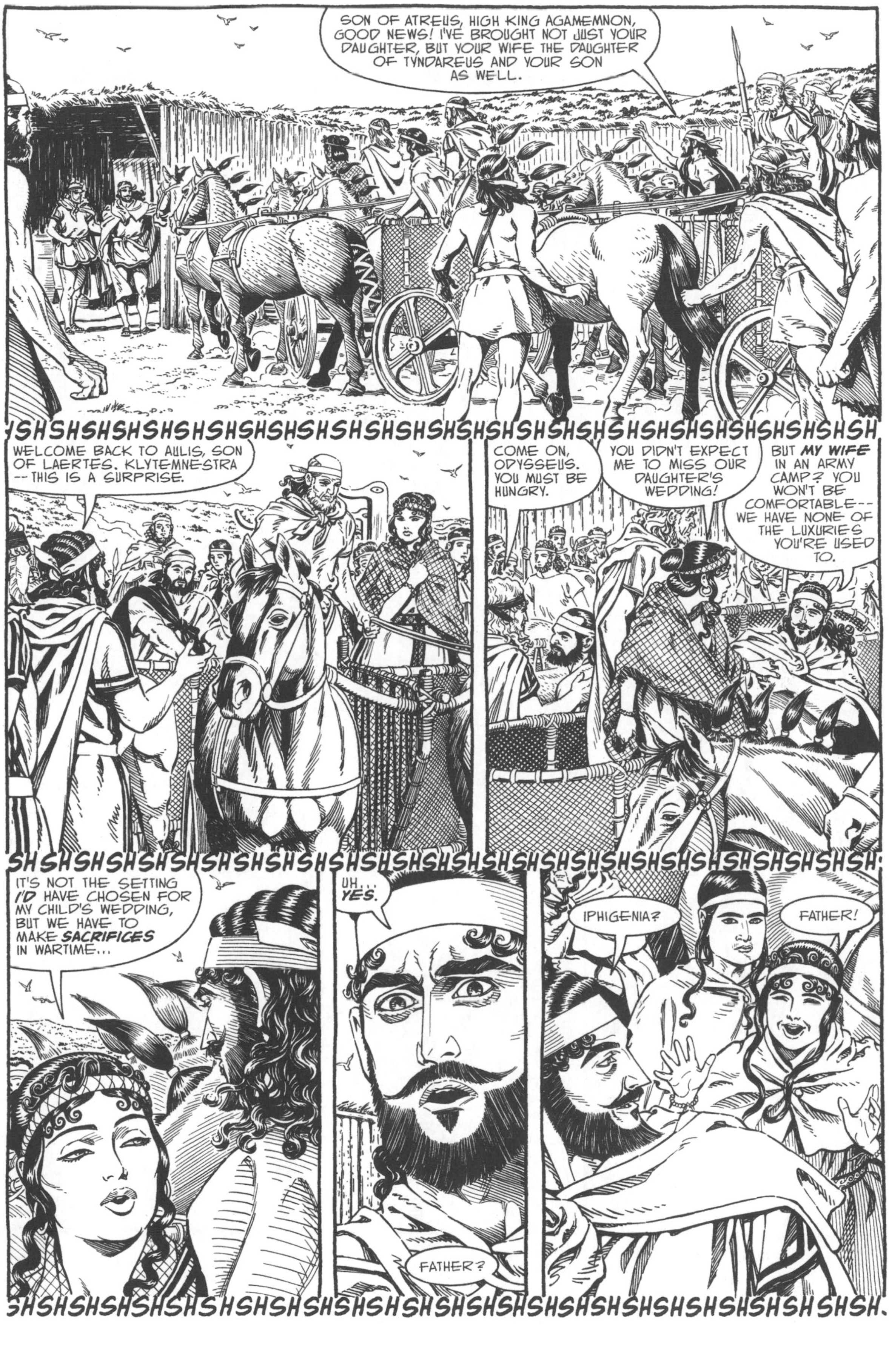
SON OF ATREUS, HIGH KING AGAMEMNON, GOOD NEWS! I'VE BROUGHT NOT JUST YOUR DAUGHTER, BUT YOUR WIFE THE DAUGHTER OF TYNDAREUS AND YOUR SON AS WELL.
SHSHSHSHSHSHSHSHSHSHSHSHSHSHSHSHSHSHSHSHSHSHSH
WELCOME BACK TO AULIS, SON OF LAERTES. KLYTEMNESTRA --THIS IS A SURPRISE.
COME ON, ODYSSEUS. YOU MUST BE HUNGRY.
YOU DIDN'T EXPECT ME TO MISS OUR DAUGHTER'S WEDDING!
BUT MY WIFE IN AN ARMY CAMP? YOU WON'T BE COMFORTABLE-- WE HAVE NONE OF THE LUXURIES YOU'RE USED TO.
SHSHSHSHSHSHSHSHSHSHSHSHSHSHSHSHSHSHSHSHSHSHSH
IT'S NOT THE SETTING I'D HAVE CHOSEN FOR MY CHILD'S WEDDING, BUT WE HAVE TO MAKE SACRIFICES IN WARTIME...
UH... YES.
FATHER?
IPHIGENIA?
FATHER!
SHSHSHSHSHSHSHSHSHSHSHSHSHSHSHSHSHSHSHSHSHSHSH

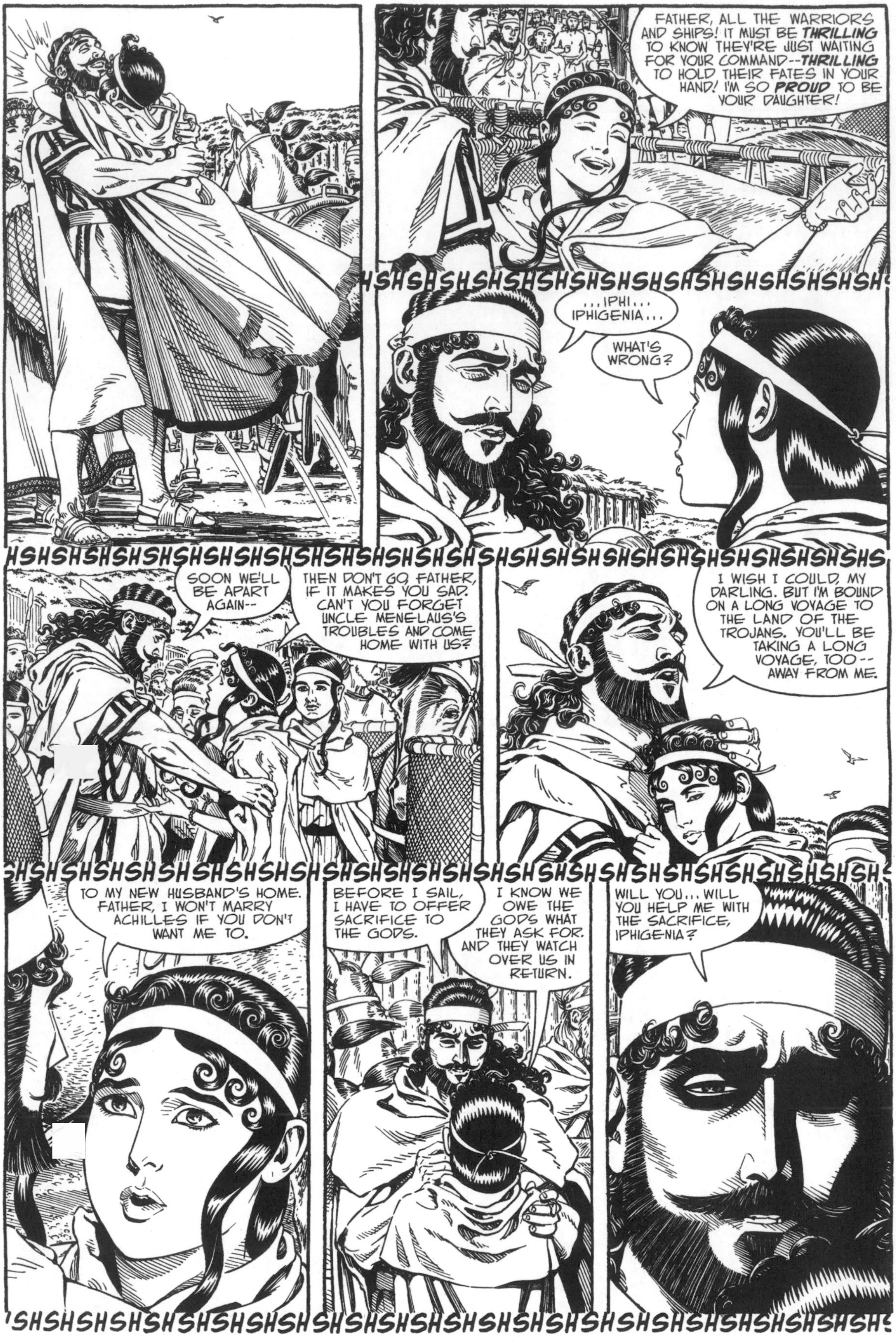
FATHER, ALL THE WARRIORS AND SHIPS! IT MUST BE THRILLING TO KNOW THEY'RE JUST WAITING FOR YOUR COMMAND--THRILLING TO HOLD THEIR FATES IN YOUR HAND! I'M SO PROUD TO BE YOUR DAUGHTER!
SHSHSHSHSHSHSHSHSHSHSHSHSHSH
...IPHI... IPHIGENIA...
WHAT'S WRONG?
SHSHSHSHSHSHSHSHSHSHSHSHSHSHSHSHSHSH
SOON WE'LL BE APART AGAIN--
THEN DON'T GO, FATHER, IF IT MAKES YOU SAD. CAN'T YOU FORGET UNCLE MENELAUS'S TROUBLES AND COME HOME WITH US?
I WISH I COULD, MY DARLING. BUT I'M BOUND ON A LONG VOYAGE TO THE LAND OF THE TROJANS. YOU'LL BE TAKING A LONG VOYAGE, TOO--AWAY FROM ME.
SHSHSHSHSHSHSHSHSHSHSHSHSHSHSHSHSHSH
TO MY NEW HUSBAND'S HOME. FATHER, I WON'T MARRY ACHILLES IF YOU DON'T WANT ME TO.
BEFORE I SAIL, I HAVE TO OFFER SACRIFICE TO THE GODS.
I KNOW WE OWE THE GODS WHAT THEY ASK FOR. AND THEY WATCH OVER US IN RETURN.
WILL YOU... WILL YOU HELP ME WITH THE SACRIFICE, IPHIGENIA?
SHSHSHSHSHSHSHSHSHSHSHSHSHSHSHSHSHSH

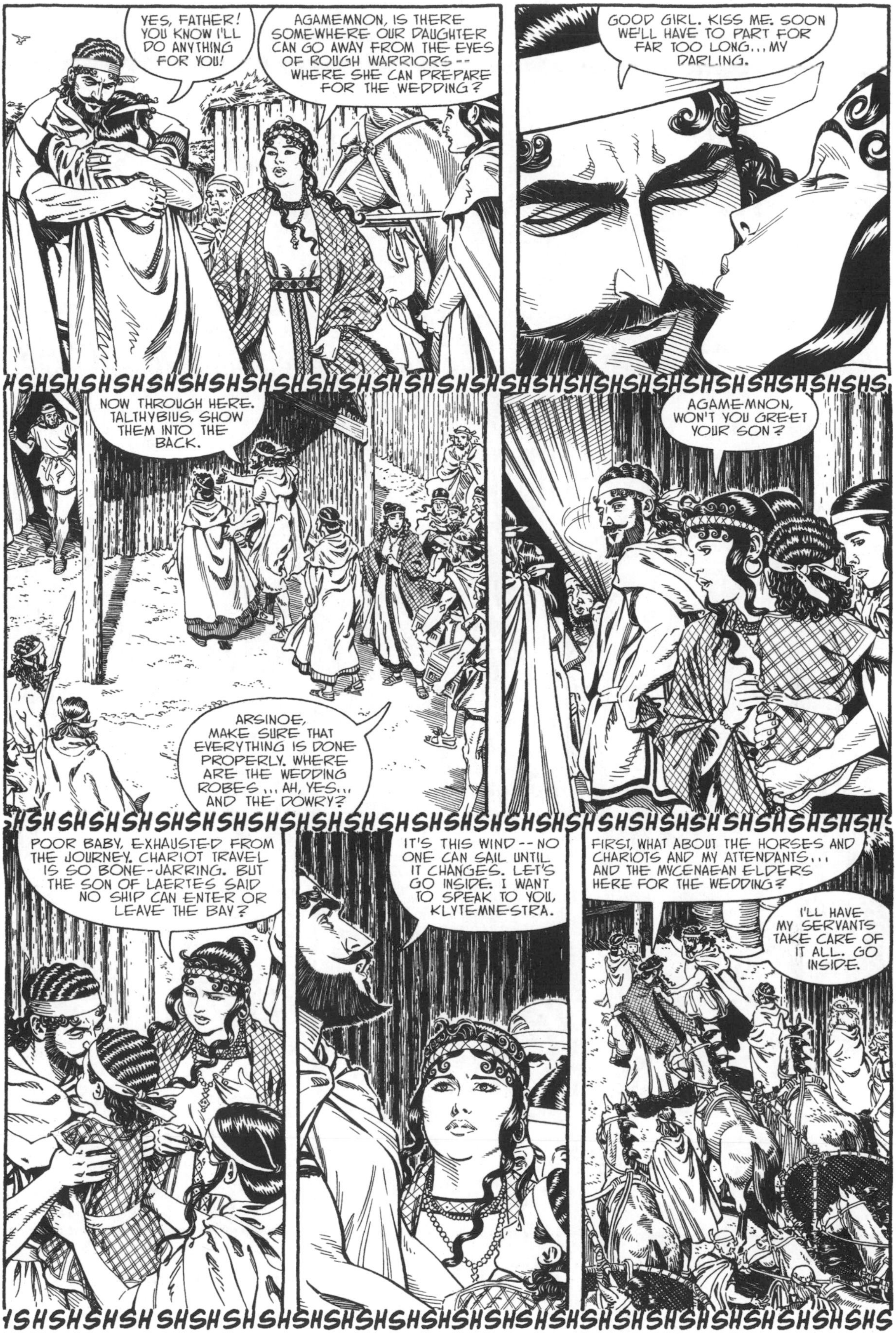
YES, FATHER! YOU KNOW I'LL DO ANYTHING FOR YOU!
AGAMEMNON, IS THERE SOMEWHERE OUR DAUGHTER CAN GO AWAY FROM THE EYES OF ROUGH WARRIORS -- WHERE SHE CAN PREPARE FOR THE WEDDING?
GOOD GIRL. KISS ME. SOON WE'LL HAVE TO PART FOR FAR TOO LONG... MY DARLING.
NOW THROUGH HERE. TALTHYBIUS, SHOW THEM INTO THE BACK.
ARSINOE, MAKE SURE THAT EVERYTHING IS DONE PROPERLY. WHERE ARE THE WEDDING ROBES... AH, YES... AND THE DOWRY?
AGAMEMNON, WON'T YOU GREET YOUR SON?
POOR BABY, EXHAUSTED FROM THE JOURNEY. CHARIOT TRAVEL IS SO BONE-JARRING. BUT THE SON OF LAERTES SAID NO SHIP CAN ENTER OR LEAVE THE BAY?
IT'S THIS WIND -- NO ONE CAN SAIL UNTIL IT CHANGES. LET'S GO INSIDE. I WANT TO SPEAK TO YOU, KLYTEMNESTRA.
FIRST, WHAT ABOUT THE HORSES AND CHARIOTS AND MY ATTENDANTS... AND THE MYCENAEAN ELDERS HERE FOR THE WEDDING?
I'LL HAVE MY SERVANTS TAKE CARE OF IT ALL. GO INSIDE.

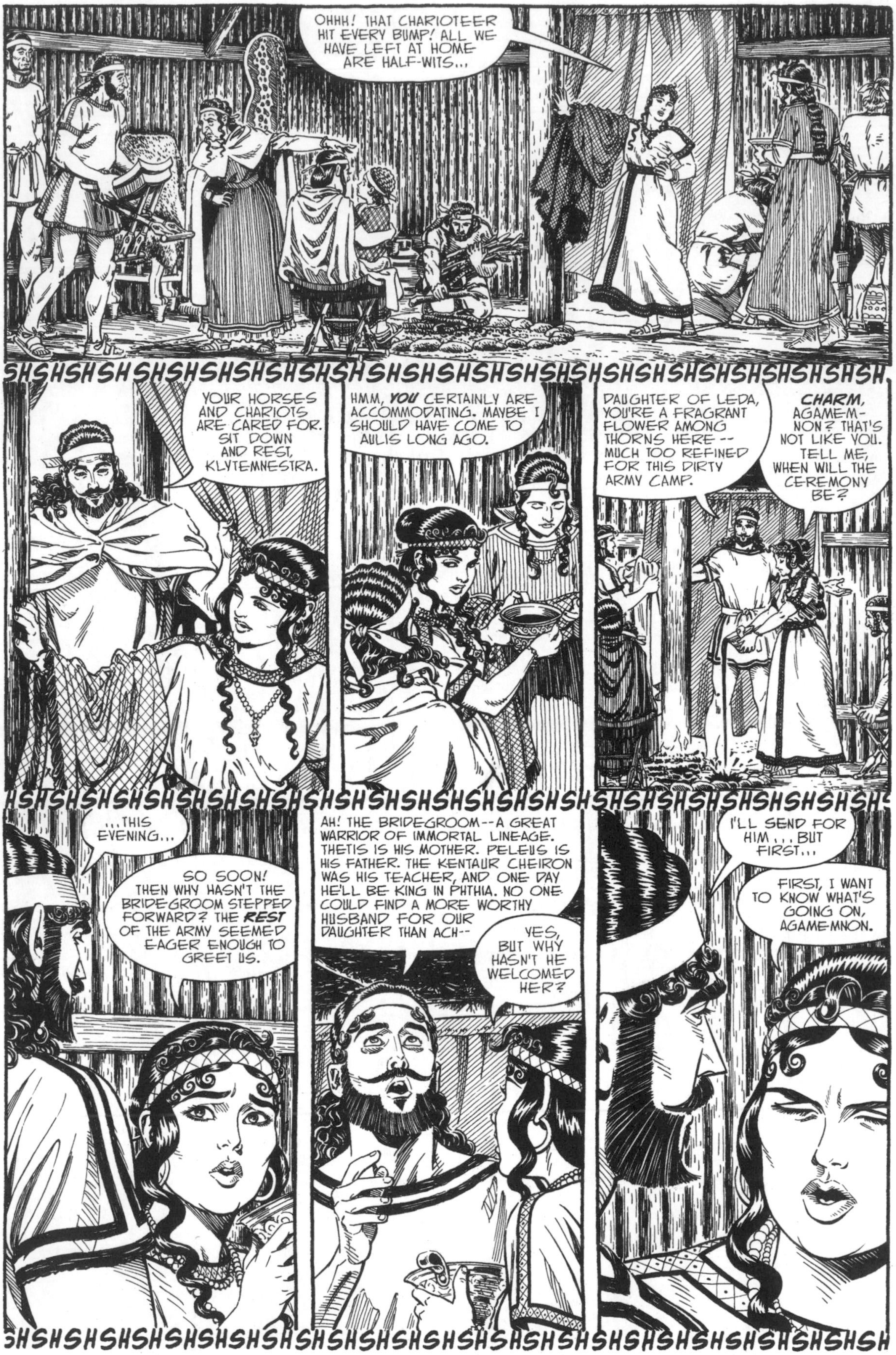
OHHH! THAT CHARIOTEER HIT EVERY BUMP! ALL WE HAVE LEFT AT HOME ARE HALF-WITS...
SHSHSHSHSHSHSHSHSHSHSHSHSHSHSHSHSHSHSHSHSHSH
YOUR HORSES AND CHARIOTS ARE CARED FOR. SIT DOWN AND REST, KLYTEMNESTRA.
HMM, YOU CERTAINLY ARE ACCOMMODATING. MAYBE I SHOULD HAVE COME TO AULIS LONG AGO.
DAUGHTER OF LEDA, YOU'RE A FRAGRANT FLOWER AMONG THORNS HERE -- MUCH TOO REFINED FOR THIS DIRTY ARMY CAMP.
CHARM, AGAMEMNON? THAT'S NOT LIKE YOU. TELL ME, WHEN WILL THE CEREMONY BE?
SHSHSHSHSHSHSHSHSHSHSHSHSHSHSHSHSHSHSHSHSHSH
...THIS EVENING...
SO SOON! THEN WHY HASN'T THE BRIDEGROOM STEPPED FORWARD? THE REST OF THE ARMY SEEMED EAGER ENOUGH TO GREET US.
AH! THE BRIDEGROOM--A GREAT WARRIOR OF IMMORTAL LINEAGE. THETIS IS HIS MOTHER. PELEUS IS HIS FATHER. THE KENTAUR CHEIRON WAS HIS TEACHER, AND ONE DAY HE'LL BE KING IN PHTHIA. NO ONE COULD FIND A MORE WORTHY HUSBAND FOR OUR DAUGHTER THAN ACH--
YES, BUT WHY HASN'T HE WELCOMED HER?
I'LL SEND FOR HIM... BUT FIRST...
FIRST, I WANT TO KNOW WHAT'S GOING ON, AGAMEMNON.
SHSHSHSHSHSHSHSHSHSHSHSHSHSHSHSHSHSHSHSHSHSH

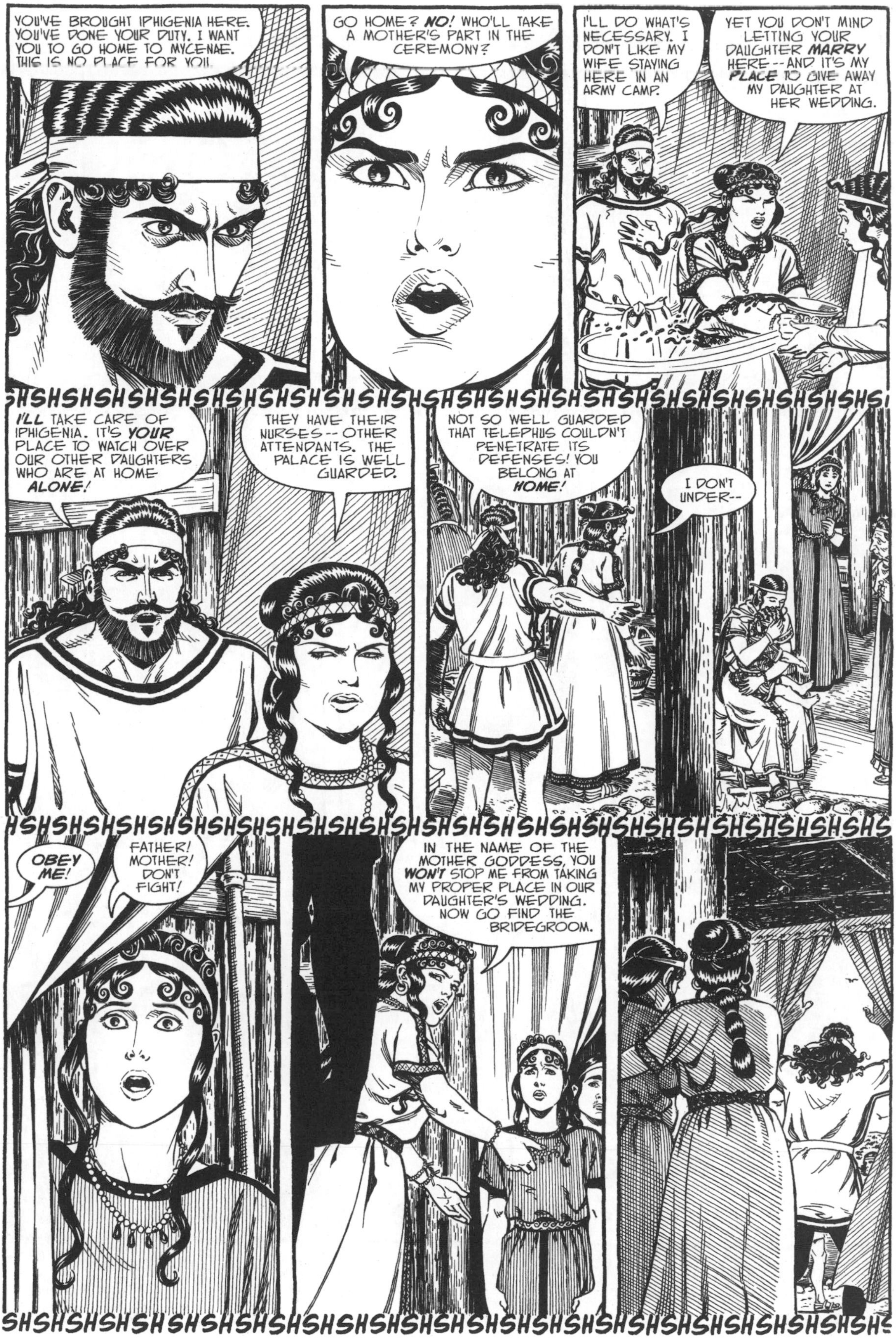
YOU'VE BROUGHT IPHIGENIA HERE. YOU'VE DONE YOUR DUTY. I WANT YOU TO GO HOME TO MYCENAE. THIS IS NO PLACE FOR YOU.
GO HOME? NO! WHO'LL TAKE A MOTHER'S PART IN THE CEREMONY?
I'LL DO WHAT'S NECESSARY. I DON'T LIKE MY WIFE STAYING HERE IN AN ARMY CAMP.
YET YOU DON'T MIND LETTING YOUR DAUGHTER MARRY HERE--AND IT'S MY PLACE TO GIVE AWAY MY DAUGHTER AT HER WEDDING.
SHSHSHSHSHSHSHSHSHSHSHSHSHSHSHSHSHSHSHSHSHSHSHSHSHS
I'LL TAKE CARE OF IPHIGENIA. IT'S YOUR PLACE TO WATCH OVER OUR OTHER DAUGHTERS WHO ARE AT HOME ALONE!
THEY HAVE THEIR NURSES--OTHER ATTENDANTS. THE PALACE IS WELL GUARDED.
NOT SO WELL GUARDED THAT TELEPHUS COULDN'T PENETRATE ITS DEFENSES! YOU BELONG AT HOME!
I DON'T UNDER--
SHSHSHSHSHSHSHSHSHSHSHSHSHSHSHSHSHSHSHSHSHSHSHSHSHS
OBEY ME!
FATHER! MOTHER! DON'T FIGHT!
IN THE NAME OF THE MOTHER GODDESS, YOU WON'T STOP ME FROM TAKING MY PROPER PLACE IN OUR DAUGHTER'S WEDDING. NOW GO FIND THE BRIDEGROOM.
SHSHSHSHSHSHSHSHSHSHSHSHSHSHSHSHSHSHSHSHSHSHSHSHSHS

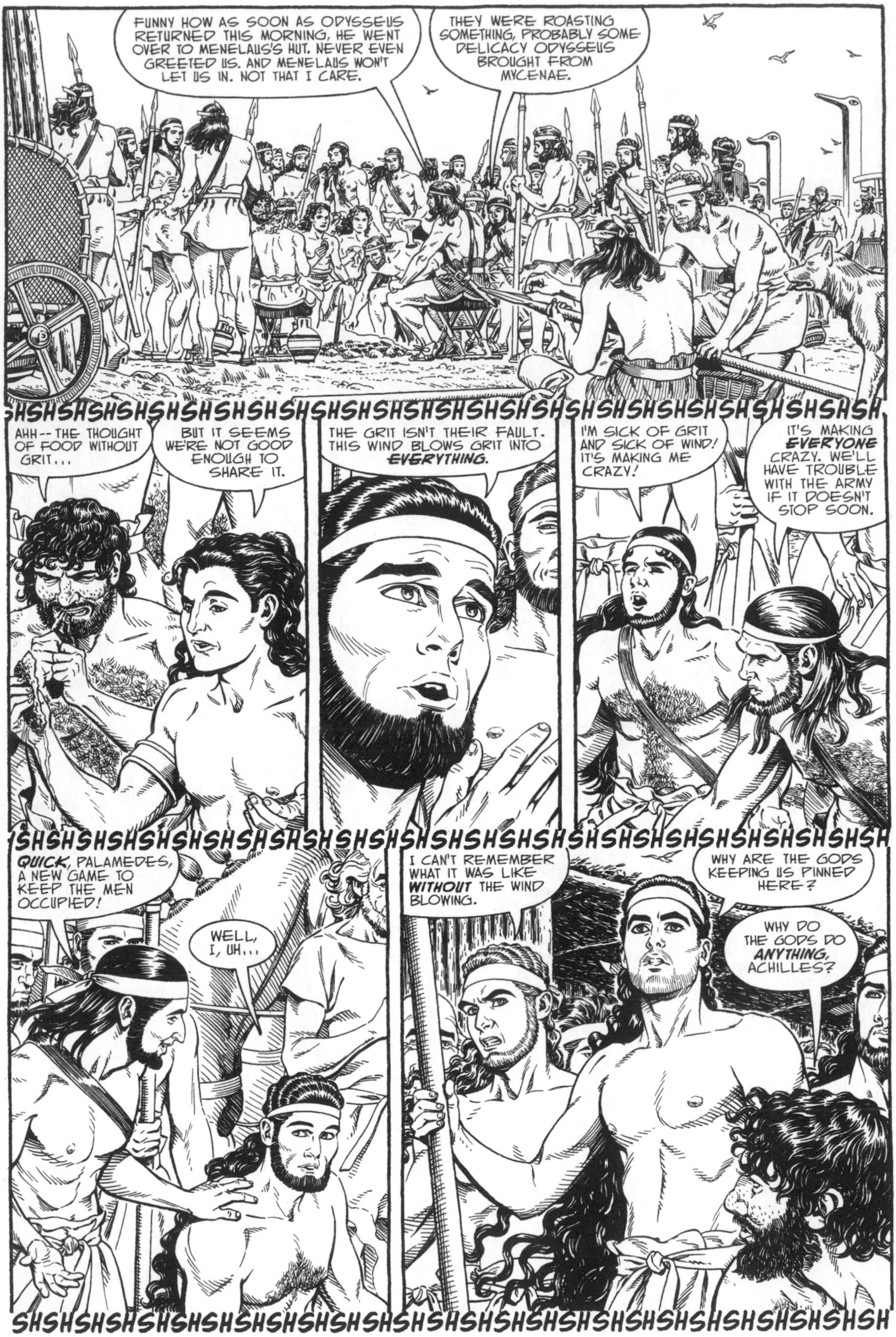

FUNNY HOW AS SOON AS ODYSSEUS RETURNED THIS MORNING, HE WENT OVER TO MENELAUS'S HUT. NEVER EVEN GREETED US. AND MENELAUS WON'T LET US IN. NOT THAT I CARE.
THEY WERE ROASTING SOMETHING, PROBABLY SOME DELICACY ODYSSEUS BROUGHT FROM MYCENAE.
SHSHSHSHSHSHSHSHSHSHSHSHSHSHSHSHSHSHSHSHSHSHSH
AHH-- THE THOUGHT OF FOOD WITHOUT GRIT...
BUT IT SEEMS WE'RE NOT GOOD ENOUGH TO SHARE IT.
THE GRIT ISN'T THEIR FAULT. THIS WIND BLOWS GRIT INTO EVERYTHING.
I'M SICK OF GRIT AND SICK OF WIND! IT'S MAKING ME CRAZY!
IT'S MAKING EVERYONE CRAZY. WE'LL HAVE TROUBLE WITH THE ARMY IF IT DOESN'T STOP SOON.
SHSHSHSHSHSHSHSHSHSHSHSHSHSHSHSHSHSHSHSHSHSH
QUICK, PALAMEDES, A NEW GAME TO KEEP THE MEN OCCUPIED!
WELL, I, UH...
I CAN'T REMEMBER WHAT IT WAS LIKE WITHOUT THE WIND BLOWING.
WHY ARE THE GODS KEEPING US PINNED HERE?
WHY DO THE GODS DO ANYTHING, ACHILLES?
SHSHSHSHSHSHSHSHSHSHSHSHSHSHSHSHSHSHSHSHSH

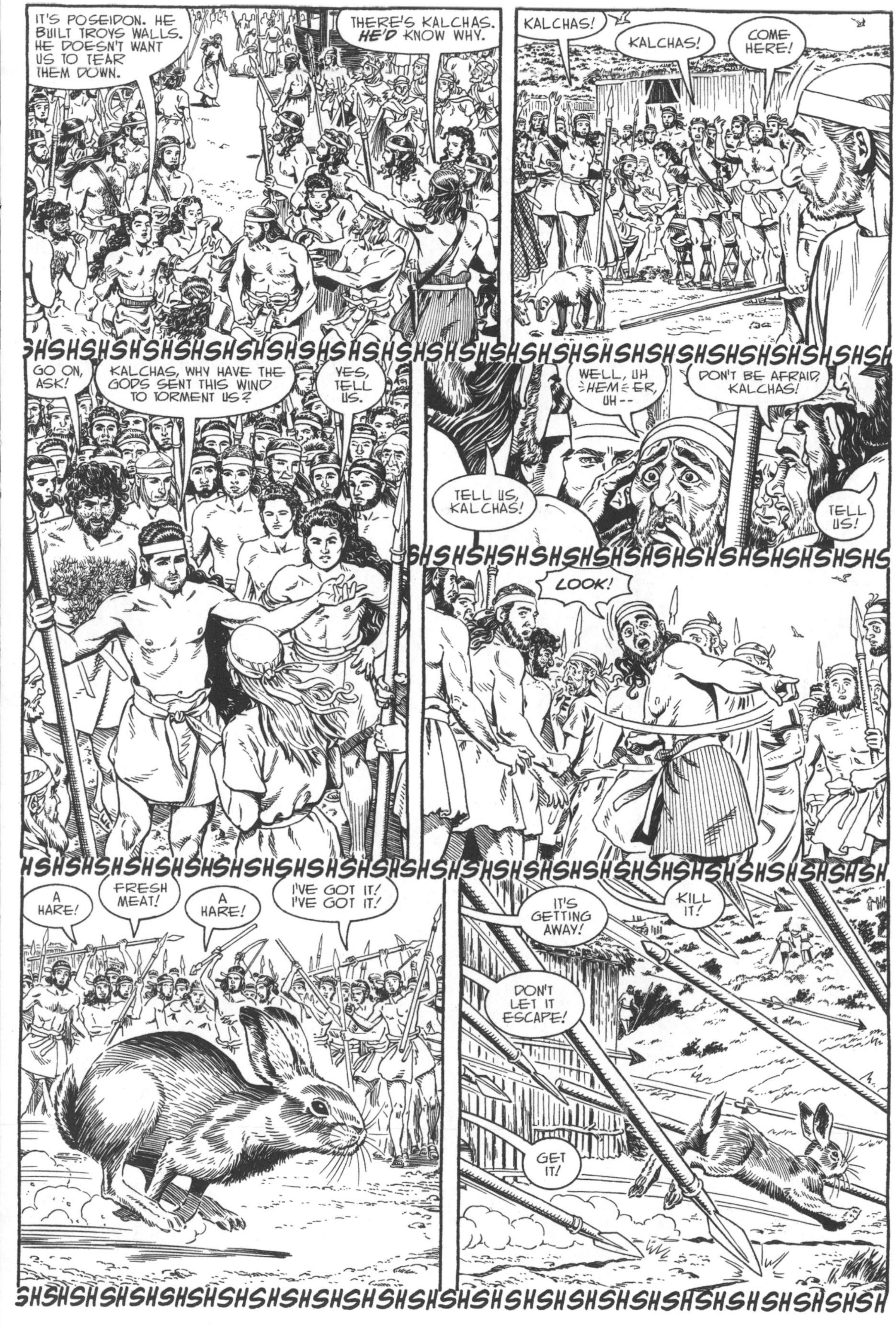
IT'S POSEIDON. HE BUILT TROYS WALLS. HE DOESN'T WANT US TO TEAR THEM DOWN.
THERE'S KALCHAS. HE'D KNOW WHY.
KALCHAS!
KALCHAS!
COME HERE!
SHSHSHSHSHSHSHSHSHSHSHSHSHSHSHSHSHSHSHSHSHSHSH
GO ON, ASK!
KALCHAS, WHY HAVE THE GODS SENT THIS WIND TO TORMENT US?
YES, TELL US.
WELL, UH HEM ER, UH --
DON'T BE AFRAID KALCHAS!
TELL US, KALCHAS!
TELL US!
SHSHSHSHSHSHSHSHSHSHSHSHSHS
LOOK!
SHSHSHSHSHSHSHSHSHSHSHSHSHSHSHSHSHSHSHSHSHSH
A HARE!
FRESH MEAT!
A HARE!
I'VE GOT IT! I'VE GOT IT!
IT'S GETTING AWAY!
KILL IT!
DON'T LET IT ESCAPE!
GET IT!
SHSHSHSHSHSHSHSHSHSHSHSHSHSHSHSHSHSHSHSHSHSHSH

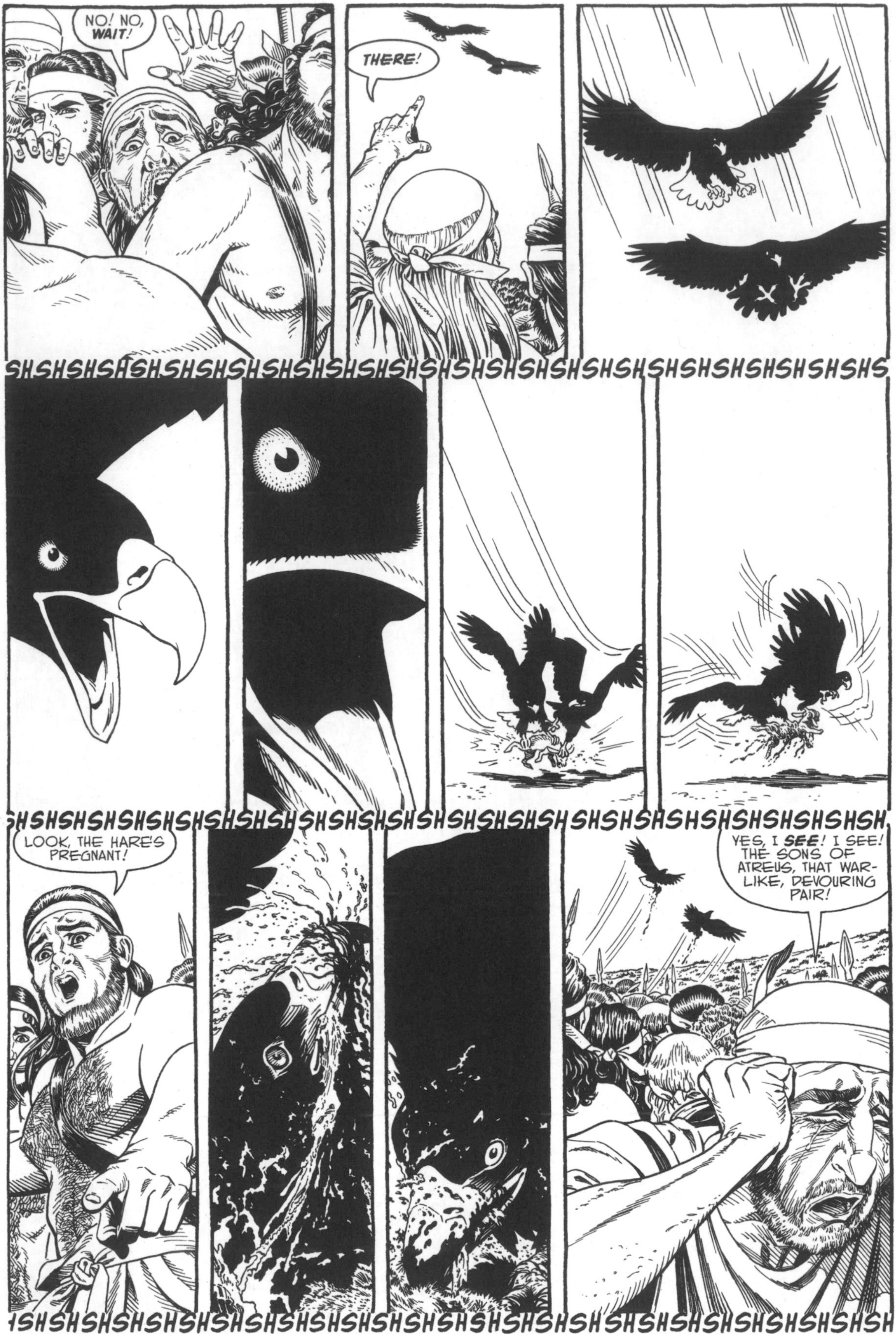
NO! NO, WAIT!
THERE!
SHSHSHSHSHSHSHSHSHSHSHSHSHSHSHSHSHSHSHSHSHSHS
SHSHSHSHSHSHSHSHSHSHSHSHSHSHSHSHSHSHSHSHSH
LOOK, THE HARE'S PREGNANT!
YES, I SEE! I SEE! THE SONS OF ATREUS, THAT WAR-LIKE, DEVOURING PAIR!
SHSHSHSHSHSHSHSHSHSHSHSHSHSHSHSHSHSHSHSHSH

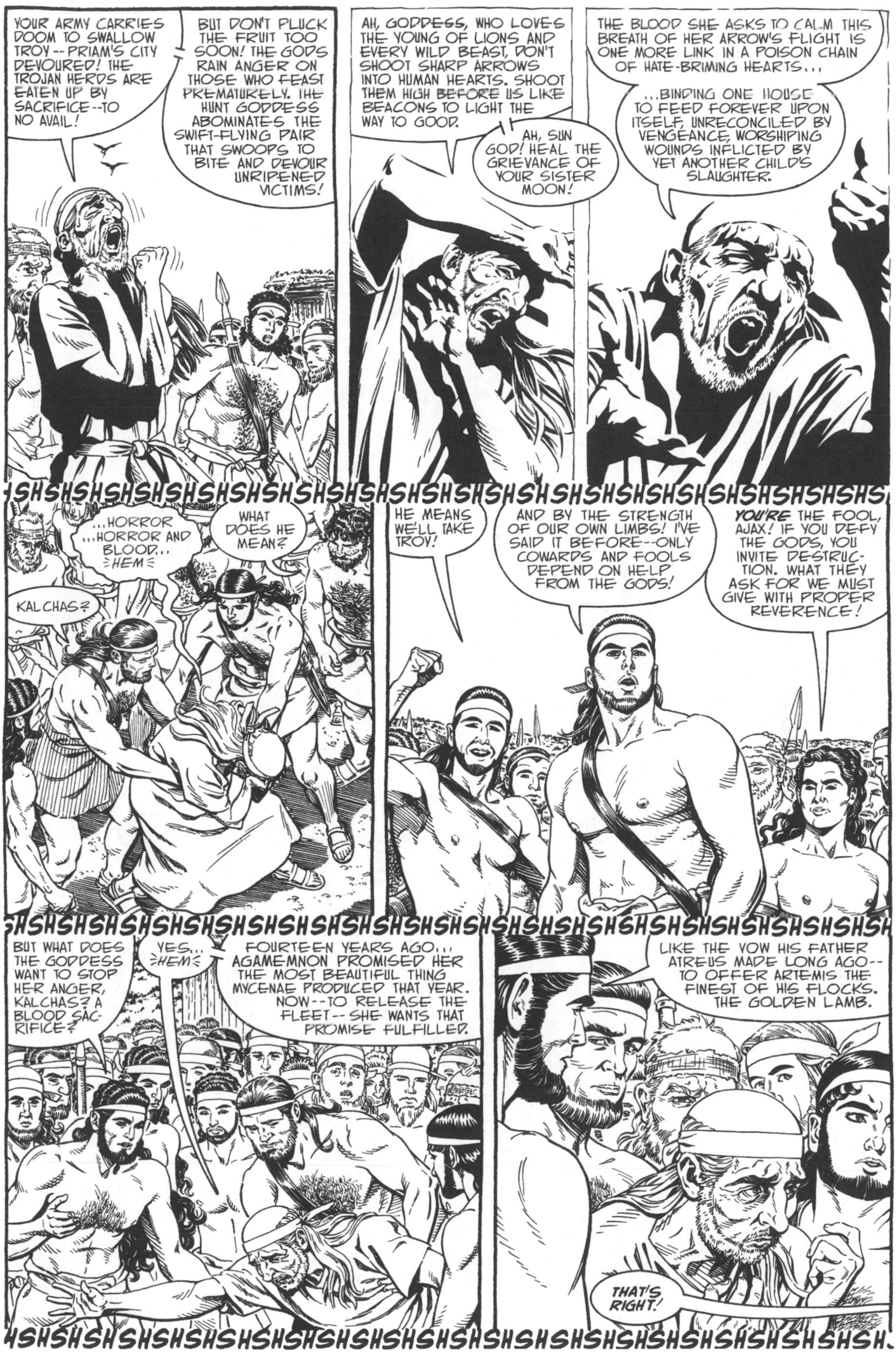
YOUR ARMY CARRIES DOOM TO SWALLOW TROY--PRIAM'S CITY DEVOURED! THE TROJAN HERDS ARE EATEN UP BY SACRIFICE--TO NO AVAIL!
BUT DON'T PLUCK THE FRUIT TOO SOON! THE GODS RAIN ANGER ON THOSE WHO FEAST PREMATURELY. THE HUNT GODDESS ABOMINATES THE SWIFT-FLYING PAIR THAT SWOOPS TO BITE AND DEVOUR UNRIPENED VICTIMS!
AH, GODDESS, WHO LOVES THE YOUNG OF LIONS AND EVERY WILD BEAST, DON'T SHOOT SHARP ARROWS INTO HUMAN HEARTS. SHOOT THEM HIGH BEFORE US LIKE BEACONS TO LIGHT THE WAY TO GOOD.
AH, SUN GOD! HEAL THE GRIEVANCE OF YOUR SISTER MOON!
THE BLOOD SHE ASKS TO CALM THIS BREATH OF HER ARROW'S FLIGHT IS ONE MORE LINK IN A POISON CHAIN OF HATE-BRIMING HEARTS...
...BINDING ONE HOUSE TO FEED FOREVER UPON ITSELF, UNRECONCILED BY VENGEANCE, WORSHIPING WOUNDS INFLICTED BY YET ANOTHER CHILD'S SLAUGHTER.
SHSHSHSHSHSHSHSHSHSHSHSHSHSHSHSHSHSHSHSHSHSHSHSH
...HORROR ...HORROR AND BLOOD... HEM
WHAT DOES HE MEAN?
KALCHAS?
HE MEANS WE'LL TAKE TROY!
AND BY THE STRENGTH OF OUR OWN LIMBS! I'VE SAID IT BEFORE--ONLY COWARDS AND FOOLS DEPEND ON HELP FROM THE GODS!
YOU'RE THE FOOL, AJAX! IF YOU DEFY THE GODS, YOU INVITE DESTRUCTION. WHAT THEY ASK FOR WE MUST GIVE WITH PROPER REVERENCE!
SHSHSHSHSHSHSHSHSHSHSHSHSHSHSHSHSHSHSHSHSHSHSHSH
BUT WHAT DOES THE GODDESS WANT TO STOP HER ANGER, KALCHAS? A BLOOD SACRIFICE?
YES... HEM
FOURTEEN YEARS AGO... AGAMEMNON PROMISED HER THE MOST BEAUTIFUL THING MYCENAE PRODUCED THAT YEAR. NOW--TO RELEASE THE FLEET--SHE WANTS THAT PROMISE FULFILLED.
LIKE THE VOW HIS FATHER ATREUS MADE LONG AGO--TO OFFER ARTEMIS THE FINEST OF HIS FLOCKS. THE GOLDEN LAMB.
THAT'S RIGHT!
SHSHSHSHSHSHSHSHSHSHSHSHSHSHSHSHSHSHSHSHSHSHSH

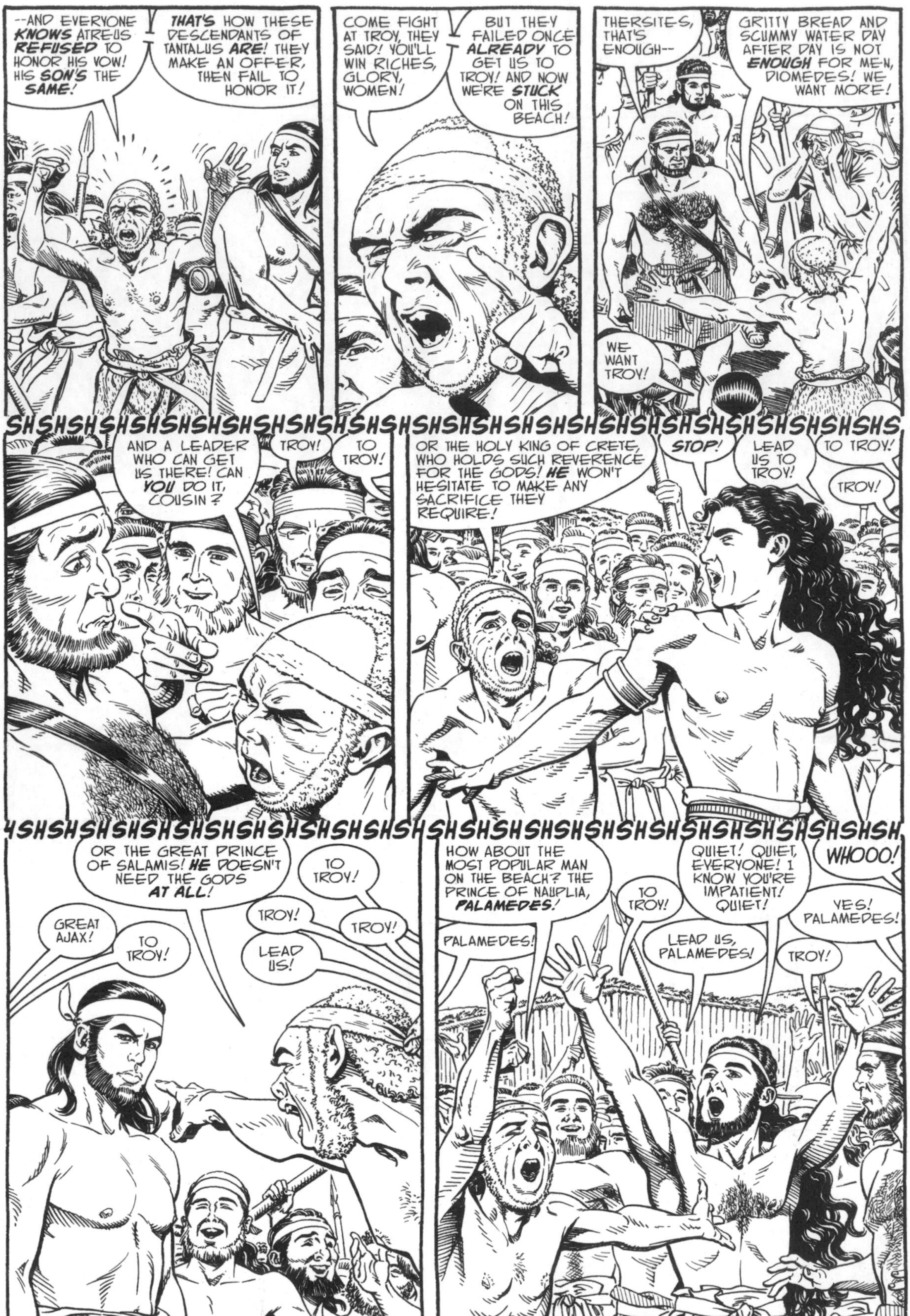
--AND EVERYONE KNOWS ATREUS REFUSED TO HONOR HIS VOW! HIS SON'S THE SAME!
THAT'S HOW THESE DESCENDANTS OF TANTALUS ARE! THEY MAKE AN OFFER, THEN FAIL TO HONOR IT!
COME FIGHT AT TROY, THEY SAID! YOU'LL WIN RICHES, GLORY, WOMEN!
BUT THEY FAILED ONCE ALREADY TO GET US TO TROY! AND NOW WE'RE STUCK ON THIS BEACH!
THERSITES, THAT'S ENOUGH--
GRITTY BREAD AND SCUMMY WATER DAY AFTER DAY IS NOT ENOUGH FOR MEN, DIOMEDES! WE WANT MORE!
WE WANT TROY!
SHSHSHSHSHSHSHSHSHSHSHSHSHSHSHSHSHSHSHSHSHSHSHS
AND A LEADER WHO CAN GET US THERE! CAN YOU DO IT, COUSIN?
TROY!
TO TROY!
OR THE HOLY KING OF CRETE, WHO HOLDS SUCH REVERENCE FOR THE GODS! HE WON'T HESITATE TO MAKE ANY SACRIFICE THEY REQUIRE!
STOP!
LEAD US TO TROY!
TO TROY!
TROY!
SHSHSHSHSHSHSHSHSHSHSHSHSHSHSHSHSHSHSHSHSHSHSH
OR THE GREAT PRINCE OF SALAMIS! HE DOESN'T NEED THE GODS AT ALL!
TO TROY!
GREAT AJAX!
TO TROY!
TROY!
TROY!
LEAD US!
HOW ABOUT THE MOST POPULAR MAN ON THE BEACH? THE PRINCE OF NAUPLIA, PALAMEDES!
QUIET! QUIET, EVERYONE! I KNOW YOU'RE IMPATIENT! QUIET!
WHOOO!
TO TROY!
YES! PALAMEDES!
PALAMEDES!
LEAD US, PALAMEDES!
TROY!
SHSHSHSHSHSHSHSHSHSHSHSHSHSHSHSHSHSHSHSHSHSHSHS

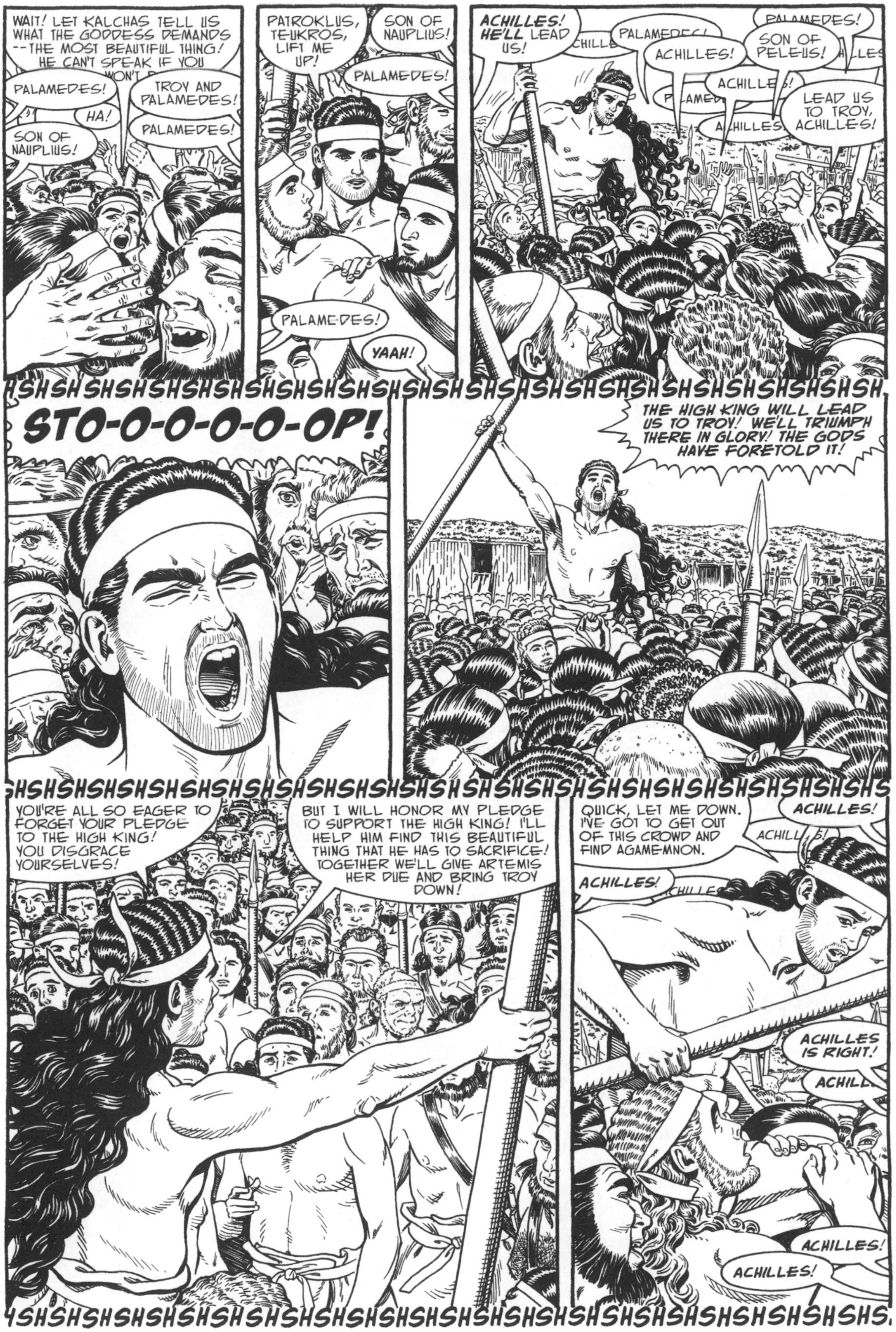
WAIT! LET KALCHAS TELL US WHAT THE GODDESS DEMANDS --THE MOST BEAUTIFUL THING! HE CAN'T SPEAK IF YOU
PALAMEDES!
TROY AND PALAMEDES!
HA!
SON OF NAUPLIUS!
PALAMEDES!
PATROKLUS, TEUKROS, LIFT ME UP!
SON OF NAUPLIUS!
PALAMEDES!
PALAMEDES!
YAAH!
ACHILLES! HE'LL LEAD US!
ACHILLES!
SON OF PELEUS!
LEAD US TO TROY, ACHILLES!
PALAMEDES!
SHSHSHSHSHSHSHSHSHSHSHSHSHSHSHSHSHSHSHSHSH
STO-O-O-O-O-OP!
THE HIGH KING WILL LEAD US TO TROY! WE'LL TRIUMPH THERE IN GLORY! THE GODS HAVE FORETOLD IT!
SHSHSHSHSHSHSHSHSHSHSHSHSHSHSHSHSHSHSHSHSHS
YOU'RE ALL SO EAGER TO FORGET YOUR PLEDGE TO THE HIGH KING! YOU DISGRACE YOURSELVES!
BUT I WILL HONOR MY PLEDGE TO SUPPORT THE HIGH KING! I'LL HELP HIM FIND THIS BEAUTIFUL THING THAT HE HAS TO SACRIFICE! TOGETHER WE'LL GIVE ARTEMIS HER DUE AND BRING TROY DOWN!
QUICK, LET ME DOWN. I'VE GOT TO GET OUT OF THIS CROWD AND FIND AGAMEMNON.
ACHILLES!
ACHILLES!
ACHILLES IS RIGHT!
ACHILLES!
ACHILLES!
SHSHSHSHSHSHSHSHSHSHSHSHSHSHSHSHSHSHSHSHSHS

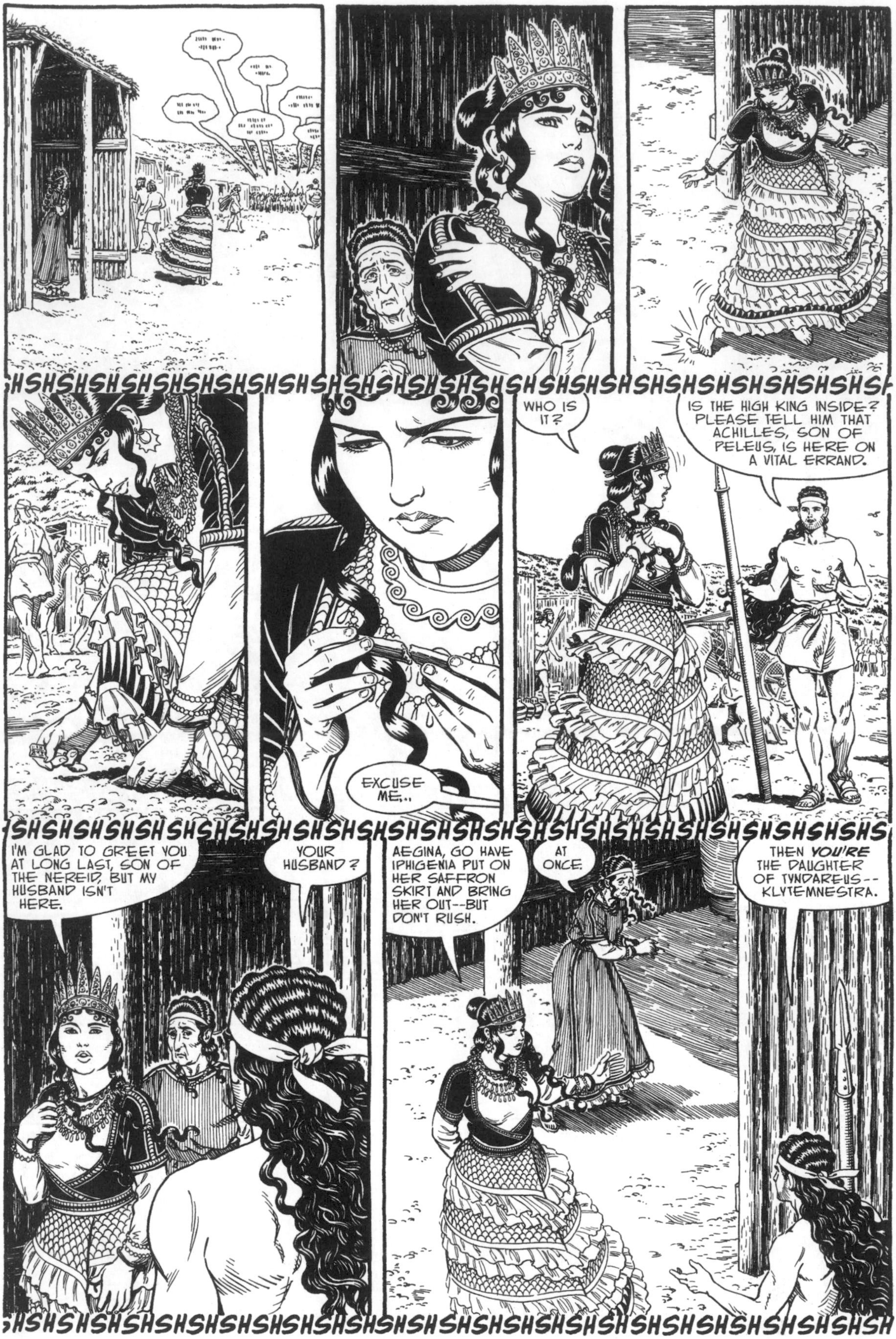

SHSHSHSHSHSHSHSHSHSHSHSHSHSHSHSHSHSHSHSHSH
EXCUSE ME...
WHO IS IT?
IS THE HIGH KING INSIDE? PLEASE TELL HIM THAT ACHILLES, SON OF PELEUS, IS HERE ON A VITAL ERRAND.
SHSHSHSHSHSHSHSHSHSHSHSHSHSHSHSHSHSHSHSHSH
I'M GLAD TO GREET YOU AT LONG LAST, SON OF THE NEREID, BUT MY HUSBAND ISN'T HERE.
YOUR HUSBAND?
AEGINA, GO HAVE IPHIGENIA PUT ON HER SAFFRON SKIRT AND BRING HER OUT--BUT DON'T RUSH.
AT ONCE.
THEN *YOU'RE* THE DAUGHTER OF TYNDAREUS--KLYTEMNESTRA.
SHSHSHSHSHSHSHSHSHSHSHSHSHSHSHSHSHSHSHSHSH

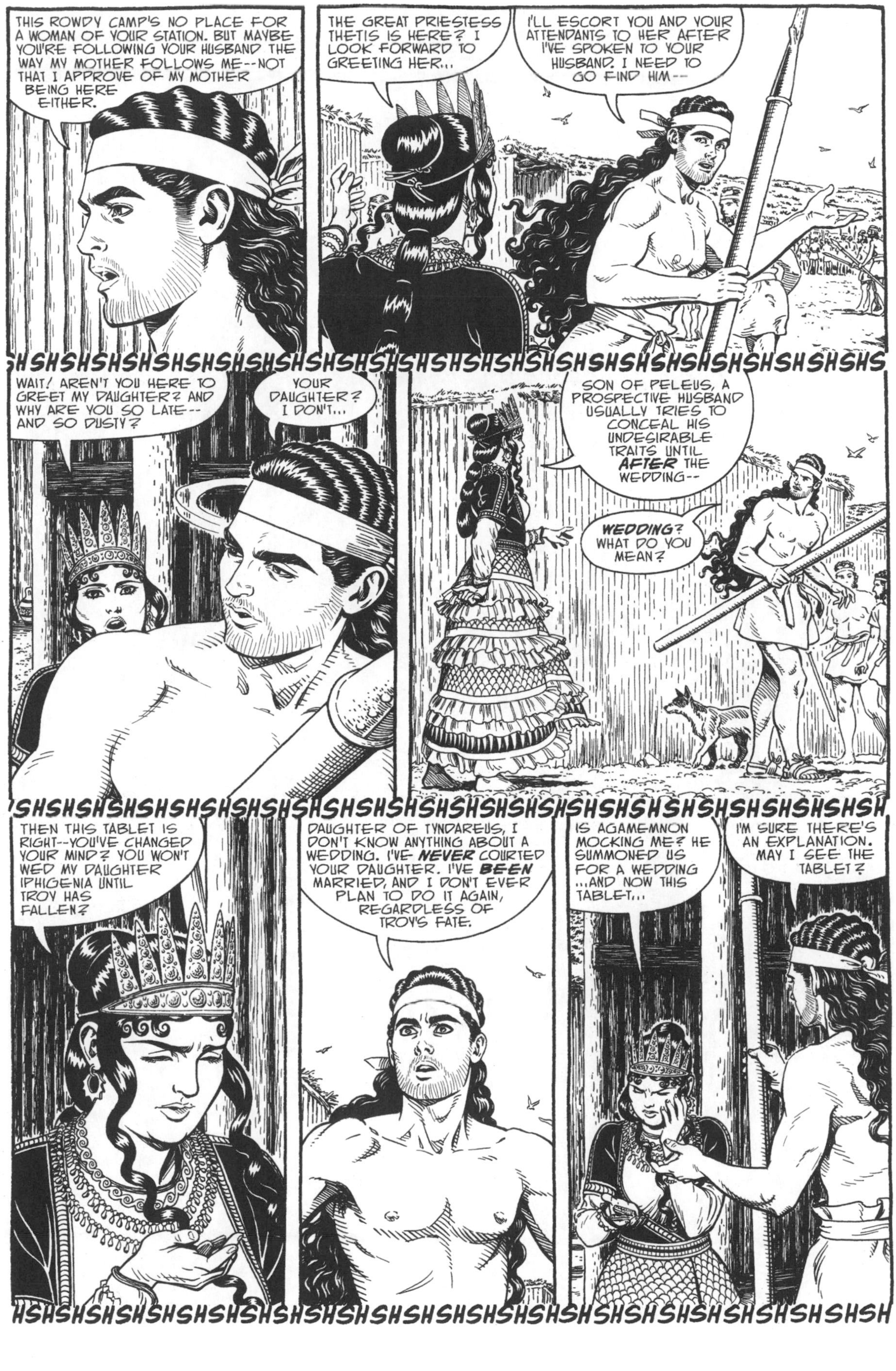
THIS ROWDY CAMP'S NO PLACE FOR A WOMAN OF YOUR STATION. BUT MAYBE YOU'RE FOLLOWING YOUR HUSBAND THE WAY MY MOTHER FOLLOWS ME--NOT THAT I APPROVE OF MY MOTHER BEING HERE EITHER.
THE GREAT PRIESTESS THETIS IS HERE? I LOOK FORWARD TO GREETING HER...
I'LL ESCORT YOU AND YOUR ATTENDANTS TO HER AFTER I'VE SPOKEN TO YOUR HUSBAND. I NEED TO GO FIND HIM--
WAIT! AREN'T YOU HERE TO GREET MY DAUGHTER? AND WHY ARE YOU SO LATE-- AND SO DUSTY?
YOUR DAUGHTER? I DON'T...
SON OF PELEUS, A PROSPECTIVE HUSBAND USUALLY TRIES TO CONCEAL HIS UNDESIRABLE TRAITS UNTIL AFTER THE WEDDING--
WEDDING? WHAT DO YOU MEAN?
THEN THIS TABLET IS RIGHT--YOU'VE CHANGED YOUR MIND? YOU WON'T WED MY DAUGHTER IPHIGENIA UNTIL TROY HAS FALLEN?
DAUGHTER OF TYNDAREUS, I DON'T KNOW ANYTHING ABOUT A WEDDING. I'VE NEVER COURTED YOUR DAUGHTER. I'VE BEEN MARRIED, AND I DON'T EVER PLAN TO DO IT AGAIN, REGARDLESS OF TROY'S FATE.
IS AGAMEMNON MOCKING ME? HE SUMMONED US FOR A WEDDING ...AND NOW THIS TABLET...
I'M SURE THERE'S AN EXPLANATION. MAY I SEE THE TABLET?

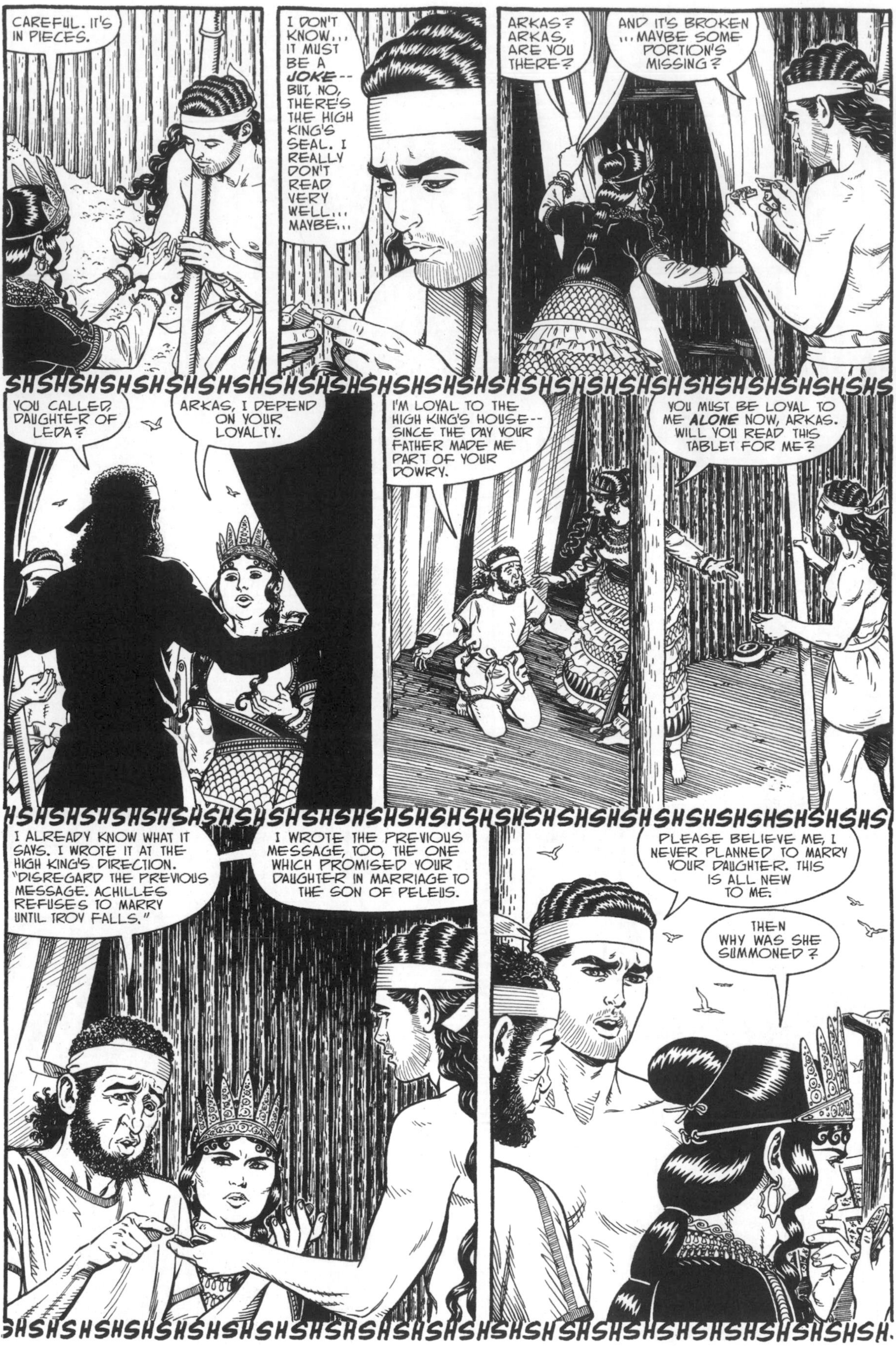

CAREFUL. IT'S IN PIECES.
I DON'T KNOW... IT MUST BE A JOKE-- BUT, NO, THERE'S THE HIGH KING'S SEAL. I REALLY DON'T READ VERY WELL... MAYBE...
ARKAS? ARKAS, ARE YOU THERE?
AND IT'S BROKEN ...MAYBE SOME PORTION'S MISSING?
SHSHSHSHSHSHSHSHSHSHSHSHSHSHSHSHSHSHSHSHSHSHSHS
YOU CALLED, DAUGHTER OF LEDA?
ARKAS, I DEPEND ON YOUR LOYALTY.
I'M LOYAL TO THE HIGH KING'S HOUSE-- SINCE THE DAY YOUR FATHER MADE ME PART OF YOUR DOWRY.
YOU MUST BE LOYAL TO ME ALONE NOW, ARKAS. WILL YOU READ THIS TABLET FOR ME?
SHSHSHSHSHSHSHSHSHSHSHSHSHSHSHSHSHSHSHSHSHSHS
I ALREADY KNOW WHAT IT SAYS. I WROTE IT AT THE HIGH KING'S DIRECTION. "DISREGARD THE PREVIOUS MESSAGE. ACHILLES REFUSES TO MARRY UNTIL TROY FALLS."
I WROTE THE PREVIOUS MESSAGE, TOO, THE ONE WHICH PROMISED YOUR DAUGHTER IN MARRIAGE TO THE SON OF PELEUS.
PLEASE BELIEVE ME, I NEVER PLANNED TO MARRY YOUR DAUGHTER. THIS IS ALL NEW TO ME.
THEN WHY WAS SHE SUMMONED?
SHSHSHSHSHSHSHSHSHSHSHSHSHSHSHSHSHSHSHSHSHSH

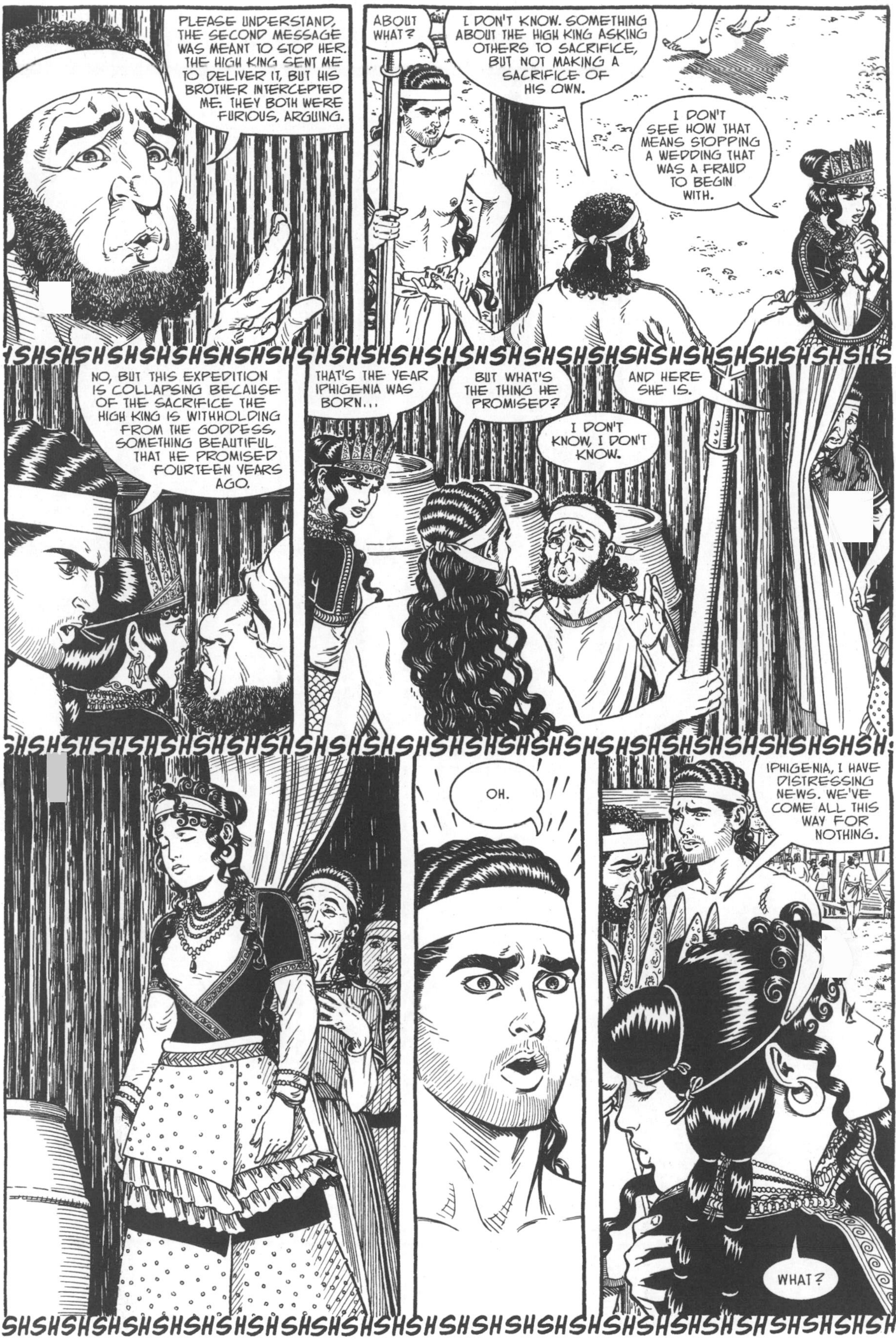
PLEASE UNDERSTAND, THE SECOND MESSAGE WAS MEANT TO STOP HER. THE HIGH KING SENT ME TO DELIVER IT, BUT HIS BROTHER INTERCEPTED ME. THEY BOTH WERE FURIOUS, ARGUING.
ABOUT WHAT?
I DON'T KNOW. SOMETHING ABOUT THE HIGH KING ASKING OTHERS TO SACRIFICE, BUT NOT MAKING A SACRIFICE OF HIS OWN.
I DON'T SEE HOW THAT MEANS STOPPING A WEDDING THAT WAS A FRAUD TO BEGIN WITH.
SHSHSHSHSHSHSHSHSHSHSHSHSHSHSHSHSHSHSHSHSHSHSHSHSHS
NO, BUT THIS EXPEDITION IS COLLAPSING BECAUSE OF THE SACRIFICE THE HIGH KING IS WITHHOLDING FROM THE GODDESS, SOMETHING BEAUTIFUL THAT HE PROMISED FOURTEEN YEARS AGO.
THAT'S THE YEAR IPHIGENIA WAS BORN...
BUT WHAT'S THE THING HE PROMISED?
I DON'T KNOW, I DON'T KNOW.
AND HERE SHE IS.
SHSHSHSHSHSHSHSHSHSHSHSHSHSHSHSHSHSHSHSHSHSHSHSHSHSH
OH.
IPHIGENIA, I HAVE DISTRESSING NEWS. WE'VE COME ALL THIS WAY FOR NOTHING.
WHAT?
SHSHSHSHSHSHSHSHSHSHSHSHSHSHSHSHSHSHSHSHSHSHSHSHSHSH

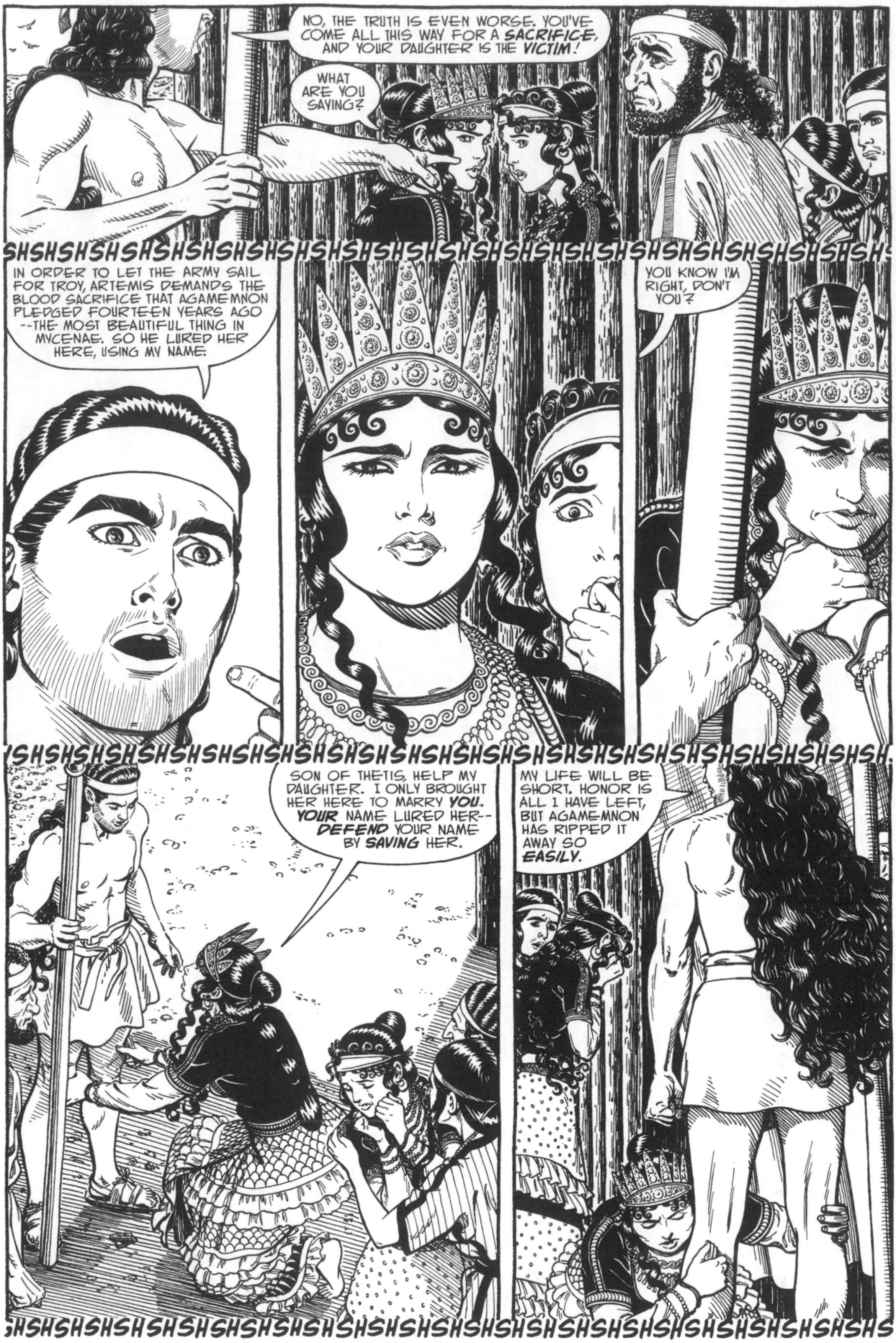

NO, THE TRUTH IS EVEN WORSE. YOU'VE COME ALL THIS WAY FOR A SACRIFICE, AND YOUR DAUGHTER IS THE VICTIM!
WHAT ARE YOU SAYING?
SHSHSHSHSHSHSHSHSHSHSHSHSHSHSHSHSHSHSHSHSH
IN ORDER TO LET THE ARMY SAIL FOR TROY, ARTEMIS DEMANDS THE BLOOD SACRIFICE THAT AGAMEMNON PLEDGED FOURTEEN YEARS AGO --THE MOST BEAUTIFUL THING IN MYCENAE. SO HE LURED HER HERE, USING MY NAME.
YOU KNOW I'M RIGHT, DON'T YOU?
SHSHSHSHSHSHSHSHSHSHSHSHSHSHSHSHSHSHSHSHSH
SON OF THETIS, HELP MY DAUGHTER. I ONLY BROUGHT HER HERE TO MARRY YOU. YOUR NAME LURED HER-- DEFEND YOUR NAME BY SAVING HER.
MY LIFE WILL BE SHORT. HONOR IS ALL I HAVE LEFT, BUT AGAMEMNON HAS RIPPED IT AWAY SO EASILY.
SHSHSHSHSHSHSHSHSHSHSHSHSHSHSHSHSHSHSHSHSH

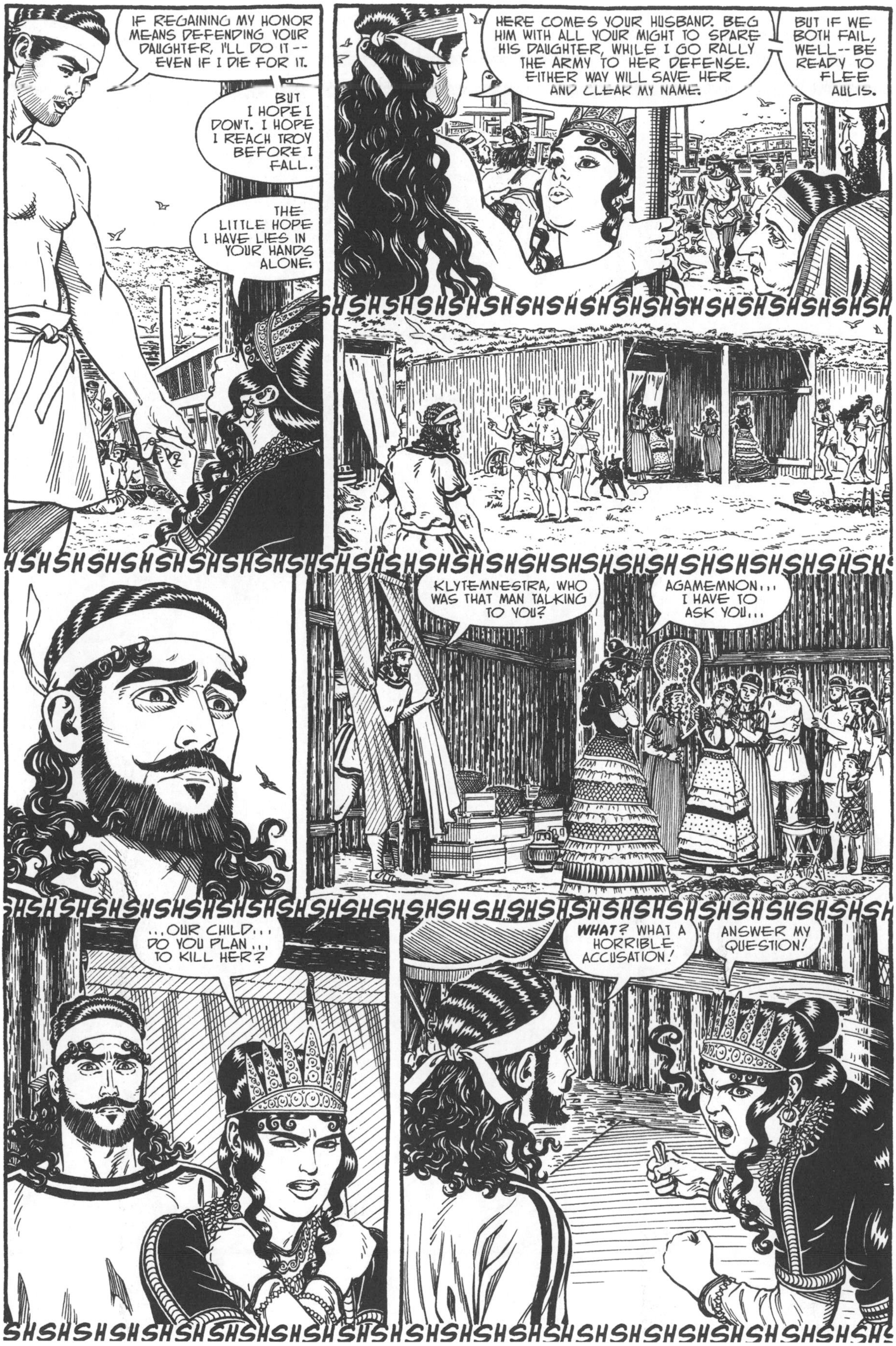
IF REGAINING MY HONOR MEANS DEFENDING YOUR DAUGHTER, I'LL DO IT -- EVEN IF I DIE FOR IT.
BUT I HOPE I DON'T. I HOPE I REACH TROY BEFORE I FALL.
THE LITTLE HOPE I HAVE LIES IN YOUR HANDS ALONE.
HERE COMES YOUR HUSBAND. BEG HIM WITH ALL YOUR MIGHT TO SPARE HIS DAUGHTER, WHILE I GO RALLY THE ARMY TO HER DEFENSE. EITHER WAY WILL SAVE HER AND CLEAR MY NAME.
BUT IF WE BOTH FAIL, WELL--BE READY TO FLEE AULIS.
KLYTEMNESTRA, WHO WAS THAT MAN TALKING TO YOU?
AGAMEMNON... I HAVE TO ASK YOU...
...OUR CHILD... DO YOU PLAN... TO KILL HER?
WHAT? WHAT A HORRIBLE ACCUSATION!
ANSWER MY QUESTION!

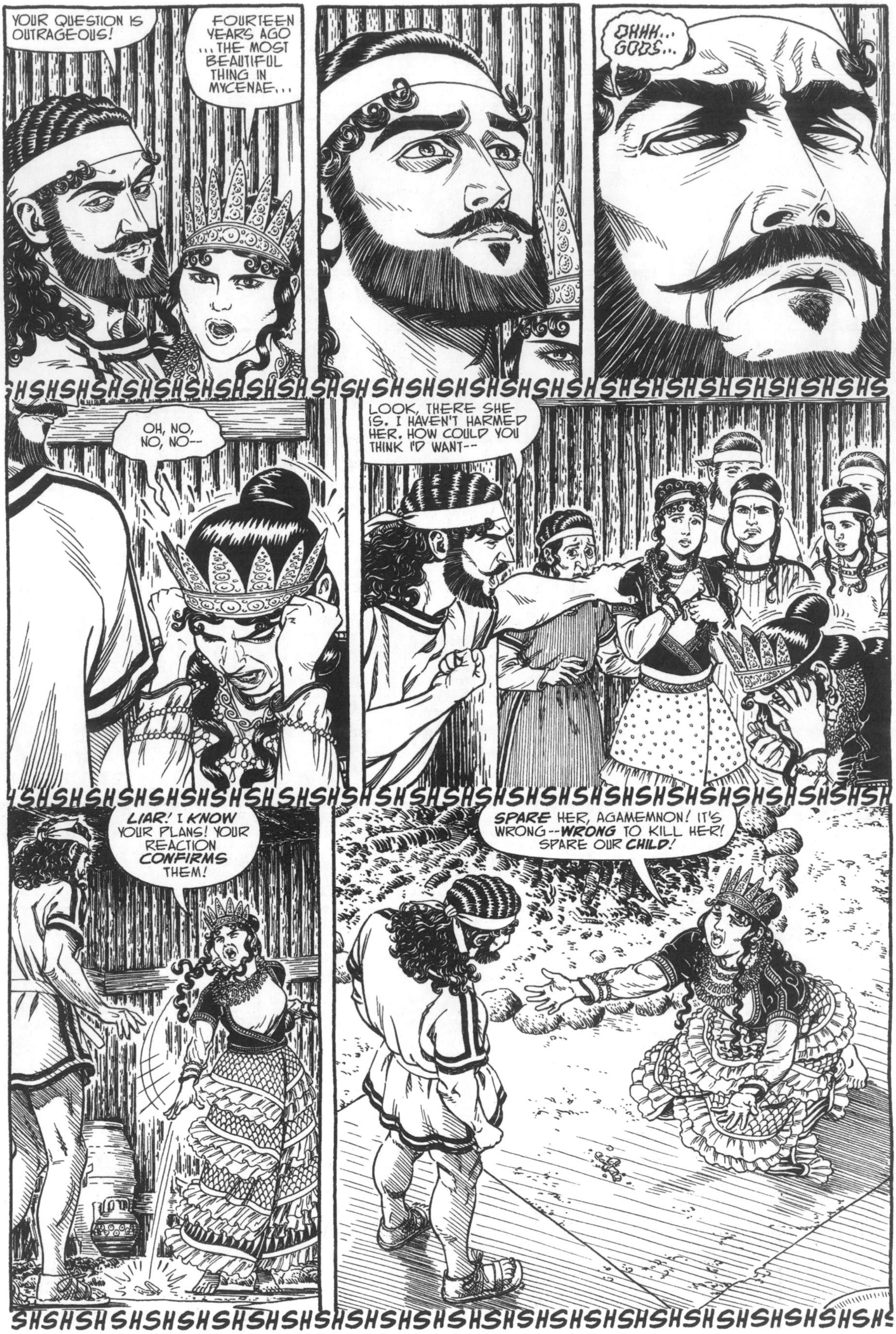
YOUR QUESTION IS OUTRAGEOUS!
FOURTEEN YEARS AGO ...THE MOST BEAUTIFUL THING IN MYCENAE...
OHHH... GODS...
SHSHSHSHSHSHSHSHSHSHSHSHSHSHSHSHSHSHSHSHSHSHSHSH
OH, NO, NO, NO--
LOOK, THERE SHE IS. I HAVEN'T HARMED HER. HOW COULD YOU THINK I'D WANT--
SHSHSHSHSHSHSHSHSHSHSHSHSHSHSHSHSHSHSHSHSHSHSHSH
LIAR! I KNOW YOUR PLANS! YOUR REACTION CONFIRMS THEM!
SPARE HER, AGAMEMNON! IT'S WRONG--WRONG TO KILL HER! SPARE OUR CHILD!
SHSHSHSHSHSHSHSHSHSHSHSHSHSHSHSHSHSHSHSHSHSHSHSH

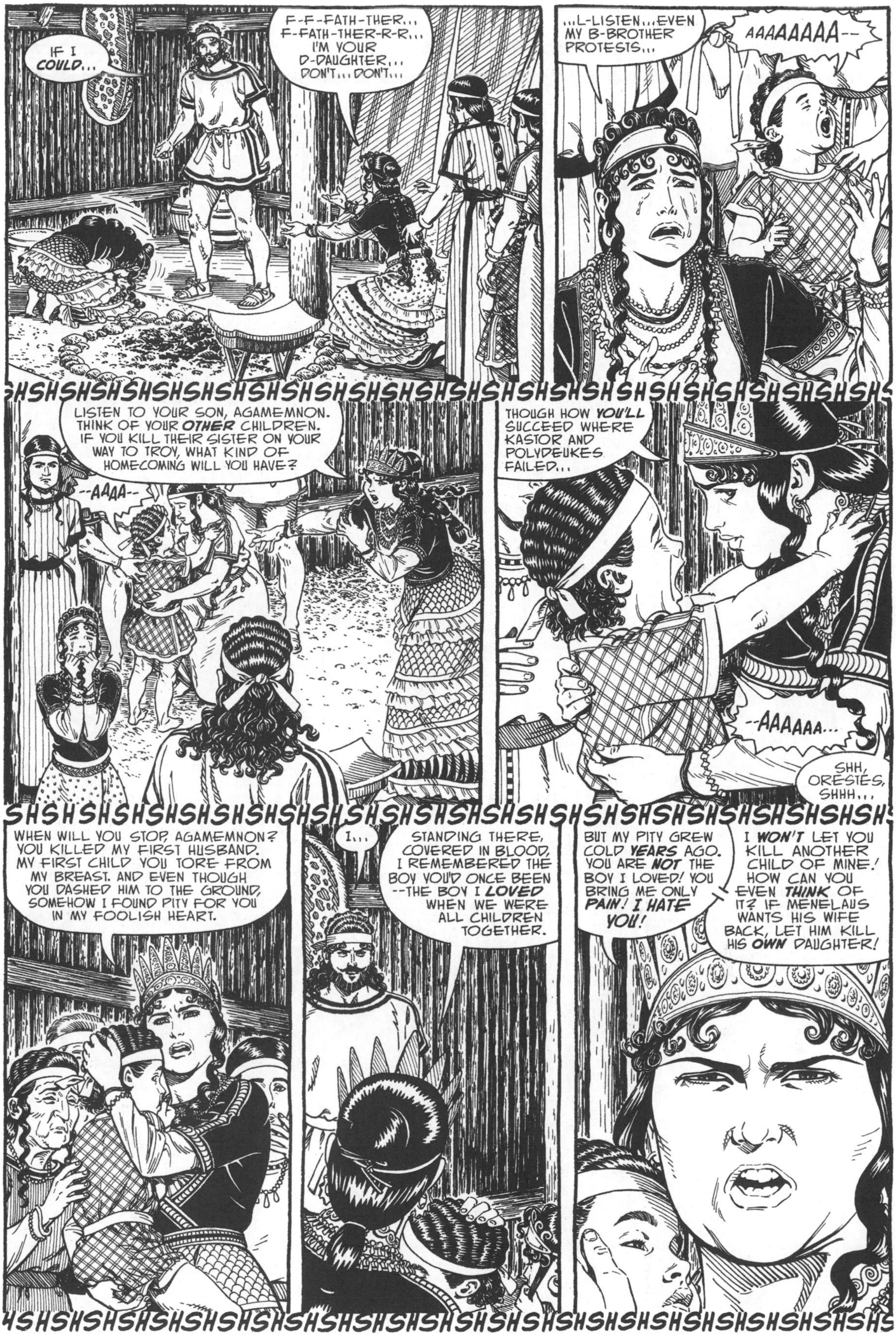

IF I COULD...
F-F-FATH-THER... F-FATH-THER-R-R... I'M YOUR D-DAUGHTER... DON'T... DON'T...
...L-LISTEN... EVEN MY B-BROTHER PROTESTS...
AAAAAAAA--
SHSHSHSHSHSHSHSHSHSHSHSHSHSHSHSHSHSHSHSHSHSHSHSHSH
LISTEN TO YOUR SON, AGAMEMNON. THINK OF YOUR OTHER CHILDREN. IF YOU KILL THEIR SISTER ON YOUR WAY TO TROY, WHAT KIND OF HOMECOMING WILL YOU HAVE?
--AAAA--
THOUGH HOW YOU'LL SUCCEED WHERE KASTOR AND POLYDEUKES FAILED...
--AAAAAA...
SHH, ORESTES, SHHH...
SHSHSHSHSHSHSHSHSHSHSHSHSHSHSHSHSHSHSHSHSHSHSHSHSH
WHEN WILL YOU STOP, AGAMEMNON? YOU KILLED MY FIRST HUSBAND. MY FIRST CHILD YOU TORE FROM MY BREAST. AND EVEN THOUGH YOU DASHED HIM TO THE GROUND, SOMEHOW I FOUND PITY FOR YOU IN MY FOOLISH HEART.
I...
STANDING THERE, COVERED IN BLOOD, I REMEMBERED THE BOY YOU'D ONCE BEEN --THE BOY I LOVED WHEN WE WERE ALL CHILDREN TOGETHER.
BUT MY PITY GREW COLD YEARS AGO. YOU ARE NOT THE BOY I LOVED! YOU BRING ME ONLY PAIN! I HATE YOU!
I WON'T LET YOU KILL ANOTHER CHILD OF MINE! HOW CAN YOU EVEN THINK OF IT? IF MENELAUS WANTS HIS WIFE BACK, LET HIM KILL HIS OWN DAUGHTER!
SHSHSHSHSHSHSHSHSHSHSHSHSHSHSHSHSHSHSHSHSHSHSHSHSH

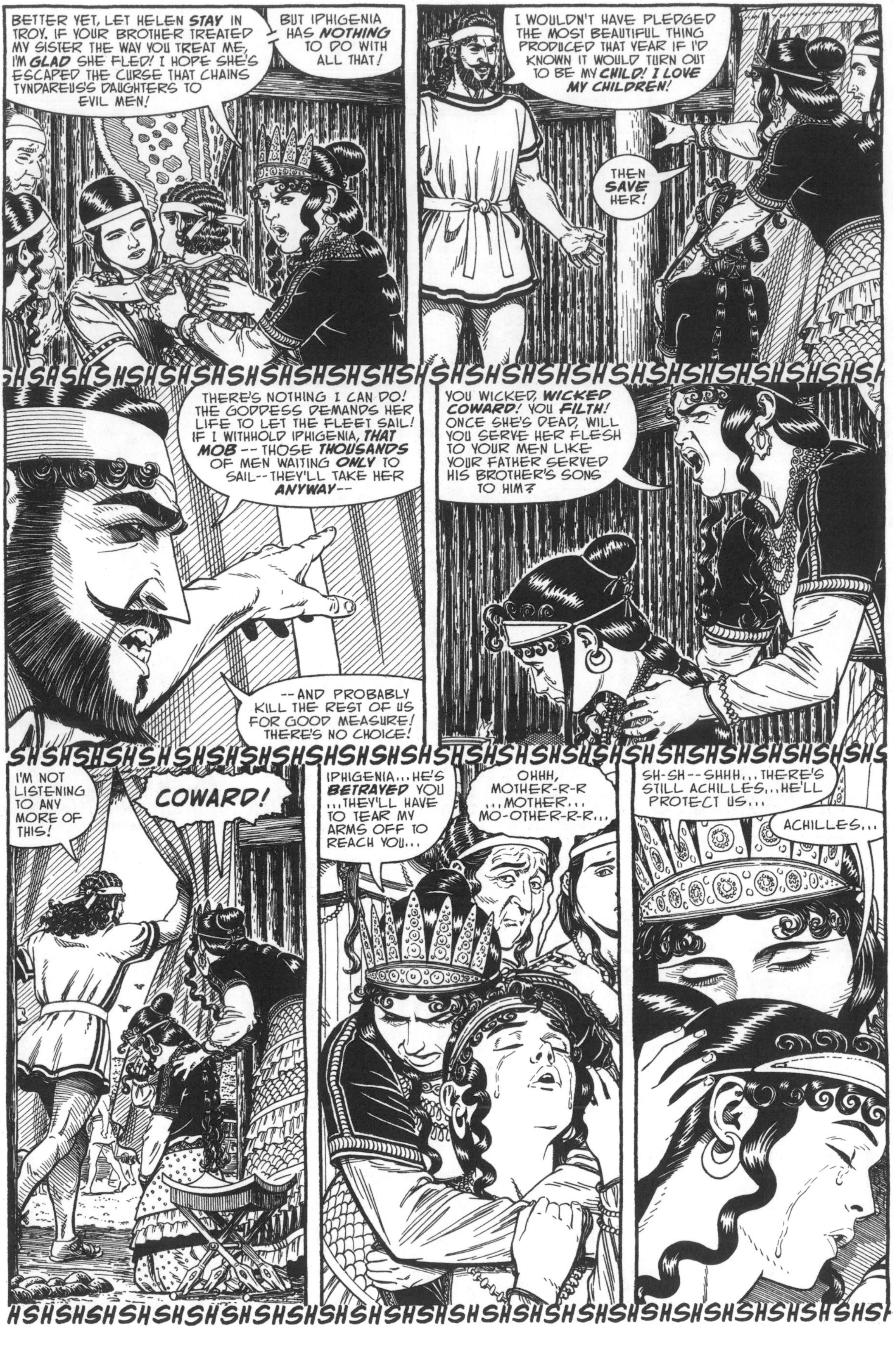
BETTER YET, LET HELEN STAY IN TROY. IF YOUR BROTHER TREATED MY SISTER THE WAY YOU TREAT ME, I'M GLAD SHE FLED! I HOPE SHE'S ESCAPED THE CURSE THAT CHAINS TYNDAREUS'S DAUGHTERS TO EVIL MEN!
BUT IPHIGENIA HAS NOTHING TO DO WITH ALL THAT!
I WOULDN'T HAVE PLEDGED THE MOST BEAUTIFUL THING PRODUCED THAT YEAR IF I'D KNOWN IT WOULD TURN OUT TO BE MY CHILD! I LOVE MY CHILDREN!
THEN SAVE HER!
SHSHSHSHSHSHSHSHSHSHSHSHSHSHSHSHSHSHSHSHSHSHSH
THERE'S NOTHING I CAN DO! THE GODDESS DEMANDS HER LIFE TO LET THE FLEET SAIL! IF I WITHHOLD IPHIGENIA, THAT MOB -- THOSE THOUSANDS OF MEN WAITING ONLY TO SAIL -- THEY'LL TAKE HER ANYWAY --
-- AND PROBABLY KILL THE REST OF US FOR GOOD MEASURE! THERE'S NO CHOICE!
YOU WICKED, WICKED COWARD! YOU FILTH! ONCE SHE'S DEAD, WILL YOU SERVE HER FLESH TO YOUR MEN LIKE YOUR FATHER SERVED HIS BROTHER'S SONS TO HIM?
SHSHSHSHSHSHSHSHSHSHSHSHSHSHSHSHSHSHSHSHSHSHS
I'M NOT LISTENING TO ANY MORE OF THIS!
COWARD!
IPHIGENIA... HE'S BETRAYED YOU ...THEY'LL HAVE TO TEAR MY ARMS OFF TO REACH YOU...
OHHH, MOTHER-R-R ...MOTHER... MO-OTHER-R-R...
SH-SH -- SHHH... THERE'S STILL ACHILLES... HE'LL PROTECT US...
ACHILLES...
HSHSHSHSHSHSHSHSHSHSHSHSHSHSHSHSHSHSHSHSHSHS

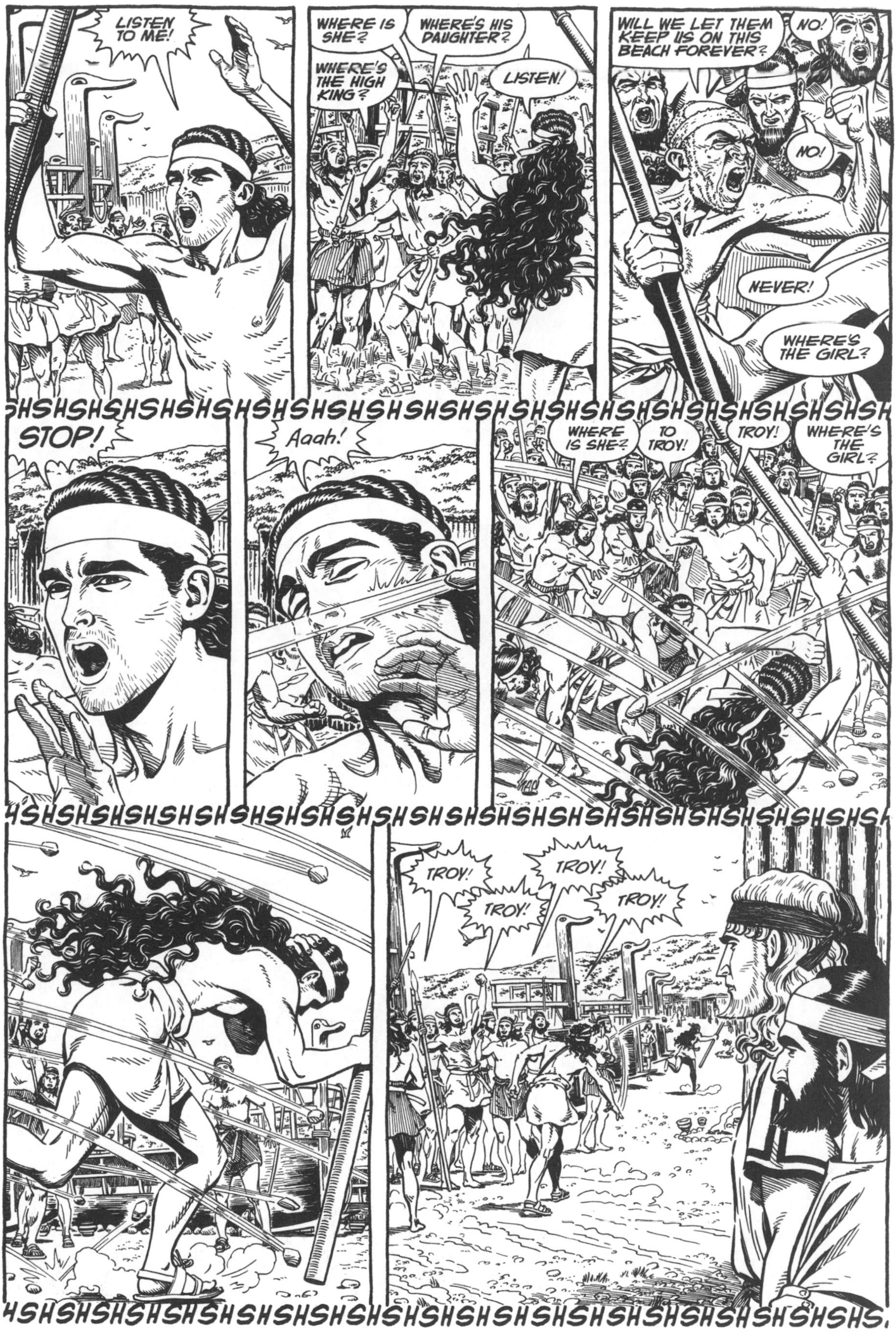
LISTEN TO ME!
WHERE IS SHE?
WHERE'S HIS DAUGHTER?
WHERE'S THE HIGH KING?
LISTEN!
WILL WE LET THEM KEEP US ON THIS BEACH FOREVER?
NO!
NO!
NEVER!
WHERE'S THE GIRL?
SHSHSHSHSHSHSHSHSHSHSHSHSHSHSHSHSHSHSHSHSHSHSHSH
STOP!
Aaah!
WHERE IS SHE?
TO TROY!
TROY!
WHERE'S THE GIRL?
SHSHSHSHSHSHSHSHSHSHSHSHSHSHSHSHSHSHSHSHSHSHSH
TROY!
TROY!
TROY!
TROY!
SHSHSHSHSHSHSHSHSHSHSHSHSHSHSHSHSHSHSHSHSHSHSHS

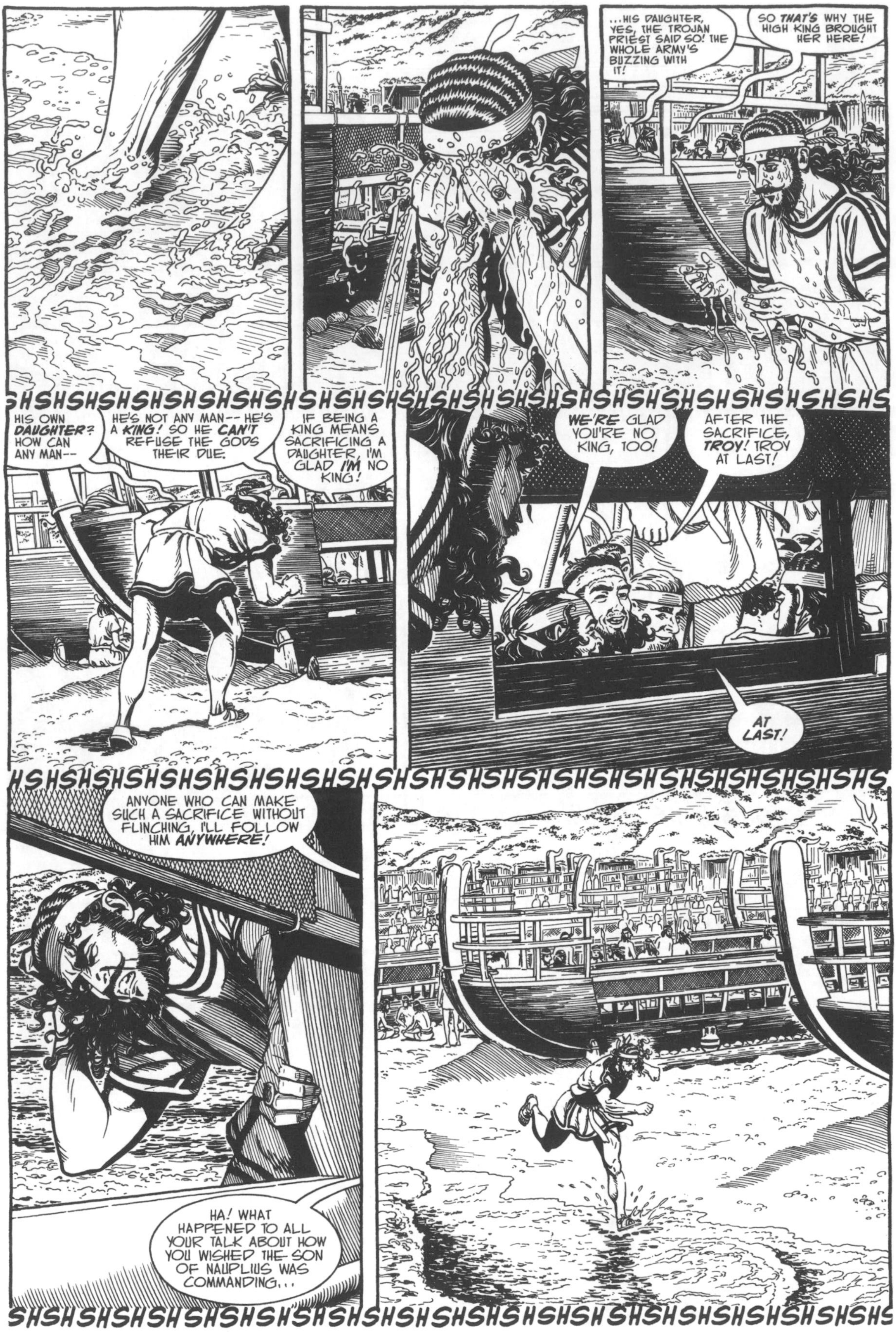
...HIS DAUGHTER, YES, THE TROJAN PRIEST SAID SO! THE WHOLE ARMY'S BUZZING WITH IT!
SO THAT'S WHY THE HIGH KING BROUGHT HER HERE!
SHSHSHSHSHSHSHSHSHSHSHSHSHSHSHSHSHSHSHSHSHSHSHS
HIS OWN DAUGHTER? HOW CAN ANY MAN--
HE'S NOT ANY MAN-- HE'S A KING! SO HE CAN'T REFUSE THE GODS THEIR DUE.
IF BEING A KING MEANS SACRIFICING A DAUGHTER, I'M GLAD I'M NO KING!
WE'RE GLAD YOU'RE NO KING, TOO!
AFTER THE SACRIFICE, TROY! TROY AT LAST!
AT LAST!
SHSHSHSHSHSHSHSHSHSHSHSHSHSHSHSHSHSHSHSHSHSHSHS
ANYONE WHO CAN MAKE SUCH A SACRIFICE WITHOUT FLINCHING, I'LL FOLLOW HIM ANYWHERE!
HA! WHAT HAPPENED TO ALL YOUR TALK ABOUT HOW YOU WISHED THE SON OF NAUPLIUS WAS COMMANDING...
SHSHSHSHSHSHSHSHSHSHSHSHSHSHSHSHSHSHSHSHSHSHSHS

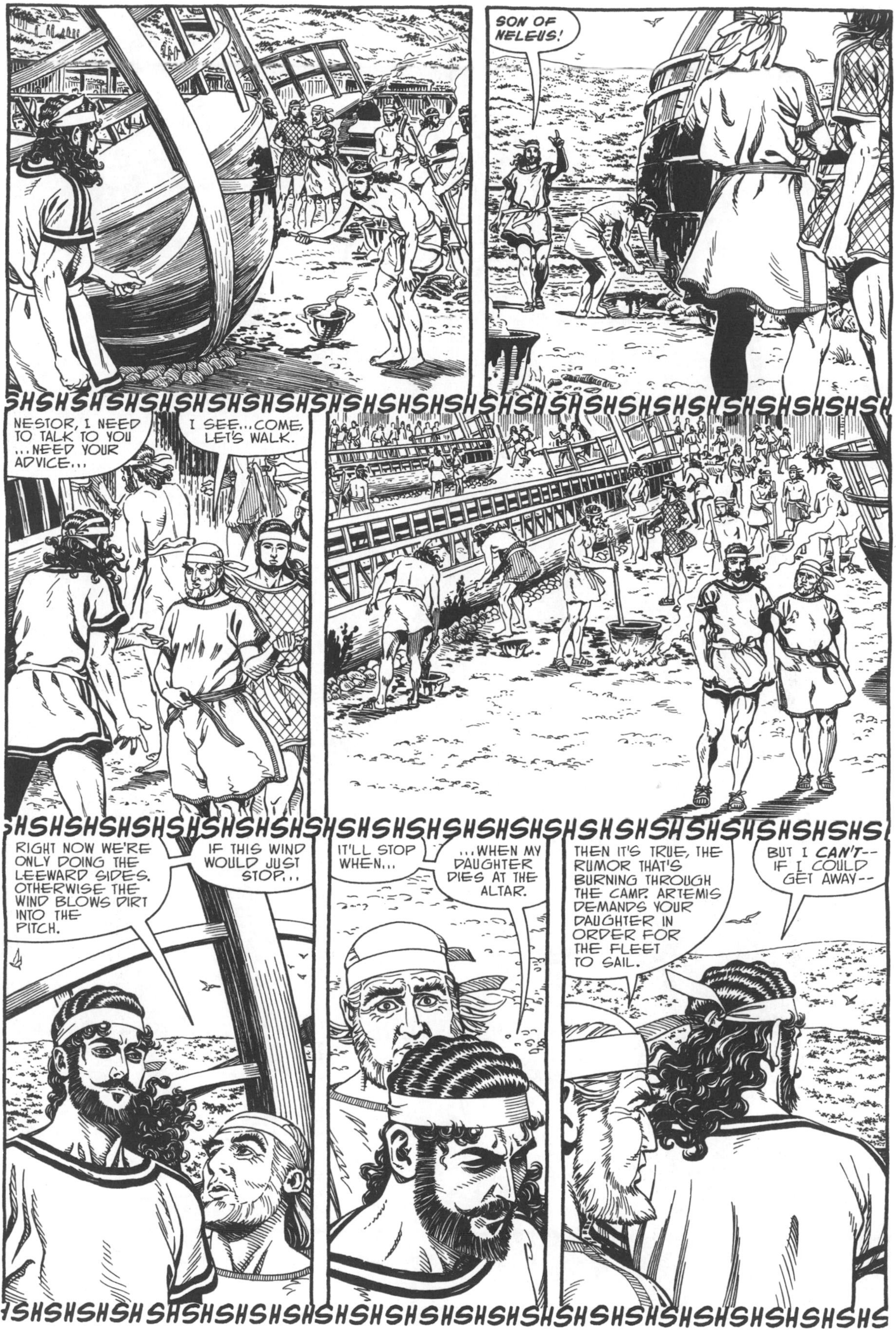
SON OF NELEUS!
SHSHSHSHSHSHSHSHSHSHSHSHSHSHSHSHSHSHSH
NESTOR, I NEED TO TALK TO YOU ...NEED YOUR ADVICE...
I SEE...COME. LET'S WALK.
SHSHSHSHSHSHSHSHSHSHSHSHSHSHSHSHSHSHS
RIGHT NOW WE'RE ONLY DOING THE LEEWARD SIDES. OTHERWISE THE WIND BLOWS DIRT INTO THE PITCH.
IF THIS WIND WOULD JUST STOP...
IT'LL STOP WHEN...
...WHEN MY DAUGHTER DIES AT THE ALTAR.
THEN IT'S TRUE, THE RUMOR THAT'S BURNING THROUGH THE CAMP. ARTEMIS DEMANDS YOUR DAUGHTER IN ORDER FOR THE FLEET TO SAIL.
BUT I CAN'T-- IF I COULD GET AWAY--
SHSHSHSHSHSHSHSHSHSHSHSHSHSHSHSHSHS

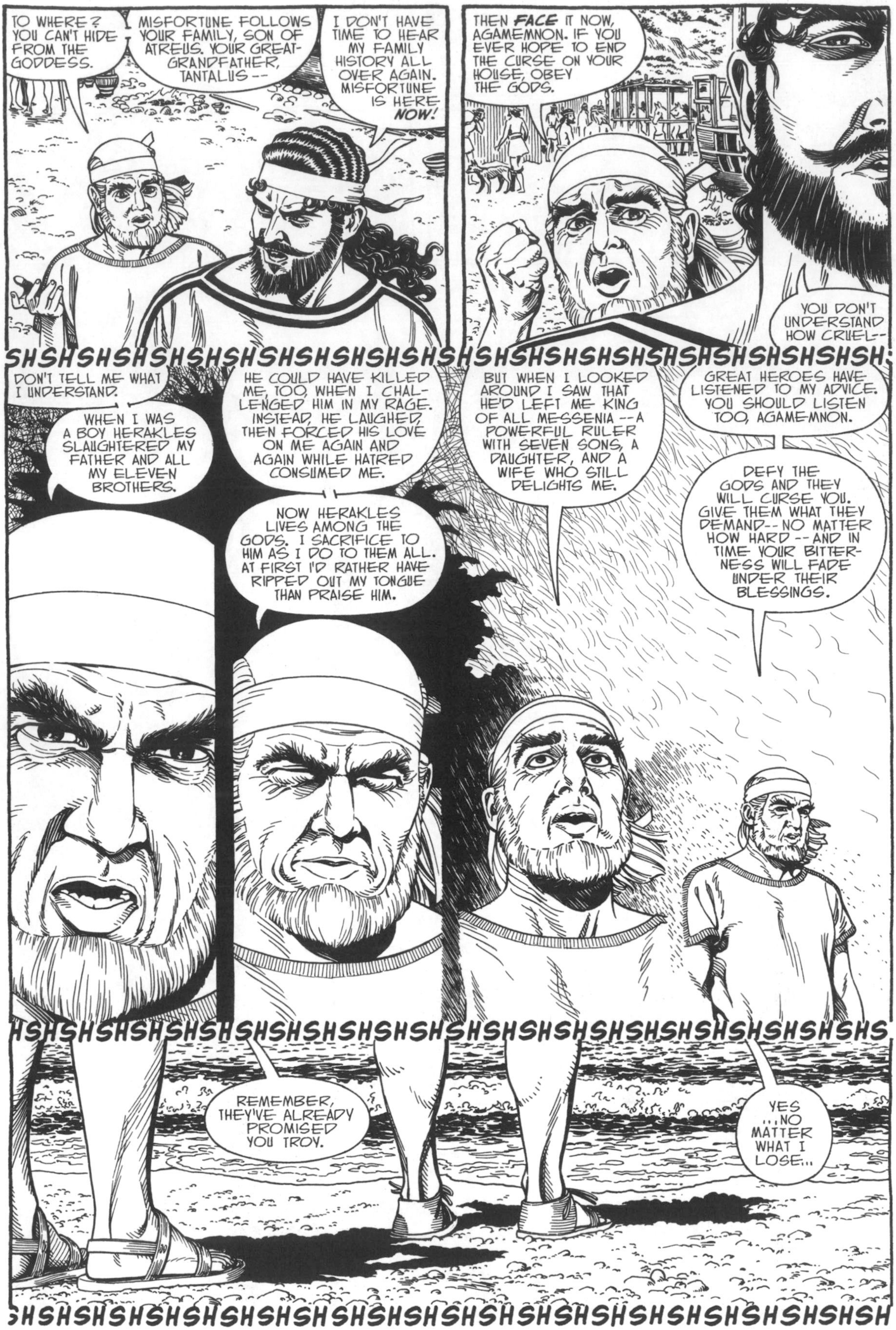
TO WHERE? YOU CAN'T HIDE FROM THE GODDESS.
MISFORTUNE FOLLOWS YOUR FAMILY, SON OF ATREUS. YOUR GREAT-GRANDFATHER, TANTALUS --
I DON'T HAVE TIME TO HEAR MY FAMILY HISTORY ALL OVER AGAIN. MISFORTUNE IS HERE NOW!
THEN FACE IT NOW, AGAMEMNON. IF YOU EVER HOPE TO END THE CURSE ON YOUR HOUSE, OBEY THE GODS.
YOU DON'T UNDERSTAND HOW CRUEL--
SHSHSHSHSHSHSHSHSHSHSHSHSHSHSHSHSHSHSHSHSHSH
DON'T TELL ME WHAT I UNDERSTAND.
WHEN I WAS A BOY HERAKLES SLAUGHTERED MY FATHER AND ALL MY ELEVEN BROTHERS.
HE COULD HAVE KILLED ME, TOO, WHEN I CHALLENGED HIM IN MY RAGE. INSTEAD, HE LAUGHED, THEN FORCED HIS LOVE ON ME AGAIN AND AGAIN WHILE HATRED CONSUMED ME.
NOW HERAKLES LIVES AMONG THE GODS. I SACRIFICE TO HIM AS I DO TO THEM ALL. AT FIRST I'D RATHER HAVE RIPPED OUT MY TONGUE THAN PRAISE HIM.
BUT WHEN I LOOKED AROUND I SAW THAT HE'D LEFT ME KING OF ALL MESSENIA -- A POWERFUL RULER WITH SEVEN SONS, A DAUGHTER, AND A WIFE WHO STILL DELIGHTS ME.
GREAT HEROES HAVE LISTENED TO MY ADVICE. YOU SHOULD LISTEN TOO, AGAMEMNON.
DEFY THE GODS AND THEY WILL CURSE YOU. GIVE THEM WHAT THEY DEMAND-- NO MATTER HOW HARD -- AND IN TIME YOUR BITTERNESS WILL FADE UNDER THEIR BLESSINGS.
SHSHSHSHSHSHSHSHSHSHSHSHSHSHSHSHSHSHSHSHS
REMEMBER, THEY'VE ALREADY PROMISED YOU TROY.
YES ...NO MATTER WHAT I LOSE...
SHSHSHSHSHSHSHSHSHSHSHSHSHSHSHSHSHSHSHSH

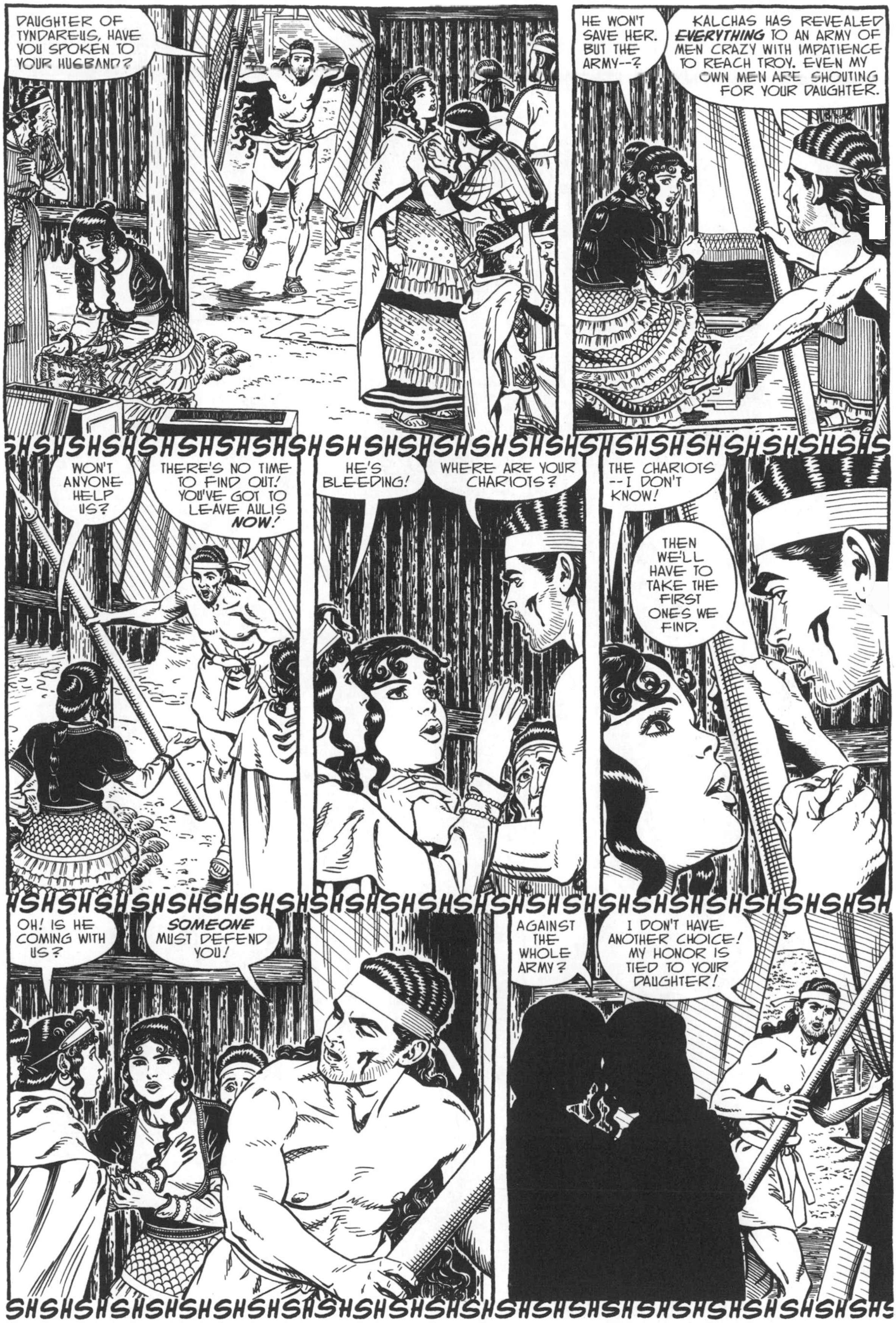
DAUGHTER OF TYNDAREUS, HAVE YOU SPOKEN TO YOUR HUSBAND?
HE WON'T SAVE HER. BUT THE ARMY--?
KALCHAS HAS REVEALED EVERYTHING TO AN ARMY OF MEN CRAZY WITH IMPATIENCE TO REACH TROY. EVEN MY OWN MEN ARE SHOUTING FOR YOUR DAUGHTER.
SHSHSHSHSHSHSHSHSHSHSHSHSHSHSHSHSHSHSHS
WON'T ANYONE HELP US?
THERE'S NO TIME TO FIND OUT! YOU'VE GOT TO LEAVE AULIS NOW!
HE'S BLEEDING!
WHERE ARE YOUR CHARIOTS?
THE CHARIOTS --I DON'T KNOW!
THEN WE'LL HAVE TO TAKE THE FIRST ONES WE FIND.
SHSHSHSHSHSHSHSHSHSHSHSHSHSHSHSHSHSHSHS
OH! IS HE COMING WITH US?
SOMEONE MUST DEFEND YOU!
AGAINST THE WHOLE ARMY?
I DON'T HAVE ANOTHER CHOICE! MY HONOR IS TIED TO YOUR DAUGHTER!
SHSHSHSHSHSHSHSHSHSHSHSHSHSHSHSHSHSHSHS

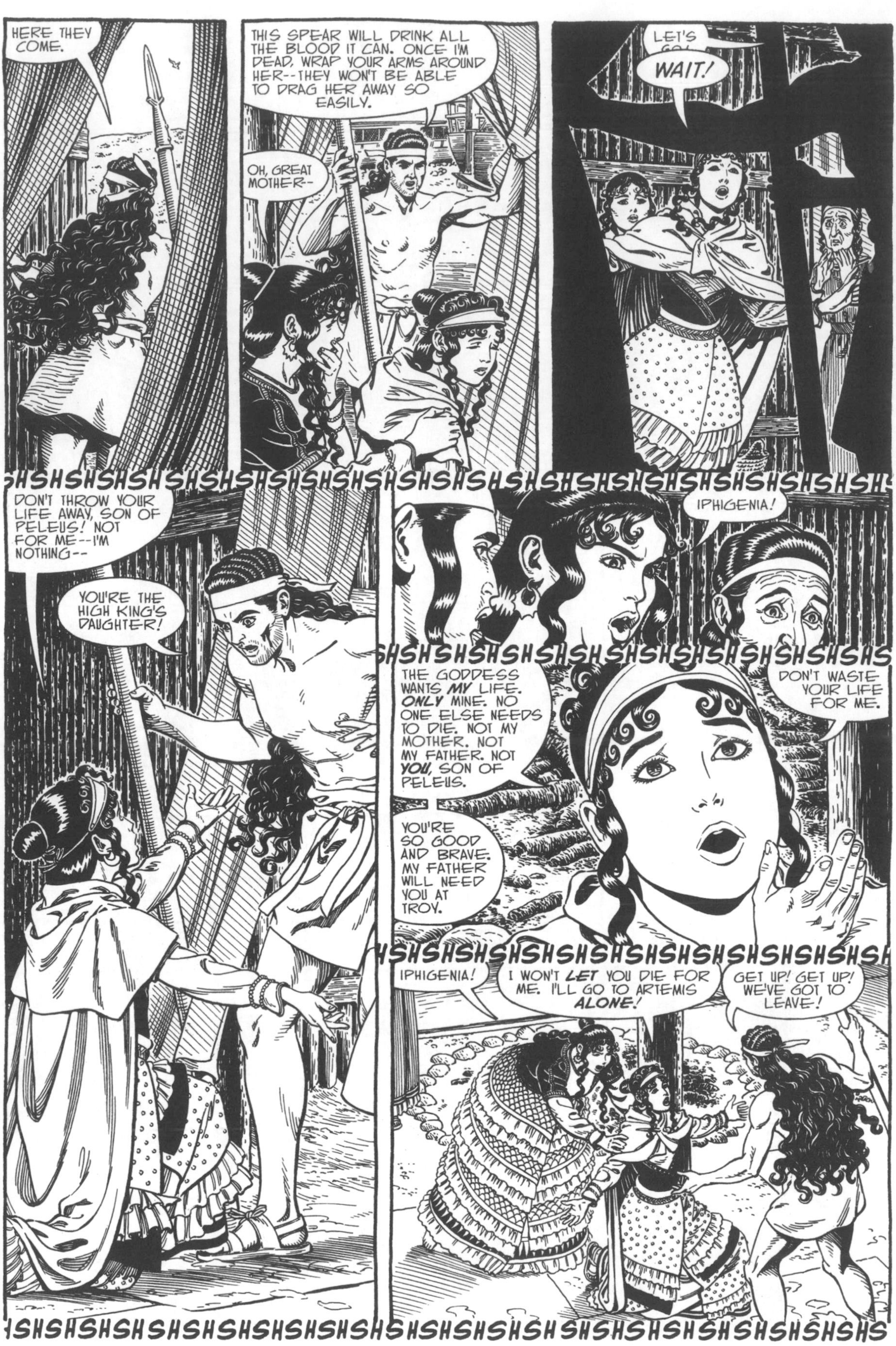
HERE THEY COME.
THIS SPEAR WILL DRINK ALL THE BLOOD IT CAN. ONCE I'M DEAD, WRAP YOUR ARMS AROUND HER--THEY WON'T BE ABLE TO DRAG HER AWAY SO EASILY.
OH, GREAT MOTHER--
LET'S
WAIT!
SHSHSHSHSHSHSHSHSHSHSHSHSHSHSHSHSHSHSHSHSHSHSHSH
DON'T THROW YOUR LIFE AWAY, SON OF PELEUS! NOT FOR ME--I'M NOTHING--
YOU'RE THE HIGH KING'S DAUGHTER!
IPHIGENIA!
SHSHSHSHSHSHSHSHSHSHSHSHSHSHSH
THE GODDESS WANTS MY LIFE. ONLY MINE. NO ONE ELSE NEEDS TO DIE. NOT MY MOTHER. NOT MY FATHER. NOT YOU, SON OF PELEUS.
DON'T WASTE YOUR LIFE FOR ME.
YOU'RE SO GOOD AND BRAVE. MY FATHER WILL NEED YOU AT TROY.
SHSHSHSHSHSHSHSHSHSHSHSHSHSHSH
IPHIGENIA!
I WON'T LET YOU DIE FOR ME. I'LL GO TO ARTEMIS ALONE!
GET UP! GET UP! WE'VE GOT TO LEAVE!
SHSHSHSHSHSHSHSHSHSHSHSHSHSHSHSHSHSHSHSHSHSHSHSHSHS

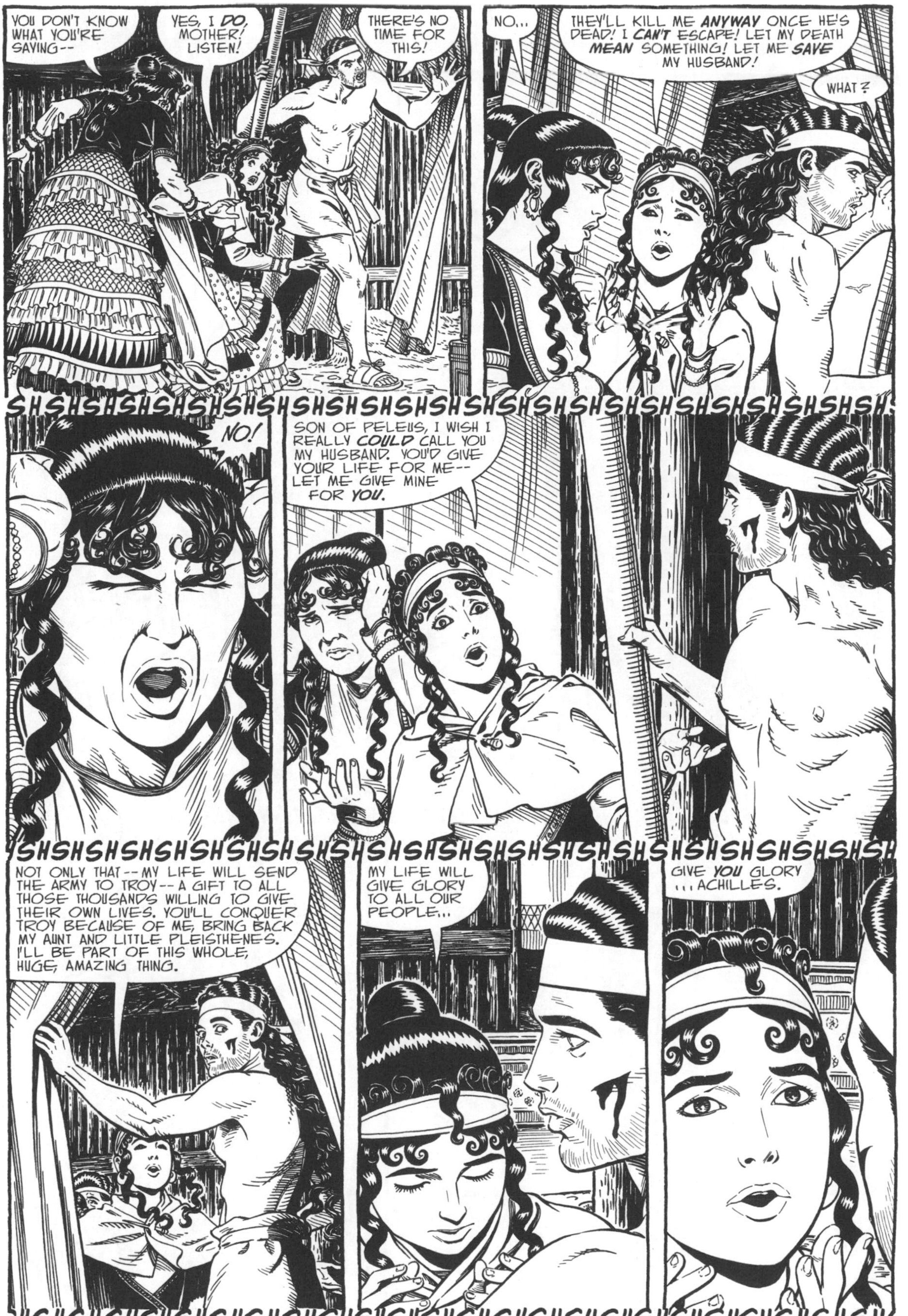
YOU DON'T KNOW WHAT YOU'RE SAYING--
YES, I DO, MOTHER! LISTEN!
THERE'S NO TIME FOR THIS!
NO...
THEY'LL KILL ME ANYWAY ONCE HE'S DEAD! I CAN'T ESCAPE! LET MY DEATH MEAN SOMETHING! LET ME SAVE MY HUSBAND!
WHAT?
SHSHSHSHSHSHSHSHSHSHSHSHSHSHSHSHSHSHSHSHSHSHSHSH
NO!
SON OF PELEUS, I WISH I REALLY COULD CALL YOU MY HUSBAND. YOU'D GIVE YOUR LIFE FOR ME-- LET ME GIVE MINE FOR YOU.
SHSHSHSHSHSHSHSHSHSHSHSHSHSHSHSHSHSHSHSHSH
NOT ONLY THAT--MY LIFE WILL SEND THE ARMY TO TROY--A GIFT TO ALL THOSE THOUSANDS WILLING TO GIVE THEIR OWN LIVES. YOU'LL CONQUER TROY BECAUSE OF ME, BRING BACK MY AUNT AND LITTLE PLEISTHENES. I'LL BE PART OF THIS WHOLE, HUGE, AMAZING THING.
MY LIFE WILL GIVE GLORY TO ALL OUR PEOPLE...
GIVE YOU GLORY ...ACHILLES.
SHSHSHSHSHSHSHSHSHSHSHSHSHSHSHSHSHSHSHSH

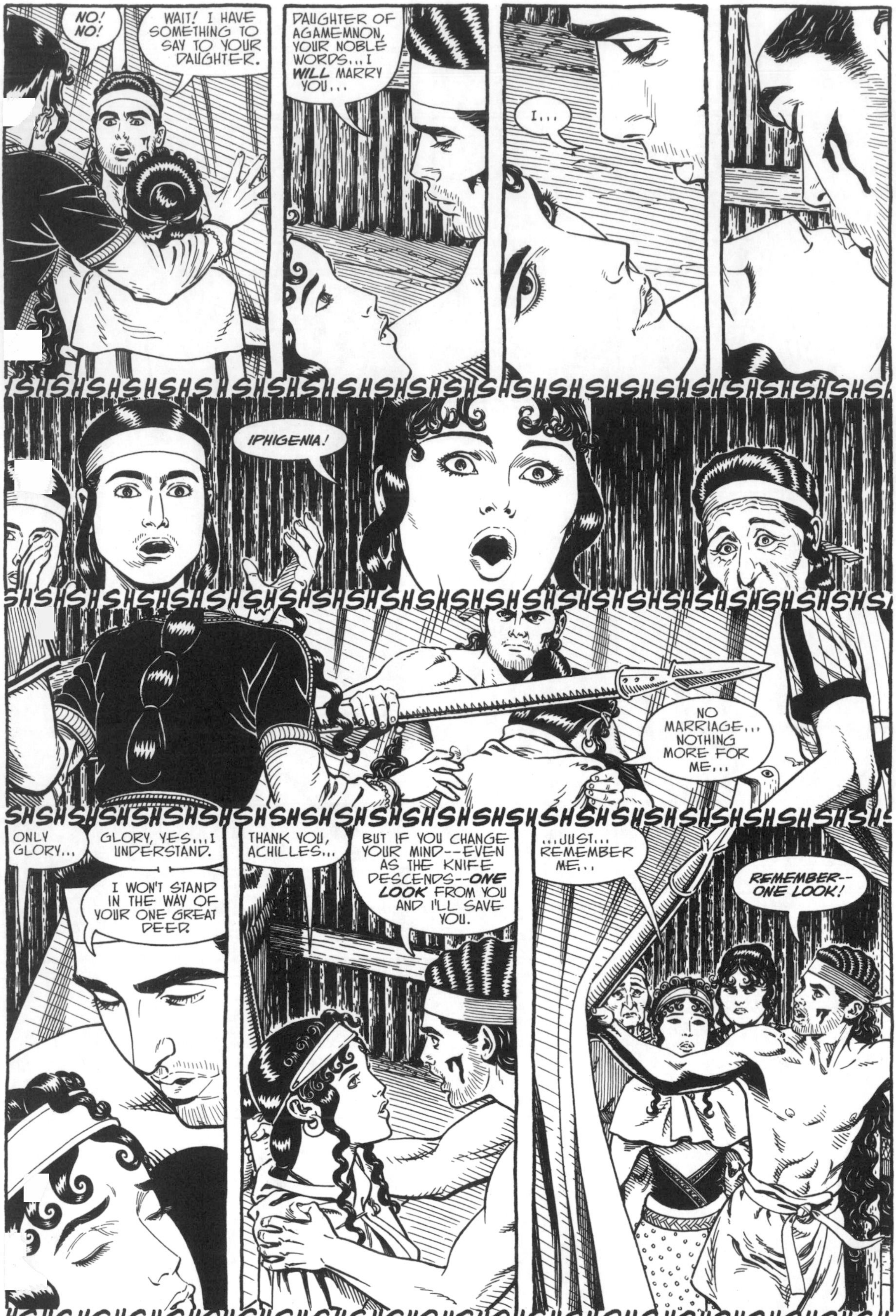
NO! NO!
WAIT! I HAVE SOMETHING TO SAY TO YOUR DAUGHTER.
DAUGHTER OF AGAMEMNON, YOUR NOBLE WORDS... I WILL MARRY YOU...
I...
SHSHSHSHSHSHSHSHSHSHSHSHSHSHSHSH
IPHIGENIA!
SHSHSHSHSHSHSHSHSHSHSHSHSHSHSHSH
NO MARRIAGE... NOTHING MORE FOR ME...
SHSHSHSHSHSHSHSHSHSHSHSHSHSHSHSH
ONLY GLORY...
GLORY, YES... I UNDERSTAND.
I WON'T STAND IN THE WAY OF YOUR ONE GREAT DEED.
THANK YOU, ACHILLES...
BUT IF YOU CHANGE YOUR MIND--EVEN AS THE KNIFE DESCENDS--ONE LOOK FROM YOU AND I'LL SAVE YOU.
...JUST... REMEMBER ME...
REMEMBER--ONE LOOK!
SHSHSHSHSHSHSHSHSHSHSHSHSHSHSHSH

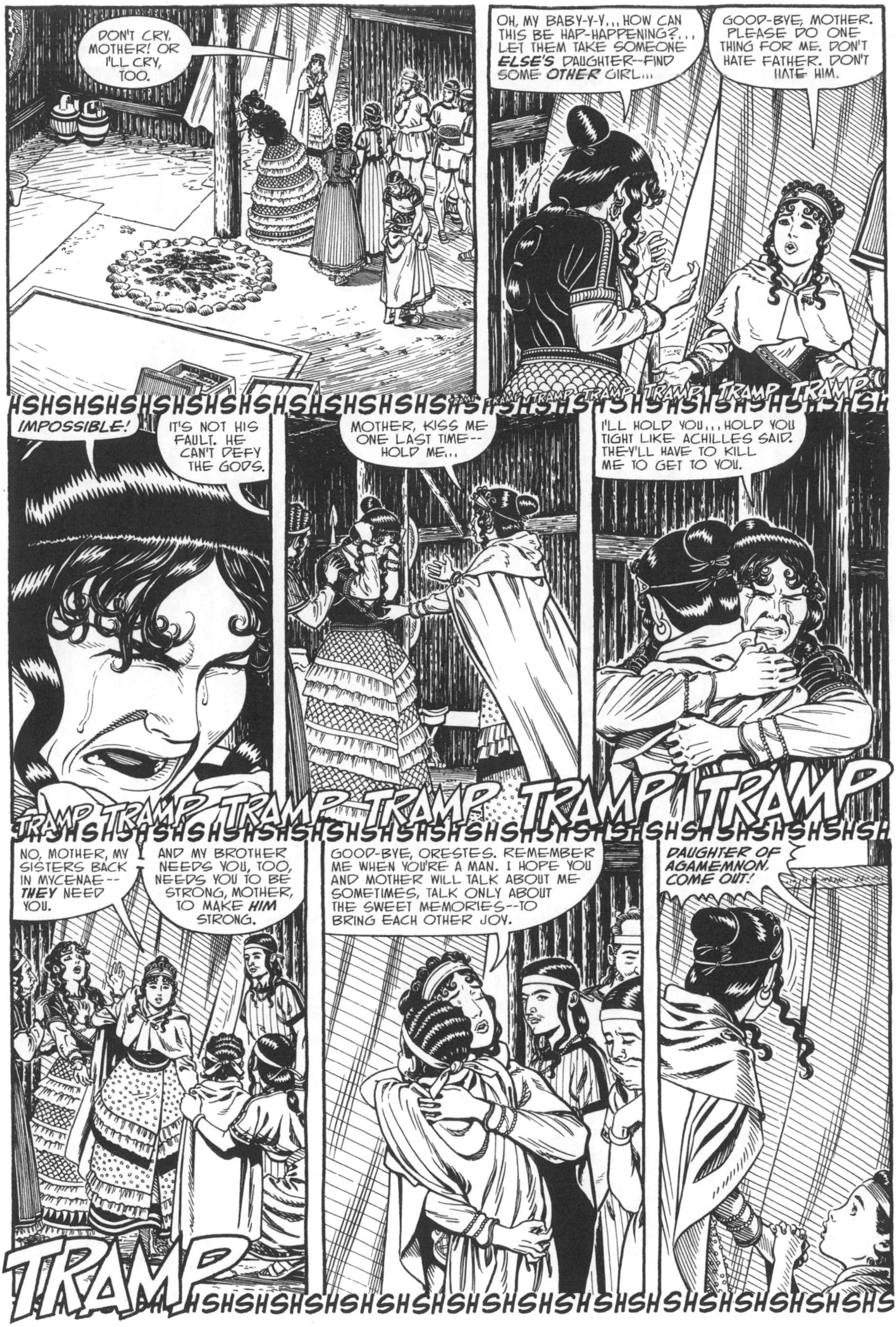
DON'T CRY, MOTHER! OR I'LL CRY, TOO.
OH, MY BABY-Y-Y... HOW CAN THIS BE HAP-HAPPENING?... LET THEM TAKE SOMEONE ELSE'S DAUGHTER--FIND SOME OTHER GIRL...
GOOD-BYE, MOTHER. PLEASE DO ONE THING FOR ME. DON'T HATE FATHER. DON'T HATE HIM.
TRAMP TRAMP TRAMP TRAMP TRAMP TRAMP TRAMP
SHSHSHSHSHSHSHSHSHSHSHSHSHSHSHSHSHSHSHSHSH
IMPOSSIBLE!
IT'S NOT HIS FAULT. HE CAN'T DEFY THE GODS.
MOTHER, KISS ME ONE LAST TIME-- HOLD ME...
I'LL HOLD YOU... HOLD YOU TIGHT LIKE ACHILLES SAID. THEY'LL HAVE TO KILL ME TO GET TO YOU.
TRAMP TRAMP TRAMP TRAMP TRAMP TRAMP
SHSHSHSHSHSHSHSHSHSHSHSHSHSHSHSHSHSHSHSHSHSH
NO, MOTHER, MY SISTERS BACK IN MYCENAE-- THEY NEED YOU.
AND MY BROTHER NEEDS YOU, TOO, NEEDS YOU TO BE STRONG, MOTHER, TO MAKE HIM STRONG.
GOOD-BYE, ORESTES. REMEMBER ME WHEN YOU'RE A MAN. I HOPE YOU AND MOTHER WILL TALK ABOUT ME SOMETIMES, TALK ONLY ABOUT THE SWEET MEMORIES--TO BRING EACH OTHER JOY.
DAUGHTER OF AGAMEMNON, COME OUT!
TRAMP
SHSHSHSHSHSHSHSHSHSHSHSHSHSHSHSHSHSHS

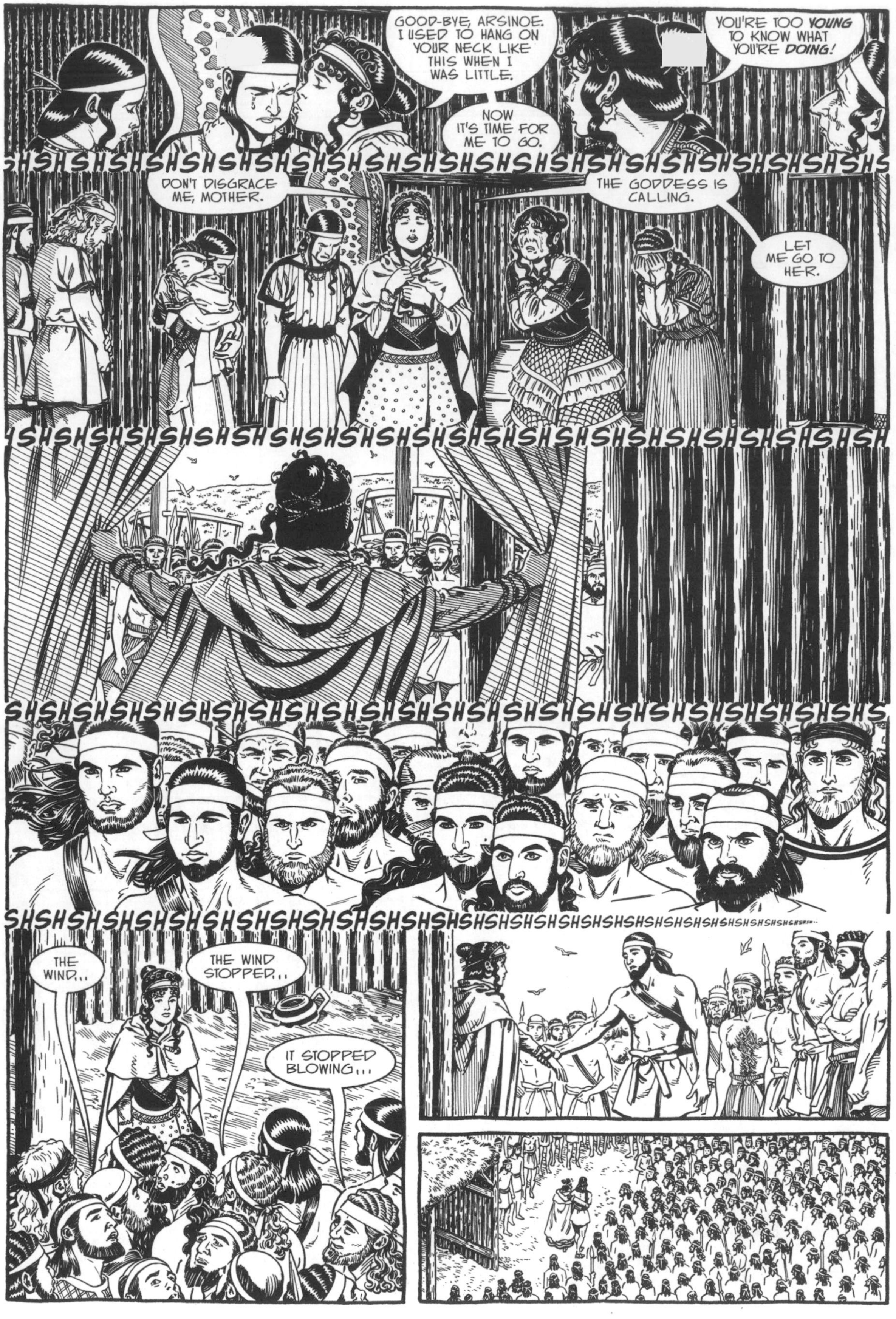

GOOD-BYE, ARSINOE. I USED TO HANG ON YOUR NECK LIKE THIS WHEN I WAS LITTLE.
NOW IT'S TIME FOR ME TO GO.
YOU'RE TOO **YOUNG** TO KNOW WHAT YOU'RE **DOING!**
SHSHSHSHSHSHSHSHSHSHSHSHSHSH
DON'T DISGRACE ME, MOTHER.
THE GODDESS IS CALLING.
LET ME GO TO HER.
SHSHSHSHSHSHSHSHSHSHSHSHSHSH
SHSHSHSHSHSHSHSHSHSHSHSHSHSH
SHSHSHSHSHSHSHSHSHSHSHSHSHSHSHSHSHSHSHSH...
THE WIND...
THE WIND STOPPED...
IT STOPPED BLOWING...

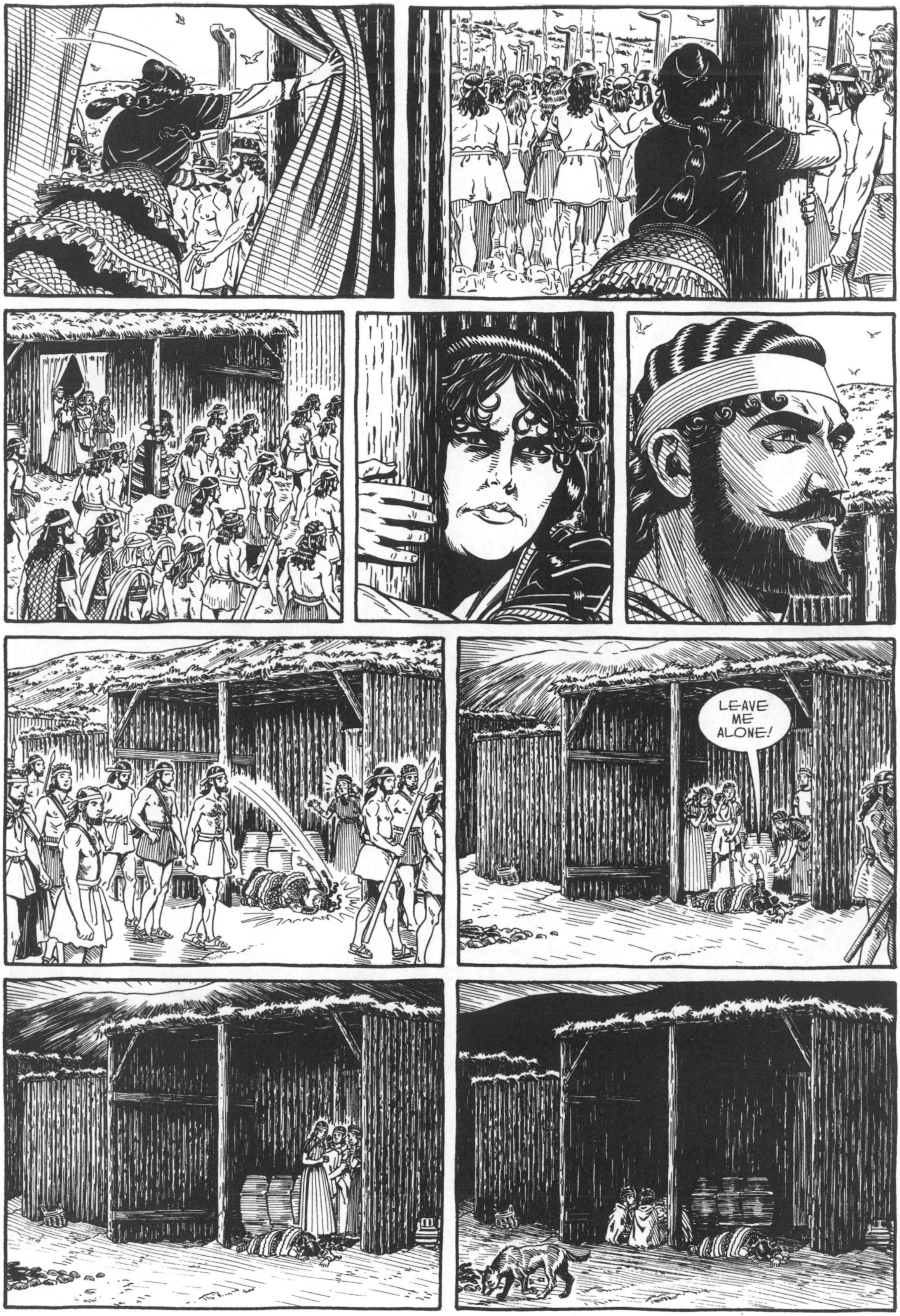
LEAVE ME ALONE!

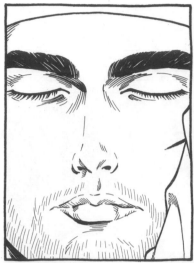

YES...

...FOR TROY TO FALL, THE FIRST-BORN DAUGHTER OF AGAMEMNON MUST DIE.

I'M BOUND BY HONOR TO RESCUE HER IF SHE ASKS ME TO, MOTHER.

IF YOU RESCUE HER, YOU WON'T SAIL FOR TROY. THAT'S WHAT I'VE WANTED ALL ALONG... BUT NOW -- I FEAR A BATTLE AT THE ALTAR.

MOTHER, DEATH LIES IN WAIT FOR EVERYONE.

YOUR DEATH WILL COME FROM THE SUN GOD IN RETRIBUTION FOR YOUR SLAYING A SON OF HIS.

I HAVEN'T SLAIN ONE YET.

I CAN MAKE SURE YOU NEVER DO.

MNEMON, COME HERE.

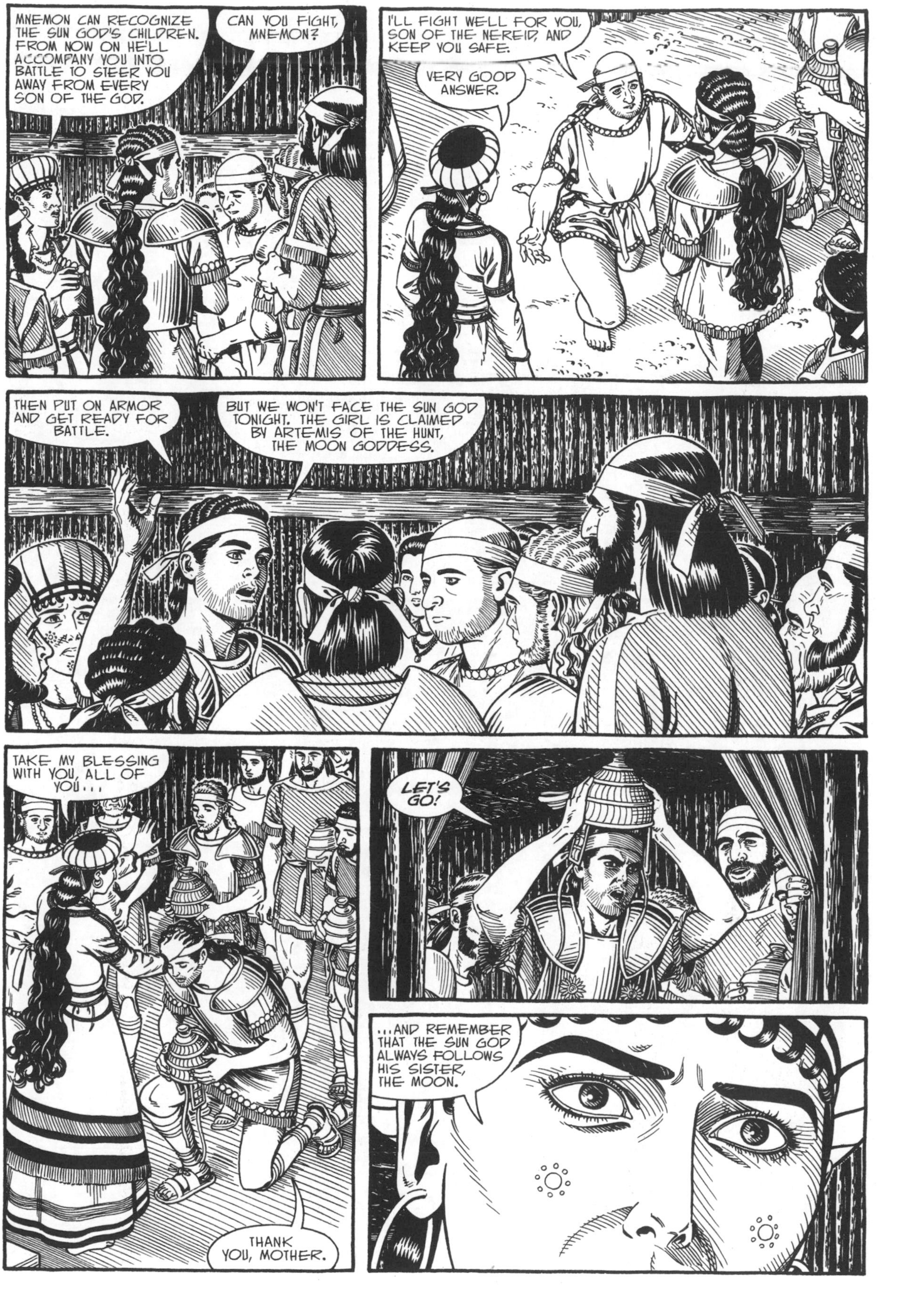
MNEMON CAN RECOGNIZE THE SUN GOD'S CHILDREN. FROM NOW ON HE'LL ACCOMPANY YOU INTO BATTLE TO STEER YOU AWAY FROM EVERY SON OF THE GOD.
CAN YOU FIGHT, MNEMON?
I'LL FIGHT WELL FOR YOU, SON OF THE NEREID, AND KEEP YOU SAFE.
VERY GOOD ANSWER.
THEN PUT ON ARMOR AND GET READY FOR BATTLE.
BUT WE WON'T FACE THE SUN GOD TONIGHT. THE GIRL IS CLAIMED BY ARTEMIS OF THE HUNT, THE MOON GODDESS.
TAKE MY BLESSING WITH YOU, ALL OF YOU...
THANK YOU, MOTHER.
LET'S GO!
...AND REMEMBER THAT THE SUN GOD ALWAYS FOLLOWS HIS SISTER, THE MOON.

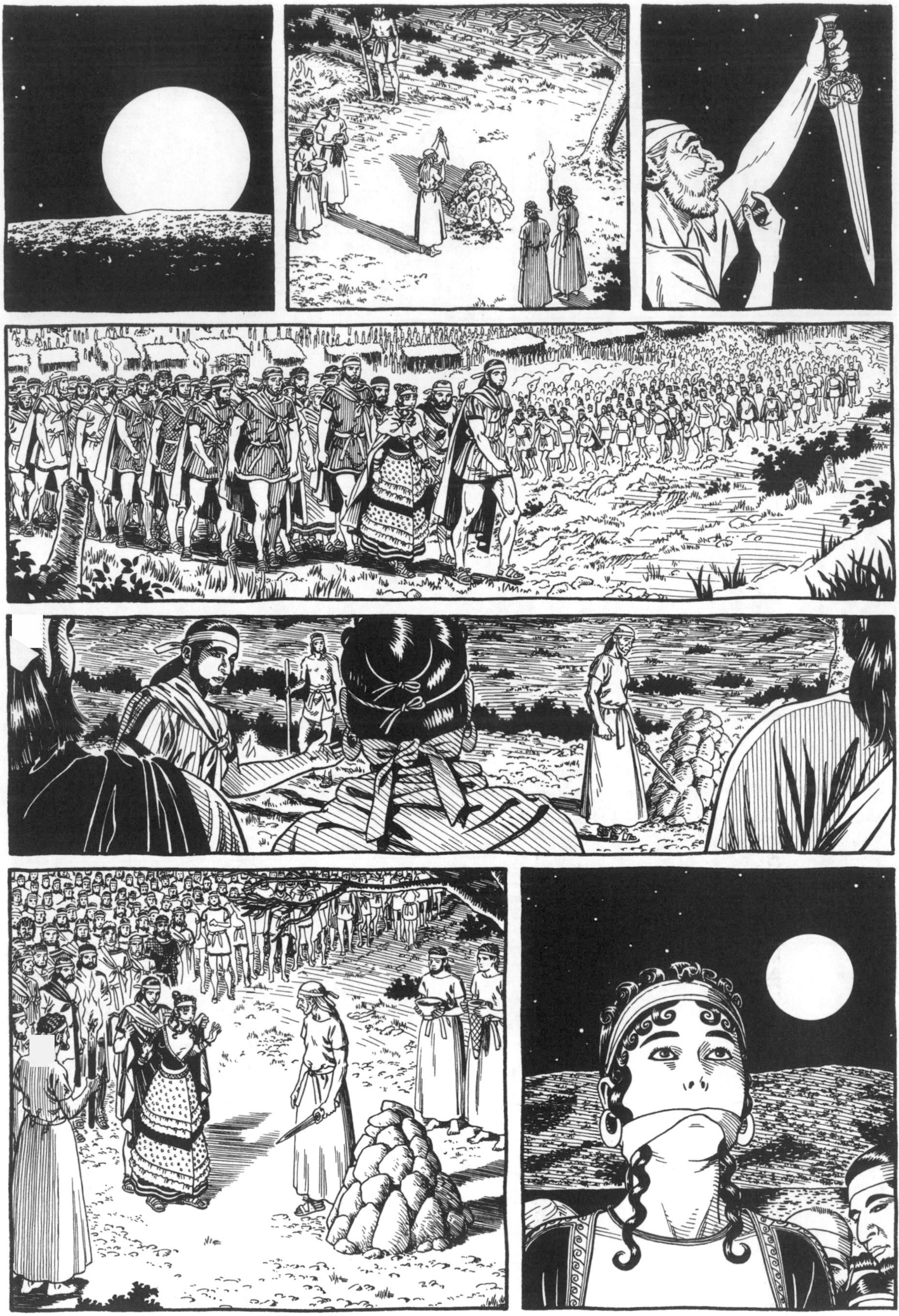

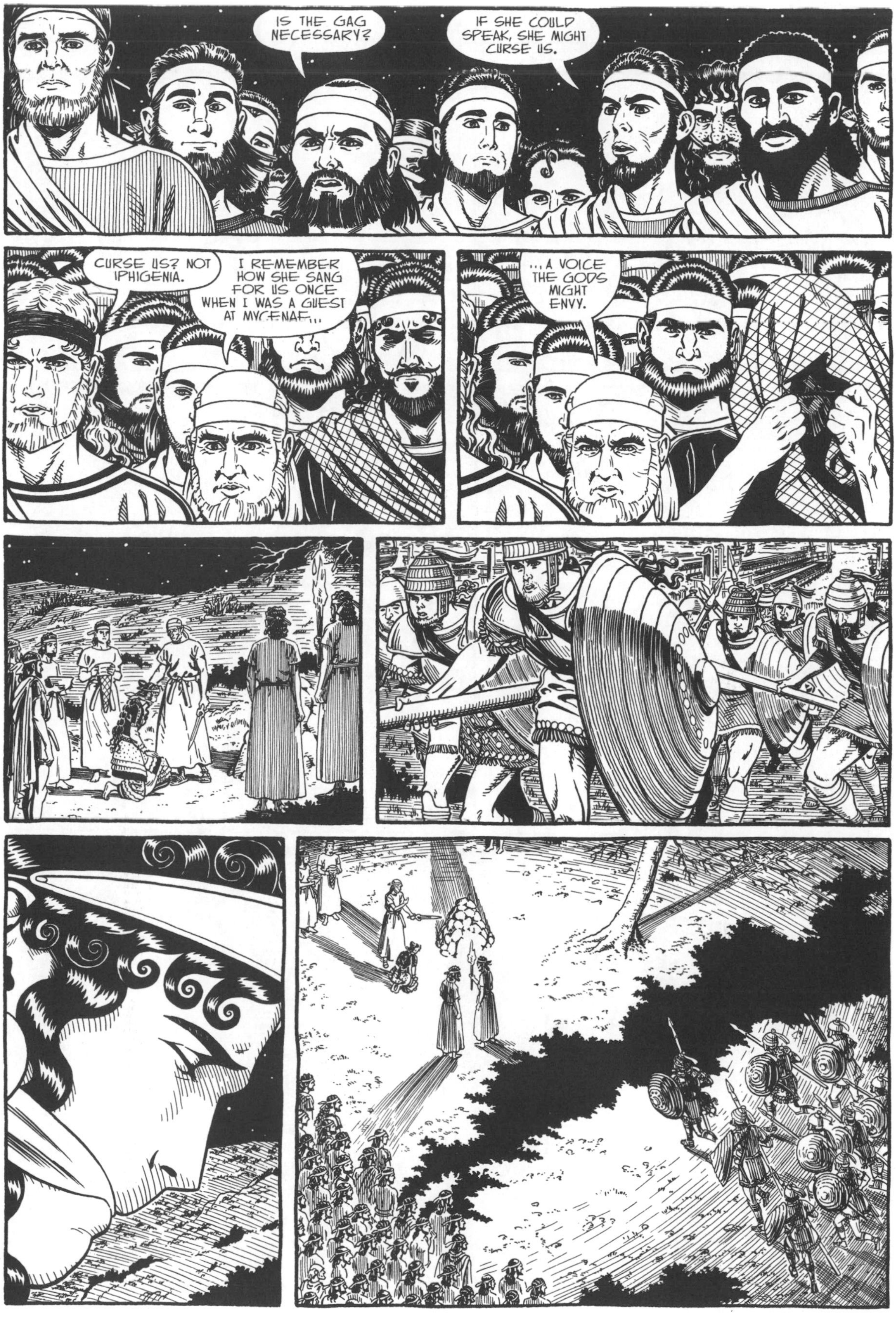

IS THE GAG NECESSARY?
IF SHE COULD SPEAK, SHE MIGHT CURSE US.
CURSE US? NOT IPHIGENIA.
I REMEMBER HOW SHE SANG FOR US ONCE WHEN I WAS A GUEST AT MYCENAE...
...A VOICE THE GODS MIGHT ENVY.

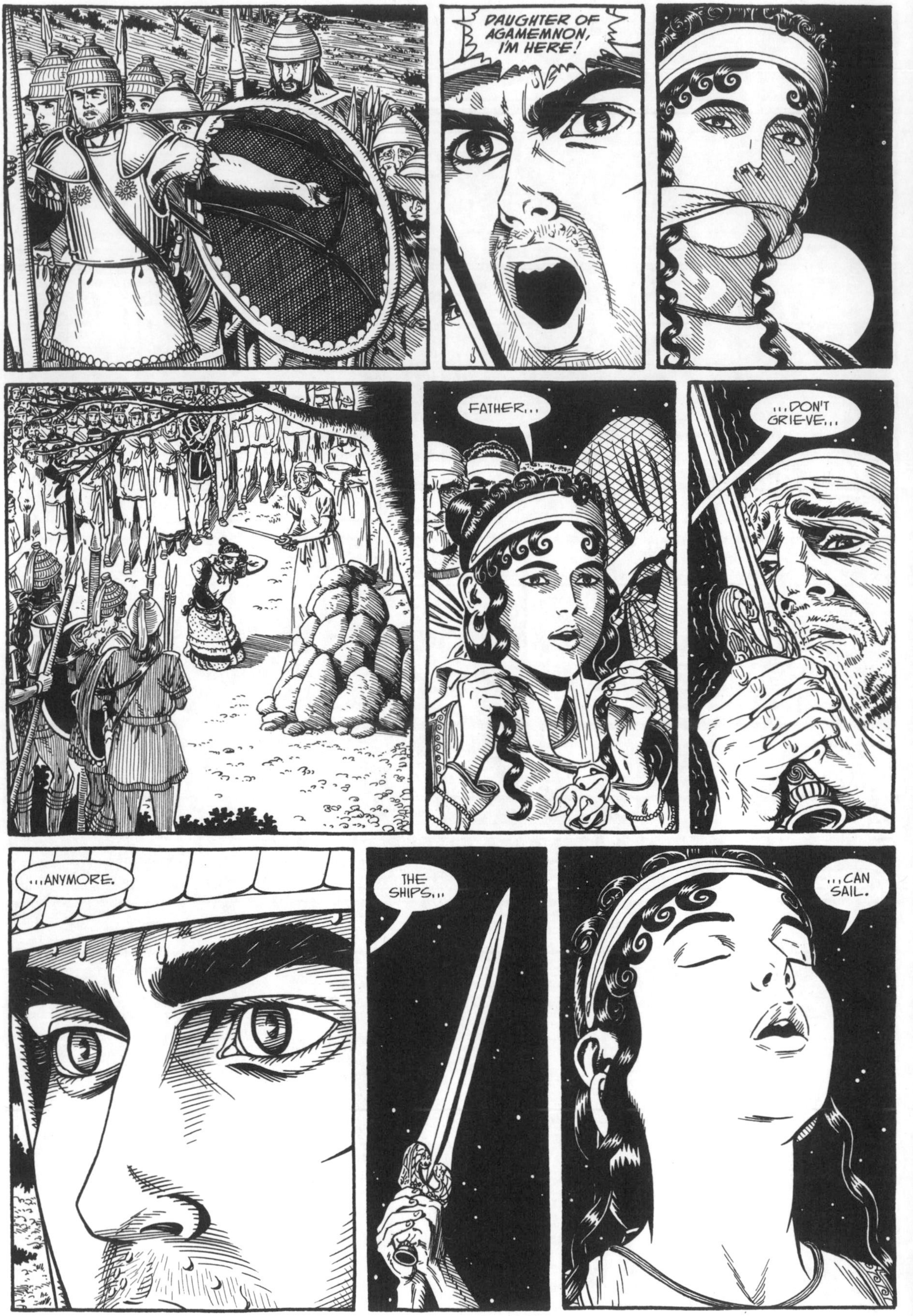
DAUGHTER OF AGAMEMNON, I'M HERE!
FATHER...
...DON'T GRIEVE...
...ANYMORE.
THE SHIPS...
...CAN SAIL.

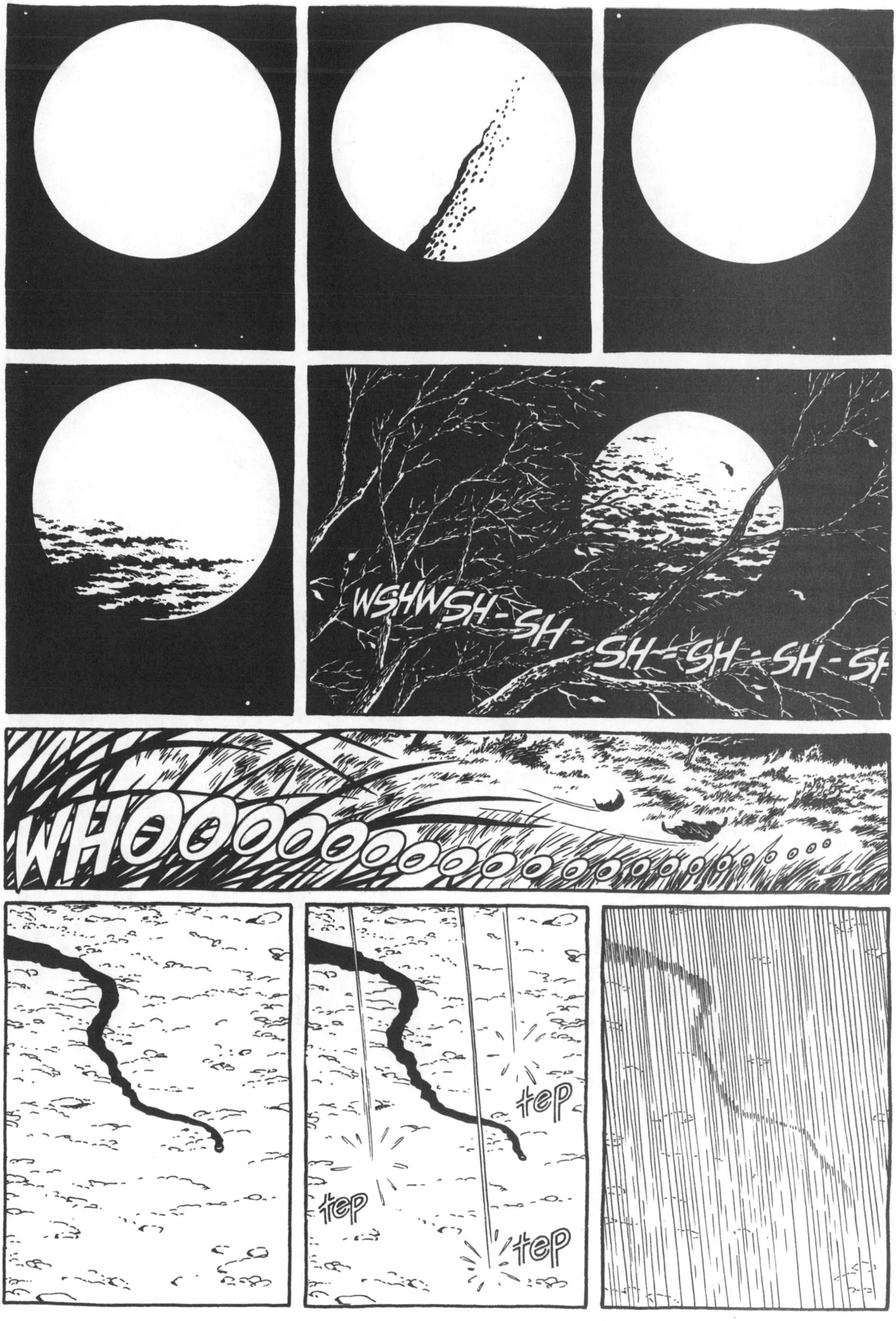
WSHWSH-SH-SH-SH-SH-SH
WHOOOOOOOOOOOOOOOOOOO...
tep
tep
tep

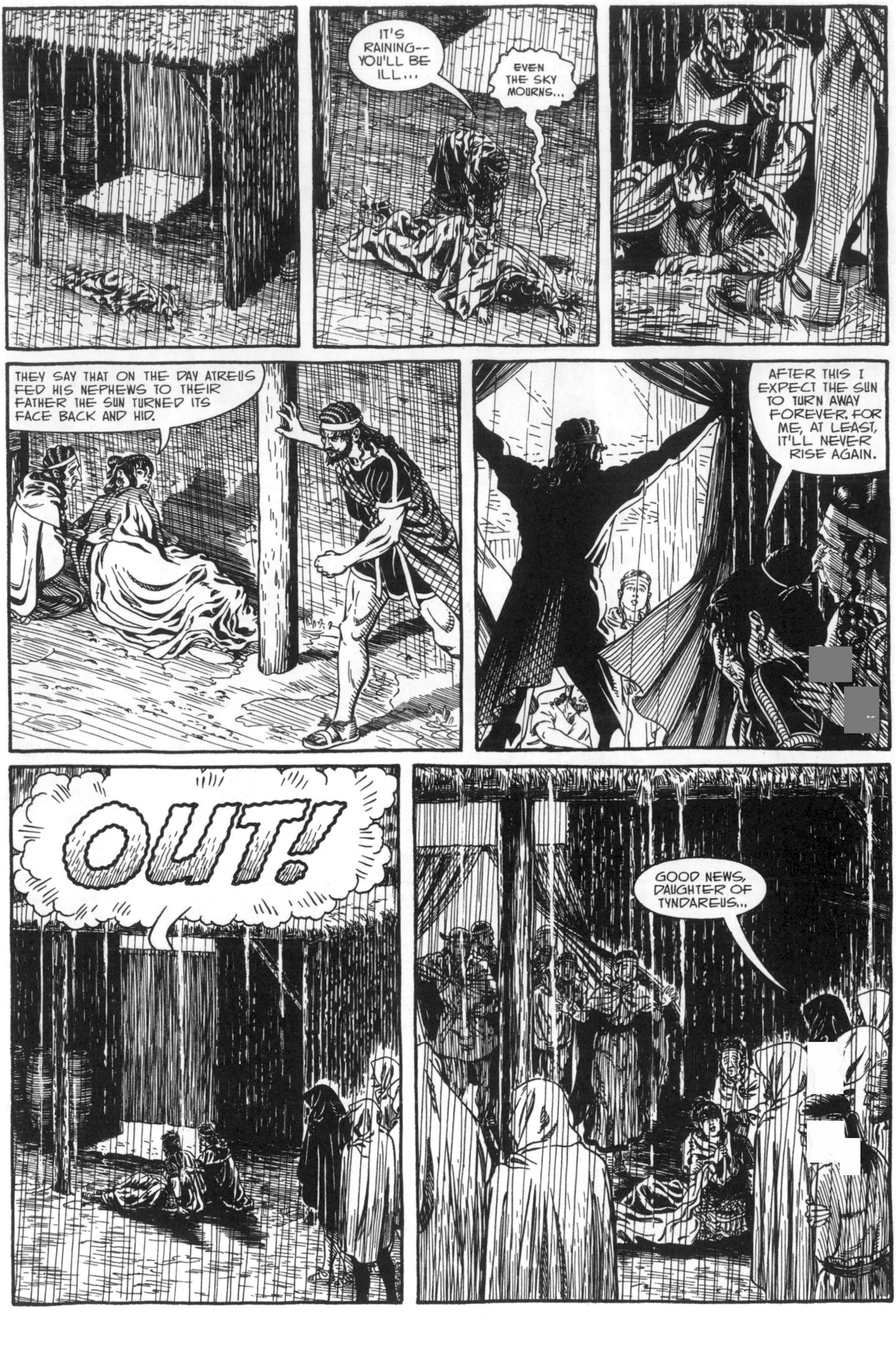

IT'S RAINING-- YOU'LL BE ILL...
EVEN THE SKY MOURNS...
THEY SAY THAT ON THE DAY ATREUS FED HIS NEPHEWS TO THEIR FATHER THE SUN TURNED ITS FACE BACK AND HID.
AFTER THIS I EXPECT THE SUN TO TURN AWAY FOREVER. FOR ME, AT LEAST, IT'LL NEVER RISE AGAIN.
OUT!
GOOD NEWS, DAUGHTER OF TYNDAREUS...

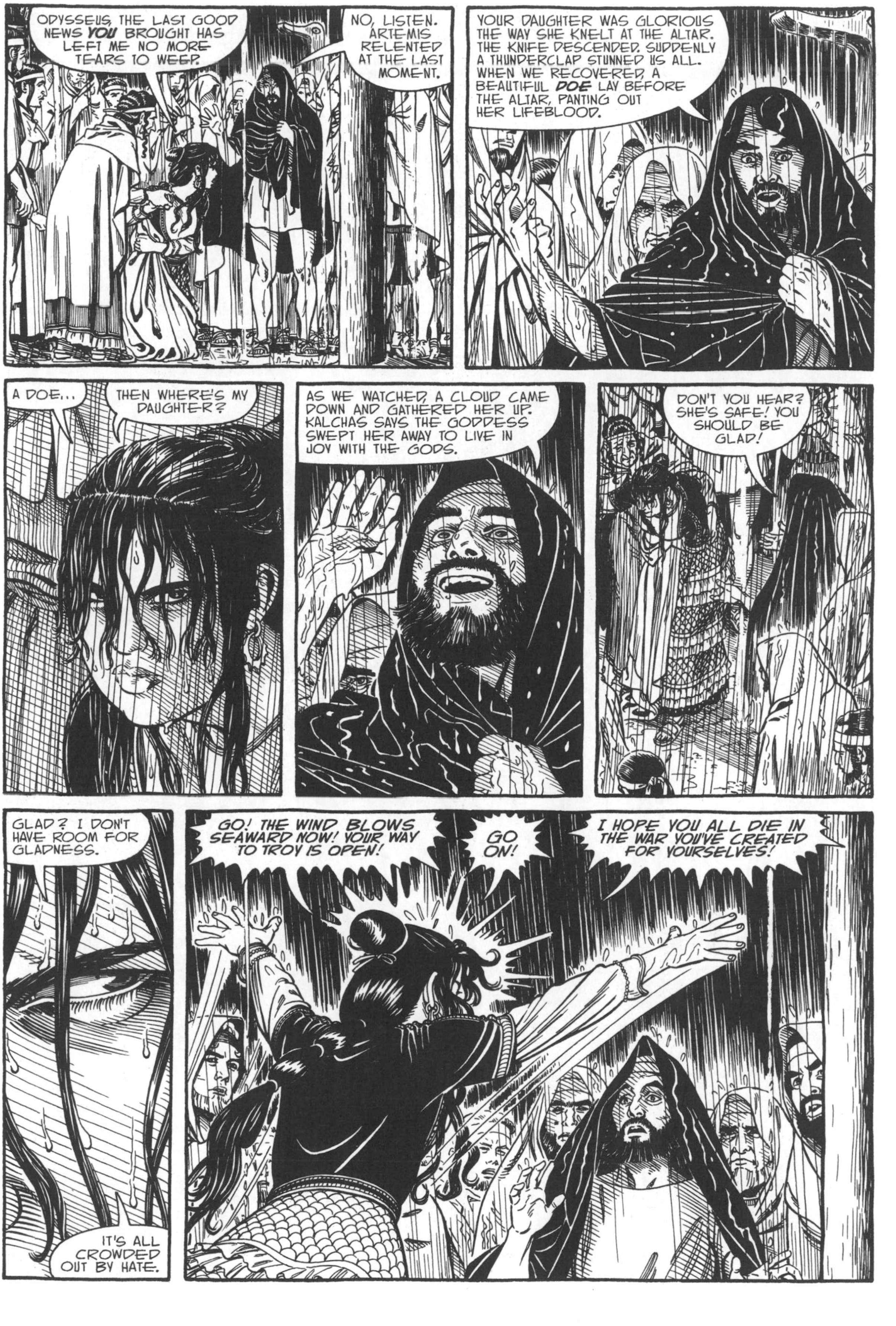
ODYSSEUS, THE LAST GOOD NEWS YOU BROUGHT HAS LEFT ME NO MORE TEARS TO WEEP.
NO, LISTEN. ARTEMIS RELENTED AT THE LAST MOMENT.
YOUR DAUGHTER WAS GLORIOUS THE WAY SHE KNELT AT THE ALTAR. THE KNIFE DESCENDED. SUDDENLY A THUNDERCLAP STUNNED US ALL. WHEN WE RECOVERED, A BEAUTIFUL DOE LAY BEFORE THE ALTAR, PANTING OUT HER LIFEBLOOD.
A DOE...
THEN WHERE'S MY DAUGHTER?
AS WE WATCHED, A CLOUD CAME DOWN AND GATHERED HER UP. KALCHAS SAYS THE GODDESS SWEPT HER AWAY TO LIVE IN JOY WITH THE GODS.
DON'T YOU HEAR? SHE'S SAFE! YOU SHOULD BE GLAD!
GLAD? I DON'T HAVE ROOM FOR GLADNESS.
IT'S ALL CROWDED OUT BY HATE.
GO! THE WIND BLOWS SEAWARD NOW! YOUR WAY TO TROY IS OPEN!
GO ON!
I HOPE YOU ALL DIE IN THE WAR YOU'VE CREATED FOR YOURSELVES!

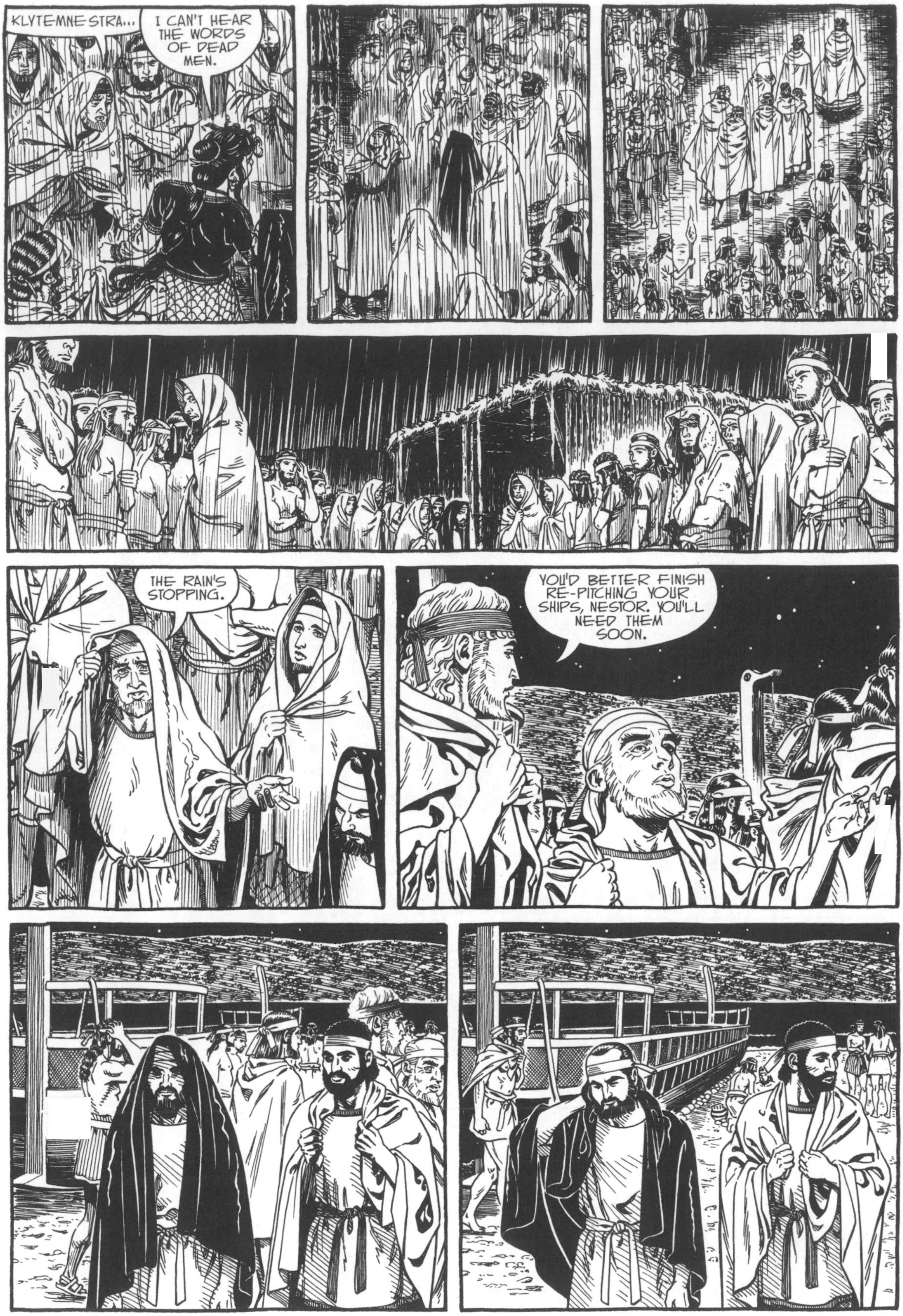
KLYTEMNESTRA...
I CAN'T HEAR THE WORDS OF DEAD MEN.
THE RAIN'S STOPPING.
YOU'D BETTER FINISH RE-PITCHING YOUR SHIPS, NESTOR. YOU'LL NEED THEM SOON.

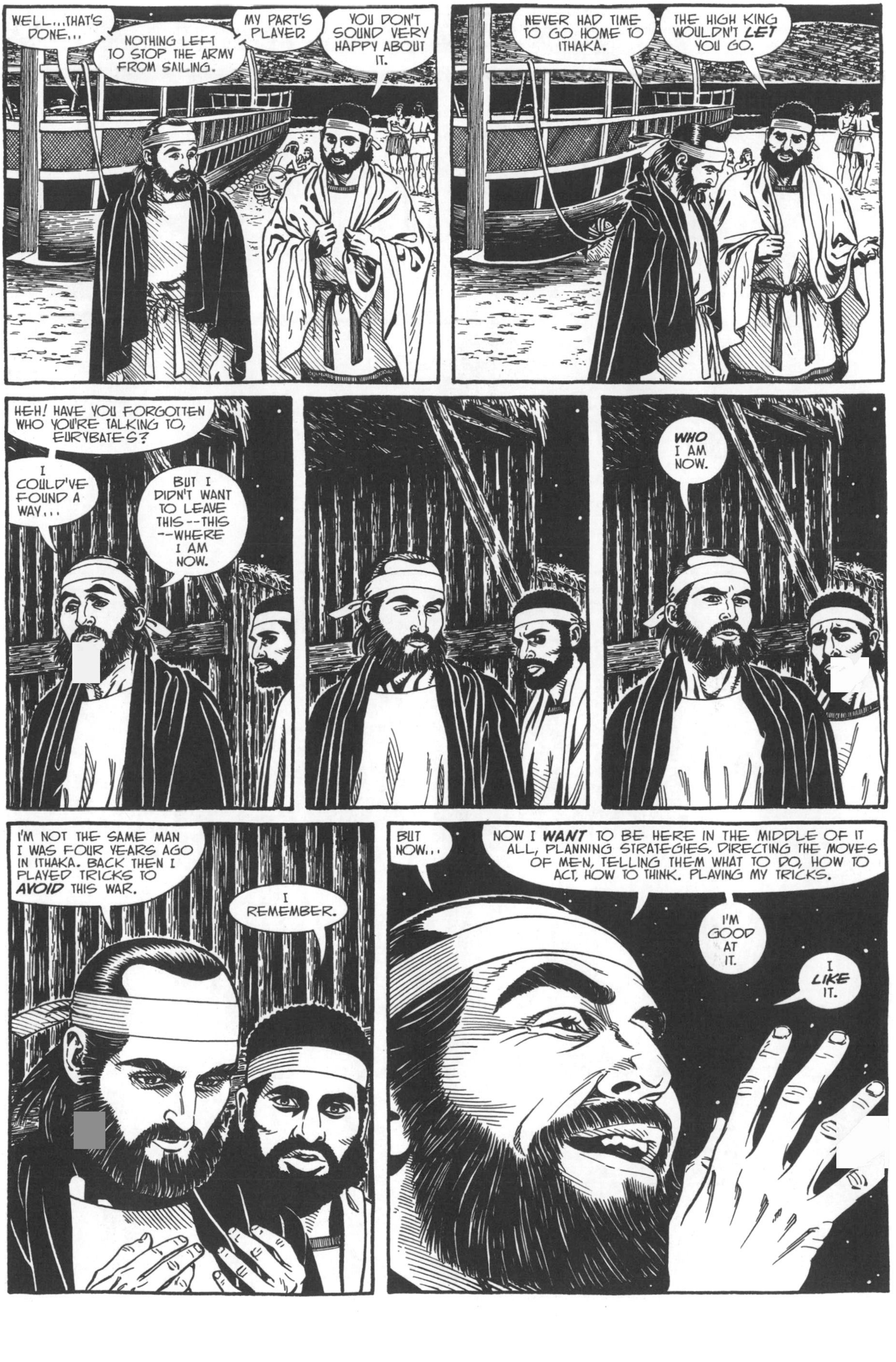

WELL...THAT'S DONE...
NOTHING LEFT TO STOP THE ARMY FROM SAILING.
MY PART'S PLAYED.
YOU DON'T SOUND VERY HAPPY ABOUT IT.
NEVER HAD TIME TO GO HOME TO ITHAKA.
THE HIGH KING WOULDN'T LET YOU GO.
HEH! HAVE YOU FORGOTTEN WHO YOU'RE TALKING TO, EURYBATES?
I COULD'VE FOUND A WAY...
BUT I DIDN'T WANT TO LEAVE THIS--THIS --WHERE I AM NOW.
WHO I AM NOW.
I'M NOT THE SAME MAN I WAS FOUR YEARS AGO IN ITHAKA. BACK THEN I PLAYED TRICKS TO AVOID THIS WAR.
I REMEMBER.
BUT NOW...
NOW I WANT TO BE HERE IN THE MIDDLE OF IT ALL, PLANNING STRATEGIES, DIRECTING THE MOVES OF MEN, TELLING THEM WHAT TO DO, HOW TO ACT, HOW TO THINK. PLAYING MY TRICKS.
I'M GOOD AT IT.
I LIKE IT.

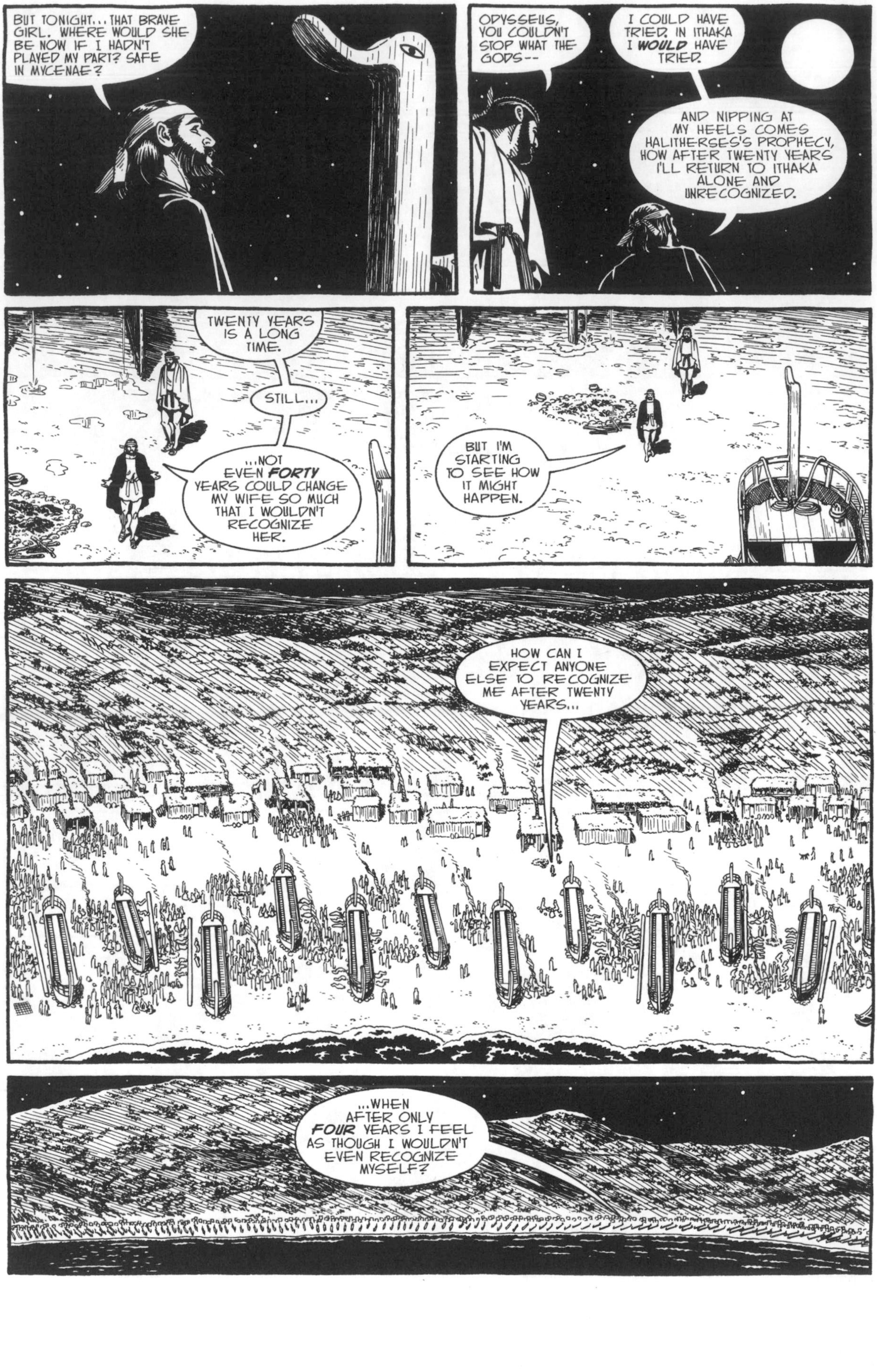
BUT TONIGHT... THAT BRAVE GIRL. WHERE WOULD SHE BE NOW IF I HADN'T PLAYED MY PART? SAFE IN MYCENAE?
ODYSSEUS, YOU COULDN'T STOP WHAT THE GODS--
I COULD HAVE TRIED. IN ITHAKA I **WOULD** HAVE TRIED.
AND NIPPING AT MY HEELS COMES HALITHERSES'S PROPHECY, HOW AFTER TWENTY YEARS I'LL RETURN TO ITHAKA ALONE AND UNRECOGNIZED.
TWENTY YEARS IS A LONG TIME.
STILL...
...NOT EVEN **FORTY** YEARS COULD CHANGE MY WIFE SO MUCH THAT I WOULDN'T RECOGNIZE HER.
BUT I'M STARTING TO SEE HOW IT MIGHT HAPPEN.
HOW CAN I EXPECT ANYONE ELSE TO RECOGNIZE ME AFTER TWENTY YEARS...
...WHEN AFTER ONLY **FOUR** YEARS I FEEL AS THOUGH I WOULDN'T EVEN RECOGNIZE MYSELF?

GLOSSARY OF NAMES

Pronunciation of names can vary widely. What I present here is merely a guide and needn't be considered definitive.

Anyone seeking consistency among the forms of character and place names should look elsewhere. In general, I've used the more familiar Roman forms for the better-known characters—for instance, Achilles instead of Akhilleos, Helen instead of Helena. Lesser-known and minor characters use a more Greek form—for instance, Teukros instead of Teucer, Polydeukes instead of Pollux.

a as in lap	ee as in see	i as in sit	oo as in wool	u as in us
ay as in say	eye as in hike	o as in not	s as in less	uh as in duh
e as in bed	g as in get	oh as in note	th as in thick	

Listed alphabetically   Stress italicized syllable

Achaea a-*kee*-a, roughly the area now known as Greece
Achaeans a-*kee*-uhnz, people of Achaea, roughly modern Greece
Achilles a-*kil*-eez, son of Peleus and Thetis, prince of Phthia
Aeakus *ee*-a-kus, father of Peleus
Aegina ee-*jee*-na, Klytemnestra's servant and former nurse
Aeneas ee-*nee*-as, prince of Dardania, cousin of Trojan royal family
Agamemnon a-ga-*mem*-non, king of Mycenae, High King of the Achaeans
Aganus a-*gay*-nus, son of Paris and Helen
Agapenor a-ga-*pee*-nor, king of Arcadia
Agenor a-*jee*-nor, common ancestor of Hekuba and Helen
Aithra *ay*-thra, Helen's servant, mother of Theseus
Ajax (Great) *ay*-jax, prince of Salamis, son of Telamon
Akamas *a*-ka-mas, son of Theseus
Alkimus *al*-ki-mus, companion of Achilles
Amyntor a-*min*-tor, father of Phoenix (1)
Antenor an-*tee*-nor, Priam's councillor, Trojan elder
Antigone an-*ti*-goh-nee, cousin of Cressida
Antiphus *an*-ti-fus, from Kos, grandson of Herakles
Arcadia ar-*kay*-dee-a, area ruled by Agapenor, west of Mycenae
Argo *ar*-go, ship on quest for Golden Fleece
Argos *ar*-gos, city ruled by Diomedes
Arkas *ar*-kas, servant of Agamemnon
Arsinoe ar-*sin*-oh-ee, Iphigenia's nurse
Artemis *ar*-te-mis, goddess of the hunt and moon
Askalaphus a-*ska*-la-fus, king of Orchomenos
Asklepius as-*klee*-pee-us, greatest Achaean healer
Astyoche as-*teye*-o-kee, sister of Priam, wife of Telephus
Astyochea as-tee-o-*kee*-a, mother of Tlepolemus
Athens *a*-thenz, city in Attika, ruled by Menestheus
Atlas *at*-las, a titan
Atreus *ay*-tryoos, father of Agamemnon and Menelaus
Auge *aw*-jee, mother of Telephus
Aulis *aw*-lis, bay where army assembles
Automedon o-*to*-me-don, Achilles's charioteer
Balius *bay*-lee-us, chariot horse of Achilles
Boeotia bee-*oh*-sha, area north of Mycenae
Borus *bor*-us, father of Menesthius, brother-in-law of Achilles
Chalkiope kal-*keye*-o-pee, grandmother of Antiphus and Phiddipus
Chalkis *kal*-kis, town on the shore of Euboea opposite Aulis
Cheiron *keye*-ron, young Achilles's teacher

216

Chrysippus kreye-*sip*-us, son of Pelops, uncle of Agamemnon and Menelaus
Chrysothemis kry-*so*-the-mis, third daughter of Agamemnon and Klytemnestra
Cressida *kres*-i-duh, daughter of Kalchas
Crete *kreet,* Achaean island ruled by Idomeneus
Cyprus *seye*-prus, island recently ruled by Kinyras
Dardania dar-*day*-nee-uh, area ruled by Anchises
Dardanus *dar*-dan-us, forefather of the Trojan royal family
Deidamia dee-i-da-*meye*-uh, eldest daughter of Lykomedes of Skyros
Deiphobus de-*if*-oh-bus, prince of Troy
Delos *dee*-los, Achaean island
Demophoon dee-*mo*-foh-on, son of Theseus
Diomedes deye-o-*mee*-deez, king of Argos and Tiryns
Diores deye-*o*-reez, father of Automedon
Elektra ee-*lek*-tra, second daughter of Agamemnon and Klytemnestra
Ephyra e-fi-ra, Achaean city
Euboea yoo-*bee*-a, island ruled by Elephenor
Eudorus yoo-*dor*-us, Myrmidon
Eumenes yoo-*mee*-neez, a farmer in Lakedaemon
Eurybates yoo-*ri*-ba-teez, herald of Ithaka, companion of Odysseus
Eurypylus yoo-*ri*-pi-lus, son of Telephus and Astyoche
Guowaxeus gwo-*waks*-yoos, a farmer in Lakedaemon
Haimos *hay*-mos, Mysian warrior
Halitherses ha-li-*ther*-seez, a seer of Ithaka
Hektor *hek*-tor, eldest prince of Troy, son of Priam and Hekuba
Hekuba *he*-kyoo-ba, queen of Troy, primary wife of Priam
Helen *he*-len, wife of Menelaus, afterward wife of Paris
Helenus *he*-le-nus, Trojan prince, twin brother of Kassandra
Helikaon he-li-*kay*-on, son of Antenor
Hellespont *he*-le-spont, body of water just north of Troy
Herakles *her*-a-kleez, greatest Achaean hero
Hermione hur-*meye*-o-nee, daughter of Menelaus and Helen
Hesione he-*seye*-uh-nee, mother of Teukros, sister of Priam
Hiera heye-*eer*-uh, wife of Telephus
Ida *eye*-da, mountain near Troy
Idaeus eye-*dee*-us, Priam's herald
Idomeneus eye-do-men-yoos, king of Crete
Ilus *eye*-lus, founder of Trojan royal family, grandfather of Priam
Iphigenia i-fi-je-*neye*-a, first daughter of Agamemnon and Klytemnestra
Iphiklus *eye*-fi-klus, former king of Phylake, father of Iolaus
Ithaka *i*-tha-ka, Achaean island ruled by Odysseus
Kaikos *kay*-kos, river in Mysia
Kalchas *kal*-kas, former Trojan priest, now ally of the Achaeans
Karians *kayr*-ee-unz, area south of Troy
Kassandra ka-*san*-druh, seer daughter of Priam and Hekuba
Kastor *kas*-tor, twin of Polydeukes, brother of Helen and Klytemnestra
Katreus *kat*-ryoos, maternal grandfather of Agamemnon and Menelaus
Kebriones ke-*breye*-o-neez, son of Priam by a secondary wife
Kilissa ki-*lis*-uh, nurse of Orestes
Kinyras *kin*-i-ras, former king of Cyprus
Klymene *kli*-mee-nee, Helen's servant
Klytemnestra kleye-tem-*nes*-tra, wife of Agamemnon, sister of Helen
Kolchis *kol*-kis, city on the eastern shore of the Black Sea
Kos *kos,* Achaean island
Kreusa kree-*oo*-suh, eldest daughter of Priam and Hekuba
Kusamenos koo-sa-*mee*-nos, a farmer in Lakedaemon

217

Laerkes lay-*ur*-keez, father of Alkimus
Laertes lay-*ur*-teez, father of Odysseus
Laius *lay*-us, father of Oedipus, former king of Thebes
Lakedaemon (1) la-ke-*dee*-mon, area ruled by Menelaus
Lakedaemon (2) la-ke-*dee*-mon, grandson of Atlas, ancestor of Helen
Laodike lay-*o*-di-kee, daughter of Priam and Hekuba
Leda *lee*-da, mother of Helen
Lykia *lik*-ya, area south of Troy ruled by Sarpedon
Lykomedes leye-ko-*mee*-deez, king of Skyros, father of Deidamia
Machaon ma-*kay*-on, Achaean healer from Trikka, Podalirius's brother
Maemalus *mee*-ma-lus, father of Pisander
Melampus me-*lam*-pus, cousin of Nestor
Menelaus me-ne-*lay*-us, king of Lakedaemon, Helen's husband, Agamemnon's brother
Menestheus me-*nes*-thyoos, king of Athens
Menesthius me-*nes*-thee-us, Myrmidon son of Borus, nephew of Achilles
Menoetius men-*ee*-shus, father of Patroklus
Messenia me-*sen*-ee-a, area ruled by Nestor
Mestor *mes*-tor, prince of Troy
Mnemon *nee*-mon, guide assigned to Achilles by Thetis
Mycenae meye-*see*-nee, Achaean city ruled by Agamemnon
Mycenaean meye-see-*nee*-an, of the area ruled by Agamemnon
Myrmidons *mur*-mi-donz, Achilles's soldiers
Mysia *mi*-sha, area south of Troy where Telephus rules
Mysians *mi*-shanz, people of the area south of Troy where Telephus rules
Nauplia *naw*-plee-uh, area ruled by Nauplius on coast of Argolid
Nauplius *naw*-plee-us, father of Palamedes and Oeax, king of Nauplia
Neleus *neel*-yoos, father of Nestor
Neoptolemus nee-op-*to*-le-mus, son of Achilles and Deidamia
Nereid *nee*-ree-id, title of Thetis, the daughter of Nereus
Nestor *nes*-tor, elderly king of Pylos
Odysseus o-*dis*-yoos, king of Ithaka
Oedipus *ed*-i-pus or *ee*-di-pus, king of Thebes, grandfather/uncle of Thersander
Opois *o*-poh-is, Achaean city
Orchomenos or-*ko*-me-nus, city ruled by Askalaphus
Orestes oh-*res*-teez, son of Agamemnon and Klytemnestra
Paeonians pee-*oh*-nee-unz, area northwest of Troy, beyond Thrace
Palamedes pa-la-*mee*-deez, prince of Nauplia
Pandarus *pan*-da-rus, uncle of Cressida, brother of Kalchas
Panthous *pan*-thoh-us, Trojan elder
Paris *pa*-ris, Trojan prince, lover of Helen
Patara pa-*tar*-a, city in Lykia
Patroklus pa-*trok*-lus, Achilles's closest companion
Peirithous peye-*rith*-oh-us, Achaean hero, brother of Phisadie, father of Polypoetes
Peleus *peel*-yoos, father of Achilles, king of Phthia
Pelops *pel*-ops, paternal grandfather of Agamemnon and Menelaus
Peneleos pee-*ne*-lee-os, Boeotian commander
Penelope pe-*nel*-o-pee, wife of Odysseus
Periboea pe-ri-*bee*-uh, mother of Great Ajax
Phalis *fay*-lis, king of Sidon
Phidippus feye-*dip*-us, from Kos, grandson of Herakles
Philoktetes fi-lok-*tee*-teez, king of Methone
Phoenicia fee-*ni*-sha, area on the coast of the Levant
Phoenix (1) *fee*-niks, companion of Achilles
Phoenix (2) *fee*-niks, son of Agenor

218

Phrygia *fri*-ja, area northeast of Troy
Phthia *ftheye*-a, area of Achaea ruled by Peleus
Pisander peye-*san*-der, a Myrmidon
Pleione pleye-*oh*-nee, lover of Atlas, ancestor of both Helen and the Trojan royal line
Pleisthenes plee-*is*-the-neez, son of Helen and Menelaus
Podalirius po-da-*leye*-ree-us, Achaean healer from Trikka, brother of Machaon
Podarge po-*dar*-jee, mare given to Peleus by the gods
Poliwos po-*lee*-wos, a farmer in Lakedaemon
Polydamas po-*li*-da-mas, son of Panthous, companion of Hektor
Polydeukes po-li-*dyoo*-keez, twin of Kastor, brother of Helen and Klytemnestra
Polydora po-li-*dor*-a, sister of Achilles
Polyneikes po-li-*neye*-keez, son of Oedipus, father of Thersander
Polypoetes po-li-*pee*-teez, son of Peirithous, nephew of Phisadie
Poseidon poh-*seye*-don, god of the sea and earthquake
Priam *preye*-am, king of Troy
Pylos *peye*-los, area ruled by Nestor
Pyrrha *peer*-uh, Achilles's name in female disguise
Pyrrhus *peer*-us, original name of son of Achilles and Deidamia
Rhodes *rohdz*, Achaean island ruled by Tlepolemus
Salamis *sa*-la-mis, Achaean island ruled by Telamon
Sarpedon sar-*pee*-don, king of Lykia
Sidon *seye*-don, area on the coast of the Levant
Skaean Gate *skee*-an, a gate of Troy
Skyros *skeye*-ros, island ruled by Lykomedes
Skythia *ski*-thee-a, area northeast of Troy across the Black Sea
Sparta *spar*-tuh, city ruled by Menelaus
Spercheus spur-*kee*-us, river in Phthia
Sthenelus *sthen*-e-lus, companion of Diomedes
Talthybius tal-*thi*-bee-us, Agamemnon's herald
Tantalus *tan*-ta-lus, great-grandfather of Agamemnon and Menelaus
Tegea te-*jee*-a, Achaean city
Telamon *tel*-a-mon, king of Salamis, father of Ajax and Teukros
Telemachus te-*lem*-a-kus, son of Odysseus and Penelope
Telephus *te*-le-fus, king of Mysia, son of Herakles
Teukros *tyoo*-kros, half-brother of Ajax, son of Telamon and Hesione
Teuthrania tyooth-*ran*-ya, Mysian city
Teuthranius tyooth-*ran*-yus, half-brother of Telephus
Teuthras *tyooth*-ras, former king of Teuthrania
Thebans *thee*-banz, people of Thebes
Thebes *theebz*, Achaean city ruled by Thersander
Thersander ther-*san*-der, king of Thebes
Thersites ther-*seye*-teez, cousin of Diomedes
Theseus *thees*-yoos, Achaean hero, former king of Athens
Thessalus *thes*-a-lus, father of Antiphus and Phidippus
Thetis *thee*-tis, Achaean priestess, mother of Achilles
Thrace *thrays*, area northwest of Troy across the Hellespont
Thyestes theye-*es*-teez, brother of Atreus, uncle of Agamemnon and Menelaus
Thymoetes theye-*mee*-teez, Trojan elder
Tlepolemus tle-*po*-le-mus, king of Rhodes, son of Herakles
Trikka *trik*-a, Achaean city of Podalirius and Machaon
Troilus *troy*-lus, prince of Troy
Tyndareus tyn-*dar*-yoos, father of Helen and Klytemnestra
Xanthus *zan*-thus, chariot horse of Achilles
Zeus *zyoos*, greatest of the gods

Genealogical Chart: The Achaeans

Characters in bold appear and are named in *Sacrifice.*

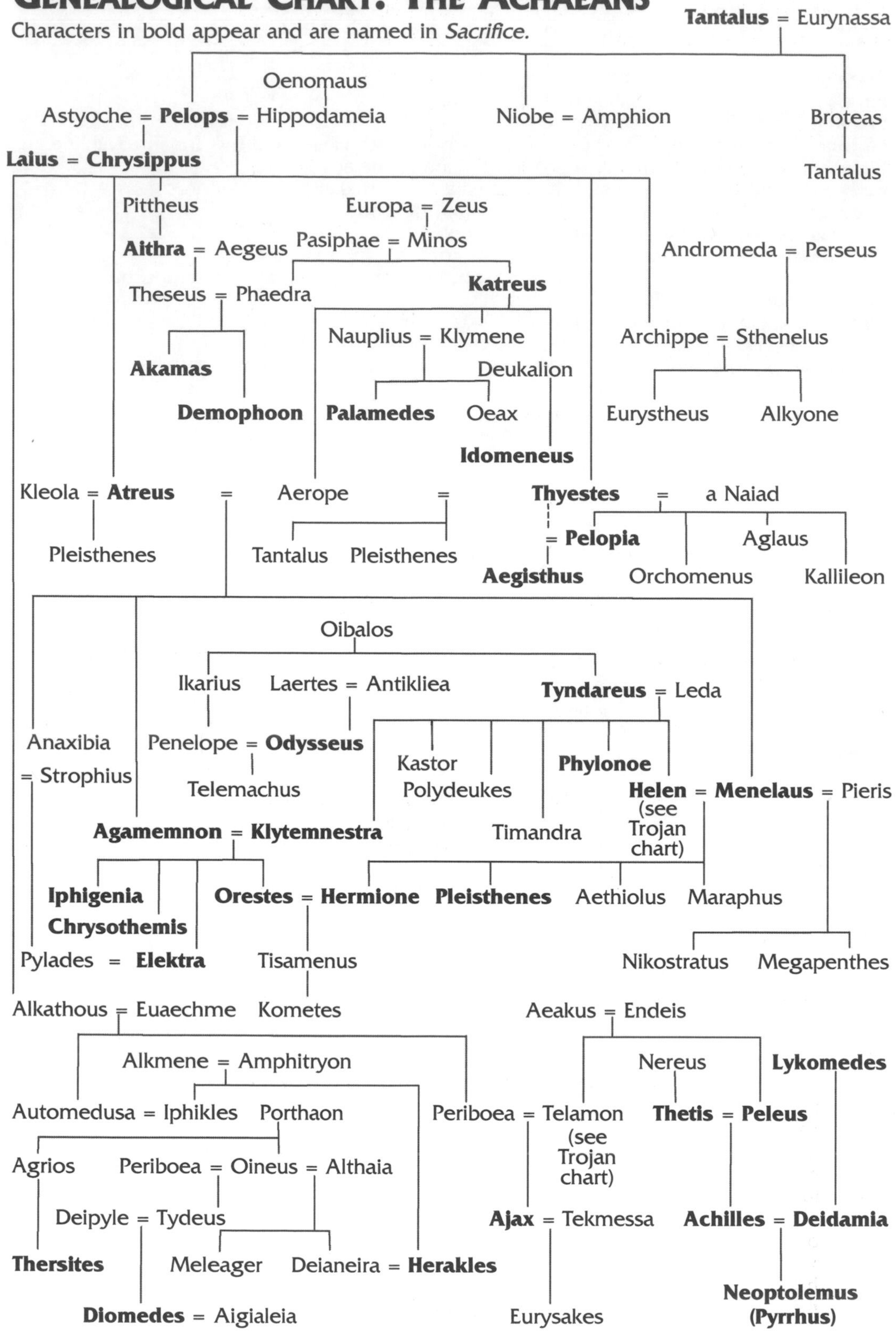
Tantalus = Eurynassa
Oenomaus
Astyoche = Pelops = Hippodameia
Niobe = Amphion
Broteas
Laius = Chrysippus
Tantalus
Pittheus
Europa = Zeus
Aithra = Aegeus
Pasiphae = Minos
Andromeda = Perseus
Katreus
Theseus = Phaedra
Nauplius = Klymene
Archippe = Sthenelus
Akamas
Deukalion
Demophoon
Palamedes
Oeax
Eurystheus
Alkyone
Idomeneus
Kleola = Atreus
=
Aerope
=
Thyestes
=
a Naiad
= Pelopia
Aglaus
Pleisthenes
Tantalus
Pleisthenes
Aegisthus
Orchomenus
Kallileon
Oibalos
Ikarius
Laertes = Antikliea
Tyndareus = Leda
Anaxibia
Penelope = Odysseus
Kastor
Phylonoe
= Strophius
Telemachus
Polydeukes
Helen (see Trojan chart)
= Menelaus = Pieris
Agamemnon = Klytemnestra
Timandra
Iphigenia
Orestes = Hermione
Pleisthenes
Aethiolus
Maraphus
Chrysothemis
Pylades = Elektra
Tisamenus
Nikostratus
Megapenthes
Alkathous = Euaechme
Kometes
Aeakus = Endeis
Alkmene = Amphitryon
Nereus
Lykomedes
Automedusa = Iphikles
Porthaon
Periboea = Telamon (see Trojan chart)
Thetis = Peleus
Agrios
Periboea = Oineus = Althaia
Deipyle = Tydeus
Ajax = Tekmessa
Achilles = Deidamia
Thersites
Meleager
Deianeira = Herakles
Neoptolemus (Pyrrhus)
Diomedes = Aigialeia
Eurysakes

GENEALOGICAL CHART: THE TROJAN ROYAL FAMILY

Characters in bold appear and are named in *Sacrifice.*

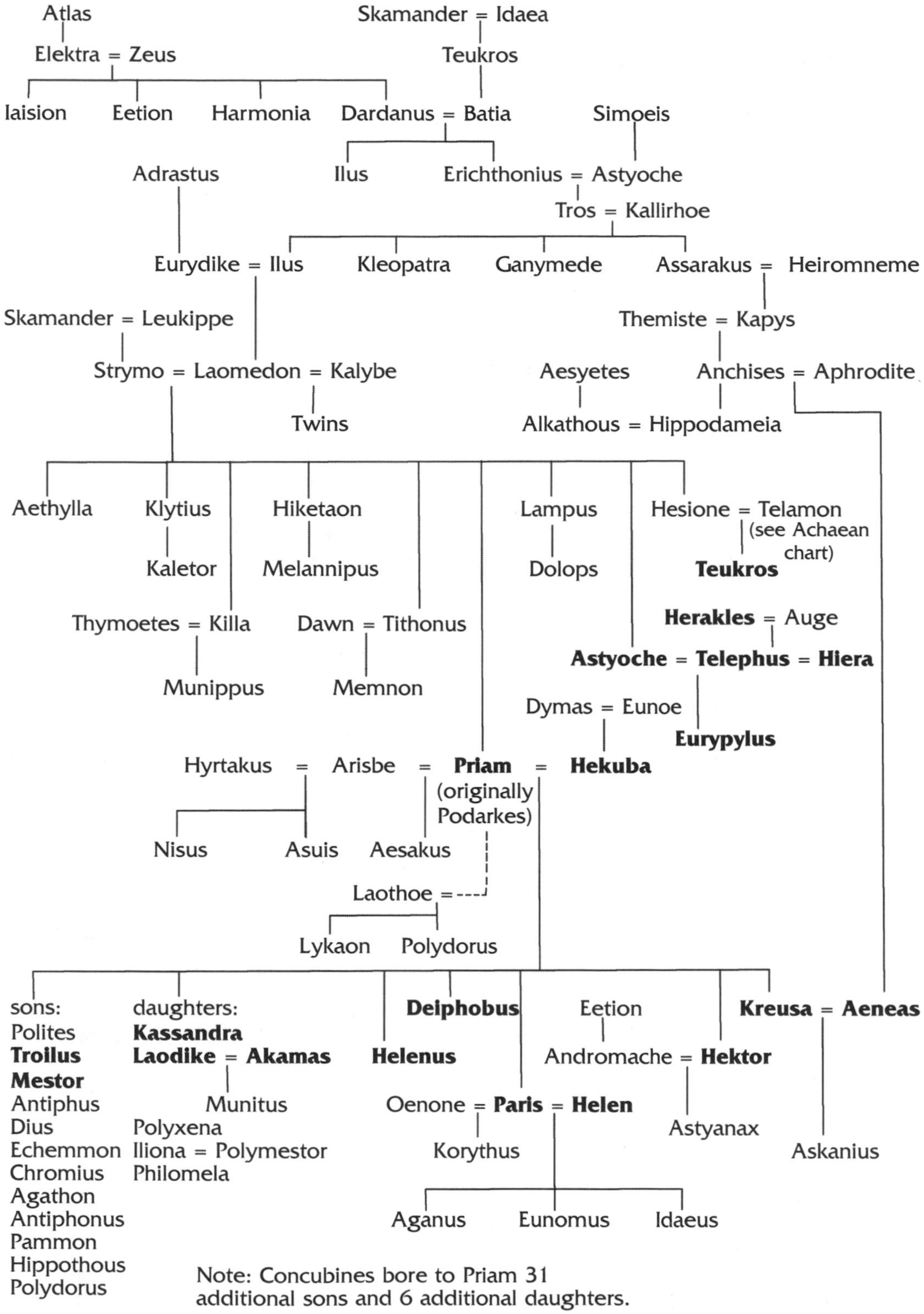
Atlas
Skamander = Idaea
Elektra = Zeus
Teukros
Iaision
Eetion
Harmonia
Dardanus = Batia
Simoeis
Adrastus
Ilus
Erichthonius = Astyoche
Tros = Kallirhoe
Eurydike = Ilus
Kleopatra
Ganymede
Assarakus = Heiromneme
Skamander = Leukippe
Themiste = Kapys
Strymo = Laomedon = Kalybe
Aesyetes
Anchises = Aphrodite
Twins
Alkathous = Hippodameia
Aethylla
Klytius
Hiketaon
Lampus
Hesione = Telamon
(see Achaean chart)
Kaletor
Melannipus
Dolops
Teukros
Thymoetes = Killa
Dawn = Tithonus
Herakles = Auge
Astyoche = Telephus = Hiera
Munippus
Memnon
Dymas = Eunoe
Eurypylus
Hyrtakus = Arisbe = Priam = Hekuba
(originally Podarkes)
Nisus
Asuis
Aesakus
Laothoe =
Lykaon
Polydorus
sons:
Polites
Troilus
Mestor
Antiphus
Dius
Echemmon
Chromius
Agathon
Antiphonus
Pammon
Hippothous
Polydorus
daughters:
Kassandra
Laodike = Akamas
Munitus
Polyxena
Iliona = Polymestor
Philomela
Deiphobus
Helenus
Eetion
Andromache = Hektor
Kreusa = Aeneas
Oenone = Paris = Helen
Korythus
Astyanax
Askanius
Aganus
Eunomus
Idaeus

Note: Concubines bore to Priam 31 additional sons and 6 additional daughters.

BIBLIOGRAPHY

The following list of sources is an addendum to the list in the previous volume, *A Thousand Ships*.

THE STORY

Aeschylus. *Agamemnon. Libation Bearers. Eumenides. Fragments.* Trans. Herbert Weir Smith (Loeb Classical Library). Cambridge and London: Harvard University Press, 1999. (Orig. edition 1926.)

Alkaios. "Helen and Thetis." In *Greek Lyric Poetry.* Trans. Willis Barnstone. New York: Bantam Books, 1962.

Atwood, E. Bagby and Virgil K. Whitaker, eds. *Excidium Troiae.* Cambridge: The Medieval Academy of America, 1944.

Bacchylides. *Complete Poems.* Trans. Robert Fagles, new edition. New Haven, CT and London: Yale University Press, 1998.

Brewer's Dictionary of Phrase and Fable, revised and enlarged. New York: Harper & Brothers Publishers, n.d.

Burgess, Jonathan S. *The Tradition of the Trojan War in Homer and the Epic Cycle.* Baltimore and London: The Johns Hopkins University Press, 2001.

Bush, Douglas. *Mythology and the Renaissance Tradition in English Poetry.* New York: Pageant Book Company, 1957.

de Pizan, Christine. *The Book of the City of Ladies.* Trans. Rosalind Brown-Grant. London: Penguin Books, 1999.

Euripides. *Electra.* Produced and directed by Michael Cacoyannis. 1 hour 53 minutes. Metro Goldwyn Mayer, 1962. Digital virtual disc.

Feder, Theodore H. "Iphigenia and Isaac, Saved at the Altar." *Archaeology Odyssey* 5 (May/June 2002): 50-62.

Forsdyke, John. *Greece Before Homer, Ancient Chronology and Mythology.* London: Max Parrish, 1956.

Gibbs, A.C. *The Gest Hystoriale of the Destruction of Troy.* In *Middle English Romances.* Evanston, IL: Northwestern University Press, 1966.

Gluck, Christoph Willibald. *Iphigenie en Aulide.* Libretto by Marie Francois Louis Gand Bailli du Roullet dit Le Blanc. Trans. John Sidgwick. Monteverdi Choir. Orchestre de L'opera de Lyon. Conducted by John Eliot Gardiner. N.P.: Radio France - Erato Disques, 1990.

Greek Epic Fragments from the Seventh to the Fifth Centuries BC. Trans. Martin L. West (Loeb Classical Library). Cambridge and London: Harvard University Press, 2003.

Haggard, H. Rider and Andrew Lang. *The World's Desire.* New York: A Del Rey Book published by Ballantine Books, 1972.

Henryson, Robert. *Testament of Cresseid,* ed. Denton Fox. London: Thomas Nelson and Sons Ltd., 1968.

Hutchinson, W.M.L. *The Sunset of the Heroes.* London: J.M. Dent & Co. and New York: E.P. Dutton & Co., 1911.

Huxley, G.L. *Greek Epic Poetry from Eumelos to Panyasis.* Cambridge: Harvard University Press, 1969.

Joseph of Exeter. *Trojan War I-III.* Trans. A.K. Bate. Warminster, Wiltshire: Bolchazy - Carducci Publishers/Aris & Phillips Ltd., 1986.

Landor, Walter Savage. "The Abbe Delille and Walter Landor." In *The Works of Walter Savage Landor,* vol. I. London: Chapman and Hall, 1868.

Landor, Walter Savage. *Pericles and Aspasia,* "Laodamia" and "Menelaus and Helen." In *The Works of Walter Savage Landor,* vol. II. London: Chapman and Hall, 1868.

Lydgate, John. *Troy Book: Selections,* ed. Robert R. Edwards. Kalamazoo, MI: Medieval Institute Publications for Western Michigan University, 1998.

Morris, William. "The Death of Paris." In *The Earthly Paradise, a Poem,* part III. Boston: Roberts Brothers, 1870.

Mozart, Wolfgang Amadeus. *Idomeneo: King of Crete.* Libretto by Giovanni Battista Varesco. Directed by Lofti Mansouri. San Diego Opera, April 2001.

Norris III, Frank Pelletier. *La Coronica Troyana: A Medieval Spanish Translation of Guido de Colonna's Historia Destructionis Troiae.* University of North Carolina's Studies in the Romance Languages and Literatures, No. 90. Chapel Hill, NC: University of North Carolina Press, 1970.

O'Neill, Eugene. *Mourning Becomes Electra.* UCSD Theatre & Dance, San Diego, CA, November 2002.

Peele, George. "Tale of Troy" and "Araygnement of Paris." In *The Life and Works of George Peele,* vol. 3. New Haven and London: Yale University Press, 1970.

Philostratus, Flavius. *Heroikos.* Trans. Jennifer K. Berenson Maclean and Ellen Bradshaw Aitken. Atlanta, GA: Society of Biblical Literature, 2001.

Pindar. *The Odes of Pindar.* Trans. Sir John Sandys (Loeb Classical Library). Cambridge: Harvard University Press, 1957.

Plautus. *The Two Bacchides.* In *The Complete Roman Drama,* vol. 1, ed. George E. Duckworth. Trans. Edward H. Sugden. New York: Random House, 1942.

Rossetti, Dante Gabriel. "Troy Town." In *Victorian Poetry and Poetics,* 2nd edition, ed. Houghton and Stange. Boston: Houghton Mifflin Company, 1968.

Sappho. "To Anaktoria, Now a Soldier's Wife in Lydia" and "Wedding of Andromache." In *Greek Lyric Poetry.* Trans. Willis Barnstone. New York: Bantam Books, 1962.

Sophocles. *Fragments.* Trans. Hugh Lloyd-Jones (Loeb Classical Library). Cambridge and London: Harvard University Press, 1996.

The Trojan War in Greek Art, A Picture Book. Boston: Museum of Fine Arts, [1975].

The Trojan Women. Produced by Michael Cacoyannis and Anis Nohra. 105 minutes. Family Home Entertainment, Inc., 1971. Videocassette.

Wordsworth, William. "When Philoctetes in the Lemnian Isle" and "Laodamia." In *The Shorter Poems of William Wordsworth.* London: J.M. Dent & Co. and New York: E.P. Dutton & Co., 1907.

Young, Arthur M. *Troy and Her Legend.* Pittsburgh, PA: University of Pittsburgh Press, 1948.

THE SETTINGS IN GENERAL

Carpenter, Rhys. *Discontinuity in Greek Civilization.* New York: The Norton Library, W.W. Norton & Company, Inc., 1968.

Connolly, Peter. *The Ancient Greece of Odysseus.* Oxford: Oxford University Press, 1998.

Leaf, Walter. *Troy, a Study in Homeric Geography.* London: Macmillan and Co., Limited, 1912.

Miller, Olive Beaupre and Harry Neal Baum. *My Book of History, A Picturesque Tale of Progress,* vol. 2, Conquests. Chicago and Toronto: The Bookhouse for Children, 1930.

Page, Denys L. *History and the Homeric Iliad.* Berkeley, CA and Los Angeles: University of California Press, 1963.

Sandars, N.K. *The Sea Peoples: Warriors of the Ancient Mediterranean, 1250-1150 BC.* London: Thames & Hudson, 1978.

TROY

Easton D.F., J.D. Hawkins, A.G. Sherratt, and E.S. Sherratt. "Troy in Recent Perspective." *Anatolian Studies* 52 (2002): 75-109.

Studia Troica. Band 9. Mainz am Rhein: Verlag Phillip von Zabern, 1999.

Studia Troica. Band 10. Mainz am Rhein: Verlag Phillip von Zabern, 2000.

Studia Troica. Band 11. Mainz am Rhein: Verlag Phillip von Zabern, 2001.

THE CHARACTERS

King, Katherine Callen. *Achilles, Paradigms of the War Hero from Homer to the Middle Ages.* Berkeley, CA: University of California Press, 1987.

Kleinbaum, Abby Wettan. *The War Against the Amazons.* New York: New Press, McGraw-Hill Book Company, 1983.

Mackie, Hilary. *Talking Trojan, Speech and Community in the Iliad.* Lanham, Boulder, New York, and London: Rowman & Littlefield Publishers, Inc., n.d.

Michelakis, Pantelis. *Achilles in Greek Tragedy.* Cambridge: Cambridge University Press, n.d.

Percy III, William Armstrong. *Pederasty and Pedagogy in Archaic Greece.* Urbana, IL and Chicago: University of Illinois Press, 1996.

Wilde, Lyn Webster. *On the Trail of the Women Warriors, the Amazons in Myth and History.* New York: Thomas Dunne Books, St. Martin's Press, 2000.

THE MYCENAEANS

Desbrough, V.R. *The Last Mycenaeans and Their Successors.* Oxford: Clarendon Press, 1964.

French, Elizabeth. *Mycenae, Agamemnon's Capital.* Stroud, Goucestershire and Charleston, SC: Tempus, 2002.

Levin, Saul. *The Linear B Decipherment Controversy Re-examined.* New York: State University of New York, 1964.

Palmer, L.R. *The Interpretations of Mycenaean Greek Texts.* London: Oxford University Press, 1963.

Tarsouli, Georgia. *Mystras—Sparta.* Athens: M. Pechlivanides and Co. S.A., n.d.

Ventris, Michael and John Chadwick. *Documents in Mycenaean Greek.* London: Cambridge University Press, 1956.

MORE GREAT BOOKS FROM IMAGE COMICS

40 OZ. COLLECTED TP
ISBN# 1582403298
$9.95

AGE OF BRONZE
VOL. 1: A THOUSAND SHIPS TP
issues 1-9
ISBN# 1582402000
$19.95
VOL. 2: SACRIFICE HC
issues 10-19
ISBN# 1582403600
$29.95

THE BLACK FOREST GN
ISBN# 1582403503
$9.95

CITY OF SILENCE TP
ISBN# 1582403678
$9.95

CLASSIC 40 OZ.:
TALES FROM THE BROWN BAG TP
ISBN# 1582404380
$14.95

CREASED GN
ISBN# 1582404216
$9.95

DEEP SLEEPER TP
ISBN# 1582404933
$12.95

DIORAMAS, A LOVE STORY GN
ISBN# 1582403597
$12.95

EARTHBOY JACOBUS GN
ISBN# 1582404925
$17.95

FLIGHT, VOL. 1 GN
ISBN# 1582403816
$19.95

FLIGHT, VOL. 2 GN
ISBN# 1582404771
$24.95

FOUR-LETTER WORLDS GN
ISBN# 1582404399
$12.95

GRRL SCOUTS
VOL. 1 TP
ISBN# 1582403163
$12.95
VOL. 2: WORK SUCKS TP
ISBN# 1582403430
$12.95

HAWAIIAN DICK, VOL. 1:
BYRD OF PARADISE TP
ISBN# 1582403171
$14.95

HEAVEN, LLC. GN
ISBN# 1582403511
$12.95

KANE
VOL. 1: GREETINGS FROM NEW
EDEN TP
issues 1-4
ISBN# 1582403406
$11.95
VOL. 2: RABBIT HUNT TP
issues 5-8
ISBN# 1582403554
$12.95
VOL. 3: HISTORIES TP
issues 9-12
ISBN# 1582403821
$12.95
VOL. 4: THIRTY NINTH TP
issues 13-18
ISBN# 1582404682
$16.95

LAZARUS CHURCHYARD
THE FINAL CUT GN
ISBN# 1582401802
$14.95

LIBERTY MEADOWS
VOL. 1:
EDEN LANDSCAPE ED TP
issues 1-9
ISBN# 1582402604
$19.95
VOL. 2:
CREATURE COMFORTS HC
issues 10-18
ISBN# 1582403333
$24.95

PUTTIN' THE BACKBONE BACK TP
(MR)
ISBN# 158240402X
$9.95

PvP
THE DORK AGES TP
original miniseries 1-6
ISBN# 1582403457
$11.95
VOL.1: PVP AT LARGE TP
issues 1-6
ISBN# 1582403740
$11.95
VOL. 2: PVP RELOADED TP
issues 7-12
ISBN# 158240433X
$11.95

REX MUNDI
VOL. 1:
THE GUARDIAN OF THE TEMPLE TP
issues 0-5
ISBN# 158240268X
$14.95
VOL. 2:
THE RIVER UNDERGROUND TP
issues 6-11
ISBN# 1582404798
$14.95

SMALL GODS, VOL. 1:
KILLING GRIN TP
issues 1-4
ISBN# 1582404577
$9.95

TOMMYSAURUS REX GN
ISBN# 1582403953
$11.95

ULTRA: SEVEN DAYS TP
ISBN# 1582404836
$17.95

THE WALKING DEAD
VOL. 1: DAYS GONE BYE TP
issues 1-6
ISBN# 1582403589
$12.95
VOL. 2: MILES BEHIND US TP
issues 7-12
ISBN# 1582404135
$12.95
VOL. 3: SAFETY BEHIND BARS TP
issues 13-18
ISBN# 1582404879
$12.95

THE WICKED WEST GN
ISBN# 1582404143
$9.95

For a comic shop near you carrying graphic novels from Image Comics, please call toll free: 1-888-COMIC-BOOK